Canadian Penology:
Advanced Perspectives
and
Research

Edited by
Kevin R. E. McCormick
and
Livy A. Visano

Canadian Scholars' Press   Toronto 1992

60109590

Canadian Penology: Advanced Perspectives and Research

Published in 1992 by
Canadian Scholars' Press Inc.
339 Bloor St. W., Ste. 222
Toronto, Ontario
Canada

Canadian Cataloguing in Publication Data

Main entry under title:

Canadian Penology

Includes bibliographical references.

ISBN 0-921627-93-9

1. Corrections - Canada. 2. Correctional institutions - Canada.
I. McCormick, Kevin R.E., 1965-. II. Visano, L.A.

HV9507.C36   1992   364.6'0971   C92-094328-4

Book design by The Dancing Puffin Co.

Dedication
To Doris and Ken for their unconditional love and support.

Acknowledgements

This endeavour would never had been possible without the assistance of many people to whom we remain deeply indebted. Firstly we would like to thank the contributors, who representing the leading scholars in the area, bring to the project theoretically and methodologically challenging perspectives. We also would like to thank the many inmates and former inmates, whose concerns and insights informed both the contributors and editors as to the current state of corrections within Canada. To them we extend our appreciation and gratitude.

Further we are indebted to a number of colleagues for their encouragement, insights and counsel. To Paul Bessler, Clifford Jansen, Tony Haddad, and Larry Lam, for their discussions concerning the shape of the text. To Richard Brown, Tony Carella and Alice Trachimovsky, for their years of dedication to teaching individuals to take scholarly debate to levels which transcend and challenge traditional rhetoric. To Arthur Hudlin, for his computer knowledge and assistance. And to the many students at both York University and the University of Toronto, who afforded the editors with comments on various drafts of the project.

Also we thank the support staff of York University, Department of Sociology: Audrey, Jackie, Myrna, Pat, Tracy and Ursula, whose time and expertise proved invaluable to the editors.

We further thank the publisher of this work, Canadian Scholars' Press and especially Jack Wayne, for undertaking this project and for maintaining the integrity of the theoretical, methodological and substantive concerns of both the editors and contributors.

Finally and most importantly we would like to thank our families for their continued love and support. To Anthony, Robynne and Renée whose patience and understanding continues to give our work and lives meaning.

Table of Contents

Foreword

This publication marks a turning point in the study of penology. The editors have succeeded in demonstrating considerable courage and conviction in providing a multi-disciplinary collection of insightful articles from a wide array of talented scholars from history, sociology, criminology, psychology, law and corrections. This volume will certainly serve as a long-overdue teaching resource as well as an attractive reference for practitioners. Specifically, McCormick and Visano should be commended for inviting a community-based agency like The Vitanova Foundation to comment on such an enterprise. Far too frequently, academics tend to overlook the reactions of the populations they study. Accordingly, we accept this challenge with gratitude.

The Vitanova Foundation is a community non-profit, voluntary organization assisting many formerly incarcerated individuals to remain drug-free. This publication is of extreme interest to service-providers for a number of reasons. Substantively, the articles examine with precision and clarity the dynamic contexts in which critical judgments are routinely made and interventions justified. As the authors consistently maintain, such structures as the political economy, state practices, and cultural reproductions are often ignored, but warrant analytic primacy. Traditionally, symptoms of "trouble" have become too conveniently individualized or pathologized thereby inhibiting an examination of institutional and systemic barriers. "Inmates," "offenders," "clients," "subjects" or whatever euphemisms one adopts, there must be a critical recognition of the failure of traditional interventive strategies to include empowering social development models. The horrific levels of alienation, powerlessness, drug dependency, unemployment, racism, sexism, violence, and illiteracy must be confronted; otherwise, all of us consent to further strategies of incarceration. Agencies like The Vitanova Foundation struggle daily to involve the community with the less advantaged and their families, in securing more healthy life-chances. A program of re-entry that offers counselling, education, employment, recreation, shelter, food, drug therapy, peer support, training, etc. constitutes a new life that is not confined by the oppressive walls of dependencies.

Founded in 1988, our agency was established to help troubled young adults with drug addictions. Support groups emerged and meetings were held in a variety of locales, responding quickly to the concerns of those who remained cast aside. Throughout the early 1990s a large number of requests from clients and their families necessitated the development of a rehabilitation centre consisting of counselling services for individuals and groups, resource materials, recreational and gymnastic facilities, meeting rooms, craft workshops, computer literacy training—to name but a few responses.

The focus of the centre's activities has always been the importance of the self—an improved mental and physical self-image. This sense of self and the opportunity to express one's individuality, creativity and skills have been effectively denied by the experiences suffered by substance abusers, many of whom have been incarcerated and dehumanized by brutal social environments. The growth of this community-based organization in a few years is remarkable. What has driven that growth is the conviction that less rhetoric and more action is needed to address a serious threat to individual life, the security of the family, and the collective health of "our" community.

Regrettably, much more is needed in providing accessible services. Restraints in state funding for more staff, more resources and outreach programs have hit those segments in our society who have been silenced and voiceless. The limited options faced by former inmates, for example, cannot be ignored. Passion in advocacy and in coalition building are not mere words with empty gestures. They are expressions of struggle which McCormick, Visano and their collaborators relentlessly pursue. No longer can we afford to relegate action-oriented research to a handful of "radical" social workers who are so often dismissed as subversives. Instead, this book admonishes all of us—from undergraduate students to law professors—to root our ideas about penology in the experiences of the human condition. Social justice, as a constitution of any society, is a collective commitment to eradicate inequality.

I salute the efforts of all the contributors of this volume for their initiative and industry in forging a challenging agenda. I thank all the many men and women with whom I have worked for sustaining their will to create and live a new life—*a vita nuova.*

Franca Damiani Carella
Founder and Executive Director
The Vitanova Foundation

Preface

Problematic Penological Prospects: Prefatory Comments

Any conceptual understanding of penology must direct us to the phenomenon of power. Unless analyses are ultimately addressed to the relationships of control and power, discussions will continue to falter. Invariably, extant studies provide interesting insights on the social consequences of crime and the social conditions under which control promotes order.

Careful investigation of "control," however, yields some interesting implications for our understanding of how various environing influences—political, legal, historical and ideological contexts—are related to behavioural and organizational variations. The emphasis on crime and control as mutually exclusive models may serve to obfuscate and mystify power. Regardless of whether the control is defined as punishment or persuasion, an analytic commitment to power provides promising directions.

The study of power is basic to an understanding of the control process and the attendant "problems of order." From the various perspectives on social control a significant theme emerges linking social order to concentrations of greater proportions of power resources. What then do we mean by power and order? A definition of order within these contexts will undoubtedly demonstrate the underlying transformation of control. Order, as an arrangement of institutions with established structures of action and systems of tools, defines the nature and quality of opportunities to act.

Historically this phenomenon can be traced to the development of the concept of peace. Crime is an intrusion of certain orders, a disruption of the peaceful order. Irrespective of whether this order is defined by a community's normative values or by specific interest groups, control becomes a political derivative.

Admittedly, control involves the management of a wide range of mechanisms and institutions for the maintenance of a certain peace, however defined. Control through the use of coercive sanctions approximates more accurately the nature of social relationships within a "power" perspective.

The processes and structures of control have been studied by writers and practitioners from many fields; diverse points of view may be discerned within this inquiry. Penology is no exception; penologists have discussed many features of sanctions, utilizing a variety of methodological and theoretical approaches. Although research on sanctions continues to grow, especially of a descriptive or exhortative nature, gaps exist with regard to crucial considerations of how sanctions are sustained and challenged; how theories of sanctions are developed, tested and compared; how new questions are provoked especially in relation to measuring the "costs" of sanctions and "to whom"; how easily sanctions may be transformed into mobilized resources controlling other types of crime; how sanctions transfer and/or exacerbate existing conflicts; to name only a few. Do sanctions, for example, as socially recognized privileges of force, provide fundamental "links" between the structures of authority and the interactional encounters on a more microlevel of analysis?

Essentially, sanctions perform legitimating services designed ultimately to make order possible in a society in which power and privilege are not equally distributed. Complete with articles of faith, sacred symbols, hardware, rituals; powerful images have thus been evoked and the veritable myth of sanctions developed.

Although no society can hope to survive without sanctions, positive or negative, the attempts to manipulate sanctions have been complex. Informal controls to suppress disruptive behaviour and prescribe behaviour in the interests of the "common good" alone become problematic as the variety of social worlds and the size of groupings that are designated as deviant increase. To maintain a minimum "common moral order" among divergent subcultures additional mechanisms have been introduced. Formal methods may, however, not be more effective in influencing the behaviour, but they have symbolic significance insofar as they are applied consistently to members of differing primary groups.

Stated differently, the co-ordination of large scale activities itself tends to be a full-time occupation necessitating enormous resources. The relative decline of informal social controls leads to demands for the imposition of formal and institutional controls.

External controls through a series of formal institutions such as law and the socialization of values become perceived as providing qualities of group conformity over a large number of people. Generally, the literature on sanctions has been primarily, and too narrowly, concerned with the production of norm conformity. The continued emphasis on deterrence or recidivism precludes any careful attention to the extremely significant and larger roles played by sanctions. It is possible that the relative importance of sanctions is far more complex than has been assumed. Almost invariably, socio-legal studies have been successful in examining in isolation, only fragmented units of the legal system, vis-à-vis, the deterrent effects of sanctions, the interactional and organizational determinants of decision making, the development of specific statutes, the characteristics of the deviants, etc., while concurrently failing to consider the wider context of which these notable elements presumably constitute integral parts. Indeed, these weaknesses in explaining, specifying and interpreting interests, forces and participants belie an understanding of the dynamic nature of sanctions. Aside from examining the impact of rules, orders and commands on conduct, it further remains incumbent upon us to interpret the contradictions as well as the conflicts arising out of these incompatibilities. In analysing the development of legal authority, control is often depicted as rigidly fixed in character. The readings included in this book argue that interactions are maintained via a complexity of contingencies operating on a number of systems—economic, social, political, etc. Similarly, the relationship between the environment and behaviour cannot be considered as static especially since these relationships change, modify and develop over time.

These contributions yield sensitizing conceptual insights by specifying ways in which control efforts engage in complicated processes of interchanges with environing systems. Admitting that an immense amount of elaboration and clarification is needed, they note that the central conception and most important characteristic of control is that they are "open." This flexibility used to describe and analyse social interactions refers to a complex of interdependent parts, components and processes that involve discernible regularities of relationship, especially as known and used by actors. They note that control systems are inherently evolving, engaged in processes of interchange with its environment, as well as consisting of interchanges among its internal units.

To elucidate, the organizational environment is construed to be directly and extremely relevant in particular ways, not in determining behaviour nor as a passive setting but rather as interacting actively with the behaving individual in such a way that certain environments are more likely to elicit certain behaviours and inhibit others. How then does the social organization affect the way people lead their lives, what they do and with whom they do it? The political environment is "permissive," providing opportunities for activities to occur within the framework of the institutional environment. Lastly, although the determinants of social control are usually construed to be centralized or organizationally oriented and independent of local historical needs, there are many behavioural strategies that fit remarkably well with certain characteristics of the local environment.

The articles in this text certainly provide useful empirical and theoretical knowledge concerning the processes and structures of sanctions. Essentially, they examine the objectives of those sanctions which fall within a general security perspective and its emphasis on efficient, smooth circulation and control of movements. They document carefully how penological issues do not exist in a vacuum but occur within certain environments which to date have been understated. For example, the historical development of the penal institution in all its manifestations is integrally related to the parallel development of the modern state. It should therefore be obvious that addressing the issues of sanctions or changes in sanctions and their relationship with institutional references is a monumental endeavour.

Penology does not exist independent of social life but emerges out of complex interactive processes. Analyses of penology may be conceptually more comprehensive by focussing on the nature of controls constructed by actors in meaningful interaction, the multiple involvements with larger relational communities and lastly, the relationships with disciplining/sanctioning agencies. The self concept, relational controls and formal controls are inextricably linked. An examination of both the impinging controls of outside structures and the emerging (responding) controls of the community is warranted. Responses therefore, include the necessary and ongoing accomplishments that develop in effective interaction in order to better cope with various problems of adjustments and commitment. That is, in fragmented and differentiated social worlds, actors come into contact and attend to the responses of others. How is response as a purposive and continuous activity, socially organized?

In discovering the nature of incarcerated social realities, we will examine how actors in their mundane and routine forms of interaction create opportunities, regulate difficulties and manage their problems. This leads us to determine the extent to which they acknowledge to themselves and to others symbolic expressions of collectivity. Essentially, this entails an investigation of how they adapt, respond and make use of their affiliations. In terms of its nature and roles, how does the subculture or community function to secure the flow of resources, information about activity, neutralizations, manipulations and coping strategies, within incarcerated settings?

The manner in which these incarcerated communities and individual actors respond to the legitimacy of labels is fundamental to any analysis of social control and change within institutionally mediated and constructed environments. Traditionally these responses have been studied in terms of accommodations and negotiations. From the readings it becomes apparent that a valuable commodity like self-identity is not a negotiable item especially from the perspective of those in subordinate positions. A recognition of their realities is sought. The mechanism used to secure this immediate end is protest or challenge.

Another more expansive interpretation considers crime and more specifically penology as expressions of challenges to authority. That is, all crimes are politically significant acts in the symbolic or real struggle for power. Regardless of the competing definitions of the foundations or accountability of state—populist, pluralist or elitist—the state must ultimately be perceived within its role as definer. Accordingly, the state is an interested party and loses its neutrality. The legal system is designed to maintain the existing distributions of powerful resources. One such resource is the certification of offenders. Political consciousness on the part of offending members is not a necessary condition of the politicization of "criminal" protests.

By definition, crime may also reflect the ineffectiveness of the persuasive and coercive resources of the authority structure in controlling "disorderly" elements. Caution must be exercised in noting that not all protests constitute a challenge to existing social relationships. For example, the label may be conveniently flexible resulting in exaggerated or even understated implications for those in authority. Simply stated, "challengeable" order becomes a pivotal concern in any discussion of protest. Consequently, these mechanisms do not remain neutral. Whether our concerns are with the "offender" or offending institutions, actors represent meaningful identities denoting their status or their "fit" in the social order. Traditionally, studies of protests have been discredited because of rhetoric, sloganeering and failure to consider non-coercive aspects of power. The last few decades, however, have witnessed the growth of critical perspectives which have provided both substantive breakthroughs in power analyses, and the methodological generation of new data bases. The term has come to denote a wide variety of activities and imputations. Clearly, crime is the subject of complex interpretations connoting contests of, or more appropriately, challenges to interests and power.

Essentially, fundamental differences in interests and influence, characterize social order. That is, a certain order will obviously satisfy some interest groups and offend others. Whether we accept the notions that normative standards are assented to by the collectivity or the ruling class, social order tends to exact civil disobedience.

In brief, responses are studied in terms of how they shape and are shaped by the nature and quality of social control. Relatively little attention has been directed to these larger contexts in which response occurs. Little effort has been made in examining how formal social controls stimulate the development of informal controls and how subcultural and community accomplishments affect relations with the outside.

From the foregoing it is apparent that power is considered to be central to social control and order. Much of social theorizing, however, has been suggestive of these relationships and it is more of a definitive application of these assumptions of control with which we now proceed.

The concept of sanction generally refers to a coercive process by which the law seeks to impose its will in the last resort upon an offender. This traditional notion limits sanctions to penalties concomitant with breaches of norms. A legal sanction is an official imposition of consequences such as civil liability, criminal punishment and rehabilitation or "diversionary" tactics. These consequences are sanctions—promises or threats of force or coercion which are supported by the power of law.

More sophisticated notions of sanctions endow the concept with even a wider meaning. Other forms of sanctions include education or socialization, that is the structural or organizational climate within which the "offender" operates.

Sanctions are based on force and conscience. Values constrain if not punish. Laws exist whenever a groups' values rule as authoritative and where there are agencies whose staff compel compliance to rules. But, coercion is legality. Is law more than merely a strongly enforced custom? If we point to state or official enforcement as the differentiating factor, a new dilemma emerges: how are we to distinguish the "legal" from the "political"? Likewise, although the legal system and political system are closely interrelated, they are presented as separate.

People obey the law because they are constrained to do so by force and also because they consent to its hegemonic operations. Such a view was in the past particularly associated with the notions that society and law are based on social contract.

The threat of punishment is believed to contribute to the development of morality and respect for law. A persuasively more powerful interpretation considers the enforcement of criminal law as inherently coercive. Under optimal circumstances, punishment is very much one-sided; the parties are unequal in strength. Penology is the study of inequality.

Control through law performs a myriad of functions, both manifest and latent. The many purposes of sanctions have become obfuscated by the state's attempts to couch them in a number of convenient models. These purposes conceal institutional-ideological or rational-bureaucratic goals. The facile dichotomous classifications of Crime Control and Due Process, further subdivided into punishment, treatment, compensation and regulation are ideologically designed to exacerbate tensions.

The articles in this book clearly contextualize the problematic relationship(s) between "corrections" and social order. Subsequently, readers are urged to confront, interrogate and locate the convenience of current correctionalist impulses within the overall political economy of control.

C h a p t e r 1

Bilateral Legitimation: The Parole Pendulum[*]

R.S. Ratner

Introduction

For all its material affluence and its apparent triumph over communist economic orders, capitalist societies are scored by deep inequalities and, consequently, suffer chronic legitimation problems (Habermas, 1975; Wolfe, 1977; Offe, 1984, 1985). When adjustments in the accumulative sphere prove inadequate to manage or dispel recurrent crises, the burden of social control falls on coercive systems—occasionally in the form of foreign military exploits, more often as intensified domestic repression. This was evident in the late 1970s when worrying economic trends precipitated in recessionary cutbacks, a weakening of democratic institutions, and the emergence of so-called "exceptional states" (Hall et al., 1978; Ratner and McMullan, 1983). The neo-conservative politics unleased by the negative trajectories of that period were no less visible in Canada, where subsequent developments accentuated problems of legitimation (Taylor, 1983, 1987).

Without doubt, the spread of a reactive political climate in this country was fuelled by growing anxiety over crime. In 1981, for example, 40% of respondents to a Canadian Urban Victimization Survey said they felt unsafe walking alone in their own neighbourhood at night.[1] A 1984 Decima Quarterly Report poll found a similar level of concern among Canadians. Of those surveyed, 44% agreed with the statement: "I don't feel safe when I go out alone at night in my neighbourhood" (Johnson, 1988: 24). Substantiating this

[*] The author wishes to thank the various members of staff at the British Columbia offices of the National Parole Board and Corrections Service Canada for granting the interviews that helped to inform this study.

fear, a 1988 survey by Statistics Canada estimates that nearly 5 million Canadians were victims of at least one crime, and that over half of the crimes were personal—theft, robbery, assault, and sexual assault.[2]

Public anxieties about crime often fixate on the issue of parole, partly because it presents the spectre of unknown offenders legitimately "at large." But controversy over the pros and cons of the parole system often reaches such crescendos as to suggest a symptomatic reading of social crisis,[3] indicative of far more than public attitudes toward the disposition of a relatively small number of offenders. For example, while only 7,000 plus federal prisoners in Canada were on some form of parole in 1991,[4] and although the National Parole Board (NPB) actually grants parole only in about one-third of the cases reviewed, a widely shared public myth persists that the NPB is "soft" on criminals and that the recidivism rate of inmates on parole is astronomical. On the other hand, recent government efforts to allay public fears and encourage a policy of community corrections have been frustrated by a rash of murders committed by prisoners who had been released on parole or on mandatory supervision[5] and who were placed in community correctional facilities despite long histories of sexual violence.[6] No more than a dozen such horrific incidents have occurred over the past several years, but these were sufficient to send up the hue-and-cry of "Scrap parole!" Oddly, government commissions and task forces have arrived at radically different recommendations about the use of prison and parole in combatting crime. The Government Task Force on Program Review (Nielsen, 1986) urged restrained use of incarceration, since imprisoning criminals had become a fiscal "luxury."[7] The Canadian Sentencing Commission (Archambault, 1987), arguing the need to make sentences "real," recommended the abolition of parole,[8] while the Parliamentary Justice Committee (Daubney, 1988) strongly supported parole, community alternatives, and improved treatment programs.[9] In the very same week that the Daubney Report was released, the then Solicitor General James Kelleher proceeded to introduce a bill to tighten the Parole Act and lengthen the proportion of sentences that inmates serve in prison. Paradoxically, the Pepino inquiry into one of the sensationalized parolee murders ended with a qualified endorsement of the halfway house concept.[10]

All of the varied proposals raise important questions about the sources of public misinformation and media bias in the reporting of parole violations, the role of privatization in the corrections service, and the general problem of restoring public credibility in the parole system. Their contradictory recommendations, however, can best be grasped through contrasting an understanding of parole geared to a concept of "rehabilitation" with parole as a mechanism of societal "regulation."

Parole as Rehabilitation

The main tenets of Enlightenment philosophy—social contract, rationality, free choice—formed the basis of the Classical School of Criminal Law (Beccaria, 1963; Bentham, 1982) during the late 18th and 19th centuries. These juristic assumptions were articulated in a tight grid of offences and corresponding punishments that prescribed a whole catalogue of property crimes, thus protecting the foundations of a nascent capitalist economy. A powerful 19th-century Tory State in Canada, bent on "peace, order, and good government" (Horowitz, 1968), eagerly incorporated classicist doctrine, so that by the turn of the century, classical modes of thinking dominated the Canadian criminal justice system and disparaged "mollycoddling" reforms.[11]

Parole began in Canada with the passage of the Ticket-of-leave Act in 1989 by the Federal Parliament. Like the British legislation from which it was drafted, the Act was vague regarding its essential purpose. Some members of Parliament believed Tickets-of-leave would assist convicts in becoming law-abiding citizens. Others thought it would solve the problem of overcrowding in the prisons. Some saw the new system simply as a means of granting clemency to young and first offenders. By 1905, the Ticket-of-leave experiment was considered to be a success, and by the end of WWI, it had become an established institution,[12] centred on the principle of rehabilitation. This focus was blurred by the social unrest after WWI, which led to increases in crime and criticisms of leniency in the criminal justice system. But the granting of Tickets-of-leave was again liberalized to counter the escalating prison population during the Depression years, and later to allow prisoners to join the armed forces or to accept employment in war industry. This development coincided with a theoretical shift away from juristic-deductive reasoning to scientific study of the offender (Lombroso, 1912). This new positivist thrust, combined with the practical need to mould a well disciplined work-force, eclipsed the classical philosophy of retribution and deterrence in favour of rehabilitation. Reformist intentions were officially endorsed by the 1938 Archambault Report, which recommended humanitarian changes in correctional institutions and commented approvingly on the "rehabilitative ideal." A subsequent government report on corrections—Fauteux Committee (1956)—went further in urging the abandonment of the retributive philosophy, the provision of treatment facilities for specific categories of offenders, the development of professional specialties to serve prisoners, probation departments and after-care agencies, and the establishment of criminology as "the study of crime and its treatment" (1956: 85). In commenting on the Ticket-of-leave system, the Fauteux Committee was "astonished" that "such antiquated legislation" could provide "such satisfactory results" (1956: 55); nevertheless, it called for creation of a parole authority organizationally independent from the parole service.

The recommendations of the Fauteux Report were implemented in 1959 with the proclamation of the Parole Act and the creation of a National Parole Board. In transferring authority to grant conditional release to the NPB, the concept of rehabilitation was incorporated into law, with parole envisioned as a logical step between confinement and freedom. Accordingly, a National Parole Service was established to prepare cases for Board consideration and to supervise parolees in the community.

In 1969, the rehabilitative strategy was extended to cover those inmates released automatically at the two-thirds mark of their prison sentence, owing to earned remission.[13] The Ouimet Committee, appointed partly in response to the civil rights movements in the late 1960s (which called the criminal justice system into question), expressed concern that inmates deemed unfit for parole were being released without any of the controls or benefits of supervision provided to the better risk parolees. On the Committee's recommendation, amendments to the Parole Act of 1969 were passed which required that inmates released as a result of remission be supervised in the community for the remainder of the sentence under a program known as Mandatory Supervision (MS).[14] The provision of counselling services to assist high-risk MS releasees through a transitional period of statutory conditional release seemed to establish the dominance of the "rehabilitative ideal."

Even with its apparent entrenchment, the rehabilitative philosophy has been continually assailed on grounds of "undue lenience," a characterization which many prisoners would regretfully dispute. This incongruity reveals the extent to which parole remains a politically charged issue, obtaining erratic and unprincipled support, at best, from public and governmental sectors. This was evident in the notorious "gating" controversy, where, between September 1982 and May 1983, 11 MS releasees with histories of violence or serious sexual offences, were "gated" (i.e., had their release revoked at the penitentiary gate).[15] The practice was then challenged in the courts as an unreasonable reading of sections of the Parole Act and as violative of S.9 of the Charter of Rights, which prohibits arbitrary detention or imprisonment. In May 1983, the Supreme Court of Canada declared gating to be illegal, and all gated individuals who were still incarcerated were released on MS. This prompted the Solicitor General to introduce amendments to the Parole Act that would, in effect, legalize gating. Bills C-67 and C-68, passed in June 1986, gave authority to the National Parole Board to "detain," until warrant expiry, prisoners deemed unsuitable for automatic release under MS.[16] While mollifying public criticism of the parole system, this legislation seemed to undermine the logic of conditional release, since mandatory supervision had been recommended by the Ouimet Committee precisely in order to prevent dangerous offenders from being discharged without first undergoing a transitional period of supervision in the community.

This inconsistency is reflected in the public's persistent failure to differentiate parole, with its moderately respectable success rate (approximately 65%), from mandatory supervision, with its significantly lower success rate (approximately 40%).[17] The reasons for the distorted public perception are not clear, but it is unlikely that media bias can be the sole explanation, since a lack of assiduousness on the part of correctional officials in clarifying these terms for public consumption have invited general confusion.[18] The conflating of parolees with MS and other high-risk offenders creates the impression of a uniformly high recidivist rate, which then negates the argument for rehabilitation. Undifferentiated high recidivism rates in the context of increasing inmate populations[19] and sharply escalating state expenditures in corrections (MacLean, 1986: 125-127; 1989), ultimately sink therapeutic expectations to the level of "nothing works" (Martinson, 1974). Moreover, inherent restraints on acclaiming the successes of parole,[20] the dwarfing of positive outcomes by newer forms of criminalization (e.g., child-abuse, wife-battering), and the failure to link the rehabilitation of offenders to opportunity-structures in the economy,[21] all undermine the "rehabilitative ideal" and contribute to its antithesis, the movement to "abolish parole."

So we are drawn to the paradoxical conclusion that while the rehabilitative approach must count as a modest success, its general impact sustains a pattern of overall failure. Parole has not reduced incarceration rates, nor halted the growth of criminal justice expenditures, nor mobilized enthusiastic public support. This brings to mind W.T. McGrath's contention that, "Parole and mandatory supervision cannot be assessed in isolation from the rest of the criminal justice system. It is the system as a whole that needs review" (1982: 10).

The question is, what is the "system as a whole"?

Parole as Regulation

In a political economy of crime control, the "system as a whole" is nothing less than the entire social formation. This means that any single institutional element, such as parole, cannot be understood in isolation from the socio-economic totality in which it functions,[22] and certainly not apart from the societal mode of production. In capitalist societies, the mode of production is characterized by relations of domination and subordination, wherein exploitation and the appropriation of surplus value do not occur smoothly or without inciting resistance. Periodic crises, reflecting economic disjunctures at the national and global levels, are registered at the political level. In order to maintain order and protect the assets of capital, power over the working and "redundant" classes must be legitimated. Continued compliance in the interests of "productive efficiency" requires that human material must be defined as "worthy" or "unworthy" in terms of "good" and "bad" investments in human capital. Through ideological hegemony ("consent armed with coercion"—Gramsci, 1971), a stable social order is achieved which seeks to ensure that production and exchange remain unimpaired. In advanced capitalist societies, the state becomes the primary mechanism to articulate, co-ordinate, and direct this rationalization process (Spitzer, 1979),[23] and the "criminal justice system" becomes an indispensable element of this "modern technology of subjection" (Foucault, 1977).

From this vantage-point,[24] parole is understood as one of the managerial solutions to the problem of surplus labour,[25] especially in recessionary periods of the capitalist economy. Structurally, it operates to harmonize institutional imperatives of the "corrections" sub-system with the ubiquitous state functions of accumulation, coercion, and legitimation.[26]

1.   Parole serves the *accumulative* function by helping to regulate the size and growth of penitentiary populations and by stimulating the development of community corrections (including needed facilities, as well as personnel). As in the case of mandatory supervision, parole allows for a level of de-institutionalization that contains prohibitive costs of prison construction while alleviating institutional overcrowding.[27] On the other hand, parole policy can also be shaped to lengthen the control of the state over penitentiary inmates, thereby fostering organizational expansion.[28] Unsurprisingly, budgetary expenditures and personnel for both Corrections Service Canada (CSC) and the National Parole Board, have increased regularly since their formation. By increasing employment in this manner, and thus facilitating the realization of surplus value, economic and political crises are to some degree averted, at least in the short term.

2.   Parole serves the *coercive* function by placing individuals officially "at risk" in the community, thus permitting an extension of surveillance in order to monitor "trouble" and widen the involvement of agencies of "criminal justice." In this respect, parolees and MS releasees each represent sectors of the population that must be subjected to unrelenting control, since their relative vulnerability to economic crisis constitutes them as a core of potential dissent.[29] By placing these groupings under permanent scrutiny (through "supervisory" powers that often result in a return to custody), dissidence can be stifled both within and beyond the penitentiary setting.

3.   Parole serves the *legitimative* function through claims of protecting the public and "rehabilitating" individual offenders. But, while the

rhetoric of "reintegration" is bruited, public safety takes priority and usually short-circuits reintegration schema. Moreover, legitimation strategies net greater political dividends when invoked on behalf of greater coercive control, such as when public outcries over egregious parole violations are used to justify more repressive policies. In this respect, parolee "failures" serve as psychological scapegoats for the systemic failures of capitalism.

Although there are no Canadian studies which offer historical validation of these correlative functions of the criminal justice system, Mandel, in attempting to account for variations in the repression rate (and for his own assessment of the 1980s as the most repressive decade in Canadian history), makes the following observation (1991: 186).

"What strikes even the casual student of the history of punishment in the twentieth century is how closely changes in the repressive rate seem to parallel changes in economic conditions or what is often called the 'business cycle.'" In tracing the relationship between recessionary periods (1930s, late 1950s, early 1980s) and steep rises in the rate of repression, Mandel, using Greenberg's analysis (1977) of the oscillatory relationship between annual *unemployment* rates and annual admissions to Canadian penitentiaries, finds that connection to be the crucial indicator, rather than the conventionally assumed relationship between *crime* and repression. Studies by Tepperman (1977) and Box (1987) also point to the significance of the employment/repression ratio, leading Mandel to adopt a qualified version of the extra-punitive hypothesis.[30] While this is short of offering adequate historical substantiation for the political economy analysis that needs to be made in this area, Mandel's interpretation is suggestive of the links between parole decision-making and labour market opportunities. His exploration offers empirical grounds to conceptualize parole and mandatory supervision as homeostatic devices for regulating the flow of surplus labour through the penitentiaries,[31] producing the "quasi-normalization of deviant populations" (Spitzer, 1975), and helping to preserve the stability of bourgeois rule (Mandel, 1985).[32]

If this depiction is correct, the ultimate effect of such palatably repressive "solutions" is to ensure the continuation of high incarceration and recidivism rates,[33] along with a consequent expansion of the carceral system. From the perspective of parole as societal regulation, we are led, therefore, to the ironic observation that the purported "failures" of the correctional system add up to an uninterrupted success. Not liberal-cynicism, but the *sardonicism* of Foucault best grasps the inverted logic of this situation:

For the observation that prison fails to eliminate crime, one should perhaps substitute the hypothesis that prison has succeeded extremely well in producing delinquency—so successful has been the prison that, after a century and a half of "failures" the prison still exists, producing the same results, and there is the greatest reluctance to dispense with it (1977: 277).

Bilateral Legitimation

Interestingly, both the rehabilitative and regulative notions of parole (and corrections, generally) infuse the recent "mission" statements of the National Parole Board and the Correctional Service:

> The Board, by facilitating the timely integration of offenders as law-abiding citizens, contributes to the protection of society. (Mission Statement of the National Parole Board, 1986, p.1)

> The Correctional Service of Canada, as part of the criminal justice system, contributes to the protection of society by actively encouraging and assisting offenders to become law-abiding citizens, while exercising reasonable, safe, secure, and humane control. (Mission of the Correctional Service of Canada, 1989, p.4)

This merger of control philosophies occurs through sequential implementation of inclusionary strategies (rehabilitation) and exclusionary strategies (regulation), as dictated by economic conditions and political exigencies.[34] Periods of relative affluence ordinarily feature inclusionary (or "re-integration") strategies emphasizing "treatment" and "community corrections" programs.[35] The expansion of community corrections, which entails a re-commodification of "bad" human material, provides an accumulative stimulus and boosts legitimation, since an increased investment in "rehabilitation" is generally perceived as enhancing social equity. Thus, domestic repression is less visible during periods of economic prosperity, operating mainly at the level of "noiseless surveillance."[36] As regards parole, a more lenient policy of conditional release is tactically appropriate.

During periods of economic crisis and downturn, the state confronts a contradictory situation. The reduced availability of funds for state-sponsored treatment and corrections, combined with a growing public resentment towards programs that provide various forms of assistance to "less-deserving" offenders,[37] makes "community corrections" politically untenable and forces the state to re-adopt exclusionary control strategies, especially since the increased economic vulnerability of the poor and working-class sectors of the population *does* result in more crime, which then "justifies" the recourse to coercion. But punishment and imprisonment is costly, requiring an investment of state revenues that must be diverted from more profitable sources of accumulation. The costs of new custodial facilities, increased policing, and more sophisticated technology, can be reduced, to some extent, via privatization,[38] but this presents a further contradiction—the dangers of abuse and non-accountability should the state lose control over the enforcement and administration of "criminal justice." In this quandary, the corrections sector performs a vital legitimative function alongside its intensified coercive activity, through such programs as victim assistance and "target-hardening," and by strident law-and-order campaigns. Such concrete manoeuvres re-invigorate the political status quo and prevent mass public disaffection. In this context, parole risks previously adjudged "assumable," become "undue risks." Parole grant rates go down and revocation rates go up.[39]

    If then, corrections performs an ideological "system-maintenance" function in good times and bad, this oscillation nevertheless poses serious problems for practitioners, especially during periods of fiscal austerity when the rehabilitative component must be curtailed. One danger in promoting carceral expansion, whatever the short-term legitimation benefits, is that it may suppress tolerable behaviour and dissent, controverting the declared principles of democratic society, principles to which most people working in corrections avowedly adhere. Moreover, the stimulation of "moral panics" as a means of coping with legitimation crises could result in an over-investment incarceral expansion, compounding the problem of fiscal instability.[40] The end result of such regulative strategies would be to alienate both managerial technocrats and rank-and-file operatives of the coercive state. Professional "training," organizational expansion, and the authority of "science"[41] offer only limited inducements to collaborate in abandonments of the rehabilitative philosophy. Either covert strategies proliferate to circumvent neo-conservative policy and rhetoric,[42] or resignation prevails, with practitioners sustained only by the belief that the "rehabilitative ideal" will be disinterred when the "new realism" fails.

    That government tinkering with conditional release policy does little to dispel these contradictions was illustrated by Solicitor General James Kelleher's 1988 proposals. Responding to constitutional challenges to Bills C-67, 68[43] (which attempted to legalize "gating"), and wishing to restore flagging public confidence in the parole system,[44] Kelleher declared that, henceforth, "risk to society" would be the overriding factor in conditional release decisions. Four major changes to parole legislation were proposed:

1. Earned remission and mandatory supervision would be abolished.[45]
2. Mandatory supervision would be replaced by a period of supervised statutory release for the last one-third of the sentence or one year before the expiry of the term of imprisonment, whichever was less.
3. The parole eligibility date would change from one-third of the sentence to one-half of the total sentence.
4. The day parole eligibility date would change from one-sixth of the sentence to a date which is six months prior to the full parole eligibility date.

Many observers surmised that the net effect of these changes would be longer prison sentences, an outcome which exacerbates the criminogenic effects of imprisonment by extending incarceration beyond the period where the inmate normally would have "earned" a remission release. Rather than contributing to a safer society, the ultimate effect of these measures could be to increase the likelihood of danger. Moreover, the proposed period of "statutory release," which limits the disciplinary incentive of earned remission to a maximum of twelve months, could well increase the difficulty of maintaining order within prison institutions since abolishment of the MS remission period reduces the incentive for "good behaviour."

    A further "balancing" proposal to improve the system's ability to differentiate between low-risk and high-risk offenders through more frequent reviews was expected to result in the expeditious release of inmates who posed little or no risk to the community. In practice, however, plans to increase the frequency of parole hearings are often waived or delayed because the system lacks the resources to conduct accelerated reviews and to supervise more releasees in the community.[46]

    In sum, the Kelleher proposals, in deferring to public demands for retribution, would have overloaded prisons and furthered the absorption of non-violent offenders into the prison subculture. In their criticism of these proposals as "hastily and speculatively formulated in response to public misconceptions," the Canadian Criminal Justice Association noted that:

> By projecting the impact of these proposals on the penitentiary admissions for 1985-86, one concludes that [the] resources would result in that group of inmates serving 23% more time, which would translate into a total of 1471 additional prison years to be served at a cost of $58,840,000 to the taxpayers for that one group of inmates.[47]

Recognizing the potential impact on prison populations, Kelleher modified his proposals to reduce parole by aiming them primarily at "violent" offenders.

Presumably this adjustment would neither undermine the principal criterion of public safety[48] nor overtax institutional capacity. But if tinkering with parole eligibility dates can purchase a temporary measure of legitimation, it cannot relieve the criminal justice system of the weight of contradictions implicit in such an opportunistic posture. Whether through "rehabilitation" or "regulation," correctionalist policy is wedded to system-maintenance, not change or transformation. The intent of either orientation is to legitimate the state and leave fundamentally unchanged the system of institutionalized class interests which the state is beholden to represent, if in an erratic and contradictory fashion. The rhetoric for popular consumption is that parole is an integral feature of the "liberal" state, but that it justifies only a limited investment. Precisely why the costs of effective rehabilitation are insupportable escapes scrutiny.

Whither Parole?

The vicissitudes of parole depend upon the flow of human merchandise through the criminal justice system, which in turn determines whether prison institutions are likely to disappear, contract, or expand. In the class-based society of Canada, prison abolition is unfortunately a quixotic goal, given the need to create and maintain an offender class whose treatment and disposition would deter those in similarly deprived circumstances from electing to misbehave.[49] The rationale for the existence of such a class will only evaporate with the disappearance of subsistence labour and derivative inequalities. Barring some major societal transformation, this prospect is inconceivable. Current de-skilling and divestment trends in the globalization phase of capital are more likely to swell the reserve labour supply.[50]

Even a moderate contraction of the prison population is unlikely, taking into account the legislative curtailments of mandatory supervision and parole, the inflexibly long sentences imposed on capital offenders, and the intensified scrutiny of those who do get discharged.[51] Bureaucratic subversion of new legislative strictures will doubtless occur, but parole and correctional officers will balk at assuming detectable risks when organizational fidelity (as well as political legitimacy) is at stake. Demographically, more people are bound to be proletarianized by the movements of international capital, increasing their susceptibility to crime and to stigmatization within the carceral order. New prison construction may be unaffordable,[52] but the cost of managing a widening pool of offenders will be reduced by technological means, a development now widespread in the U.S. (McCarthy, 1987) and taking root in Canada with the paired use of electronic monitoring and home confinement.[53] In correctional terminology, these developments are euphemistically described as "striving for consistency and balance between *rehabilitation* and *deterrence*,"[54] but either orientation yields similar overall results—continuing high recidivism rates, an expansion of the carceral system, and reinforcement of the dominant ideology. Whether it be economic boon or crisis that impacts social order, state policy is adjusted to shift the parole pendulum so as to recoup legitimation and ensure the continued commodification of crime control. But what else should we expect of a "downstream" auxiliary control institution functioning in a dependent role and demonstrating its puerility against the more salient priorities of capitalist society?[55]

We must ask, however, whether the minimalist strategy of bilateral legitimation is necessarily all that the state can hope to achieve within the structural conditions imposed by capital. Does the ideologically fixed arc linking rehabilitation and regulation mean that rehabilitation is necessarily a spurious concept or one that cannot be implemented to real effect? Is genuine reform not possible within the system-imperatives outlined herein? Let us assume, for the moment, that the most profound pessimism is never total, and that possibilities for progressive action do reside even in the present situation. The report of the Parliamentary Justice Committee (Daubney), as well as a like-minded report of the Canadian Bar Association, did, after all, urge the retention of parole and a switch of priorities from imprisonment to community alternatives. And partly owing to such recommendations, the government did reject the advice of the Canadian Sentencing Commission to abolish parole and adopt a system of fixed sentences. While the mandatory supervision program *is* being eroded, and though more stringent rules now govern the release of violent criminals, the need for fiscal constraint and the realization, however grudging, that there can be no "responsibility" without rehabilitation, has, at least, halted a headlong shift to the right. But for rehabilitation to be more than a mere shibboleth, "community corrections" must become a priority of correctional reform, and Citizens' Advisory Committees (CACs), acting as liaisons between the public and prison institutions, must become an important and valued catalyst of change. In fact, there has been a rapid growth in Corrections Service Canada's use of existing community residential facilities,[56] and CSC is on record as favouring an expansion of the role of the CACs.[57] Yet there is little evidence of CSC plans to open new halfway houses under its aegis, despite the fact that a periodic shortage of beds impedes the National Parole Board in carrying out its parole plans for specific inmates.[58] Many federal inmates remain in prison despite reaching eligibility for parole, not only because of information logjams in the federal parole bureaucracy, but because assignments to community projects are often made before such projects even exist.[59] Moreover, increased concern over residential standards and staff safety issues such as security requirements, staff quality, and financial liability, have sapped morale amongst halfway house workers and induced private agencies to drop contracts with CSC.[60] A Toronto CAC was abruptly disbanded by the Correctional Service because it became too critical of CSC's hurried efforts to privatize more of its community facilities.[61]

Amidst these contradictions, the "community" side of program services was given a decided boost with the appointment of Ole Ingstrup, a reform-minded veteran of the Danish correctional system, to the office of Corrections Commissioner. A main architect of the parallel Mission Statements of the NPB and CSC, Ingstrup fought public cynicism and reactionary staff attitudes in channelling resources toward more institutional treatment programs and community corrections, partly by using incentives such as higher pay rates or favourable parole evaluations to entice prisoners into programs.[62] While this new momentum is continually jeopardized by bureaucratic intransigence, public disapprobation, and various "privatization" fiascos, for now it appears that Ingstrup's reforms have halted the slide back to "warehousing" offenders. Under his leadership, the "challenge of re-integration" restored fading correctionalist motifs of rehabilitation, treatment, and community corrections. Since 1987, the pages of *Liaison*, *Let's Talk*, and *Justice Report* have been filled with exhortations linking expanded programming to "long-range protection against recidivism."

Seeking a balance between the "tough-minded" reforms that had been proposed by former solicitor general James Kelleher—proposals sidetracked by the 1988 federal election—and the liberal-reformist ideology implicit in the Mission Statements engineered by Ingstrup, the government tabled the Corrections and Conditional Release Act (Bill C-36), October 8, 1991, an omnibus bill to reform sentencing, prison, and parole, replacing the Penitentiaries Act (1868) and the Parole Act (1958). While the proposed Act is purportedly aimed at public safety and protection in order to rebuild trust in the corrections system, it also contains elements that project a rehabilitative scope. Significant changes to conditional release policy are the following:[64]

1. Eligibility for full parole for violent offenders can be delayed, at a judge's discretion ("judicial determination"), for one-half of the sentence from the current one-third.

2. Sexual offences against children and serious drug offences are re-categorized as crimes for which offenders can be detained in prison custody until warrant expiry (i.e., these offenders are eligible for "gating").

3. Day parole eligibility, which currently becomes available at one-sixth of the sentence, is now fixed at six months before the date of full parole eligibility.

4. More resources will be focussed on violent eligible offenders by streamlining the parole review process for less serious, non-violent,

first-time offenders ("accelerated review"), who will now ordinarily be released as soon as they become eligible for parole at the one-third mark in their sentence.

5. Earned remission is abolished and converted to statutory release of inmates at the two-thirds mark in their sentence, unless they are paroled earlier or detained by the parole board past the two-thirds mark. Mandatory supervision is retained from the time of statutory release to sentence expiry, to ensure control and assistance.

6. The system of granting passes from prison is tightened. No unescorted temporary absence passes will be allowed for those classified as maximum security inmates.

Whether the above proposals merely represent a pastiche of concessions that will have little effect on re-integrating offenders and reducing prison populations, depends upon the development of institutional and community programming for both violent and non-violent offenders. The provision of such programs is crucial and would refute the main criticism of the new legislation that it is all "smoke and mirrors."

Some indication that the desired array of programs might not materialize was hinted in earlier statements by Ingstrup that tied the Mission's strategic objectives "to the realities of government restraint."[65] While Ingstrup offered grounds for claiming a relationship between "good programs" and a "positive effect on recidivism,"[66] leading to estimates that the overall effect of the provisions of Bill C-36 would result in no more than 160 added penitentiary inmates in the six years after the bill became law,[67] the Correctional Investigator's assessment of programming options and prospects belies such optimism.[68] There is no reason to believe that current shortages in institutional programming, of personnel to enable timely access of inmates to existing programs, and of occupational employment and training to boost after-release employment prospects, will significantly improve with the passage of Bill C-36.[69] Framers and supporters of the bill hope, of course, that a delicate balancing of priorities (alternating between retribution and rehabilitation) can be sustained, and that enough "legitimation" will be purchased at either end of the liberal-conservative arc so that "justice" and "reform" need not be construed as mutually exclusive objectives.[70] Barring a complete failure to fund programming and to manage public disapproval, a minimalist strategy of bilateral legitimation does seem tenable, although this would not fulfil the more thoroughgoing reformist vision advanced by correctionalists such as Ingstrup. A genuinely reformist vision, however, would prove difficult to establish if not grounded in a new understanding of social order and change, one that transcends the limited discourse of corrections.[71] Unless a wider commitment is won for the redistribution of resources that could extend the possibilities for "law-abiding" behaviour, unless the role of control institutions in societal regulation is plainly acknowledged, and until the communal re-integration of offenders is generously supported, no significant change can occur, and the present option will have the sole virtue of preventing rehabilitation from dissolving into the punitive cauldron of law and order. Is any other option possible? Not so long as we engage in the ideological practices that validate the current order.

Endnotes

1. 1981 was a peak year for victimization in the United States (Bastian and Deberry Jr., 1991).
2. "Nearly 24 percent of Canadians Victims of Crime," *Globe and Mail,* April 26, 1989. Violent crimes increased steadily from 648 to 856 per 100,000 between 1980 and 1987 (*Canadian Social Trends,* Statistics Canada, No. 11, Winter, 1988, p.31).
3. The past U.S. presidential election between Bush and Dukakis may have been won/lost on the symbolic politics of the "furlough" issue.
4. The reality is that Canada has the highest incarceration rate in the Western world, 112.7 per 100,000, surpassed only by the United States. See, *Basic Facts About Corrections in Canada, 1991* (hereafter referred to as BFACC, 1991), Correctional Service Canada, August, 1988, p. 11. See, also, Waller and Chan, 1974, for an earlier comparison of international incarceration rates.
5. Parole is the discretionary conditional release of an inmate prior to the end of the court's sentence. Mandatory supervision is automatic release of the inmate at the two-thirds mark of the court sentence, owing to earned remission.
6. The most troubling incident was the 1985 murder of Celia Ruygrok, a young correctional employee working in an Ottawa halfway house. She was sexually assaulted and murdered by a resident of the facility who was a diagnosed sexual psychopath on parole from a sentence of non-capital murder.
7. See, *Improved Program Delivery: Justice System*, chapter on "Parole," pp. 325-348.
8. See, *Sentencing Reform: A Canadian Approach*, Chapter 10, "The Meaning of a Sentence of Imprisonment," pp. 231-268.
9. See, *Taking Responsibility*, Chapter 12, "The Future of Conditional Release," pp. 185-196.
10. See, "Man who raped...." *Globe and Mail,* August 24, 1989, and, "Commission Praises Stricter Convict-release System," *Globe and Mail,* June 9, 1990.
11. See, for example, the *Reports of the Inspectors of Penitentiaries* in the early 1900s, which defined the object of imprisonment in strictly classicist terms.
12. In 1913, a special section called the Remission Service was created in the Justice Department to advise on matters coming under the Royal Prerogative of Mercy and the Ticket-of-Leave Act. (For a "short history of parole" in Canada, see MacLean and Ratner, 1987).

13. Remission, or "time off for good behaviour," can comprise as much as one-third of an inmate's sentence.
14. For a detailed review of the history of MS legislation, see Ratner, 1987. See, also, Shewan, 1985, for a comparative evaluation of MS and Parole legislation and policy outcomes.
15. See summary of the then Solicitor General Robert Kaplan's "Rationale for Gating," *Contact*, Vol. 2, No. 1, Summer, 1983, National Joint Committee of the CACPG FCS, pp. 5-6.
16. 810 detentions orders have been issued since Bill C-67 became law in 1986. (Testimony of current National Parole Board Chairman, Fred Gibson, at the hearings of the Justice and the Solicitor General Standing Committee regarding the provisions of Bill C-36, November 28, 1991).
17. Estimates obtained from data supplied by the NPB Pacific Regional Office, Abbotsford, British Columbia—follow-up of all full parole releases in Canada (15,340) and all mandatory supervision releases (25,660) for the 1975-1985 period.
18. NPB Chairpersons habitually apologise for the failure to communicate adequately with the public, without analysing or publicly stating the reasons for that failure. (See, "An Interview with the Chairman," *Liaison*, Vol. 15, No. 2, February 1989, pp. 9-14).
19. See *Let's Talk*, Vol. 11, No. 11, September 1986, Corrections Service Canada, pp. 1-2.
20. Successful parolees are not inclined to divulge their "criminal" backgrounds just in order to tout the virtues of rehabilitation.
21. "Rehabilitation" traditionally focusses on *individual* attitudes and behaviour, but opportunities for employment, without which rehabilitation seldom succeeds, are largely determined by structural factors (e.g., the labour market) rather than individual factors.
22. The geo-political boundaries of such totalities are usually equated with "nation-states," although the effects of the internationalization of capital now render such definitions moot.
23. This synopsis of the political economy of crime control draws on the work of Spitzer (1975, 1979).
24. The "political economy" lineage of crime control is not traced in this paper. For a highly condensed review, see Cohen (1985: 107-111).
25. A "reserve army of labour" is an inherent feature of capitalist society, created and reproduced directly by the accumulation of capital itself. The size of this pool in advanced capitalist economies is increasing under the pressures of capital flight to low wage unregulated regions, shifts in world markets, and "post-industrial" transformations to either capital-intensive works sites or a low-paying service sector.

26. This discussion of the regulatory effects of parole is adapted from a previous analysis of the functions of mandatory supervision in the penal economy (Ratner, 1987). The gross impact of correctional policy on the two groups of inmates is roughly similar.

27. Over 13,000 individuals at an annual average cost of approximately $51,000 per inmate are presently incarcerated in Canadian federal correctional institutions. The average monthly number of federal offenders on parole, day parole, and mandatory supervision is over 8,000. The average annual cost of supervising an offender on parole or mandatory supervision is approximately $8,000 (BFACC, 1991). The combined number of federal inmates released annually on parole and mandatory supervision amounts to about one-third of the total federal inmate population.

28. Approximately 50% of the combined total of federal parolees and MS releasees are revoked on technical grounds or for new offences. This obviously augments the carceral power of both the NBB and CSC, enabling an expansion of correctional resources.

29. For a description of how technical restrictions imposed on parolees by the Parole Board accomplish this objective, see Ratner, 1986.

30. The "greater punitiveness" hypothesis assumes that higher unemployment leads to greater official punitiveness (e.g., through tougher sentencing) due to rising fears of a restive surplus labour force. Mandel concludes that, "…on the best evidence, we seem to be left with this: downturns in the business cycle cause real crime to rise, and this is met by increased repression, but in a way that exaggerates, sometimes to a great extent, the real increase in crime" (1991: 192).

31. Numerous studies document that the great majority of penitentiary inmates come from the poor working class or "lumpenproletariat" underclass (e.g. Gosselin, 1982; Reiman, 1984; Braithwaite, 1979; Nettler, 1984). Although criminality is spread throughout the class structure, anomic pressures *are* unevenly distributed (Merton, 1938); moreover, the system-ethos requires that the "criminal class" be equated with the economic "underclass." Samuelson (1991) argues that the criminal justice system of post-industrial states has moved from "normalizing deviants for labour" to "managing the marginalized." Of course, mainstream analyses focussing on individual rehabilitation (and its failures) show little cognizance of class analysis. Marxist analytic categories are disdained and conceptions of state class conjunctures are embryonic or dissolve into pluralist fictions of state neutrality.

32. A detailed analysis along the analytic lines suggested here would require an integration of the "economic regulationist" model with the symbolic

model of the "blameworthy" group herded into penitentiaries or otherwise punitively controlled.

33. Approximately 40% of Canadian federal penitentiary inmates have served one or more previous sentences in federal penitentiaries (BFACC, 1991).

34. For an insightful analysis of "inclusive" and "exclusive" visions of social control, see Cohen, Chapter 6, 1986. The alternation of these complementary strategies is only sketched in this paper and awaits empirical substantiation, a task that correctionalist researchers appear to studiously avoid. Indeed, correctionalists deny that reducing prison populations is one of the purposes of parole. As the NPB Chairman recently asserted, "The National Parole Board is not a mechanism for controlling prison or penitentiary populations.... Parole in Canada explicitly rejects this approach. The Parole Act does not allow it. The National Parole Board's commitment to public protection does not allow it" (Gibson, 1990: 488). That this is sheer rhetoric is connoted by the fact that Canada has one of the highest imprisonment rates in the western world, yet prison over-crowding is not a major problem. Brodeur, too, notes that, "The use of parole to reduce the prison population has been repeatedly disclaimed by the NPB.... It is nonetheless occurring, sometimes on a massive scale" (1990: 507).

35. See, *Let's Talk*, Vol. 123, No. 5, June 1988, pp. 9-10; and, *Let's Talk*, November/December, 1988, pp. 6-9, Correctional Service Canada.

36. i.e., social control operates *most* effectively through state *ideological* apparatuses rather than through state *repressive* apparatuses. See Althusser, 1971.

37. In more formal terms, a re-activation of the "principle of less eligibility." See Rusche and Kirchheimer, 1939.

38. See *Let's Talk*, Vol. 11, No. 8, June 1, 1986, p. 3.

39. An observation offered by a senior member of the British Columbia National Parole Board, August 11th, 1988.

40. A daily average of approximately 30,000 federal and provincial prisoners are held in 225 correctional institutions in Canada, involving a staff of over 26,000 (BFAAC, 1991). The total annual cost of adult correctional services in Canada is now approximately two billion dollars. Two new penitentiaries have been built, and others are being renovated, mainly in order to avoid new capital construction costs. But even the costs of renovation are astronomical (10 to 30 million dollars per institution). The construction of more custodial facilities seems inevitable, however, since Canada's 10-25 year sentences prior to parole eligibility for capital offences has already resulted in a population of over 1900 "lifers" (BFAAC, 1991). Attempts to cope with overcrowding by "double-

bunking"—the practice of containing two inmates in a single cell—have raised constitutional questions and are generally deemed unsatisfactory.

41. Behaviourist treatment modalities and socio-biology, each of which places the onus of blame/change/incorrigibility on the individual offender, are the privileged perspectives of neo-conservative criminology.

42. With uncommon candor, Fred Gibson, the new Chairman of the National Parole Board, commented that, "Any abolition of earned remission and mandatory supervision would put pressure on the Board to take further risks and exercise discretion positively, since a progressive parole policy absolutely requires a period of supervision in the community." (Remarks following his lecture on, "Parole in Canada Today," Douglas College, New Westminster, B.C., September 19, 1988).

43. In a 1986 court challenge in British Columbia, the Supreme Court of Canada held that the plaintiff, Perry Ross, was deprived of fundamental rights guaranteed by the Canadian Charter, since his defence counsel had been refused the right of cross-examination regarding "evidence" pertaining to his detention under Bills C-67, 68.

44. Suspicion abounded that Kelleher's chief intent was to gain some political mileage through "anti-crime" legislation introduced just prior to a federal election.

45. For further details of the Kelleher plan, see *Let's Talk*, Vol. 13, No. 6, July 1988, pp. 5-8; also, *Liaison*, Vol. 14, No. 7, July-August, 1988, pp. 4-9.

46. This was the experience under the parole eligibility review provision of Bill C-67 where hearings were supposed to be held for all inmates at the one-sixth mark of their confinement. Such hearings were frequently waived, often upon the recommendation of case management officers, and usually because treatment programs within the prison and/or community were simply unavailable.

47. See *Justice Report*, Vol. 5, No. 3, Summer 1988, pp. 1-2, 9-10.

48. *Vancouver Sun*, August 4, 1988.

49. This theoretical requirement for an offender class nullifies the otherwise plausible arguments put forth by abolitionists such as Claire Culhane (1980, 1985) and the prisoners contributing to the inaugural issue of the Canadian *Journal of Prisoners on Prison*, Vol. 1, No. 1, Summer, 1988. The British "left realist" wing of critical criminology also concedes the unlikelihood of eliminating prisons from class society (Matthews, 1989).

50. Even Simon Reisman, Canada's chief negotiator in the Canada-U.S. Free Trade Agreement, has joined the chorus of protests against U.S. implementation of the deal, which has so far resulted in a massive transfer of capital and jobs from Canada to the U.S. and Mexico. ("Top Trade Negotiators Assail U.S.," *Vancouver Sun*, January 18, 1992).

51. See *Let's Talk*, Vol. 13, No. 8, September 1988, pp. 4-5.

52. "Double-bunking" may soon be viewed as an acceptable solution to the problem of prison overcrowding. A state court of appeal in California recently overturned a blanket ban on the controversial practice, ruling that it was *not* cruel and unusual punishment in violation of the Eighth Amendment (*Los Angeles Times,* December 13, 1988). Also in support of institutional confinement, a recent U.S. Justice Department study has tried to show that it costs less to build new prisons than to relieve overcrowding in jails by releasing repeat offenders, given the cost of crimes they commit in the community ("New Prisons Make Sense, Study Says," *Vancouver Sun,* July 4, 1988).

53. An electronic monitoring pilot project sponsored by the British Columbia Solicitor General's Department was recently completed and is now being replicated in other Canadian provinces. The B.C. project has won the confidence of correctional administrators and is now being slotted into the provincial corrections system on an enlarged scale. (See the Report of the Electronic Monitoring Advisory Committee, submitted to the Corrections Branch of the Ministry of Solicitor General of British Columbia, March 2, 1989). Utilization of electronic monitoring has also increased rapidly in the U.S. since its first implementation in 1984 (Schmidt, 1989).

54. See *Liaison*, Vol. 14, No. 8, September 1988, pp. 14-18.

55. Assuming that the correctional component of the criminal justice system did have the wherewithal to promote an aggressive reform agenda, clearly one major constraint on its "relative autonomy" would be the danger of reducing its clientele and jeopardizing its own organizational base. Not much relative autonomy is evident when the Chairman of the National Parole Board remarks that, "I think that co-operation and co-ordination are nearly as important to the Board as its independence, and I think we should not lose sight of the fact that we are still part of the Government of Canada. The way we do business should be in tune with government policies." (Ingstrup, 1986:19).

56. See *Let's Talk*, Vol. 14, No. 3, May 1989, pp. 12-13.

57. See *Let's Talk*, Vol. 14, No. 2, March 1989, pp. 12-14.

58. Currently, there are beds available in many community residential facilities, primarily because fewer inmates are being granted day parole. The reason for this seems to be that inmates who don't participate in treatment programs within the prisons are not likely to qualify for day parole. Since few programs are available (especially for sex offenders), day parole is granted in fewer instances.

59. "Paperwork Delaying Parole Hearings," *Globe and Mail,* September 23, 1988.

60.   "Halfway Houses ending Contracts because of Corrections' Policies," *Globe and Mail,* December 10, 1988.

61.   "Ottawa Fires Watchdog Group Critical of Halfway House Plans," *Globe and Mail,* October 19, 1988.

62.   Ingstrup has acknowledged that some discharged inmates, especially some of those released on mandatory supervision, *are* quite dangerous. In such cases, he favours recourse to "dangerous offender" legislation, which, on application by the Crown, allows a judge to apply an "indeterminate sentence" with release contingent on a parole board determination that the inmate can be safely discharged (*Vancouver Province,* September 22, 1987).

63.   "The primary mandate of Canada's criminal justice system is protection of the public" (Campbell and Cadieux, 1990).

64.   See *Directions for Reform: A Framework for Sentencing, Corrections, and Conditional Release,* 1990, pp. 21-24.

65.   See *Let's Talk,* Vol. 14, No. 5, July 1989, p. 4; and Vol. 14, No. 6, August 1989, p. 7.

66.   Testimony before the Standing Committee of Justice and the Solicitor General on Bill C-36, House of Commons, Issue No. 17, November 27, 1991, p. 10.

67.   Ibid., p. 30.

68.   Testimony before the Standing Committee of Justice and the Solicitor General on Bill C-36, House of Commons, Issue No. 19, December 3, 1991, pp. 7, 10, 11, 16.

69.   This is especially so when judges continue to believe that the courts are "hog-tied" by reforms (*Vancouver Sun,* December 13, 1991), and when the penitentiary system serves the government as a readily available source of cost-cutting, as was the case, for example, when Ottawa slashed spending ($14 million taken from the prison service) to pay for Canadian forces in the Persian Gulf (*The Province,* November 25, 1990).

70.   Criminologists who evaluate correctionalist quandaries by locating the merits of a position at one end of the arc or the other, ignore the plausibility of bilateral legitimation. Mohr (1990) for example, is strongly opposed to retribution and punishment as correctional guidelines, while Brodeur (1990) argues for the abolition of parole, granting too much importance to the issue of the "effectiveness" of rehabilitation. The fact that rehabilitation prospects are compromised by the "attrition of parole" is irrelevant to whether it can nevertheless obtain some measure of legitimation. Appearances are crucial, so failure to "act" on the rehabilitation-parole front can contribute to disorder and consequent legitimation crisis.

71. Even the most sympathetic liberal analyses fail to emphasize the necessity of fundamental social and economic change in order to reduce crime (e.g., Cullen and Gilbert, 1982: 268-291; Reiman, 1984: 143-162). Identifying the starting points of such change is no easy matter, but they are unlikely to originate within the criminal justice system.

References

Althusser, Louis. 1971. "Ideology and Ideological State Apparatuses," in *Lenin and Philosophy and Other Essays*. London: New Left Books.

Andrews, D.A. 1990. "Some Criminological Sources of Anti-rehabilitation Bias in the Report of the Canadian Sentencing Commission," *Canadian Journal of Criminology*, Vol. 32, No. 3, 511-524, 525-529.

Archambault, J. 1938. Report of the Royal Commission to Investigate the Penal System of Canada. Ottawa: King's Printer.

Archambault, J.R. 1987. *Sentencing Reform: A Canadian Approach*. Report of the Canadian Sentencing Commission, Canada.

Bastian, Lisa D. and Marshall M. Deberry Jr. 1991. "Criminal Victimization 1990," *Bureau of Justice Statistics Bulletin*, October, U.S. Department of Justice; see, also, 1992. "National Update," *Bureau of Justice Statistics*, Vol. 1, No. 3, January.

Beccaria, Cesare. 1963. *An Essay on Crimes and Punishments*. Bobbs-Merrill, Indianopolis.

Bentham, Jeremy. 1982. *An Introduction to the Principles of Morals and Legislation*, J.H. Burns and H.C.A. Hart (eds.). London: Methuen.

Box, Steven. 1987. *Recession, Crime, and Punishment*. Totowa, New Jersey: Barnes and Noble Books.

Braithwaite, John. 1979. *Inequality, Crime, and Public Policy*. London: Routledge & Kegan Paul.

Brodeur, Jean-Paul. 1990. "The Attrition of Parole," *Canadian Journal of Criminology*, Vol. 32, No. 3, 503-509.

Campbell, A. Kim and Pierre H. Cadieux. 1990. *Directions for Reform: A Framework for Sentencing, Corrections and Conditional Release*, Minister of Supply and Services, Canada.

Cohen, Stanley. 1985. *Visions of Social Control*. Cambridge: Polity Press.

Culhane, Claire. 1980. *Barred From Prison*. Vancouver: Pulp Press.

_____. 1985. *Still Barred From Prison: Social Inequities in Canada*. Montreal, Black Rose Books.

Cullen, Francis and Karen E. Gilbert. 1982. *Reaffirming Rehabilitation*. Cincinnati: Anderson Publishing Co.

Daubney, David. 1988. *Taking Responsibility*, Report of the Standing Committee on Justice and Solicitor General on its Review of Sentencing, Conditional Release, and Related Aspects of Correction. Canadian Government Publishing Centre, Ottawa.

Doob, Anthony N. and Jean-Paul Brodeur. 1989. "Rehabilitating the Debate on Rehabilitation," *Canadian Journal of Criminology*, Vol. 31, No. 2, 179-192.

Fauteux, G. 1956. Report of a Committee Appointed to Inquire into the Principles and Procedures Followed in the Remission Service of the Department of Justice of Canada. Ottawa: Queen's Printer.

Foucault, Michel. 1977. *Discipline and Punish: The Birth of the Prison*. New York: Pantheon Books.

Gendreau, Paul. 1989. "Programs that do not Work: A Brief Comment on Brodeur and Doob," *Canadian Journal of Criminology*, Vol. 31, No. 2, 193-195.

Gibson, Fred E. 1988. "The Future of Parole in Canada," *The State of Corrections* (Proceedings: ACA Annual Conferences), ed. Jeanne-Marie Etkins, The American Correctional Association, pp. 123-130.

―――. 1990. "The Renewal of Parole," *Canadian Journal of Criminology*, Vol. 32, No. 3, 487-491.

Gosselin, Luc. 1982. *Prisons in Canada*. Montreal: Black Rose Books.

Gramsci, Antonio. 1971. *Selections from the Prison Notebooks of Antonio Gramsci*. Q. Hoare and G. Nowell Smith (eds.). Lawrence & Wishart.

Greenberg, David F. 1977. "The Dynamics of Oscillatory Punishment Processes," *The Journal of Criminal Law and Criminology*, Vol. 68, 643-651.

Habermas, Jurgen. 1975. *Legitimation Crisis*. Boston: Beacon Press.

Hall, Stuart et al. 1978. *Policing the Crisis: Mugging, the State, and Law and Order*. London: MacMillan Press Ltd.

Horowitz, Gad. 1968. *Canadian Labour in Politics*. Toronto: University of Toronto Press.

House of Commons, Minutes of Proceedings and Evidence of the Standing Committee on Justice and the Solicitor General, Chairperson, Bob Horner, Issue No. 16, November 26, 1991, Honourable Doug Lewis, Solicitor General of Canada, pp. 3-35; Issue No. 17, November, 27, 1991, Ole Ingstrup, Commissioner of Corrections, pp. 3-34; Issue No. 18, November 28, 1991, Fred Gibson, National Parole Board Chairman, pp. 3-32; Issue No. 19, December 3, 1991, Ron Stewart, Correctional Investigator, pp. 3-26. Ingstrup, Ole. 1986. Mission Statement of the National Parole Board, Ottawa.

―――. 1986. "Setting a New Course," *Liaison*, Vol. 12, No. 11, 16-19.

―――. 1989. Mission Statement of the Correctional Service of Canada, Correctional Service Canada, Ottawa.

Johnson, Holly. 1988. "Violent Crime," *Canadian Social Trends*, Statistics 1988 Canada. Summer, 24-29.

Lombroso Cesare. 1912. *Crime: Its Causes and Remedies*. Boston: Little Brown and Company.

MacLean Brian. 1986. "State Expenditures on Canadian Criminal Justice," *The Political Economy of Crime*, Brian D. MacLean (ed.). Prentice-Hall, 106-133.

———. 1988/89. "What is to be done about the Correctional Enterprise in Canada?" *Journal of Prisoners on Prisons*, Vol. 1, No. 2, Winter 59-74.

MacLean, Brian and R.S. Ratner. 1987. "An Historical Analysis of Bills C-67 and C-68: Implications for the Native Offender," *Native Studies Review*, Vol. 3, No. 1, 31-58.

Mandel, Michael. 1985. "Democracy, Class, and the National Parole Board," *The Criminal Law Quarterly* Vol. 27, No. 2, 159-181.

———. 1991. "The Great Repression: Criminal Punishment in the Nineteen-Eighties," in *Criminal Justice: Sentencing Issues and Reform*, eds. Les Samuelson and Bernard Schissel. Toronto: Garamond Press, pp. 177-226.

McCarthy, Belinda. 1987. *Intermediate Punishments: Intensive Supervision, Home Confinement and Electronic Surveillance*. New York: Criminal Justice Press.

McGrath, W.T. 1982. "Parole and Mandatory Supervision," *Bulletin of the Canadian Association for the Prevention of Crime*, Vol. XI, No. 6, March, 10.

Martinson, R.M. 1974. "What Works?—Questions and Answers about Prison Reform," *Public Interest*, Vol. 55, Spring, 22-54.

Matthews, Roger. 1989. "Alternatives to and in Prison: A Realist Approach," eds. P. Carlen and D. Cook, *Paying for Crime*. Milton Keynes: Open University Press, pp. 128-150.

Merton, Robert. 1938. "Social Structure and Anomie," *American Sociological Review*, Vol. 3, 672-682.

Mohr, J.W. 1990. "Sentencing Revisited," *Canadian Journal of Criminology*, Vol. 32, No. 3, 531-535.

Nettler, Gwynn. 1984. *Explaining Crime*. New York: McGraw-Hill.

Nielsen, Erik. 1986. *Improved Program Delivery: Justice System*, A Study Team Report to the Task Force on Program Review. Canadian Government Publishing Centre, Ottawa.

Offe, Claus. 1984. *Disorganized Capitalism*. Cambridge: MIT Press.

———. 1985. *Contradictions of the Welfare State*. Cambridge: MIT Press.

Ouimet, A. 1969. Report of the Canadian Committee on Corrections. Ottawa: Queen's Printer.

Ratner, R.S. 1986. "Parole Certificate as Dominant Hegemony" in *The Administration of Justice*, Dawn H. Currie and Brian MacLean (eds.). Social Research Unit, Department of Sociology, University of Saskatchewan, 205-214.

———. 1987. "Mandatory Supervision and the Penal Economy," in *Transcarceration: Essays in the Sociology of Social Control*, John Lowman,

Robert Menzies, Ted Palys (eds.). Gower Publishing Co., 291-308, 391-392.

Ratner, R.S. & John L. McMullan. 1983. "Social Control and the Rise of the 'Exceptional State' in Britain, the United States, and Canada," *Crime and Social Justice*, No. 19, Summer, 31-43.

Reiman, Jeffrey. 1984. *The Rich get Richer and the Poor get Prison*, 2nd edition, New York: Macmillan.

Rusche Georg & Otto Kirchheimer. 1939. *Punishment and Social Structure*. New York: Columbia University Press.

Samuelson, Les. 1991. "Social Reproduction and Social Control: A Political Economy of Sentencing Reform in Canada," in *Criminal Justice: Sentencing Issues and Reform*, eds. Les Samuelson and Bernard Schissal. Toronto: Garamond Press, pp. 59-80.

Schmidt, Annesley K. 1989. "Electronic Monitoring of Offenders Increases," National Institute of Justice, *NIJ Reports*, January/February, No. 212, pp. 2-5.

Shewan, Ian. 1985. "The Decision to Parole: Balancing the Rehabilitation of the Offender with the Protection of the Public," *Canadian Journal of Criminology*, Vol. 27, No. 3, 327-339.

Spitzer, Steven. 1975. "Toward a Marxian Theory of Deviance," *Social Problems*, Vol. 22, 638-651.

———. 1979. "The Rationalization of Crime Control in Capitalist Society," *Contemporary Crises*, No. 3, 187-206.

Taylor, Ian. 1983. *Crime, Capitalism and Community: Three Essays in Socialist Criminology*. Butterworths: Toronto.

———. 1987. "Theorising the Crisis in Canada," in *State Control: Criminal Justice Politics in Canada*, eds. R.S. Ratner and John L. McMullan. Vancouver: University of British Columbia Press, pp. 85-125.

Tepperman, Lorne. 1977 *Crime Control: the Urge Toward Authority*. Toronto: McGraw-Hill Ryerson.

Waller, Irvin and Janet Chan. 1974/75. "Prison Use: A Canadian and International Comparison," *The Criminal Law Quarterly*, Vol. 17, No. 1, 47-71.

Wolfe, Alan. 1977. *The Limits of Legitimacy: Political Contradictions of Contemporary Capitalism*. New York: Free Press.

Chapter 2

Punishing for Profit: Reflections on the Revival of Privatization in Corrections*

Richard V. Ericson, Maeve W. McMahon and Donald G. Evans

Cet article fait appel aux théories sociologiques de la peine pour comprendre les tendances récentes de la privatisation de la correction. Même si la participation contemporaine du secteur privé à la correction comporte des caractères distinctifs, le fait de cette participation est une chose qui n'a cessé d'exister depuis longtemps. Dans sa manifestation actuelle, la privatisation résume une évolution apparente vers la dispersion du contrôle social, laquelle fait intervenir un tissu complexe d'organismes publics et privés. Ces derniers agissent de plus en plus á l'extrémité douce du système; ils administrent une panoplie de programs communautaires et ce qui reste des services sociaux dans le système carcéral. Les organismes publics continuent d'assurer le personnel et le fonctionnement des prisons de l'extrémité dure et des services de sécurité et d'administrer les activités de l'extrémité douce des organismes privés.

L'idéologie de la privatisation étend la diminution de l'aspect gouvernemental de l'idéologie de la correction communautaire en soutenant que les entrepreneurs du secteur privé peuvent mieux diriger que le gouvernement les entreprises de contrôle. Dans les années 80, l'idéologie du marché libre a été revivifiée par le truchement non seulement du modèle de la justice par rapport aux délinquants, mais aussi de celui de la privatisation par rapport aux agents de contrôle et surveille ses contrats pour récompenser ceux qui font du bon travail de contrôle et punir les autres.

La privatisation comporte des coûts et des ramifications économiques, politiques et sociaux. Du point de vue économique,

---

* Reproduced by permission of the *Canadian Journal of Criminology*, Volume 29, No. 4, pp. 355-387. Copyright by the Canadian Criminal Justice Association.

c'est un moyen de réduire la taille et l'influence de certains éléments du service public. Elle cadre aussi avec la tendance historique à utiliser la main-d'oeuvre délinquante à l'avantage de l'Etat. Sur le plan politique, elle s'inscrit dans l'effort fait afin de déplacer les priorités dans la dépense publique et de créer l'Etat-providence minimum. C'est aussi un moyen de faire intervenir les organismes privés dans les processus de réforme et de contrôle social établis: tous les programs de privatisation sont des créatures de l'Etat et la privatisation ne déplace pas mais plutôt de vue social, le public et le privé sont entremêlés dans le même tissu complexe. Les organismes publics et privés sont solidaires dans le contrôle et la réforme. Dans le contrôle, leur relation n'est pas cyclique ni complémentaire, mais additive; ils accroissent les uns et les autres leur capacité. Dans la réforme, ils coupent ensemble l'herbe sous le pied à d'authentiques méthodes extra-publiques de contrôle et de progrès. Par conséquent, la privatisation en correction n'entraine pas la réforme, mais une réforme du système.

Introduction

The contemporary debate over the "privatization" of corrections raises fundamental questions about the penal system. At issue is the locus of the power to punish; the nature of the penal reform process; the relation between the state and civil society regarding both punishment and reform; and the role of the political economy in both punishment and reform. Since these issues are at the core of recent theorizing about punishment,[12, 27, 28, 35, 60] it is surprising that there has been very little attention to the privatization of corrections by academic analysts. In this paper, we analyse the public debate and practices that transpire in the name of privatization within the context of contemporary themes and issues in penology.

Does Privatization Represent Change?

Typical of correctional reform,[56] privatization is talked about as if it represents cataclysmic change with the potential to transform the system. However, a little reflection should make one sceptical about claims that privatization will alter the system radically. This is not to deny that there are distinct developments transpiring in the name of privatization, and that these may be the precursors of some change. It is simply to caution that these developments are best understood in the context of the history of penal systems and broader contemporary trends in the power to punish.

An historical constant is the fact that the vast majority of deviance and deviants, including crime and criminals, has been handled without the involvement of state agents and agencies. Even in the contemporary context of the enormous growth of the state apparatus for the control of crime[9, 12, 65] the vast majority of behaviours that could be designated as criminal are not reported to the authorities in the first place[64, 66] and if they are reported only a fraction are actually recorded as criminal and treated as such.[18] Citizens tend to use the formal, state mechanisms when the informal or private mechanisms of control are absent or have failed.[6] Indeed, while there has been a very substantial expansion in the state apparatus for crime control, the state often resists citizens' demands for control at various levels.[18, 54] In practice, the control of deviance has always involved a combination of state and non-state responsibility. At issue are the nature and implications of state and non-state responsibilities for control at different historical junctures.

In Anglo-American legal jurisdictions, there has been considerable scope for non-state interests to become involved in, and profit from, formal mechanisms of crime control. In the seventeenth and eighteenth centuries in England, the formal and state-sponsored systems for detection, prosecution, and punishment were typically in the control of for-profit operators.[5] For example, the keeper of the local prison was a private entrepreneur who received only a portion of his compensation from the county allowance. The largest portion of his income was derived from the prison taproom, where he sold beer, liquor, tobacco, and other profitable items. He also supplemented his income by other means, including an entry fee for visitors. In return for such benefits, the keeper had burdens, including a responsibility to recapture escapees and to pay the costs of advertising, detection and apprehension in doing so.[5]

The English system for transportation of convicts to America was also a matter for private enterprise. A merchant was paid by government for the transportation, and again by the person in America who purchased the convict as an indentured servant. That this was lucrative is indicated by the fact that after the 1718 *Transportation Act*, one merchant kept the London contract for twenty years, and merchants who held the contract subsequently also kept it for long periods.[5, 34]

In the United States,[67] and especially in the South,[3] the penal system thrived on its connection to private enterprise. Through a convict lease system, prisoners were not only "slaves of the state" legally (as enunciated in the classic statement in *Ruffin* v. *Commonwealth*, 62 Va 790 [1871]) but also slaves of the local entrepreneurs who contracted with the state to make capital gains from prisoners' labour. Officials in the state capital joined with private capital to profit from the labour of prisoners. In the South, even after the slavery of blacks ended officially, state legislatures passed enabling laws (e.g., regarding vagrancy) which allowed former slaves and other marginal members of society to be incarcerated and hired out for profit. "The size of the prison population was determined not by the amount of crime or the need for social control or the efficiency of the police, but by the desire to make crime pay—for the government and private employees."[50] The Mississippi prison system celebrated the fact that it turned a profit every year until the Second World War. It was only in the late 1920s and into the 1930s that legislation extinguished the convict lease system, apparently in response to pressure from rural manufacturers and labour unions who could not stand the competition, especially with the coming of the Depression.[61, 77]

In Canada, and more specifically at the Kingston Penitentiary, a convict lease system existed through the nineteenth century. Here too the system was encouraged when there was a shortage of non-prison labour, and discouraged when the labour market tightened and organized opposition arose from manufacturers and workers. In a revealing statement in Parliament in 1985, George Ryerson indicated that while there should no longer be competition between privately contracted prison labour and free labour, the quintessential Canadian cultural view that "good people work hard" was still to be upheld by keeping "prisoners employed in carrying balls and chains or digging holes in the sand and filling them up again."

In North America, the longstanding involvement of non-state agencies in penalizing has not been limited to prisoners. In the United States, non-state halfway house operations thrived until the 1920s, when newly formed probation and parole boards emerged with the political clout to force them out for a few decades. They re-emerged in the 1950s as an economic and administrative necessity in the face of deteriorating and overcrowded prisons. In Canada, the first remission service community supervision was undertaken under the auspices of the Salvation Army at the turn of the century. After the Second World War, other non-state agencies became involved as "parole pioneers,"[58] providing service to ex-inmates, and, in 1970, this expanded to actual supervision of those on parole and mandatory supervision. Probation too had its origins in non-state agency involvement. In Quebec, probation was the preserve of non-state agencies until as late as 1967. In the 1970s non-state agencies—led especially by the John Howard Society and the Salvation Army—became heavily involved in contracts to operate community-based residential facilities. This made them look more like jailers than like assailers of the penal system in their traditional advocacy role.

These recollections from the historical record indicate that non-state agency involvement has a long and unbroken record in Anglo-American systems of punishment. While there have been distinctive and definite alterations in the content of this involvement, the form of formal crime control as a blend of state and non-state interests remains a constant.

Who Profits?

Crime control is big business. In recent decades, crime control has been at or near the lead as a growth sector of Canadian government employment and expenditure.[9, 65] While the greatest proportionate growth has been in police personnel—over 50%, controlling for population, from the early 1960s to the late 1970s[9, 65]—the correctional/punishment component of the system has also thrived as a growth industry. In 1983-84, Canadian prisons accommodated standing populations of 27,595 inmates and 19,283 staff, a ratio of 1:1.4. In the United States, it is estimated that it costs $10 billion annually to look after 750,000 incarcerated people.[26] In the United States in particular, prison is a growth sector: one survey found that at the state level alone 77,000 new prison beds were added in the first half of this decade, and that there are plans for 104,700 new beds at a cost of $5 billion over the next ten years.[39,46] Over 8 million people were admitted to jails in the United States during 1983.[75]

The Concise Oxford Dictionary includes in the definition of profit the terms "benefit" and "advantage," and defines profitable in part as "beneficial" and "useful." Defined in terms of benefit and use, it can be said that there is always profit to be made from the policing and processing of offenders. The questions are: Who profits? Under what circumstances? Why? What are the consequences?

As developed in latter sections, it is evident that both state and non-state interests find punishment beneficial and useful. The state profits from the use of crime control or "law and order" as a vehicle for trafficking in its preferred ideologies and reproducing its legitimacy. Criminal punishment has always been at the very core of citizens' assessment of the state as a moral agent, and is used as a barometer of lesser exercises of authority by the state. More directly, state involvement in the crime industry had entailed benefits to civil servants who are employed as control agents; they have been provided with handsome incomes, a career structure with attendant prestige, and a context in which to advance professional interests. Even more directly the state can use crime control to offset its costs enforcement. This is most obvious in the case of the fine, a criminal sanction that has increased dramatically in proportion to other sanctions for indictable offences.[8] It is becoming more obvious in other parts of the system. For example, the Correctional Service of Canada (C.S.C.) has an expansion program to generate revenue from prison industries. The C.S.C. projects an increase in revenue from this source from $8.6 million in 1983 to $32 million in 1989. The C.S.C. justifies this by saying it "has a goal of cost reduction rather than profit-making." As any accountant knows, this is a matter of semantics.

It is clear that non-state organizations also find penalizing a beneficial and useful enterprise. The employee of the John Howard Society, Salvation Army, or other non-state agency is as much interested in his or her income, career status, and professional interests as is the civil servant. This applies to all those—medical doctors, educators, chaplains, criminologists, social workers, etc.—who contract with the system to provide their professional services. There is also great profit to be made from the provision of material goods and services to the penal system, including those required for the construction of prisons and "community residential facilities" as well as those supplied on a regular basis (food, clothing, stationery, surveillance technology, etc.).

These benefits should raise difficulty for non-state correctional employees who continue to claim that their basic interest is to "do good" for the "clients" of the penal system. However, as in the more established private markets in psychiatric services, health care, and helping the elderly, there seems to be little difficulty in this regard. Tinges of guilt in profiting from the dependent are dealt with by reverting to the more traditional "voluntary" and "charitable" imagery of non-state agency involvement in "human service delivery." This is sometimes accompanied by a moralistic "filthy lucre" stance regarding more obvious signs of profit-making out of human misery. For example, it has been asserted that the "new" profit motive is downright bad and "runs counter to all notions of democratic justice and accountability."[36] However, as we now consider, the real problem may be that of "social control entrepreneurship"[76] which blends both economic and moral interest. In all forms of capitalism there is a need to create new markets and expand perpetually. State and non-state agencies seem to be working together to foster and facilitate the very things they seek to control.[12, 41]

Privatization as Franchising

Privatization is a "buzz word," summarizing what has been developing in the penal system over a long period. It summarizes the evolution toward the dispersal of social control involving a complex web of state and non-state interests, organizations, and social forces. The fact that it pertains to all facets of the penal enterprise, and beyond explains why people use the word privatization to consider everything from prison garbage collection to parole supervision contracts with non-state agencies.

As evidenced in the massive Neilsen reports on privatization initiatives within the federal government of Canada, privatization is the favourite "frame" of government in the 1980s. In Canada, as in Thatcher's Britain and Reagan's

America, privatization is at the forefront of conservative ideology and is represented in a wide range of practices. The Ministry of Defence contracts with private industry to supply equipment, just as the Ministry of Corrections contracts with private industry to do likewise. The government sells off state industries to private shareholders and operators, including not only aircraft manufacturers and oil companies, but also nursing homes and residential facilities for criminal offenders.

In the areas of human service delivery and control, including corrections, much of what is occurring is simply a minor adjustment of existing practices to fit the 1980s frame of "privatization." The state currently favours a fairly broad definition of privatization because it articulates with the ideology it is striving to make dominant. If the political climate changes, there may be an attendant reversion to the older charitable rhetoric of "grants-in-aid" to "voluntary agencies," or "transfer payments," while the involvement of non-state agencies continues unabated. Indeed, at the present juncture it may not be privatization that is occurring but rather a "publicization" of the voluntary sector.

One way to think about this "publication" is by analogy to the highly successful franchising phenomenon that has become characteristic of private business over the past two decades, and that is exemplified by the McDonald's Restaurant Corporation. In correctional franchising, the state functions as the franchisor and the various non-state correctional agencies as the franchisees. The franchisor is careful to select franchises based on their ability to conduct the proposed business in terms of fiscal resources and responsibility. The prospective franchisees do not need technical knowledge in advance since the franchisor requires intensive training and strict adherence to its system and methods. The franchisor establishes a careful reporting and auditing capacity, with the omnipresent threat of termination if the franchisee does not measure up to the standards.

Franchising allows for the *apparent* decentralization of control of offenders, community involvement, and distancing from the state. In effect, however, it secures "publication": centralized control of non-state agencies through the conditions of contracts and attendant monitoring and auditing functions.

As in private business franchising, such as the fast-food industry, the conditions are ripe for monopoly by a few industry giants. The McDonalds, Harveys and Burger Kings of the fast food industry may soon have their counterparts in the John Howard Societies, St. Leonard's Societies and Salvation Armies of the corrections industry.

In the franchise system, employees are "free" to quit and work for other chains in the industry. However, this freedom is severely circumscribed by the fact that conditions of employment are very similar across the industry. Employees are also "free" to quit and to set up their own independent businesses. Again, the option is extremely limited. The power of the corporate giants is usually too overwhelming to compete. The only realistic hope is to be able to obtain a franchise from one of the corporate giants, which of course means falling back into line with the restrictions imposed by the franchisor. What is left for the franchise hold is the expectation of personal capital gains. A "captain" for the ship of state, the franchisee can at least operate as a privateer: "a ship privately owned and manned but authorized by a government to attack and capture enemy vessels...the commander or one of the crew of such a ship." (*The American Heritage Dictionary*, 1969).

Privatization and the Carceral Continuum

Since the nineteenth-century transformation of the penal system, and its refinement in the twentieth century, there has developed a very long "carceral continuum"[24] that stretches deeply into the prison and widely into the community. Deep inside the prison and moving outward, there are punitive dissociation, special handling units, regional psychiatric centres, administrative dissociation, and maximum, medium and minimum security, each with their own finer gradations of security. Toward the community, there are residential centres, which are more finely graded as three-quarter-way houses, halfway houses, and one-quarter-way houses. The fact that these are a step to freedom, and yet prison-like, is indicated by the contradictory term "open custody" used for residential facilities for young offenders. Inhabitants have the sensation of being simultaneously halfway in, out and back. Also toward the community end of the carceral continuum are temporary absence programs, day parole, parole, and mandatory supervision. Further into the community are probation, community service orders, fine option programs, and pre-trial diversion schemes.

This panoply of carceral alternatives indicates how far we have evolved (most would say progressed) from penalization as the public infliction of pain toward subtle and hidden forms of control. This evolution has been marked by increasing classification for differentiation of offenders according to the degrees of segregation they seem to require. It has been accompanied by increasing administrative discretion concerning who best fits what classification and where on the carceral continuum they should be placed. "The creation of all those new agencies and services surrounding the court and the prison, the generation of new systems of knowledge, classification and professional interests...is little more than a widening and diversification of the last century's archipelago, made possible by resources, investment, ingenuity, technology and vested interest on a scale that befits 'post-industrial society.'"[12]

The extension of the carceral "ladder" into the community, and placing more rungs on it, has been accomplished with the ideology of community control, and more recently, the attendant ideology of privatization. The ideology of community control directs that the interventionist and repressive reach of the state must be blunted by having "the community" more involved in the day-to-day business of control. No one has quite worked out what "the community" is, except by reference to the glorious past, by pointing to the dispute resolution mechanisms of selected African tribes, or by beaming that "small is beautiful." Meanwhile in the large city and its condition of social distance, the reality is not communal anarchy.[73] Instead, we find large, bureaucratized, professionalized non-state agencies such as the John Howard Society and the Salvation Army moving in for a slice of the control pie. They are poised to benefit from the ideology of privatization, which has translated the diminution of the government aspect of the ideology of community into a belief that private entrepreneurs can operate control businesses more efficiently than government. The discourse that constitutes this ideology is examined further in the next section.

Under the symbolic canopy of community involvement and privatization, some real developments are taking place. At a recent meeting between interested community organizations and officials for the Alberta Ministry of the Solicitor-General, it was stated boldly by the officials that "there's nothing not on the agenda for privatization." For 1985-86, C.S.C. projected that they would enter into 358 contracts with non-state agencies. These contracts were valued at $19 million, an increase in value of 86% compared to 1983-84.[26] The Ontario Ministry of Correctional Services also has more than 300 contracts with non-state control agencies, valued at $13.2 million in 1985.[13] The rapid expansion of community service orders in Ontario[45] accounts for a significant proportion of these contracts, and for the diverse and dispersed involvement of community organizations in the control business (e.g., a Social Planning Council, Y.M.C.A., community service clubs such as Lions and Rotary, the Salvation Army and other religious groups, John Howard Society).

With these developments, the system bifurcates. Non-state organizations are involved at the soft-end of the system. As one John Howard Society official put it, here they "can extend their reach to areas where government may not have the resources or capability to extend."[58] In Canada, the "hardest" it gets for non-state agencies is the operation of halfway houses and parole supervision. Even in the United States, where there are strong political as well as fiscal pressures for privatized prisons, the reality is that, apart from immigration holding facilities, only a couple of prisons are run by private corporations and these are minimum security institutions. Moreover, a recent survey found that there are only 26 private prison industry programs in the United States, with a total investment of a paltry $2 million, and employing only 1,000 inmates (0.2% of the prison population).[61]

The state reserves the harder end of the penal system for its direct and sole control. It has trafficked in the "renaissance of dangerousness"[7] to classify security risks into the deeper entrails of the prison system and to justify new institutions with "super" security classifications. Prison stages on the carceral continuum are also used for those who foul up on "softer" programs: there must always be one worse punishment for those who cannot conform to a given system.

It is clearly the intention of the state's authorities to reserve their control contracts for soft-end activity. In a publication with the revealing title, *Everyone's Business*, the Ontario Ministry of Correctional Services enumerates the areas for its 300+ contracts: the operation of community resource centre residences (the "hardest" it gets); the administration of community service order contracts; drug and alcohol awareness programs; bail supervision; life skills training; employment programs; and, special services for native offenders. A statement by the John Howard Society of their penal involvements in Ontario indicates their soft-end orientation even when they enter into the institutional sphere: prevention (juvenile education, community education); early intervention (attendance centres, juvenile drug and alcohol counselling, youth employment service, literacy and/or life skills, juvenile group work, juvenile counselling, juvenile community service orders, juvenile victim/offender reconciliation/restitution); courts (bail verification, bail supervision, probation supervision, victim services, victim/offender reconciliation, restitution, counselling the developmentally handicapped, fine options youth residences, community service orders, driving while impaired program); institutional (remand visiting, inmate counselling, temporary absence supervision, release planning, advocacy, recreation, group-work, chapter [inmate group] support, federal community assessment, family support); and post-institutional (Family counselling, voluntary counselling, federal parole supervision, employment service, group-work, residential centres, intake and referral, inhouse workshops).

This range of activity for non-state agencies at the soft end of the penal system is part of the wider "informal" justice and community control movement.[2] State agencies, and the large non-state agencies they contract with, mobilize citizens to become more involved in controlling each other through prevention, surveillance, and service delivery. Citizens are to be watchers as well as watched, the bearers of their own control. They can do so by paying for it, contracting with private security firms.[62, 63] They can do so by getting involved in it, becoming paid employees or volunteers for non-state control organizations. They can do so by making believe that they are doing something about it, having "Neighbourhood Watch" signs placed at the end of their streets and in the windows of their homes.

Selling Privatization: The Discourse of Reform

The privatization frame is accompanied by a shift in the terms of penal discourse. This shift reflects contradictions in modern liberalism more generally. On the one hand, there is a continuing pull to maintain the state as parent. On the other hand, there is a push toward independence formulated as a distrust of benevolence and articulated as the ideology of the minimum state.

Penal reform discourse has conventionally emphasized the "holy trinity" of cost, effectiveness, and humaneness. In the discourse of privatization, however, the moral position of humaneness has been relegated to a marginal place under the dominant theme of efficiency (cost effectiveness). For example, in an article by Gooderham in the CSC newspaper, *Let's Talk*, privatization is described as "only a 'new' word for contracting outside for services…. The current thrust of privatization is the result of government rethinking its position, its growth, its expenditures. The burning question seems to be how can government services like CSC do its job better, at lower cost and using fewer person years."[29]

In operating the penal system, as in other modern enterprises, the belief is created that "the private sector" can do it more efficiently than the public sector. As a common in the history of penal reform, there are no adequate research studies to support the claim. Changes are advocated and made without sufficient evidence, and without incorporating research to generate evidence.[26,45] Indeed even if adequate research designs were provided for, it would still be problematic to chart efficiency because penal goals are so fuzzy, the norms remain unspecifiable and efficiency itself is inherently a matter of ideology. Advocates of privatization are thus left to argue efficiency in a rhetorical mode, and things get decided on the basis of what can be reasonably counted: the cost in relation to the numbers served.

There is a certain moral tone to this rhetoric. Discourse on privatization conflates the issue of cost and effectiveness into a moral sensibility emphasizing rationality. It is presently a virtue to be seen to be cutting back on government spending, especially in relation to the socially marginal who least deserve it. In a survey of American correctional administrators regarding the benefits of contracting for services, the benefits signified as most important were cost savings and more economical use of resources; these were deemed twice as important as improvements in the quality of services.[26]

The rhetoric of humaneness, the third component of conventional reform discourse, has been reformulated into a conception of rationality more readily identifiable with free market ideology. A few decades ago, as the progressive era burgeoned, the dominant sensibility was to embrace the benevolent state and its presumed knowledge and power to do good.[27, 56] Thus at the turn of this century Charlton Lewis, head of the US National Prison Association, argued for elastic periods of treatment and correction in the hands of the benevolent state, and castigated the justice model as "witchcraft." [T]he method of apportioning penalties according to degrees of guilt...is as completely discredited and as incapable of a part in any reasoned system of social organization, as is the practice of astrology or...witchcraft.... [T]he time will come when the moral mutilations of fixed terms of imprisonment will seem as barbarous and antiquated as the ear lopping, nose slitting and hand amputations of a century ago."[56] In the 1980s, we are back to the "witchcraft" of "fixed penalties" and the justice model, in the wake of cogent arguments that intervention for rehabilitation of offenders is "witchcraft." Offenders are deemed to be conscious, rational actors who choose to commit crime with knowledge of burdens and benefits. The choice to commit crime or refrain from it is depicted in the same terms as choice in any other commodity market. The discourse of the private market has been revived in the discourse about criminality.

In reform talk about privatization, this free market ideology is applied equally to control agents. If the offender is to be viewed as responsive to the free market of rewards, benefits and burdens, then why not the control agents as well? The state will offer slices of the control pie for competitive bidding, and monitor its contracts to reward those who do good control work and punish those who do not.

This model lays bare that there are people and organizations out to profit from the misery of others. As mentioned previously, this causes moral indignation in some quarters especially those who define themselves as in the non-state, "voluntary" sector, and who continue to adhere to the traditional conception of humaneness emphasizing compassion and benevolence. The moral indignation is expressed in a "filthy lucre" attitude to the non-state, "for profit" sector: how can you possibly do good and be motivated by financial gain at the same time? This indignation is augmented if the agency retains remnants of an advocacy role on behalf of offenders: how can you be motivated by profit and at the same time be critical of and sometimes in opposition to those who supply the money? Put more colloquially, how can you bite the hand that feeds? The moral indignation is also expressed as a "filthy bureaucracy" attitude to government: how can you possibly do good when bureaucratic control and political popularity interests are paramount?

At the soft end of the system, the rhetoric of "doing good" has always found fertile ground. It insulates the penal system from criticism, explaining away failure and justifying more doses of the same.[12] It is difficult to criticize the righteous. Within the current sensibility of humaneness, while the state and its armies of control agents often "do bad," non-state agencies such as the Salvation Army can only "do good."

Ultimately the "success" of the penal system and its carceral network does not depend on its "success" through effectiveness research and a morally correct position. Rather, it thrives on a discourse of failure, an assertion that what went before is inefficient and wrong and can only be corrected and improved through progressive alternatives. In combining a "cognitive passion" that they are more efficient, with a "righteous passion" that they are more humane, non-state agencies are able to ensure their "success" without attention to the facts of the matter. In short, they are beneficiaries of the contradictions in modern liberalism.

Analysing the Reform Discourse of Privatization

In penal reform, there is typically more talk than action. So far, this is the case with privatization. There is no privatized prison in Canada or Britain. In the United States, private agencies have secured contracts for managing special operations, such as holding facilities for aliens, but "[n]o contracts [have been] reported for the confinement of mainstream adult operations."[46] There are a few private prison industry developments in Canada, and a few more in the United States, but these pertain to far less than one percent of the inmate population. There is an escalation of contracting out control business at the soft end of the system, but this is simply a progression of long standing policy initiatives of the past two decades.

This leads us to question the reform, discourse itself. Why is there a disjunction between words and deeds? Why does penal policy talk always claim major change and breakthrough when little is new and change evolves in complex ways over long periods? Why do we need different rationalizations for a relatively constant practice?

One key to understanding the disjunction between words and deeds is to appreciate that reform is as much a part of the crime control system as the police, courts, prisons, etc.[20, 24] Taking this view there is no incongruity in the dual mandate of non-state agencies, such as the John Howard Society, to function as an advocacy group on behalf of offenders and as an agency directly involved in controlling offenders. Reform and direct control constitute the mandate of all those involved in the crime control business. As part of effecting direct social control, there is a need to rationalize it so as to improve it. Thus the Ontario Ministry of Correctional Services stresses that its contracts with non-state agencies not only effect crime control, but also foster controlled reform. "The involvement of private, non-profit and commercial agencies in corrections increases and improves rehabilitative opportunities for offenders...offers new sources of innovation and promotes advocacy for positive reform of justice and social policies."[13]

This is no different from what the state expects of its own control agencies and agents.[20] At the level of research, programs, and policy, the largest single concentration of criminology in Canada has resided with the Ministry of the Solicitor General. Its graduate trained staff does nothing but monitor trends and developments, and constitutes a cadre of "inside" reformers who initiate major reforms.[54] At another level of the system, the police are not only at the forefront of direct and coercive social control, they are also leaders in the reform politics of crime control. The police control the very public definition of what constitutes crime in official terms. They comment upon and lobby about amendments to the law and legal process, including the appropriateness of the system of sentencing and punishment. Beyond the criminal control system *per se*, they are also consulted on community planning, urban development, educational programs, etc. Their control mandate is accomplished at this symbolic level of reform politics as well as at the everyday level of direct control. Precisely the same can be said for non-state agencies contracting for a slice of the control business. While in the distant past they may have been "outside" reformers advocating for offenders and victims against the state, they are now absorbed by the state and made useful as "inside" reformers as well as administrators of penal sanctions.

We need to appreciate that words are also deeds.[78] Regardless of what is actually transpiring in penal practice, the reform talk is of value in the public, political culture.[30] As introduced previously, talk about criminal punishment has always been at the forefront of debates in the political culture because it is a primary arena in which citizens assess the moral authority of the state and grant it degrees of legitimacy. As Durkheim,[17] Mead,[43] Erikson,[23] and many others have emphasized, the rituals of crime and punishment, in words and deeds, give shape to the economic, political and social boundaries of society. We now turn to a consideration of how everything that goes under the name of privatized corrections serves to reproduce particular contours of economic, political, and social order.

The Economy of Privatization

The privatization of corrections is directed at reducing the power of certain forms of labour. It is a means of undercutting the size and influence of selected components of the civil service. It is also part of the historical trend of using offenders' labour to the advantage of the state. The assault on the labour of civil servants and offenders occurs at both the symbolic and instrumental levels.

An explicit and intentional aspect of community corrections over the past decade has been the expansion of formal social control options without expansion of the civil service to do the extra work. Non-state control agencies are able to pay lower wages, offer fewer benefits, and turn over staff without bothering with the employment security accorded to civil servants. They can also use "ability to pay" arguments to reduce staff when their profitability becomes a problem, whereas in the public sector there is the problem that " 'ability to pay' means simply that the employer does not want to pay. It does not want to pay usually for reasons which are political."[74]

As early as 1975, an Ontario Task Force justified a move to contracting with non-state agencies on the ground that it would be more economical than expanding the civil service.[55] This was also stated as a reason for contracting out the operation of community service order programs in Ontario.[45] In Ontario there was an incentive to corrections managers to seriously consider privatization as a means of "managing the cutback" in civil service complement. This came in the form of a policy that there were to be no dollars allotted for complement civil servants, but the salary dollars would be converted into service dollars in the budget if the services were contracted out.

In British Columbia there has been a parallel thrust to privatize some areas to reduce costs of government services and the size of the civil service. Assessing efforts in this direction between 1983 and 1985, Harrison and Gosse[32] conclude

> [E]xperience with privatization can be summarized as generally, though not universally, positive. First, all of the privatized services remain and continue to be provided to consumers of justice services. This is a major plus. Second, no contract resulted in an overall increase in cost to government and many resulted in substantial savings. Another major plus. In each case of privatization, a significant contribution to the goal of reducing the number of public servants directly employed by government was realized. This is a third major benefit of privatization, particularly when one realizes that the goal of reducing the number of public servants had such strong political commitment that were it not for privatization, these services or others would have been eliminated in order to achieve the reduction target.

At the Canadian federal level, advisors on corrections to the Neilsen Task Force observed that savings in using the private sector "have come largely from lower overhead costs, much lower salaries in the private sector, and limited programming and staffing."[48] This accords with the American experience in justifying privatization in corrections by arguing non-state labour is cheaper.[40] In a recent editorial in the *American Journal of Economics and Sociology* (Vol. 45, 1986 at p. 402), the conclusion is reached that:

> It is difficult to see how a private company can provide custodial, training and institutional services cheaper than the state, unless

it does so by exploiting the prison guards. One governor said it cost his state between $30 and $35 a day to provide services to each prisoner. That is about double the federal minimum wage. To maintain prisoners on the fare of the very poor would require reducing the quality of prison of life to an extraordinary level.

In Canada it is particular parts of the civil service that are jeopardized in privatization plans and initiatives. Those involved in security functions at the hard end have nothing to fear, while those toward the soft end are threatened. For example, the CSC publication *Let's Talk* (15 February, 1986) states, "Many people are concerned that privatization will mean lost person years.... However, in the future, CSC must work with fewer person years and yet provide more services [i.e., they should be concerned!]. One solution to this demand for higher productivity is to privatize services which the private sector can handle more economically, and use the person years we have, for example, in security and classification."

The Neilsen Task Force advisors make similar threatening statements about rehabilitative service and soft end employment. Concurrently, they strengthen hard end security employment by remaining silent about it. For example, there is no talk about security staff "burnout" and their many other job related problems. In contrast, educational and vocational staff are recommended for complete privatization because under contracts it is easier to turf them out when they burn out. "Experience suggests that further privatization of these services would not be less expensive overall, but does improve the quality of the training received because burnout is less likely under a privatized system where staff turnover is more frequent."[48]

Getting more for less is always at the expense of someone. With privatization, control agents are forced to take lesser working conditions and to increase their risk of unemployment. In the United States, and in British Columbia, commercial firms involved in administering punishments are characterized by having no unions and the lack of basic benefits such as pension plans. As Gandy observers: "It is no accident that in the United States the privatized institutions are located in states where public sector unions and/or the right-to-work laws make it difficult for unions to organize."[26] The greatest touch of humanity offered by the Neilsen Task Force advisors in this regard is to suggest that civil servants who are terminated might be given first crack at punishing for profit franchises: "Protection of former civil servants: CSC employees should be given priority in hiring by private contractors and an opportunity to incorporate and bid on contracts for service delivery."[48]

There is another factor which undercuts the position of civil servants involved in soft end control activities. This is the reserve army of citizen volunteers who have been convinced that it is virtuous to do control work without financial remuneration. Under the headline, "Volunteers offer Time, Talent and Caring," the Ontario Ministry of Correctional Services publication *Everyone's Business* proudly declares, "There are more than 5,000 citizen volunteers who assist the Ministry of Correctional Services and its agencies." As Sapers observes, "volunteerism is seen as one of the primary factors contributing to the growth of privatization."[58] It has the instrumental value of free labour, providing thousands of people to counsel offenders, run errands, and keep a more watchful eye than is possible for a paid control agent with a large caseload. It also has the symbolic value of public relations, providing thousands of people to tell fellow citizens about the virtues of the system and how they too might show "responsibility" by helping to run it on the cheap.

Turning to offenders, the economics of privatization fits squarely with the way their labour has been used in the past at both the symbolic level and the instrumental level. Symbolically, offenders are used as a sign that "good people work hard."[10,34,44] This was seen as the virtue of the precursor of penitentiaries, the Houses of Correction. Writing in 1661, and referring to Houses of Correction in England, Dalton declared that inmates, "by labour and punishment of their bodies, their forward natures may be bridled, their evil minds bettered and others by their example terrified."[14] An early proposal for naming penal institutions was "hard labour houses" rather than penitentiaries.[5]

Today the Correctional Corporation of America proudly describes its Silverdale institution as a "workhouse." Also a source of pride is the fact that prisoners are paid only in the currency of penal time, not money. "Prisoners work outside the institutions with some 137 possible job assignments with the County Highway Department, County Parks, County Nursing Home, etc. They are not paid for this work but can earn up to 50 percent remission of their sentence with a good work record."[26]

The economic ideology and rationale is revealed especially in privately run prison industry programs. In these programs, it is stated that the key is to duplicate the working conditions that the person would experience as an employee of the same industry outside. This includes paying a similar wage, and then deducting from the wage the cost of living, support of dependents, and taxes. Here wages take on a moral character. It is morally sound to have offenders pay their way, even if this means that their deductions in fact leave them with virtually no surplus income. Thus, in extolling the virtues of the abattoir plant at the Guelph institution, Pahapill says, "The estimated annual family support payment of $120,000 eases burden on welfare payments."[51] The Neilsen Task Force advisors advocate having more prisoners work for outside industry because, "it reduces CSC costs in inmate pay and overhead and maintenance, while allowing the inmate to pay taxes, family support, higher room and board, and to save more towards eventual release."[48] We are back to the prison as factory.[44] This is not just a practical matter. The prisoner is being used as a sign of free market ideology, and in particular as a sign of the movement to the minimal welfare state. Moreover, while they may have more opportunity to work (in prison industries, community service), offenders still come out with far less than other labourers in the free market and thereby help to perpetuate the principle of lesser eligibility.

These components have been exported to community punishments. Offenders earn money to support dependents, they are taxed, and they do some "volunteer" community service work without remuneration.[13] Ontario community service order programs are the epitome of this. They were originally popularized by the then Minister of Corrections as "community *work* orders," which turns out to be a more frank view than the official term. As Menzies[45] observes in citing the following passage from a Peterborough, Ontario newspaper, community service order programs were not sold locally in terms of welfare and help. Rather they were promoted in terms of saving tax dollars, and within the sensibility that every decent person works hard:

> Jane Moher spends a lot of her time with shoplifters, thieves, and other petty criminals. She doesn't counsel them or chastize them or judge them—she puts them to work.... The program is designed to keep minor criminal offenders out of jail to save taxpayer's money. It is also hoped the program will prevent first offenders from being exposed to hardened criminals in jail while providing a work force for community service.

Canadian jurisdictions have to this point stopped short of making offenders pay cash for the community supervision they receive, although Ontario studied the possibilities during 1984 and and 1985. In contrast, several American states make offenders pay for their punishment. Misdemeanants under probation orders in Florida are charged a fee for the privilege of being supervised by the Salvation Army. In Texas, there is a major problem with offenders refusing to pay, with the result that other penal measures, especially jail, have to be invoked. In Canada and the United States, the idea is very much alive to have offenders pay as a means of funding victims programs. In any case, Canadian offenders are expected to work hard for little or no financial compensation, paying back the community both ideologically and instrumentally with their labour.

Enthusiasm for the labour of offenders has always been tied to particular instrumental needs for labour. Transportation of offenders was criticized on the ground that young labourers should be kept in England to contribute to the English economy rather than be exported for use in the economy of the Americas.[5] Convict lease schemes in the United States[77] and Canada[26] were only terminated in the face of a deteriorating labour market in the wider society. There is a significant tradition of research documenting the ebb and flow of incarceration, and use of inmate labour, according to prevailing economy conditions in society.[38,53,57]

In face of the contemporary economic climate of recurrent recession and persistent high unemployment, it is not surprising that offenders working in the community usually receive little or no financial remuneration. Typically, what they are asked to do is the "dirty work"[33] of looking after, and providing service for, others who are dependent, deprived, and/or depraved. Just as ex-mental patients are used to service nursing homes for the elderly as part of their welfare, and welfare payments, so offenders are conscripted to serve the elderly, handicapped, and other offenders. According to the Ontario Ministry of Correctional Services, in 1985 "offenders on probation in Ontario provided more than 550,000 hours of unpaid community service work."[13] In being used in this way, the "conscript clientele"[25] of offenders is forming a new sector of the control industry, what might be termed the "non-voluntary, voluntary sector."

Again this is portrayed publicly as a virtue. Thus a feature article on community service order in the *Niagara Falls Review* newspaper (September 18, 1986, p. 3) opens with the lead, "Ordering convicted criminals to do community work is the greatest thing since sliced bread, says Niagara Region's senior provincial court judge." The article features a 27-year-old woman identified as "Carol." Carol was required to do social service work no one else would touch, but through the hard work of doing good is doing well.

> Carol was ordered to perform 200 hours of community work. "It doesn't sound like much but when you work one or two hours now and then, it's a hell of a long time, she said. Carol's first task of community service work was looking after three "severely retarded" boys at a bowling alley every Friday night. Giving up her Friday nights was hard enough to bear but what made things more difficult was knowing she was in charge of three boys no volunteers at the Welland home wanted. Carol managed to adjust to her new surroundings which she found with the help of a volunteer from the John Howard Society. However, the job was available for only a portion of her 200 hours, new work had to be found in order to fulfil her probation term. Once again with the help of the society, Carol was able to find employment at the Bethesda Home for the mentally handicapped in Vineland. The Bethesda Home scheduled her for 20 hours per week. With a full-time job Carol knew her hands would be full but she said she would do her best. As was the case in Welland, she was placed with the very worst behaviour problem people at the home. It

was a challenge, she said, but she was once again able to adapt to her new position and hopes to continue at the Bethesda Home long after her probation order is complete.

Meanwhile inside the prison, penal labour continues to be exploited. While programs allowing private industries to operate in prison espouse the ideal of making the working conditions as close as possible to those on the outside, the reality is a labour force without the working conditions or rights of workers on the outside. In Ontario there is one positive sign: inmates working in the abattoir at the Guelph institution are paying union members and they are granted temporary absence passes to attend union meetings. Elsewhere inmates as workers receive less consideration. Weiss concludes his analysis of private industry programs in American prisons by observing. "Nowhere else in the United States can capital get away with paying the minimum wage, and providing no unemployment compensation or health insurance, while enjoying free use of facility space, political stability, and the efforts of a disciplined work force." With specific reference to a model program in Minnesota involving Control Data Corporation, Weiss notes there are no benefits such as layoff or unemployment provisions, there is no question of unionization, and discipline provisions "would have pleased Henry Ford." While all of these factors encourage private industries to set up an operation inside prisons, they are also conducive to having them leave. In January 1986, Control Data Corporation moved their computer assembly plant from Minnesota to West Germany. According to their manager, "Control Data's prison experience has been positive and successful."[47]

Some friends of privatization of prison industries even depict prison labour as the functional equivalent of a "third world" labour market that can be exploited to help America displace the third world economic threat of cheap labour. Thus Auerbach et al.,[4] argue,

> Four many years now labour intensive industrial operations have been fleeing the United States in search of a cheaper third world labour.... [S]ome manufacturers have identified the American prisons as an attractive alternative to the sometimes expensive move to foreign-based production.... It is not at all unrealistic to assert that, in the future, prison manufacturing operations will pose a greater threat to Hong Kong and Seoul than they do to Detroit or Pittsburgh. Jeremy Bentham's principle of "lesser eligibility" has been twisted inside out, with American prison labour's status enhanced at the expense of the foreign worker.

In the United States, the use of prisoners as "slave" labour is not a problem legally; in fact it is explicitly written into the United States Constitution, despite United Nations resolutions favouring the absolute abolition of slavery, without exception for prisoners.

There is a fundamental feature of a prison with privatized industry that does reproduce the world outside the prison gates. As Weiss[77] shows, a class structure is formed that parallels the class structure of society. The prisoners in the private industry program form an elite within the institution. Part of their discipline, their learning to labour, is derived from the experience of a floating surplus population ready to take over their jobs if they prove unproductive. There is also a stagnant surplus population who prefer not to work, instead seeking their profits within the inelastic demand structure of vices such as drugs, gambling and illicit sex. Finally, there is a handicapped population unable to work, the welfare class. As in the world outside, these folks are to be given some assistance but never the equivalent of what the worker receives.

> Industrial wages should not be linked with this institutional welfare payment in the sense that such a payment *becomes* the wage. As in the free world, the minimum industrial wage should be set at a level above this welfare payment, to ensure that it does in fact constitute a legitimate incentive to work.[59]

So Jeremy Bantham's principle of lesser eligibility has been turned outside in, and all inmates receive further lessons in the class structure and the working relations it produces.

There are several additional economic aspects of privatization in corrections that bear consideration. It is worthwhile to ask whether the penal system should devote so much effort to disciplining people for the labour market when the labour market itself is the problem? The problem of unemployment persists, especially for the working class youths who are over-represented in prisons and other penal programs. At best, they are trained for jobs that will keep them at the margins of society economically. At worst, they are given the hope that they do have something to sell to the labour market, only to have it dashed by the unavailability of meaningful and reasonably lucrative employment.

Consideration must also be given to the role of monopoly capital in the penal industry. Contrary to the "small is beautiful" ideal and decentralized programs urged by the community corrections movement, most of the business in Canadian jurisdictions is monopolized by the franchise conglomerates such as the Salvation Army and John Howard Society. In the United States, too, large organizations are pushing the small ones out of business, and the need to compete and grow has led some non-profit organizations to convert to for-profit status.[68,49] This is evident in the dramatic move to private sector "community control" of juveniles in Massachusetts, a $300 million industry in 1981. As Cohen observes. "[T]his is genuine commodification—not 'Little House on the Prairie' families looking after deprived children, but large corporations, experienced contract lawyers and organized lobbying of the state legislature."[12]

The obvious issue raised by all of this is the implications for the welfare of offenders. Experience in the United States suggests that an efficiency orientation in privatized services is often at the expense of inmate programs and services.[26] Privatized programs in other sectors also indicate this tendency. For example, over 300 of the 332 nursing homes in Ontario are operated by private entrepreneurs. The public nursing homes compared to private ones spend 25% more on food, 300% more on nursing supplies, and 400% more on recreational activity.[36] The system is also riddled with persistent allegations of mistreatment and abuse (*The Globe and Mail*, 31 October, 1986: 1). The underlying thrust of privatization appears to be a move to reduce welfare costs, and of course it is welfare recipients who receive the brunt of it.

The Politics of Privatization

It is fantasy to assume the private sector will displace the state in operating the penal system because that system, and crime control more generally, is too dear to the state's claims to legitimacy. What the state is after through privatization is a reduction of welfare expenditures while retaining the use of the penal system in the reproduction of its legitimacy.

As Taylor has argued cogently,[71, 72] the real meaning of the "minimum state" is the "minimum welfare state." In Canada at least, the state continues to grow along with its deficit, but iis priorities are shifting away from welfare provision. Moreover, there are differences internationally in both the symbolic and practical importance of welfare. Britain has certainly adopted an American-style conservative ideology through its Conservative government, and yet retains a substantial welfare infrastructure and shows no signs of American-style privatization in its penal system. Indeed, in Britain, the prison system and military are the only two areas that receive 100% of their funding from the central government. In Canada, too, there is a significant state commitment to health, education and welfare that differs from the United States.[39]

Regardless of the realities we have documented previously, Canadian politicians are happy to emphasize that our political/cultural identity includes a commitment to welfare, even of inmates. For example, speaking on the private CTV network program "W5," former solicitor General MacKay declared, "I'm far more interested in the welfare of inmates and getting them back into society...than I am in the cost factor and getting them into an institution where we can be too crass and business-like" (cited in *Liaison*, March, 1985: 17).

In Canadian politics, the preferred form of "community correction" seems to involve a well-placed politician arranging to have a penitentiary built in his home community because the economic stimulus it brings also has a certain political purchase. Witness Prime Minister Mulroney's arrangement to have a penitentiary built in his home constituency even though locating there will cost tens of millions of dollars more than what was planned by his civil servants in the CSC, and even though his civil servants' planning suggests that a different type of facility is required than the "super maximum" one being built for the Prime Minister's riding (cf. *The Globe and Mail*, 22 October, 1986: 1). In Ontario, the MPP for Muskoka, as part of the May 1983 budget, announced plans to add on another 500 beds in 10 institutions as "part of a job creation initiative." That the government as well as the unemployed were expected to benefit financially from this is evident in the subsequent statement by the former Minister of Corrections that a prefabricated unit would be constructed in some cases and "we anticipate marketing the unit to other correctional jurisdictions in Canada once our own needs are met" (Hansard, J-132, 133, 1984).

The involvement of non-state agencies in certain forms of penalizing helps to reproduce the legitimacy of the state. When community programs directed at self-help and inclusion are run by the state directly they appear totalitarian, but when managed and operated by responsible citizens they appear much less so. Hence non-state agency involvement is a way for the state to extend its reach more legitimately. Moreover, if a non-state agency is operating a penal program and particular problems arise, responsibility for the problems can be displaced to the non-state agency. In addition, the involvement of reputable citizens in community programs allows absorption of criticism in the wake of problems. For example, community correctional boards that developed with the Ontario community service order programs, and which were "a direct result of fee-for-service contracting," function to "deflect criticism of community correctional programming at their level since the boards are usually comprised of reputable concerned citizens."[55]

Through non-state agencies, the state also manages to canalize the reform process. As addressed earlier, through contracting with government, non-state agencies are co-opted as both controllers and reformers. The state uses its power, including especially its money, to stimulate non-state community organizations to be its servants and critics in the quest for progressive reform.[52] This is exemplified in the process by which the Ontario community service order programs came into being and quickly flourished. An enormous range of community organizations joined with the full range of state criminal justice agencies in producing a consensus rarely seen in any area of political policy.[45]

The strong state is still with us. As Cohen[12] has show so ably, community corrections policies and programs are "creatures of the state" in every aspect: conception, sponsorship, financing, evaluation, and rationalization. These state-directed efforts to recreate community are signs of the demise of community: "It is unlikely, to say the least, that the very same interest and forces which destroyed the traditional community—bureaucracy, professionalization, centralization, rationalization—can now be used to reverse the process."[12]

The Social Aspects of Privatization

In this political economy, the notion of separate public and private realms extinguishes. This notion is from the nineteenth century, and makes little sense with the twentieth-century evolution of "the social" realm.[11, 16, 27, 56] The public and private are entwined in the complex and seamless web of the social, constituting the realm of social work, social administration, and so on. The history of crime control is the history of "publicizing" and "politicizing" private spheres and concerns and bringing them into the social. Publication, politicization, and legislation relating to violence in domestic settings is a recent manifestation of this evolution.[49]

In the social realm, the relation between the state and non-state agencies is not cyclical or complementary but additive. State agencies increase their capacity while non-state agencies do likewise. In the process, genuine extra-state modes of informal control are often suffocated.

State agents take on a broader range of responsibilities. As outlined previously, they become hard-end controllers of dangerous populations. They also police non-state soft-end controllers of troublesome populations. They develop standards, inspection procedures, reward structures, and so on for policing the non-state controllers. Correctional classification is no longer reserved for offenders, but is also elaborated for correctional programs and the control agents they employ. Typical of bureaucratic life,[31] the emphasis is placed on procedural form, and ferreting out procedural strays. In this policing function, state agents also become reformers. Finding errors, faults and cracks allows them to sustain the perpetual sense of failure that is needed to justify tinkering, repair work, and the perpetual sense of progress.

In continuing the realm of the social, non-state agencies join in diminishing the prospect for substantial reform. They engage in re-form rather than reform.[15, 19, 20, 21, 22, 42] Talk about privatization shifts the discourse away from abolition of particular components of the penal system and even away from arguments about alternatives to the penal system.

We are left with technical discussions of different ways to keep doing the same thing. The prevailing question is whether it will be done "privately" or "publicly" and who will profit from it. As usual, the recipients of the penal system are rarely consulted. They remain silent, or have been silenced, it is difficult to say which.

No one is saying much any more about altering the structures that lead to criminalization. No one is saying much any more about letting at least some unfortunate people go. No one is even urging that we might reduce the reliance on prisons substantially by eliminating their predominant use as a sanction for debtors. Just imagine how many people the John Howard Society or the Salvation Army could keep out of prison if they paid the fines of debtors! Indeed, taking the example of the John Howard Society in Ontario, their limited involvement with fine defaulters provides the organization with both financial and ideological capital. According to a former Ontario Minister of Corrections, "it would be cheaper for us to pay the fines for these offenders than to operate the program" of fine options run by the John Howard Society in Niagara (Hansard, J-165, 1984).

As Taft observes about experiences in the United States, when the state puts the fiscal squeeze on non-state control agents, "The reformist spirit that has driven so many of them is...snuffed out..." and some have even joined state control agencies "hoping to reform the system from within."[68] Even if they do not join the state formally, non-state agencies are prone to join it in every other respect in the realm of the social. There is no clearer indication of this than the way the Salvation Army has embraced the state in running the entire misdemeanant probation program in Florida.[70] Indeed, the Florida state legislation enabling this social relation is simply titled, *The Salvation Army Act.* This solidifies the social monopoly, and its hold on the process of re-form.

An indication of how non-state crime control agencies have embraced the state in the social realm comes from a paper by Howard Sapers,[58] Provincial Executive Director, John Howard Society of Alberta. Sapers records the increasing heavy reliance of the Alberta JHS on government service contracts, which now constitute the substantial majority of Alberta JHS funding. He expresses the view that the relative autonomy of Alberta JHS has contracted with each increment in the proportion of funding that is dependent on government contracts. This is because contract funding is tied to programs that "are sanction-based and are overtly social control oriented." Overall, contract-dependency "has tended to reinforce notions of social control...[but] social control is not an aim compatible with the stated objectives of the Alberta John Howard Society."

Sapers seems to have a point if one examines the stated objectives that were formulated at the inception of the Alberta John Howard Society in 1947. "Although the major aim of the Society was directed primarily to aiding individual dischargees in re-establishing themselves in the community, the officially stated goals of the Society originally included a much wider definition.

This definition included: reform for justice legislation; help to prisoners' families; removal of criminogenic conditions; and prison reform."[58] However, if one examines the new set of objectives adopted by the Society in 1983, it is very evident that the ideals have been adjusted to the new reality that the Society is primarily a control agency dependent on the state. These new objectives are, "The prevention of crime through: a) the development and implementation of improved policies and techniques within the criminal justice system [i.e., re-form in the form of refining control techniques]; b) the provision of services to those in conflict with the law, including the provision of community and residential services to ex-offenders [i.e. running carceral institutions]; c) the promotion of awareness within society of those circumstances that contribute to crime [i.e., education]; d) the promotion of acceptance of responsibility and accountability to society to change those circumstances that contribute to crime [i.e., re-form for crime prevention]."[58]

As refiners of control techniques, jailers, educators, and re-formers in the interest of crime prevention, the Alberta John Howard Society is no different from state criminal justice agencies. A further indication of this is an informant's statement that an Alberta John Howard Society official responsible for initiating the adoption of these revised aims subsequently became an advisor on penal system matters to the Neilsen Task Force, and is now a civil servant specializing in privatization of penal programs. In the realm of the social, state and non-state personnel converge in interests and objectives as both controllers and re-formers.

Conclusions

All agencies, whether state, commercial or voluntary, constitute the realm of the social and are part of the penal system. They all function as controllers and reformers simultaneously, disciplining their conscript clientele as well as each other.

We are reminded of the institutional parallels in academic criminology. There is the sphere of "criminology for cash," undertaking research contracts for government ministries that are lucrative, but limited intellectually. In recent years, there has been increasing competition for these contracts from commercial companies. Regardless of who does the work, the dominant discourse of criminology is shifted into the administrative efficiency discourse of the state. Since questions of efficiency are inherently ideological, the criminologist cannot avoid becoming an ideologue of the state.

Another funding possibility is sustaining grants from government ministries. These of course allow greater autonomy, although due deference must be given to the ministry in publications and on other public occasions. Moreover, as in any form of sponsorship, the recipient must always be half-watching in terms of another show, the expectations of the sponsor.

The academic criminologist can seek other sponsorship, for example from the Social Sciences and Humanities Research Council and from private foundations. Furthermore, teaching provides income that brings a measure of independence. However, all this hardly constitutes independence from the state since the Canadian academic is wholly dependent on the state for his base salary.

State and non-state control agencies are left to criticize and educate within the cost-effectiveness-humaneness discourse of re-form, while simultaneously getting on with their direct control task of capturing people and putting them in their place. They thereby continue to contribute to the acceleration and dispersal of social control. In face of this, it is still viable to take a "least worst" position. Since somebody has to do the "dirty work"[33] of looking after the dependent, deprived and depraved it might as well be one's own agency because one believes it can do the work better than competitors. This faith is based on a feeling of superiority over other possibilities. For example, as we identified earlier, "voluntary, non profit" agencies express a superiority over the "filthy lucre" of "for-profit" agencies and the "filthy bureaucracy" of state agencies.

This is fine. A sense of superiority, of moral worthiness, is, after all, what motivates people and their organizations to take initiatives and get on with the task. However, before rushing into things, it is important to reflect on the history of good intentions being enveloped and suffocated by the demands of administrative convenience, and the wider economic, political and social aspects we have raised.

Endnotes

1.   Richard Ericson presented an earlier version of this paper to the Annual Couchiching Conference, John Howard Society of Ontario. We are grateful to Professor Stanley Cohen of the Hebrew University of Jerusalem for his comments on an earlier version of this paper. The development of this paper was assisted by the Contributions Program of the Centre of Criminology, University of Toronto of the Ministry of the Solicitor General. Canada.

2.   Abel, Richard, ed. *The Politics of Informal Justice*. New York: Academic Press. 1982.

3.   Adamson, Christopher. "Punishment after Slavery: Southern State Penal Systems, 1865-1890," *Social Problems*, 30: 555-569. 1983.

4.   Auerbach, Barbara et al. *A Guide to Effective Prison Industries, Volume I, Creating Free Venture Prison Industries: Program Considerations*. Chatham, N.J.: Chatham House Publishers. 1979.

5.   Beattie, John. *Crime and the Courts in England 1660-1800*. Princeton: Princeton University Press. 1986.

6.   Black, Donald. *The Behaviour of Law*. New York: Academic Press. 1976.

7.   Bottoms, Anthony. "Reflections on the Renaissance of Dangerousness," *Howard Journal of Penology and Crime Prevention*, 16: 70-76, 1977.

8.   Bottoms, Anthony. "Neglected Features in Contemporary Penal Systems," in D. Garland and P. Young, eds., *The Power to Punish: Contemporary Penalty and Social Analysis*. London: Heinemann. 1983.

9.   Chan, Janet and Richard Ericson. *Decarceration and the Economy of Penal Reform*. Toronto: Centre of Criminology, University of Toronto. 1981.

10.   Chunn, Dorothy. "Good Men Work Hard: Convict Labour in Kingston Penitentiary, 1835-1850," *Canadian of Criminology Forum*. 4: 13-22. 1981.

11.   Chunn, Dorothy. "From Punishment to Doing Good: The Origins and Impact of Family Courts in Ontario, 1888-1942." Ph.D. Thesis, Department of Sociology, University of Toronto. 1986.

12.   Cohen, Stanley. *Visions of Social Control: Crime, Punishment, and Classification*. Cambridge: Polity. 1985.

13.   "Corrections in Ontario," *Everyone's Business*. Toronto: Ontario Ministry of Correctional Services. 1986.

14.   Dalton, Michael. *The Country Justice*. 1661.

15.   Dittenhoffer, Tony and Richard Ericson. "The Victim/Offender Reconciliation Program: A Message to Correctional Reformers," *University of Toronto Law Journal*. 33: 314-347. 1983.

16.   Donzelot, Jacques. *The Policing of Families*. New York: Pantheon. 1979.

17. Durkheim, Emile. *The Division of Labor in Society*. New York: Free Press. 1933.
18. Ericson, Richard. *Reproducing Order: A Study of Police Patrol Work*. Toronto: University of Toronto Press. 1982.
19. Ericson, Richard. "Legal Inequality," in S. Spitzer and A. Scull, eds., *Research in Law. Deviance and Social Control*. Greenwich, Connecticut: JAI Press. 1985.
20. Ericson, Richard. "The State and Criminal Justice Reform," in R. Ratner and J. McMullan, eds., *State Control: Criminal Justice Politics in Canada*. Vancouver: University of British Columbia Press. 1987.
21. Ericson, Richard and Patricia Baranek. *The Ordering of Justice*. Toronto: University of Toronto Press. 1982.
22. Ericson, Richard and Patricia Baranek. "Criminal Law Reform and Two Realities of the Criminal Process," in A. Doob and E. Greenspan, eds., *Perspectives in Criminal Law: Essays in Honour of J.U.J. Edwards*. Toronto: Canada Law Book. 1984.
23. Erikson, Kai. *Wayward Puritans: A Study in the Sociology of Deviance*. New York: John Wiley. 1966.
24. Foucault, Michel. *Discipline and Punish: The Birth of the Prison*. New York: Pantheon. 1977.
25. Friedenberg, Edgar. *The Disposal of Liberty and Other Industrial Wastes*. New York: Double-day. 1975.
26. Gandy, John. *Privatization of Correctional Services for Adults*. Reports to the Ministry of the Solicitor General of Canada. 1985.
27. Garland, David. *Punishment and Welfare: A History of Penal Strategies*. Aldershot: Gower. 1985.
28. Garland, David and Peter Young. *The Power to Punish: Contemporary Penalty and Social Analysis*. London: Heinemann. 1983.
29. Gooderham, H. "The Controversy over Privatization," *Let's Talk, 11(3)* (February). 1986.
30. Gusfield, Joseph. *The Culture of Public Problems: Drinking-Driving and the Symbolic Order*. Chicago: University of Chicago Press. 1981.
31. Habermas, Jurgen. *Legitimation Crisis*. London: Heinemann. 1975.
32. Harrison, E. and M. Gosse. "Privatization: A Restraint Initiative," Policy Report. British Columbia Ministry of Corrections. September 9, 1985.
33. Hughes, Everett. "Work and Self," in J. Rohrer and M. Sherif, eds., *Social Psychology at the Crossroads*. New York: Harpers. 1951.
34. Ignatieff, Michael. *A Just Measure of Pain: The Penitentiary in the Industrial Revolution 1750-1850*. London: Macmillan. 1978.
35. Ignatieff, Michael. "State, Civil Society and Total Institutions: A Critique of Present Social Histories of Punishment," in M. Tonry and N. Morris,

eds., *Crime and Justice: An Annual Review of Research.* Volume 3. Chicago: University of Chicago Press. 1981.

36. John Howard Society of Ontario. *Privatization and Commercialization of Correctional Services.* Draft manuscript (September), 1986.

37. John Howard Society of Ontario. *The John Howard Society Services Across Ontario.* Toronto: J.H.S. Ontario. 1986.

38. Kellough, Gail, Steven Brickey and William Greenaway. "The Politics of Incarceration: Manitoba, 1918-1939," *Canadian Journal of Sociology* 5: 253-271. 1980.

39. Lowman, John and Robert Menzies. "Out of the Fiscal Shadow: Carceral Trends in Canada and the United States," *Crime and Social Justice.* (Fall/Winter) 1986/87.

40. Maghan, Jess and Edward Sagarin. "The Privatization of Corrections: Seeking to Anticipate the Unanticipated Consequences," Paper presented to the American Society of Criminology. San Diego (November). 1985.

41. Marx, Gary. "Ironies of Social Control," *Social Problem.* 28: 221-266. 1981.

42. McMahon, Maeve and Richard Ericson. "Reforming the Police and Policing Reform," in R. Ratner and J. Mcmullan, eds., *State Control: Criminal Justice Politics In Canada.* Vancouver: University of British Columbia Press. 1987.

43. Mead, George, H. "The Psychology of Punitive Justice," *American Journal of Sociology.* 23: 586-592. 1918.

44. Melossi, Dario and Massimo Pavarini. *The Prison and the Factory: Origins of the Penitentiary System.* New Jersey: Barnes and Noble. 1981.

45. Menzies, Ken. "The Rapid Spread of Community Service Orders in Ontario," *Canadian Journal of Criminology.* 28: 157-169. 1986.

46. Mulllen, Joan. "Corrections and the Private Sector," *Research in Brief.* Washington: National Institute of Justice. 1985.

47. Mulcrone, R. "A Private Sector Perspective on Prison Industries," Paper to the Workshop on Corrections and the Private Sector, Toronto, February, 1986.

48. Neilsen, Eric. *Improved Program Delivery Justice.* Ottawa: A Study Team Report to the Task Force on Programming Review, Neilsen Task Force. 1986.

49. Neilsen, Barbara. *Making an Issue of Child Abuse: Political Agenda Setting for Social Problems.* Chicago: University of Chicago Press. 1984.

50. Novak, Michael. "Mediating Institutions: The Communicatarian Individual in America," *The Public Interest.* 68: 3-20. 1982.

51. Pahapill, J. "The Private Enterprise and Inmate Employment Joint Ventures: Some Experiences by Ontario Corrections," Paper to

conference, "New Partnerships: Corrections and Private Enterprise," Toronto (February). 1986.

52. Pifer, Alan. *The Nongovernmental Organization at Bay*. New York: Carnegie Corporation of New York. 1966.

53. Platt, Tony and Paul Takagi, eds., *Punishment and Penal Discipline: Essays on the Prison and the Prisoners' Movement*. Berkeley: Crime and Justice Associates. 1980.

54. Rock, Paul. *A View from the Shadows*. Oxford University Press. 1986.

55. Roe, John. "Private Sector Contracts," *Correctional Options*. 1: 54-61. 1981.

56. Rothman, David. *Conscience and Convenience: The Asylum and Its Alternatives in Progressive America*. Boston: Little, Brown. 1980.

57. Rusche, Georg and Otto Kirchheimer. *Punishment and Social Structure*. New York: Columbia University Press. 1939.

58. Sapers, Howard. "Contracting in Context: The Selling of Criminal Justice Services," Paper presented to the American Society of Criminology, San Diego (November). 1985.

59. Schaller, Jack. "Normalizing the Prison Work Environment," in D. Fogel and J. Hudson, eds., *Justice and Fairness: Perspectives on the Justice Model*. Cincinnati: Anderson. 1981.

60. Scull, Andrew. *Decarceration: Community Treatment and the Deviant—A Radical View*: Second Edition. Cambridge: Polity. 1984.

61. Sexton, George, et al. "The Private Sector and Prison Industries," *Research in Brief*. Washington: National Institute of Justice (August). 1985.

62. Shearing, Clifford and Philip Stenning. "Private Security: Its Growth and Implications," in M. Tonry and N. Morris, eds., *Crime and Justice: An Annual Review of Research*, Volume 3. Chicago: University of Chicago Press. 1981.

63. Shearing, Clifford and Philip Stenning. "Private Security: Implications for Social Control," *Social Problems*. 30: 493-506. 1983.

64. Skogan, Wesley. "Crime and Crime Rates," in W. Skogan, ed., *Sample Surveys of Victims of Crimes*. Cambridge, Mass.: Ballinger Press. 1976.

65. Solicitor General of Canada. *Selected Trends in Criminal Justice*. Ottawa: Ministry of the Solicitor General, 1985.

66. Sparks, Richards et al. *Surveying Victims: A Study of the Measurement of Criminal Victimization, Perceptions of Crime, and Attitudes to Criminal Justice*. London: Wiley. 1977.

67. Spitzer, Steven and Andrew Scull. "Social Control in Historical Perspective: From Private to Public Responses to Crime," in D. Greenberg, ed., *Corrections and Punishment*. Beverly Hills: Sage. 1977.

68. Taft, Philip. "The Fiscal Crisis in Private Corrections," *Corrections Magazine*. 8(6): 27-32. 1982.

69. Taft, Philip. "Survival of the Fittest," *Corrections Magazine*. 9(1): 36-39, 41-43. 1983.

70. Taft, Philip. "The Salvation Army Conquers Florida," *Corrections Magazine*. 9(1): 40-41.

71. Taylor, Ian. *Law and Order: Arguments for Socialism*. London: Macmillan. 1981.

72. Taylor, Ian. *Crime, Capitalism and Community: Three Essays in Socialist Criminology*. Toronto: Butterworth. 1983.

73. Taylor, Michael. *Community, Anarchy and Liberty*. Cambridge: Cambridge University Press. 1982.

74. Teplitsky, Martin. Address to the Ontario Labour Law Section of the Canadian Bar Association (November). 1983.

75. United States Department of Justice. *The 1983 Jail Census*. Washington: U.S. Department of Justice Bulletin NCJ—95536. 1984.

76. Warren, Carol. "New Forms of Social Control: The Myth of De-Institutionalization," *American Behavioural Scientist*. 24: 724-740. 1981.

77. Weiss, Robert. "The Reappearance of the 'Ideal Factory': The Entrepreneur and Social Control in the Contemporary Prison," in J. Lowman, R. Menzies and T. Palys, eds., *Transcarceration: Essays in the Sociology of Social Control*. Aldershot: Gower. 1986.

78. Wittgenstein, Ludwig. *Philosophical Investigations*. Oxford: Blackwell. 1972.

Chapter 3

Risky Business: The Classification of Dangerous People in the Canadian Carceral Enterprise[*]

Robert Menzies, Dorothy E. Chunn and Christopher D. Webster

If there is an overall political issue around the prison, it is not therefore whether it is corrective or not; whether the judges, the psychiatrists or the sociologists are to exercise more power in it than the administrators or the supervisors; it is not even whether we should have prison or something other than prison. At present, the problem lies rather in the steep rise in the use of these mechanisms of normalization and the wide-ranging powers which, through the proliferation of new disciplines, they bring with them.

Michel Foucault. *Discipline and Punish* (1977: 306)

[*] Thanks are expressed to Debbie Slomen, Diana Sepejak, Shelley McMain and Shauna Staley, who co-ordinated data collection during various stages of the project described in this chapter. Acknowledged as well is the assistance of the many research assistants, and representatives of mental health, police, justice and correctional agencies (too numerous to list here by name), who collaborated in the compilation of the information described below. Funding was supplied by the Social Sciences and Humanities Research Council of Canada, the Canadian Psychiatric Research Foundation, the Solicitor General Canada, the LaMarsh Research Program on Violence and Conflict Resolution, the Ontario Department of Health, Simon Fraser University, the University of Toronto Centre of Criminology, and the Clarke Institute of Psychiatry.

Introduction

The idea for this chapter emerged out of our individual and collective writing, on a number of convergent topics in the areas of critical social control and feminist theory (Chunn and Gavigan, 1991; Chunn and Gavigan, 1988; Lowman, Menzies and Palys, 1987; Menzies, 1989; Webster, 1990), homicide and violence (Grant, Boyle and Chunn, forthcoming; Menzies, Webster and Sepejak, 1987), the clinical prediction of dangerousness (Webster and Menzies, 1987; Webster, Hucker and Ben-Aron, 1985), and the forensic evaluation of women and other medico-legal subjects in pre-trial assessment clinics (Chunn and Menzies, 1990; Menzies, 1989; Menzies, Chunn and Webster, 1992; Webster, Menzies and Jackson, 1982).

Permeating these related subjects are various recurrent themes reflecting structures of control and cultural concerns about the securing of social order in private and public realms of contemporary society; about the apprehension of various forms of risk to that order; about the development of policies and practices for the regulation of threatening people, thoughts and things; and about the circulation of knowledge and emergence of experts in the identification of the endangered and the dangerous, the protection of the former, and the surveillance, containment and control of the latter. The idea of dangerousness—whether applied to the crimes and victimization of women, the social construction of homicide, the relationship between violence and mental disorder, or the psychiatric prediction of criminal and violent conduct—is a central feature of contemporary correctional and therapeutic systems. In its various manifestations the construct throws open many important windows for comprehending the complex processes through which the carceral apparatus is constituted, and through which, conversely, it can potentially be deconstructed and rearranged.

In what follows we examine the expert attribution of dangerousness in the Canadian penal apparatus. In the context of current developments in the critical revisionist literature on penality and social control (Chunn and Gavigan, 1988; Cohen, 1985; Cohen and Scull, 1983; Garland, 1985, 1990; Garland and Young, 1983; Lowman, Menzies and Palys, 1987; Melossi, 1990), we look at the classification of danger and risk as a central property of contemporary carceral discourses and practices in this country. We review some recent trends in the administration of danger by legal and mental health institutions and professionals. We review contemporary movements towards the bifurcation of systems designed to treat and control psychiatric populations, and we address current trends in the Americanization of the Canadian mental architecture.

Following the observations of Foucault (1977, 1978), Garland (1985, 1990) and Castel (1991), we argue that the mutual attractions of parallel and frequently overlapping control systems, along with the increasingly scientized, technocractic, and managerial character of the penal business itself (Chan, 1990; Cohen, 1988; Ericson and Shearing, 1986; Lowman and MacLean, 1992; Young, 1988), have been instrumental in both proliferating and fundamentally transforming the dangerousness construct. Finally, by enlisting some of our own work on the outcomes of forensic evaluation activities in a medico-legal assessment agency in Toronto (Chunn and Menzies, 1990; Menzies, 1989; Menzies, Chunn and Webster, in press; Webster and Menzies, 1987; Webster, Menzies and Jackson, 1982), we consider the implications of dangerousness decisions for the careers of penal and psychiatric subjects and for the deployment of judicial and therapeutic organizations in which they are immersed.

The Dangerousness Discipline in Perspective

Like a variety of allied and inter-related constructs—endangerment, disorder, dependency, delinquency, depravity, deficiency, and so forth—dangerousness is deeply engrained in the correctional culture and in the knowledge systems embraced by its practitioners (Castel, 1991; Foucault, 1977, 1978; Menzies, 1986, 1989; Petrunik, 1983; Pfohl, 1978, 1979; Rennie, 1978). From the late eighteenth century to the present (Monahan, 1981; Shah, 1978; Webster, Ben-Aron and Hucker, 1985), ideas about punishment and treatment have been recurrently fuelled both by the imagery of dangerousness circulating through public and private realms, and by official claims to scientific expertise in its diagnosis, prediction, prevention and treatment (cf. Britzer and Crowner, 1988; Brody, 1990; Hamilton and Freeman, 1982; Hall, 1987; Hinton, 1983; Toch and Adams, 1989).

The notion that risky people—and classes of people—can be precisely calibrated and contained has a powerful discursive and pragmatic appeal. It offers assurances that public protection is to be found not just in the law's retroactive response to criminal behaviour, but more so in the capacity of science to extend the reach of law beyond human behaviour and into the future tense. A purely reactive penal system, constrained by its reliance on formal categories of legality, individual responsibility, evidence and guilt, is a relatively blunt, if potentially brutal, instrument of punishment. It measures up violent behaviour and other social wrongs, and it responds in kind.

In comparison, the infusion of scientific and technical knowledge in the service of criminal law opens and re-focusses the carceral lens on the multitude of threats posed by defective human subjects across a broad and potentially indefinite band of time and space. For the purposes of penal intervention, dangerous people are dangerous because they present personalities, patterns and possibilities that transcend their own behaviour and seemingly elude the normal safeguards conferred by law.[1] So to neutralize the apparent threat, specialist systems are constructed at the frontiers of criminal law and in parallel institutions such as mental health, and psychiatrists and other professionals are designated as authoritative experts in the detection and defusion of social danger. And according to Foucault's well-known passage from *Discipline and Punish,* this dispersal of normalizing power is by no means exclusively confined to the attribution of dangerousness alone:

> Throughout the penal procedure and the implementation of the sentence there swarms a whole series of subsidiary authorities. Small-scale legal systems and parallel judges have multiplied around the principal judgment: psychiatric or psychological experts, magistrates concerned with the implementation of sentences, educationalists, members of the prison services, all fragment the legal power to punish.... The whole machinery that has been developing for years around the implementation of sentences, and their adjustment to individuals, creates a proliferation of the authorities of judicial decision-making and extends its powers of decision well beyond the sentence (Foucault, 1977: 21).

None of the above should be read as an essentialization of the construct (see Cameron, 1990; Diamond and Quinby, 1988; Eisenstein, 1988; Harding, 1987; Nicholson, 1990; Palmer, 1990), nor as a suggestion that understandings of dangerousness are in any way autonomous from historical process or from the structural-cultural context of state and civil control institutions. To the contrary, we conceive dangerousness as a highly elastic, even "protean" idea (Rennie, 1978), which indexically reflects and conditions historically specific moments in the life cycles of carceral programs and practices. From its overtly class-conscious usage in nineteenth-century social commentary (Brace, 1872; Mayhew, 1861), dangerousness has undergone a number of discursive shifts through its absorption, respectively, into the words and deeds of criminal anthropologists (Rennie, 1978), turn-of-century social reformers (Bacchi, 1983; McLaren, 1990; Rothman, 1980; Valverde, 1991), second-wave psychiatrists (Castel, Castel and Lovell, 1982), sexual and chemical prohibitionists (Boyd 1991; Coward, 1985; Dorn, 1987; Mort, 1987; Weeks, 1989) and, more recently and most intriguingly, of deinstitutionalists, social critics and civil libertarians (Floud and Young, 1981; Stone, 1984; Warren, 1982).

What unites these various incarnations of the construct is their common adherence to pervasive belief systems about the causes, consequences and cures of social (dis)order. Whereas the symbolic assailants may be consistently changing faces and forms, and while new cohorts of social defence specialists may be in constant succession or rotation, still the constructed dangerosities of any given society open up important windows toward an understanding of its main problems and preoccupations. The people, practices and ideas which are defined as most dangerous at any conjunction of time and space, however real or ideological in substance, are sharp representations of the social order's main vulnerabilities and contradictions. Taking the shape of witches or foreigners or homosexuals or heretics or communists or unmarried women or drug dealers or paedophiles, they hold up a mirror to the most profound apprehensions of those who invest in established formations and practices, and hence they paradoxically reveal the power relations and hegemonies that perpetuate the status quo and hold these structures in place.

In practice, of course, these collective iconographies of danger are often woefully misconstrued and misapplied. The personalization of dangerousness in the twentieth century, like the individualization of carceral practices more generally (Foucault, 1977; Garland, 1985; Rose, 1990; Smart, 1989), has functioned to drain the dangerousness construct of its social and political content.

Images of peril become inscribed on solitary human subjects, typically pathological or psychopathic, and social defence becomes a matter of simply segregating the dangerous and potentially dangerous from the endangered through authoritative exercises in scientific sorting. The diagnosis and prevention of inter-personal violence and other individual harms become the main task of penal systems, which are increasingly cut off from the collective and normalized hazards inherent in modern life, whether these take the form of nuclear arsenals, genocidal wars, ecological atrocities, state terrorism, institutionalized poverty, racism, sexism, or violations of human rights. Such dangers are typically seen to fall outside the realm of penality, and hence are left to other, more "politicized" institutions. The criminal law and its supporting systems are instead concerned with the depredations of sick and sinful beings. And while the legal power to punish and correct is immense (Garland, 1990; Garland and Young 1983; Pepinsky and Quinney, 1991; Smart, 1989), the weaponry is trained downward and inward, away from the structures and ideas that spawn the most terrifying kinds of collective endangerment. Constrained by such a myopic conception of risk, the state's carceral apparatus is simply not equipped to protect its citizens from the most systemic and supreme perils.

More than this, through the twentieth-century interventions of psychiatry and other mental sciences, danger has become increasingly pathologized and equated with a wide range of personal defects and disorders. Amid a sustained exercise in Foucauldian normalization (Diamond and Quinby, 1988; Garland, 1985; Rose, 1990), the routine, mundane features of violence and other social harms have been progressively submerged in political and public culture, and supplanted by the sense that dangerous people are somehow different and unique—walled off from the rest of us by some discoverable material, mental or moral barrier. From Garofalo's theories of dangerosity (1914) to contemporary sociobiologies of homicide and violence (Daly and Wilson, 1988; Wilson and Herrnstein, 1985; see Caputi, 1987; Hanmer and Maynard, 1987), experts have time and again been commissioned to chart the correlates of dangerous conduct; to draw distinctions between the innocuous and the threatening; to mine for cues and clues in the bodies and minds of risky subjects; and to construct actuarial scales and clinical methods for the scientific forecasting of dangerous events (Deitz, 1985; Dix, 1980; Hall, 1987; Mulvey, Blumstein and Cohen, 1986; Schmidt and Witte, 1990; von Hirsch, 1987).

These efforts continue, despite recurrent demonstrations of the construct's ontological orneriness—its stubborn resistance to the overtures of technicians or clinicians who propose to classify dangerous people and predict their transgressions (Menzies, 1986, 1989; Monahan, 1981; Steadman and Cocozza, 1974; Thornberry and Jacoby, 1979; Webster, Dickens and Addario, 1985; Webster and Menzies, 1987).

According to critics, the scientific normalization of dangerousness is a hapless pursuit, condemned by the ideological character of the concept itself, and by the political contexts in which it is typically invoked (Castel, 1991; Petrunik, 1983; Pfohl, 1978, 1979). And a small library of research is now available to document the meagre correspondences between violent behaviour and such personal categories and conditions as psychiatric status, criminal history and social class (Bieber, Pasewark, Bosten and Steadman, 1988; Menzies, Webster and Sepejak, 1987; Mesnikoff and Lauterbach, 1975; but see Harris, Rice and Cormier, 1991). Even those factors that do demonstrate a differential effect—for example age, gender, and prior violence—are notoriously deficient in predictive power (American Psychiatric Association, 1974; Monahan, 1981). The intuitive judgments of practising psychiatrists and other experts, in turn, show little promise (Coleman, 1984; Dix, 1980; Menzies, Webster and Sepejak, 1985a; Webster and Menzies, 1987). Statistical and psychometric instruments, while less strikingly inaccurate, are nonetheless of little practical value in the clinical or penal classification of perilous persons (Menzies, Webster and Sepejak, 1985b; Monahan, 1981; von Hirsch, 1987).

Yet the enterprise endures. Indeed, perhaps the most remarkable aspect of the danger sciences is their resilience in the face of such a prolonged legacy of unremittingly bad reviews. Over the past decade, in fact, the power to apply dangerous labels to legal and medical subjects, and to confine and correct them on the grounds of these imputations, has escalated. Moreover, some of the most vocal critics of these practices 15 or 20 years ago (Ennis and Litwack, 1974; Monahan and Cummings, 1975; Steadman, 1973; Morris and Hawkins, 1970) have revised their positions and are now endorsing the qualified use of the dangerousness construct, or some variant, in carceral and psychiatric decision-making (Litwack, 1985; Monahan, 1988; Steadman, Robbins and Monahan, 1991; Morris and Miller, 1985).

None of this should come as much of a shock to anyone versed in the behaviour of scientific paradigms, and in their power to propel "normal" theory and practice through countless minefields of empirical anomalies (Harding, 1987; Kuhn, 1970; Lakatos and Musgrave, 1968; Ritzer, 1975; Spruill, 1983). Nor should we be surprised that the dangerousness concept survives and thrives in medico-legal settings, given its embeddedness in the very fabric of forensic discourse (Menzies, 1986; Castel, 1991), and given its many contributions to the projects of penal systems and the ventures of their agents (Garland 1985; Garland and Young, 1983). Indeed, in the Canadian carceral complex as elsewhere, we are witnessing yet another in a long series of dangerousness revivals (see Bottoms, 1977), and the new versions of this vintage construct are taking a variety of legal, institutional and discursive forms.

Dangerous Trends in the Canadian Carceral Complex

The renaissance of dangerousness in Canadian correctional and therapeutic systems has been gathering momentum since the middle 1970s. The authors of provincial mental health laws across the country, caught in the convulsions of the "deinstitutionalization" movement (Dear and Wolch, 1987; Johnson, 1990; Lerman, 1982; Scull, 1984, 1989; 1990; Torrey, 1988), and inspired by the rights rhetoric emanating from the Charter and from developments in the United States (Gordon and Verdun-Jones, 1988; Robertson, 1987; Savage and McKague, 1987; Stone, 1984; Wexler, 1981), have turned to dangerousness as a focal criterion for the involuntary confinement of psychiatric subjects.

The remarkable depopulation of inclusionary mental institutions over the past quarter-century has been largely premised on and justified by expert assertions that ex-patients present no threat to the "communities" into which they are being unloaded (Ashford, 1989; Brahams and Weller, 1986; Steadman, Cocozza and Melick, 1978). Conversely only those persons evaluated to be *both* mentally ill *and* dangerous (to others, or to themselves through risk of suicide or grave disablement) are legally liable to be mentally confined against their will (Robertson, 1987; Savage and McKague, 1987; Schiffer, 1978, 1982).

The results have been predictable. The grim realities of the "community mental health movement"—the fiscal minimalism of right-wing legislators, the naive deconstructionist mentality of their liberal counterparts, the condemning of an entire generation of emotionally damaged and poor people to lives of urban decay, homelessness, petty crime and endless cycles of psycho-legal discipline—are obscured by a danger discourse that indelibly colours psychiatric practice and legal process, and purports to inform these policies with just measures of both scientific precision and legalistic propriety. In practice, the predication of involuntary mental hospitalization on diagnoses of dangerousness has led to the bifurcation of mentally disordered populations. The non-dangerous are cast into the transcarceral complex (Lowman, Menzies and Palys, 1987; Webster and Menzies, 1987), and into a desultory drift through the inner-city landscape, and between the assortment of state and private agencies left to contend with the chaos. The dangerous, often so defined on the grounds of their violent histories and carceral records, come to typify chronic hospital populations and in the process to escalate the general criminalization of psychiatric settings.

Dangerousness has also been an organizing theme in recent amendments to the *Criminal Code of Canada*. After an initial latency period following its passage in 1977, Part XXIV of the *Code* (formerly Part XXI), providing for the indefinite incarceration of convicted offenders judged to be dangerous in a quasi-criminal sentencing tribunal involving expert testimony, has been invoked over recent years with increasing regularity (Jakimiec, Porporino, Addario and Webster, 1986).[2] Dangerous offender legislation was originally proposed by the 1969 federal Ouimet Committee (see Petrunik, 1983; Price, 1970; Webster, Dickens and Addario, 1985), and was conceived in the tradition of various statutes in other jurisdictions which permit extraordinary sentences for individuals posing a perpetual risk to the public (Floud and Young, 1981; Morris and Miller, 1985; von Hirsch, 1987). Following the conviction of criminal offenders for specified violent or sexual offences, the Attorney-General has the discretion to order a dangerous offender hearing, which is conducted under civil standards of evidence and proof, and which enlists expert testimony about the subject's alleged dangerousness in determining whether to invoke an indeterminate prison sentence. Ultimate parole or release is at the discretion of the National Parole Board which reviews cases after three years, and every year thereafter. To date, of the more than 100 Canadians declared to be dangerous offenders since 1977, only one has been discharged from prison.

Dangerous offender legislation has been widely denounced by socio-legal scholars and civil libertarians who dispute its constitutionality, its efficacy in protecting the public from violent offenders, and its reliance on dubious expert judgments about the dangerousness of criminal defendants (Grant, 1985; Klein, 1976; Price, 1970; Menzies, 1986). Indeed, the Canadian Sentencing Commission (1987: 213) has recommended that it be revoked. But in response to numerous legal challenges under the *Charter of Rights*, the courts have consistently upheld its provisions (Gordon and Verdun-Jones, 1988; Webster, Dickens and Addario, 1985).

The 1986 dangerous offender trial of Robert Noyes, a British Columbia teacher convicted of 19 counts of indecent and sexual assault involving school children, was a watershed case. Noyes' offences involved no violent coercion or penetration; the previous average sentence for such sex crimes was a three year prison term; and witnesses testified at the hearing that Noyes was a "classic" paedophile who presented little risk to re-offend while under appropriate supervision and medication. Nonetheless the court rejected defence arguments that an indefinite sentence was in violation of Charter sections 7, 9 and 12,[3] and declared Noyes a dangerous offender. Six years later he remains in prison, and the appeal is still before the courts (Koutetes, forthcoming; see Caputi, 1987).

During the 1980s the dangerousness construct also converged increasingly with decisions to release federal prisoners into the community. Prompted by a few highly publicized instances of violent crime perpetrated by ex-inmates on parole or mandatory supervision[4] during the early part of the decade (Birnie, 1990; Taylor, 1981; Voumvakis and Ericson, 1984), Parliament passed amendments in 1986 to the *Parole Act* and the *Penitentiary Act*[5] which authorized the "gating" of persons otherwise eligible for MS after two-thirds of their sentence, on the grounds that they are likely to commit a violent crime during their term of supervision (MacLean, 1986; Mandel, 1986; Ratner, 1987).

Parole boards, which have since their inception been involved in the evaluation of criminal recidivism, and been institutionally endowed with exceptional discretionary powers, are now also firmly entrenched in the business of predicting dangerousness. But there is little evidence that they are any more successful in these endeavours than their clinician colleagues, or that the many actuarial and semi-structured instruments designed to facilitate release decisions (see Farrington and Tarling, 1985; Gottfredson and Gottfredson, 1986; Nuffield, 1982; von Hirsch, 1987) are capable of separating dangerous from non-dangerous parole or MS applicants with any degree of validity or regularity. The 1986 amendments were a textbook Canadian occurrence of "political prediction" (Thornberry and Jacoby, 1979), designed to impress the public and press with a display of raw carceral power in the middle of the most repressive decade in Canadian penal history (Mandel 1991). As an operation in correctional management or social defence, it has had no demonstrable impact.

The 1991 Supreme Court of Canada decision in *Regina v. Swain*[6] has opened one further aperture for admission of the dangerousness construct. This case promises to have the greatest bearing on the disposition of criminally insane Canadians since Daniel McNaughtan himself was acquitted of murder in 1843 and shipped off to Bedlam at the "pleasure" of the sovereign.[7]

In *Swain,* the Court found section 614(2) of the *Criminal Code,* ordering the mandatory indeterminate hospitalization of persons judged not guilty by reason of insanity under Warrants of the Lieutenant-Governor,[8] to violate both the *Charter of Rights* guarantee of life, liberty and security of the person under section 7, and the protection against arbitrary detention contained in section 9. The holding on its surface appeared to effectively dismantle the Canadian system for confining NGRI subjects at the discretion of provincial Advisory Review Boards and Cabinets (Schiffer 1982; Hucker, Webster and Ben-Aron, 1981; Whitley, 1984). Moreover, it was to hasten parliamentary amendments to the Criminal Code[9] designed to place upper limits on the length of detention to which persons found "not criminally responsible on account of mental disorder"[10] are subject. The civil libertarian dimensions of the case seemed self-evident. Yet, despite initial enthusiasm from some legal quarters, particularly on the apparent abolition of indeterminacy as a sentencing principle for mentally disordered offenders, the recently enacted legislation (Bill C-43, S. 4) passed by Parliament in February 1992, soon proved to hold out some potentially dangerous prospects.

The amendments restrict the court's initial hospital order to 90 days maximum. In addition, insanity acquittees will now receive absolute or conditional discharges. The provincial review boards[11] are empowered to render initial dispositional decisions in the absence of a court decision, and to administer all cases which have not received an absolute discharge. The initial order for custody or discharge is to be governed by "the need to protect the public from dangerous persons, the mental condition of the accused, the reintegration of the accused into society and the other needs of the accused" (Verdun-Jones, 1991: 20). Ceilings are imposed on the duration of psychiatric detention, namely life for murder and high treason, ten years (or the maximum Criminal Code penalty, whichever is less) for a variety of indictable offences, and two years or the maximum (again, whichever is shorter) for all other crimes. As Verdun-Jones (1991) observes, it is unlikely, given the length of these proposed ceilings, that the period of confinement for most insanity acquittees will be measurably reduced. Further, there are provisions for the court to extend the internment to life where the defendant has been acquitted of a "serious personal injury offence" and found upon application to be a "dangerous mentally disordered accused" (Verdun-Jones, 1991: 21).[12]

Once more we find dangerousness being inserted into law as a symbolic palliative, affirming the alleged capacity of judicial and forensic specialists to classify people on the basis of mental status and violent propensities, and in the apparent interests of public safety. The amendments reproduce on a different institutional terrain several of the tendencies reviewed earlier in this chapter. Dangerousness is summoned as a signifier which infuses these legal manoeuvres with discursive meaning, paradoxically allowing the perpetuation, and even escalation, of carceral power to be accomplished using the language of law reform, individual rights, and scientific method.

In effect, the legislation is yet another instance in the continuing trend toward a mutual merging of criminal and therapeutic systems (Lowman, Menzies and Palys, 1987; Menzies, 1989, 1991). It is also consistent with the hastening transformation of legal psychiatrists and other forensic practitioners from therapists into experts in mental classification (Castel, 1991; Foucault, 1977; Garland, 1985; Garland and Young, 1983; Rose, 1990). In future, the Canadian criminal defendant pleading an insanity defence will be exposed to a protracted series of diagnoses of her or his psychiatric condition and danger to others, beginning with pre-trial examinations by defence and Crown witnesses, and continuing into the judicial judgment to order custody or discharge; the determination of "dangerous mentally disordered accused" status for violent offenders; the 90-day initial confinement, which becomes in essence a protracted post-dispositional psychiatric assessment under review board authority; and finally, for custodialized subjects, the annual evaluations by the board to decide about eligibility for release (again based on ascriptions of mental status, dangerousness to the community, the prospects of successful "reintegration into society," along with unspecified "other" considerations).

This also imports yet another kind of dichotomy into the social control of psycholegal subjects. For mentally disordered persons acquitted of homicide and other personal injury offences, on the one hand, lengthy terms of security hospitalization will remain the status quo. Their purported danger to the public will become a more explicit rationale to justify what amounts to their indeterminate mental detention by another name. On the other hand, for those deemed non-dangerous (in practice, mentally disordered non-violent offenders) there will be a proliferation of insanity pleas, given the new two-year maximum for minor crimes and even the possibility for absolute or conditional discharge at trial. These people will become the criminal equivalent of non-dangerous informal psychiatric patients, who move rapidly and repeatedly through and between systems. They will become an increasingly prevalent feature of criminal trials, expert assessments and forensic institutions. Many will circulate into the civil hospital system, or will be deinstitutionalized or trans-institutionalized into alternative agencies (or more likely the streets), upon their release.

And in the process, psychiatric and psychological classification work, concentrating on the criminal responsibility and public risk of mentally disordered subjects, will escalate in frequency and significance. There will be yet another influx of professional gatekeepers, alternatively aligned with judicial authorities, defence attorneys and review boards, into these critical junctures between court, criminal and civil hospitals, prison and community. Much of this process has already unfolded in various U.S. states (Sales and Hafemeister, 1984), where reforms to the insanity defence have resulted in elevated numbers of insanity acquittees, confined for shorter periods if assessed to be non-dangerous, who are subjected to more classification and less treatment while under criminal control, and who flow with accelerating volume and speed between penal, psychiatric and other institutional settings (Cohen, 1985; Lowman, Menzies and Palys, 1987; Menzies, 1989; Ryan, 1987). Simultaneously, provisions for the designation of "mentally disordered dangerous offenders"

(BC-43, S 4) will undoubtedly multiply populations of persons deemed to be criminally dangerous. Here above the 49th parallel, with Swain and the proposed legislation we are experiencing the Americanization of our own criminal insanity apparatus.

What bridges these various scenarios is the disarming facility through which danger discourse gets injected into the routine operations of carceral control. It is no coincidence that the construct has achieved such prominence on so many parallel fronts over the past few years. The law-and-order culture of the 1980s was in many respects an ideal environment for a new wave of anti-crime projects, of "great and desperate cures" (Valenstein, 1986), and of political promises to secure a brave new world of public safety and security (Box, 1987; Ericson and Baranek, 1982; Hall, Critchley, Jefferson, Clarke and Roberts, 1978; Spitzer, 1987; Taylor, 1983). Experts in the diagnosis and containment of dangerousness simply rode the wave. And the impetus continues into the 1990s. More and more people are becoming self-professed authorities on violence. Predictive tests and instruments abound. The danger business has become an extraordinarily profitable enterprise, with numerous branch plants, a nearly insatiable clientele, and a seemingly endless supply of raw material. So the search for the magic bullet marches relentlessly onward.

The Construction and Deconstruction
of Dangerousness at METFORS

In the research conducted over the past 15 years at a pre-trial assessment agency called the Metropolitan Toronto Forensic Service (METFORS), one major focus has been on predictions about the dangerousness of criminal defendants that are formulated by psychiatrists and other clinical practitioners during the course of brief and protracted forensic remands. METFORS originally opened in 1977, and over the intervening years its personnel have conducted assessments of such attributes as fitness to stand trial, general mental status, treatability, and dangerousness to self and others in the service of criminal courts throughout the greater Toronto area (Chunn and Menzies, 1990; Menzies, 1989; Menzies, Chunn and Webster, in press; Menzies and Webster, 1988; Webster and Menzies, 1987; Webster, Menzies and Jackson, 1982).

METFORS occupies a central position in Toronto's forensic infrastructure. It is funded by the provincial Ministry of the Attorney-General; administered by a board under the auspices of the A-G along with the Ministries of Health and Community and Social Services; located on the grounds of the Queen Street Mental Health Centre on the west side of the city; and affiliated with the Clarke Institute of Psychiatry and the University of Toronto. Nearly 10,000 subjects have been evaluated at the agency since its inception. It was originally intended as a prototype for the development of other such agencies across the country, and its research unit has attracted a wealth of public and private funding on a variety of socio-legal and clinical subjects (Webster, Menzies and Jackson, 1982).

From the outset, dangerousness was a key interest. When METFORS opened its doors and the work began in earnest during the late 1970s and early 1980s, the concept had already attained a high profile in the literature of the time, and was clearly a focal concern in forensic practice across judicial and correctional contexts (Hinton, 1983; Monahan, 1981; Walker, 1978; Webster, Ben-Aron and Hucker, 1985). For the purpose of establishing a research agenda and amassing data, the initial mandate seemed obvious, namely, an appraisal of the clinical forecasting of violent and other dangerous conduct. Only a few methodologically sound evaluations of dangerousness predictions had yet been performed (Monahan, 1981; Pfohl, 1978; Steadman and Cocozza, 1974; Thornberry and Jacoby, 1979), and this void needed to be filled.

Consequently one of us (CDW), then in charge of research, set out to assess the accuracy of clinical predictions of dangerousness at METFORS. A research team was assembled, funds secured, clinicians recruited, and protocols developed to facilitate an intensive series of investigations into the correspondences between clinical judgments about the dangerousness of METFORS forensic subjects, and the institutional and community violence and criminality of these people during the years subsequent to their psychiatric evaluation. With the participation of the clinical teams (including psychiatrists, psychologists, social workers, nurses and correctional officers) detailed research instruments were constructed, a dangerousness rating scale was produced, files were tracked down and compiled on more than 800 accused persons remanded during 17 months of the clinic's operation, and Ontario correctional and hospital records were secured on the subsequent activities of these people for a period of 24 months after their initial assessments.

As the results came in during the early and mid-1980s, it soon become apparent that the relationships between the danger predictions and outcomes were at best tenuous, and at worst non-existent or even inverted. We could establish positive associations (signifying a measure of predictive accuracy) for some of the clinicians some of the time, and we could entice at least a fragment of forecasting validity out of semi-structured instruments applied by trained coders (Menzies, Webster and Sepejak, 1985b), but there was little doubt that we were consistently falling far short of the .40 "sound barrier" for prediction correlations that was a prominent threshold image in the prevailing research literature on dangerousness (Hall, 1987; Menzies, Monahan, 1981; Webster and Sepejak, 1985a).

Some of these findings were published in 1984 and 1985 (Menzies, Webster and Sepejak, 1985a,b; Webster, Sepejak, Menzies, Slomen, Jensen and Butler, 1984), complete with myriad caveats about the methodological limitations associated with work of this kind, and about the relative invalidity of the prediction scale that we had invented (called the Dangerous Behaviour Rating Scale or DBRS). Therefore the authors of these papers were dumbfounded to find themselves soon being inundated with requests for the instrument coming from clinicians and agencies across North America and Europe (including the US Secret Service), all of whom were evidently desperate for whatever "scientific" tools they could enlist in aid of their predictive practices, to the point of ignoring what we had guilelessly believed were the irrefutable indications of our near-total failure.

These developments were highly interesting for a number of reasons. Researchers and clinicians were apparently reading our work through a variety of different ideological screens.[13] At the same time, we found *ourselves* surrounded too by a swarm of similar interpretive alternatives, which inevitably forced us back onto the very political, discursive and epistemological terrain that was carved out in earlier sections of this chapter. Put crudely, why the failure to establish any compelling evidence for the clinical or technical ability to predict dangerousness in this particular clinic? Was this a purely methodological problem or empirical limitation? Was the difficulty situation-specific? Were the inadequacies our own? Had we failed to meet the minimal standards for a critical test of predictive validity? What about the specificity of the prediction indicators, or the cavernous black holes in the outcome data set,[14] or the absence of information on subjects outside the province of Ontario, or the restrictions imposed by a mere two-year outcome term? Was our study, in short, methodologically unsound? Had we "under-tested" (Webster, 1990) our clinical and actuarial subjects? Was there insufficient science in our evaluation?

These queries led to one line of theorization. On another front, a very different set of considerations emerged that propelled our thinking more towards a challenging of dangerousness itself as a discursive construct, and as an institutionalized idea that is as deeply and dialectically embedded in the understandings of researchers as it is in the practices of the clinicians being studied. Perhaps, in other words, we had been asking the wrong questions altogether. Maybe "the-clinical-and-scientific-ability-to-predict-dangerousness" is an entirely inappropriate frame for structuring research of this kind. What if the entire problem is not a matter of predictive acumen at all, or even of establishing the standards and conditions for improving performance? What if the researchers are as ideologically and institutionally confined as their clinical subjects, and that only through a fundamental and paradigmatic reworking of the entire issue—through a devolving of dangerousness and of the accepted meanings which have been built up around it over decades of "scientific" activity—will they stand any prospect of liberating the idea of dangerousness and engaging it for progressive ends?

Clearly, such a self-consciously deconstructionist approach lends itself to a very different mode of inquiry. The evaluation of dangerousness becomes an exploration of scientific authority itself, and of the material and cultural conditions that authorize the attribution of danger to some people and problems to the exclusion of others. New subjects emerge, for example: (1) the constitution and impact of the dangerousness construct itself in relation to hierarchies of dominance and subordination, in realms of social life beyond the walls of mental and carceral institutions; (2) how ideas about danger and related categories flow through organizational structures to condition the beliefs and judgments of professional experts, and in turn to shape the carceral careers of their subjects; and (3) how ideologies and institutions, law and science, people and practices are recursively bound together in the implementation of dangerousness depictions along with such related constructs as endangerment, dependency, delinquency, deficiency, disorder, and so on (see above).

These two competing strands—the empiricist and the deconstructionist—have been woven together, with no small degree of intermittent friction, in subsequent research on the subject of dangerousness at METFORS. Over the past five years a new project has been undertaken in an effort simultaneously to refine the conceptual and empirical bases of the earlier work, and to situate it within this more overtly critical framework. The return to METFORS for what can loosely be called a "replication" represented an attempt to push up against the methodological boundaries of this kind of longitudinal study, on the presumption that a more ambitious approach might reveal something about the nature of the limitations themselves (along with the forces that influence forensic practices and outcomes), and could possibly get more completely at the structures and discourses that make dangerousness such a pivotal phenomenon in psychiatry and law.

The current project, then, represents an enhancement of the work both internally and externally: *internally*, to elaborate the data base, supplement background, prediction and outcome variables, and extend the follow-up to a full six years covering the entire breadth of the country; and *externally*, to design the research not only as an evaluation of predictive validity, but in addition this time as a survey of the organizational currents and legal-scientific understandings to which both experts and subjects are exposed in the forensic construction of carceral and therapeutic careers.

Accordingly, beginning in 1986 two cohorts of defendants were selected from the original METFORS dangerousness studies (see Menzies, 1989; Menzies, Webster and Sepejak, 1985a,b), and the project has been designed to elicit as much information as possible about these people from their official judicial, correctional and hospital records. The exercise for one of these groups—162 subjects who were originally assessed at METFORS between March and June 1979—has now been completed. Detailed files were collected on these defendants' legal and clinical histories, their criminal and psychiatric condition at the time of assessment, and their socio-demographic attributes and social circumstances. Information was assembled on the original clinical decisions about a variety of medico-legal issues from all members of clinical teams, which included the completion of the Dangerous Behaviour Rating Scale (see above), and added were myriad measures of dangerousness furnished at the time of original assessment by three trained coders. This was followed by an attempt to collect the most comprehensive pool of data possible on the institutional experiences and conduct of these people for the six years subsequent to their initial METFORS remand, which included federal and provincial correctional records from across the country,[15] hospital records from 15 different institutions, National Parole Board files, Canadian Police Information Centre (CPIC) printouts, and Ontario Death Registry records. For each case the final data set totalled 5040 variables, comprising detailed information on background, assessment and outcomes (the latter specifying each correctional and psychiatric contact during the 72 months, along with year-by-year synopses of experiences and activities in correctional and mental institutions and in the community).

Armed with this comprehensive collection of materials we have been hoping to shed some light on the issues raised in earlier sections of this chapter, and perhaps to address questions that were left largely unanswered in our earlier work. How, for example, is the perceived and lived dangerousness of forensic subjects related to the expectations and decisions of authorities and to institutional parameters? To what degree do refinement of the measures, and extension of the knowledge base, contribute to predictive accuracy when it comes to dangerous behaviour? Who predicts well and badly, and under what circumstances? How do the experts fare in relation to laypersons, and what do systematization and science contribute to these comparisons? Is dangerousness person-, situation- or institution-specific? Is it chronologically structured—does it amplify or decay with the passage of time? In general does dangerousness emerge from these data as a stable construct that retains its reality across time, space and perception? Or are we dealing with a construct so mired in the complexities of cultural and institutional life that it necessarily resists the ontological overtures of clinical, criminological and other "scientific" classifiers?

Given limitations of time and space, we can barely scratch the surface of these phenomena and problems in what follows. Elsewhere (Menzies, Webster, McMain and Staley, forthcoming a,b) we present a far more detailed review of the research findings and their implications for the dangerousness construct and its place in carceral practice. Here we offer just a brief synopsis in the context of this chapter's main themes. Among the most striking observations:

1. The subjects of METFORS assessments, like the subjects of most medico-legal institutions, had already experienced extensive levels of correctional control and treatment prior to their initial forensic remand. Nearly three-quarters (73.0 percent) had been charged with a previous criminal offence, and more than two out of every five (43.5 percent) had been incarcerated. One-third were unemployed, 34 percent had attempted suicide at some time in their lives, and 64 percent and 33 percent were moderate or heavy users respectively of alcohol or other non-prescription drugs. For a large segment of the cohort this forensic stopover at METFORS was just one in a series of carceral interventions in their continuing experiences of marginality and trans-institutionalization.

2. As in the earlier prediction assessment work involving two-year outcomes, there was little demonstration of either clinical or psychometric capacity to forecast the future dangerous conduct of METFORS subjects. The strongest positive correlations among the grouped clinical disciplines (for presiding psychiatrists) were about +.20, indicating that less than five percent of future dangerousness (measured in three different ways: by total number of recorded official incidents, number of violent incidents, and number of criminal charges) was being accounted for by the predictions. Some individual practitioners, on the other hand, fared better than others, with one nurse, one correctional officer and two psychiatrists achieving correlations above +.30 (explaining about 10 percent of the six-year outcome conduct). For most groups and individuals, the correlations peaked at about two to three years, and there was a subsequent deterioration in predictive capacity with the further elapse of time.

3. Efforts to construct complex predictive instruments generally met a similar fate. The Dangerous Behaviour Rating Scale, item- and factor-analysed and honed down to 13 items[16] to maximize efficiency, contributed negligibly at best to the predictive power of clinical and other raters of dangerousness. In the hands of psychiatrists in particular, the psychometric instruments were virtually useless (see Menzies, Webster, McMain and Staley, forthcoming a,b).

4. Predictions of dangerousness based solely on the background attributes of subjects were clearly more successful than generic clinical judgments, raising important questions about the relevancy of expert input into the decision-making process. For example, multiple classification analyses involving just three variables (age, prior

violence and prior number of psychiatric hospitalizations) elicited a multiple correlation of .48 with total violent incidents during the subsequent six years. Although these operations still embraced less than one-quarter of the officially recorded dangerousness exhibited by METFORS subjects, the simple scrutiny of prior records generated far better results than either the professional projections of clinical practitioners or the technical instruments of social researchers.

5.   During the six years of intensive follow-up through carceral institutions, psychiatric settings and the community, it became apparent that the measure of dangerousness, and its very construction, varied dramatically across time and space. One dimension of this volatility was the extraordinary range of registered deviance and danger according to institutional context. For every subject-year spent in the community during the outcome period, for example, there were 2.82 official incidents and 0.34 acts of violence. In prison the respective figures were 2.70 and 0.50. This contrasts starkly with the records of mental hospitals, where 19.30 incidents and 3.38 acts of violence were reported for every patient-year.[17] It is highly doubtful that psychiatric inpatients are substantially more dangerous or prone to violence than prisoners or persons at liberty to any remote approximation of these statistics (cf. Mesnikoff and Lauterbach, 1975; Steadman, Cocozza and Melick, 1978). Instead, the diverse patterns of surveillance and containment, and the differential sensitivity of various organizations to acts of non-compliance and violence, necessarily become central features in the understanding and measurement of dangerousness. Such powerful institutional forces consistently have been ignored in writing on the subject of social danger. Yet without a comprehension of structure and discourse, and of the complex practices that infuse the production and distribution of dangerous knowledge, the predictive enterprise is unlikely to progress.

6.   One final preliminary observation from this new research pertains to the cycles of carceral and psychiatric contact to which the 159 defendants were subject. In general through the years after their forensic "diversion" these people remained highly institutionalized. Over the course of the follow-up over 90 percent experienced pre-trial jail; about the same got parole, probation or bail; 7 out of 10 were sentenced to at least one term of imprisonment; 57 percent were psychiatric inpatients; and 27 percent were outpatients. Altogether they averaged 4.47 psychiatric contacts and 3.92 carceral contacts each. At the same time there was evidence of a decay in the

intensity of control and supervision over time. For example, only 45 of 159 people experienced any period of full liberty in the community during the first year after their assessment, whereas the number gradually rose to 128 by year six. Still—and this may be the single most graphic finding of the entire project—the sheer volume of criminal and mental censures was quite spectacular. Even in the final year one-quarter of the sample spent time in prison, another one-fourth was on probation, parole or bail, 15 percent in pre-trial lock-up, and 14 percent in psychiatric hospital. The story of dangerousness is very much the story of penal and therapeutic institutions, and how it is that they converge to shape the dangerous careers of psycho-legal subjects.

Conclusion: From Dangerousness to Risk

In arguably the most important paper to be written on the subject of dangerousness since the English translations of Foucault's work (1977, 1978) first appeared, Robert Castel recently (1991) published his observations on the currently evolving transformation, in the theories and activities of academics and practitioners alike, from dangerousness into *risk* (see Floud and Young, 1981; Monahan, 1988; Steadman, Robbins and Monahan, 1991). Castel argues that the positive idea of a dangerous subject in psychiatry has always been an uncertain and fallible instrument of power. In focussing on the individual attributes of dangerous people, the experts can too easily be proven wrong, with potentially dire consequences for both clinical authority and public security. Moreover, the inclination "to treat dangerousness as an internal quality of the subject" (Castel, 1991: 284) is itself a cumbersome and inefficient control device, limited in scope and confined to the sporadic detection and prevention of isolated forms of danger: "One cannot confine masses of people just out of simple suspicion of their dangerousness, if only for the reason that the economic cost would be colossal and out of all proportion to the risks prevented" (Castel, 1991: 284).

In response to these contradictions, in concert with massive innovations in the constitution of postmodern knowledge systems (with new forms of instrumentation, data inscription and governmentality [Foucault, 1977; Garland, 1985; Rose, 1990]), the attribution of social liability is becoming increasingly objectified, depersonalized, actuarialized, applied to whole populations instead of isolated individuals, and transferred from the clinical scrutiny of experts into the hands of administrators and managers (see Cohen, 1988; Young, 1988). In the process, the designators of risk become insulated from the negative consequences of erroneous ascriptions, because their judgments are no longer applied to single subjects, but rather to entire categories of people and populations whose status is "based on the collation of a range of abstract factors deemed liable to produce risk in general...which render more or less probable the occurrence of undesirable modes of behaviour" (Castel, 1991: 281, 287).

In other words, to be risky (or to be at risk), ceases to be an attribute emerging from within and discoverable only by those with the appropriate scientific or technical "gaze" (Foucault, 1978). It is simply a set of probabilities, a position in statistical relation to a cluster of variables, to be applied from without by anyone with the requisite data. It is not a "prediction" at all, but merely an allocation, a correlation of indices and classes: "To be suspected, it is no longer necessary to manifest symptoms of dangerousness or abnormality, it is enough to display whatever characteristics the specialists responsible for the definition of preventive policy have constituted as risk factors" (Castel, 1991: 288). And the range of risky categories, once detached from the bodies and minds of dangerous individuals, can become virtually infinite: "[n]ot just those dangers that lie hidden away inside the subject, consequences of his or her weakness of will, irrational desires or unpredictable liberty, but also the exogenous dangers, the exterior hazards and temptations from which the subject has not learnt to defend himself or herself, alcohol, tobacco, bad eating habits, road accidents, various kinds of negligence and pollution, meteorological hazards, etc." (Castel, 1991: 289).

These are expansive powers, which are manifesting themselves not only in the legislative and systemic trends we reviewed earlier in this chapter, but throughout the carceral complex and beyond. Paradoxically, the very failings of the dangerousness construct have become a catalyst (yet again) for its re-emergence in new form, as an organizing concept for the bureaucratic mapping and managing of damaged and damaging cohorts in accordance with their socio-demographic configurations, their actuarial risk gradients and test profiles, their cross-referencing on composite data banks and computer libraries, their approximation to the attributes of typical risk classes and categories. Throughout the remainder of this decade, we can expect these developments to continue and expand, with profound implications for social understandings and programs on the subject of social danger, and for the practices of experts invested with the authority to define the dangerous and prevent them from inflicting harm. And efforts to curb these powers, to hold authorities accountable and define the limits of carceral interventions, will need increasingly to contend with these profound transformations in the detection and detention of "dangerous" people.

Now whether any of these reflections have any lingering value beyond their basic heuristics is another question altogether. The tenuous lines of communication between correctional research and practice, and more generally between knowledge and policy in the carceral realm, present some daunting obstructions to the formation of any kind of progressive or humane approach to the phenomenon of social danger. Old mythologies die hard, and it not at all certain that social, legal and clinical researchers—working as they usually do outside of the public eye and political arena—can effectively neutralize or even contend with the relentless deluge of imagery about malignant monsters and pathological beings that is being endlessly reproduced in the media and public culture (Caputi, 1987; Jones, 1980). Nor is it easy to deconstruct the hegemonic promises of a danger-free and secure society to be somehow achieved through tougher laws, more professional police, more painful punishment, more effective treatment, bigger prisons, better science, more rigorous classifications and precise predictions.

But the effort to deconstruct is at least a beginning (Code, 1991; Mitchell and Oakley, 1976; Smart, 1989; Spelman, 1988). And perhaps through the vehicle of research we can inch toward new discourses and practices that offer a more realistic appraisal of dangerousness, shaped by the understanding that what is to be feared most is not the random and rare assaults of predatory psychopaths and unwell beings, but the systematic ideological and structural conditions that create these people and throw them into our midst, just as they foster the celebration of war and weaponry, the economic partitioning of the planet into north and south, the industrial poisoning of the biosphere, the co-existence everywhere of outrageous affluence and poverty, the subordination of women and minorities in private and public, in the workplace and homeplace, and the kind of criminogenic criminal justice system that makes this society, for virtually everyone, a very dangerous place to live.

Endnotes

1.   Even the pursuit of peace during time of war can be defined as dangerous activity. See Wiltsher's (1985) history of women peace campaigners during World War I.

2.   Section 753 of the *Code* reads in part: "Where, upon an application made under this Part following the conviction of a person for an offence but before the offender is sentenced therefor, it is established to the satisfaction of the court (a) that the offence for which the offender has been convicted is a serious personal injury offence [defined in s.752(a)]...and the offender constitutes a threat to the life, safety or physical or mental well-being of other persons on the basis of evidence establishing (i) a pattern of repetitive behaviour by the offender, of which the offence for which he has been convicted forms a part, showing a failure to restrain his behaviour and a likelihood of his causing death or injury to other persons, or inflicting severe psychological damage on other persons, through failure in the future to restrain his behaviour, (ii) a pattern of persistent aggressive behaviour by the offender, of which the offence for which he has been convicted forms a part, showing a substantial degree of indifference on the part of the offender respecting the reasonably foreseeable consequences to other persons of his behaviour, or (iii) any behaviour by the offender, associated with the offence for which he has been convicted, that is of such a brutal nature as to compel the conclusion that his behaviour in the future is unlikely to be inhibited by normal standards of behavioural constraint, or (b) that the offence for which the offender has been convicted is a serious personal injury offence [defined in s.752(b)]...and the offender, by his conduct in any sexual matter including that involved in the commission of the offence for which he has been convicted, has shown a failure to control his sexual impulses and a likelihood of his causing injury, pain or other evil to other persons through failure in the future to control his sexual impulses, the court may find the offender to be a dangerous offender and may thereupon impose a sentence of detention in a penitentiary for an indeterminate period, in lieu of any other sentence that might be imposed for the offence for which the offender has been convicted."

3.   Section 7 of the Charter reads: "Everyone has the right to life, liberty and security of the person and the right not to be deprived thereof except in accordance with the principles of fundamental justice." Section 9 stipulates that: "Everyone has the right not to be arbitrarily detained or imprisoned." Section 12 provides that: "Everyone has the right not to be subjected to any cruel and unusual punishment or treatment."

4. Introduced through revisions to the *National Parole Act* in 1969, mandatory supervision provides for the supervised release of inmates not qualifying for regular parole after two-thirds of their sentence has been served (cf. Ratner, 1987: 294).
5. *Bill C-67,* R.S.C. 1986.
6. *Regina v. Swain* (1991), 63 C.C.C. (3d) 481.
7. *MacNaughtan's Case.* (1843), 8 E.R. 718. See Moran (1981) and West and Walk (1977).
8. *Criminal Code of Canada* s.614(2).
9. The Court originally gave Parliament six months to enact replacement legislation. The "grandparenting" period was later extended to nine months (expiring in February 1992).
10. This is the new wording, which will supplant the present legal category of "not guilty by reason of insanity."
11. Under the new legislation, each province must have a review board comprising no fewer than 5 people, 1 of whom must be a registered psychiatrist. The board chair must be a senior or retired judge or someone so qualified. The provisions resemble those pertaining to restriction orders (Peay 1989) in England and Wales (Verdun-Jones, 1991: 20).
12. The criteria for release review, under the auspices of the Advisory Review Boards, will approximate those currently applying to parole boards in the case of dangerous offenders (see Verdun-Jones, 1991: 21). Not insignificantly, the Dangerous Offender provisions, formerly contained in Part XXIV of the Criminal Code, have been moved into these new sections.
13. For a more recent illustration of the same phenomenon, see Arboleda-Florez, 1991; Rogers and Bagby, 1990; Menzies, 1991, in press.
14. In this initial two-year outcome study, the correctional data search was restricted to Canadian Police Information Centre (CPIC) and Ontario correctional files, along with six provincial mental hospitals other than METFORS.
15. Access to National Parole Board files permitted the documentation of incarcerations, transfers and releases for persons confined in the federal system, along with incarceration misconducts incurred during terms of imprisonment. Similar information was obtained at the provincial level, from all provinces with the exception of Manitoba and Nova Scotia, for all persons who registered a criminal offence in the specified province in CPIC records.
16. These are passive aggressive, hostility, anger, rage, guilt, capacity for empathy, capacity for change, self-perception as dangerous, control over

actions, tolerance, environment support, and ability to manipulative, and provides accurate information.

17. Altogether the 159 METFORS subjects spent 8931 months in the community, during which they registered 2102 incidents and 252 acts of violence. The corresponding statistics for prison and hospital were, respectively, 1784 months, 401 incidents and 74 violent occurrences (prison) and 462 months, 743 incidents and 130 violent acts (hospital).

References

American Psychiatric Association. 1974. *Clinical Aspects of the Violent Individual.* Washington DC: APA.

Arboleda-Florez, J. 1991. Book review. "Survival of the Sanest: Order and Disorder in a Pre-trial Psychiatric Clinic," *Canadian Journal of Criminology* 33: 215-220.

Ashford, J.B. 1989. "Offence comparisons between mentally disordered and non-mentally disordered inmates," *Canadian Journal of Criminology* 31: 35-48.

Bacchi, C.L. 1983. *Liberation Deferred? The Ideas of the English-Canadian Suffragists, 1877-1918.* Toronto: University of Toronto Press.

Bieber, S.L., R.A. Pasewark, K. Bosten and H.J. Steadman. 1988. "Predicting criminal recidivisn of insanity acquittees," *International Journal of Law and Psychiatry* 11: 105-112.

Birnie, L.H. 1990. *A Rock and a Hard Place: Inside Canada's Parole Board.* Toronto: Macmillan.

Bottoms, A.E. 1977. "Reflections on the renaissance of dangerousness," *The Howard Journal of Penology and Crime Prevention* 16: 70-96.

Box, S. 1987. *Recession, Crime and Punishment.* London: Macmillan.

Boyd, N. 1991. *High Society.* Toronto: Key Porter.

Brace, C.L. 1872. *The Dangerous Classes of New York and Twenty Years' Work Among Them.* New York: Wynkoop and Hallenbeck.

Brahams, D. and M. Weller. 1986. "Crime and homelessness among the mentally ill," *Medico-Legal Journal* 54: 42-53.

Britzer, D.A. and M. Crowner (eds.). 1988. *Current Approaches to the Prediction of Violence.* Washington DC: American Psychiatric Press.

Brody, B.A. 1990. "Prediction of dangerousness in different contexts," *Ethical Practice in Psychiatry and the Law* 7: 185-196.

Cameron, D. (ed.). 1990. *The Feminist Critique of Language: A Reader.* London: Routledge.

Canadian Sentencing Commission. 1987. *Sentencing Reform: A Canadian Approach.* Ottawa: Supply and Services Canada.

Caputi, J. 1987. *The Age of Sex Crime.* Bowling Green OH: Bowling Green State University Popular Press.

Castel, R. 1991. "From dangerousness to risk," in G. Burchell, C. Gordon and P. Miller (eds.), *The Foucault Effect: Studies in Governmentality.* Chicago: University of Chicago Press.

Castel, R., J. Castel and A. Lovell. 1982. *The Psychiatric Society.* New York: Columbia University Press.

Chan, J. 1990. "Decarceration: A case for theory building through empirical research," *Law in Context* 8: 32-77.

Chunn, D.E. and S.A.M. Gavigan. 1988. "Social control: Analytic tool or analytic quagmire?" *Contemporary Crises* 12: 107-124.

————. 1991. "Women and crime in Canada," in M.A. Jackson and C.T. Griffiths (eds.), *Canadian Criminology: Perspectives on Crime and Criminality.* Toronto: Harcourt, Brace and Jovanovich.

Chunn, D.E. and R.J. Menzies. 1990. "Gender, madness and crime: The reproduction of patriarchal and class relations in a pre-trial psychiatric clinic," *Journal of Human Justice* 2: 33-54.

Code, L. 1991. *What Can She Know? Feminist Theory and the Construction of Knowledge.* Ithica NY: Cornell University Press.

Cohen, S. 1985. *Visions of Social Control: Crime, Punishment and Classification.* Cambridge UK: Polity.

————. 1988. *Against Criminology.* New Brunswick NJ: Transaction.

Cohen, S. and A. Scull. 1983. *Social Control and the State: Historical and Comparative Essays.* Oxford UK: Martin Robertson.

Coleman, L. 1984. *The Reign of Error: Psychiatry, Authority and Law.* Boston: Beacon.

Coward, R. 1985. *Female Desires: How They Are Sought, Bought and Packaged.* New York: Grove Press.

Daly, M. and M. Wilson. 1988. *Homicide.* New York: A. de Gruyter.

Dear, M. and J. Wolch. 1987. *Landscapes of Despair—From Deinstitutionalization to Homelessness.* Princeton NJ: Princeton University Press.

Diamond, I. and L. Quinby (eds.). 1988. *Feminism and Foucault: Reflections on Resistance.* Boston MS: Northeastern University Press.

Dietz, P.E. 1985. "Hypothetical criteria for the prediction of individual criminality," in C.D. Webster, M.H. Ben-Aron and S.J. Hucker (eds.), *Dangerousness: Probability and Prediction, Psychiatry and Public Policy.* New York: Cambridge.

Dix, G.E. 1980. "Clinical evaluation of the 'dangerousness' of 'normal' criminal defendants," *Virginia Law Review* 66: 523-581.

Dorn, N. 1987. *A Land Fit for Heroin? Drug Policies, Prevention and Practice.* London: Macmillan.

Eisenstein, Z. 1988. *The Female Body and the Law.* Berkeley: University of California Press.

Ennis, B.J. and T.R. Litwack. 1974. "Psychiatry and the presumption of expertise: Flipping coins in the courtroom," *California Law Review* 62: 693-752.

Ericson, R.V. and P.M. Baranek. 1982. *The Ordering of Justice: A Study of Accused Persons as Dependants in the Criminal Process.* Toronto: University of Toronto Press.

Ericson, R.V. and C.D. Shearing. 1986. "The scientification of police work," in G. Bohme and N. Stehr (eds.), *The Knowledge Society: The Growing*

Impact of Scientific Knowledge on Social Relations. Dordrecht GER: Reidel.

Farrington, D.P. and R. Tarling (eds.). 1985. *Prediction in Criminology.* Albany: State University of New York Press.

Floud, J. and W. Young. 1981. *Dangerousness and Criminal Justice.* London: Heinemann.

Foucault, M. 1977. *Discipline and Punish: The Birth of the Prison.* New York: Pantheon.

————. 1978. "About the concept of the 'dangerous individual' in 19th-century legal psychiatry," *International Journal of Law and Psychiatry* 1: 1-18.

Garland, D. 1985. *Punishment and Welfare: A History of Penal Strategies.* Aldershot UK: Gower.

————. 1990. *Punishment and Modern Society: A Study in Social Theory.* Chicago: University of Chicago Press.

Garland, D. and P. Young. 1983. *The Power to Punish: Contemporary Penality and Social Analysis.* London: Heinemann.

Garofalo, R.. 1964. *Criminology.* Trans. R.W. Millar. New York: Patterson Smith [1914].

Gordon, R.M. and S.N. Verdun-Jones. 1988. "The trials of mental health law: Recent trends and developments in Canadian mental health jurisprudence," *Dalhousie Law Review* 11: 833-863.

Gottfredson, S.D. and D.M. Gottfredson. 1986. "Accuracy of prediction models," in A. Blumstein, J. Cohen, J.A. Roth and C.A. Visher (eds.), Criminal Career and Career Criminal. Vol. 2. Washington CD: National Academy Press.

Grant, I. 1985. "Dangerous offenders," *Dalhousie Law Journal* 9: 347-382.

Grant, I., C. Boyle and D.E. Chunn. Forthcoming. *The Law of Homicide.* 2nd ed. Toronto: Carswell.

Hall, H.V. 1987. *Violence Prediction: Guidelines for the Forensic Practitioner.* Springfield IL: Charles C. Thomas.

Hall, S., C. Critchley, A. Jefferson, S. Clarke and B. Roberts. 1978. *Policing the Crisis: Mugging, the State, Law and Order.* London: Macmillan.

Hamilton, J.F. and H. Freeman (eds.). 1982. *Dangerousness: Psychiatric Assessment and Management.* London: Gaskell.

Hanmer, J. and M. Maynard (ed.). 1987. *Women, Violence and Social Control.* Atlantic Highlands NJ: Humanities Press International.

Harding, S. (ed.). 1987. *Feminism and Methodology.* Bloomington: Indiana University Press.

Harris, G.T., M.E. Rice and C.A. Cormier. 1991. "Psychopathy and Violent Recidivism," *Law and Human Behaviour* 15: 625-637.

Hinton, J.W. (ed.). 1983. *Dangerousness: Problems of Assessment and Prediction.* London: Allen and Unwin.

Hucker, S.J., C.D. Webster and M.H. Ben-Aron (eds.). 1981. *Mental Disorder and Criminal Responsibility.* Toronto: Butterworths.

Jakimiec, J., F. Porporino, S. Addario and C.D. Webster. 1986. "Dangerous offenders in Canada, 1977-1985," *International Journal of Law and Psychiatry* 9: 479-489.

Johnson, A.B. 1990. *Out of Bedlam: The Truth About Deinstitutionalization.* New York: Basic.

Jones, A. 1980. *Women Who Kill.* New York: Fawcett Crest.

Klein, J.F. 1976. "The dangerousness of dangerous offender legislation: Forensic folklore revisited," *Canadian Journal of Criminology and Corrections* 18: 109-123.

Koutetes, B., Forthcoming. *I, Robert Olav Noyes.* Unpublished M.A. Thesis. Simon Fraser University School of Criminology.

Kuhn, T.S. 1970. *The Structure of Scientific Revolutions.* 2nd ed. Chicago: University of Chicago Press.

Lakatos, I. and A. Musgrave (eds.). 1968. *Problems in the Philosophy of Science.* Amsterdam: North-Holland.

Lerman, P. 1982. *Deinstitutionalization and the Welfare State.* New Brunswick NJ: Rutgers University Press.

Litwack, T.R. 1985. "The prediction of violence," *The Clinical Psychologist* (Fall): 87-91.

Lowman, J. and B.D. MacLean (eds.). 1992. *Realist Criminology: Crime Control and Policing in the 1990s.* Toronto: University of Toronto Press.

Lowman, J., R.J. Menzies and T.S. Palys (eds.). 1987. *Transcarceration: Essays in the Sociology of Social Control.* Aldershot UK: Gower.

MacLean, B.D. 1986. *The Political Economy of Crime: Readings For a Critical Criminology.* Scarborough ON: Prentice-Hall.

McLaren, A. 1990. *Our Own Master Race: The Eugenic Crusade in Canada.* Toronto: McClelland and Stewart.

McMain, S., C.D. Webster and R.J. Menzies. 1989. "The post-assessment careers of mentally disordered offenders," *International Journal of Law and Psychiatry* 12: 189-201.

Mandel, M. 1986. "The legalization of prison discipline in Canada," *Crime and Social Justice* 26: 79-94.

————. 1991. "The great repression: Criminal punishment in the nineteen-eighties," in L. Samuelson and B. Schissel (eds.), *Criminal Justice: Sentencing Issues and Reform.* Halifax NS: Garamond.

Mayhew, H. 1861. *London Labour and the London Poor.* London: Griffin.

Melossi, M. 1990. *The State of Social Control: A Sociological Study of Concepts of State and Social Control in the Making of Democracy.* New York: St. Martin's Press.

Menzies, R.J. 1986. "Psychiatry, dangerousness and legal control," in Neil Boyd (ed.), *The Social Dimensions of Law.* Scarborough ON: Prentice-Hall.

————. 1989. *Survival of the Sanest: Order and Disorder in a Pre-Trial Psychiatric Clinic.* Toronto: University of Toronto Press.

————. 1991. "Counterpoint: Response to book review." *Survival of the Sanest: Order and Disorder in a Pre-trial Psychiatric Clinic* (by Richard Rogers and Michael Bagby). *Health Law in Canada* 11: 79-83.

————. 1992. "The empire strikes back: Response to book review." *Survival of the Sanest: Order and Disorder in a Pre-trial Psychiatric Clinic. Canadian Journal of Criminology* 34: In press.

Menzies, R.J., D.E. Chunn and C.D. Webster. 1992. "Female follies: The forensic psychiatric assessment of women defendants," *International Journal of Law and Psychiatry* 15: In press.

Menzies, R.J. and C.D. Webster. 1988. "Fixing forensic patients: Psychiatric recommendations for treatment in pre-trial settings," *Behavioural Sciences and the Law* 6: 453-478.

Menzies, R.J., C.D. Webster, S. McMain and S. Staley, Forthcoming. *Dangerous liaisons: Part 1. The formulation of dangerousness decisions.*

————. Forthcoming. *Dangerous liaisons: Part 2. The outcome behaviour of dangerous people.*

Menzies, R.J., C.D. Webster and D.S. Sepejak. 1985a. "Hitting the forensic sound barrier: Predictions of dangerousness in a pre-trial psychiatric clinic," in C.D. Webster, M.H. Ben-Aron and S.J. Hucker (eds.), *Dangerousness: Probability and Prediction, Psychiatry and Public Policy.* New York: Cambridge University Press.

————. 1985b. "The dimensions of dangerousness: Evaluating the accuracy of psychometric predictions of violence among forensic patients," *Law and Human Behaviour* 9: 35-56.

————. 1987. "'At the mercy of the mad': Examining the relationship between violence and mental disorder," in R.W. Rieber (ed.), *Advances in Forensic Psychology and Psychiatry.* Vol. 2. Norwood NJ: Ablex.

Mesnikoff, A.M. and C.G. Lauterbach. 1975. "The association of violent dangerous behaviour with psychiatric disorders: A review of the research literature," *Journal of Psychiatry and Law* 3: 1-31.

Mitchell, J. and Ann Oakley (eds.). 1976. *The Rights and Wrongs of Women.* Harmondsworth UK: Penguin.

Monahan, J. 1981. *Predicting Violent Behaviour: An Assessment of Clinical Techniques.* Beverly Hills CA: Sage.

———. 1988. "Risk assessment of violence among the mentally disordered: Generating useful knowledge," *International Journal of Law and Psychiatry* 11: 249-257.

Monahan, J. and L. Cummings. 1975. "Social policy implication of the inability to predict violence," *Journal of Social Issues* 31: 153-164.

Moran, R. 1981. *Knowing Right From Wrong: The Insanity Defence of Daniel McNaughtan.* New York: The Free Press.

Morris, N. and G. Hawkins. 1970. *The Honest Politician's Guide to Crime Control.* Chicago: University of Chicago Press.

Morris, N. and M. Miller. 1985. "Predictions of dangerousness," in M. Tonry and N. Morris (eds.), *Crime and Justice: An Annual Review of Research.* Vol. 6. Chicago: University of Chicago Press.

Mort, F. 1987. *Dangerous Sexualities.* London: Routledge.

Mulvey, E.P., A. Blumstein and J. Cohen. 1986. "Reframing the research question of mental patient criminality," *International Journal of Law and Psychiatry* 9: 57-65.

Nicholson, L.J. 1990. *Feminism/Postmodernism.* London: Routledge.

Nuffield, J. 1982. *Parole Decision Making in Canada: Research Toward Decision Guidelines.* Ottawa: Supply and Services Canada.

Palmer, B.D. 1990. *Descent into Discourse: The Reification of Language and the Writing of Social History.* Philadelphia PA: Temple University Press.

Peay, J. 1989. *Tribunals on Trial: A Study of Decision-Making Under the Mental Health Act 1983.* Oxford UK: Oxford University Press.

Pepinsky, H.E. and R. Quinney (eds.). 1991. *Criminology as Peacemaking.* Bloomington IN: Indiana University Press.

Petrunik, M. 1983. "The politics of dangerousness," *International Journal of Law and Psychiatry* 5: 225-246.

Pfohl, S.J. 1978. *Predicting Dangerousness: The Social Construction of Psychiatric Reality.* Lexington MA: Heath Lexington.

———. 1979. "Deciding on dangerousness: Predictions of violence as social control," *Crime and Social Justice* 5: 28-40.

Price, R.R. 1970. "Psychiatry, criminal-law reform and the 'mythophilic' impulse: On Canadian proposals for the control of the dangerous offender," *Ottawa Law Review* 4: 1-61.

Ratner, R.S. 1987. "Mandatory supervision and the penal economy," in J. Lowman, R.J. Menzies and T.S. Palys (eds.), *Transcarceration: Essays in the Sociology of Social Control.* Aldershot UK: Gower.

Rennie, Y.F. 1978. *The Search for Criminal Man: A Conceptual History of the Dangerous Offender.* Lexington MA: Heath Lexington.

Ritzer, G. 1975. *Sociology: A Multiple Paradigm Science.* Boston: Allyn and Bacon.

Robertson, G.B. 1987. *Mental Disability and the Law in Canada.* Toronto: Carswell.

Rogers, R. and R.M. Bagby. 1990. Book review. "Survival of the Sanest: Order and Disorder in a Pre-trial Psychiatric Clinic," *Health Law in Canada* 11: 251-244.

Rose, N. 1990. *Governing the Soul: The Shaping of the Private Self.* London: Routledge.

Rothman, D.J. 1980. *Conscience and Convenience: The Asylum and its Alternatives in Progressive America.* Boston: Little, Brown.

Ryan, L. 1987. *Harry and the Bus.* University of Toronto Centre of Criminology. Unpublished.

Sales, B. and T. Hafemeister. 1984. "Empiricism and Legal Policy on the Insanity Defence," in L.A. Tepplin (ed.), *Mental Health and Criminal Justice.* Newbury Park, California: Sage.

Savage, H. and C. McKague. 1987. *Health Law in Canada.* Toronto: Butterworths.

Schiffer, M.E. 1978. *Mental Disorder and the Criminal Trial Process.* Toronto: Butterworths.

———. 1982. *Psychiatry Behind Bars.* Toronto: Butterworths.

Schmidt, P. and A. Dryden Witte. 1990. "Some thoughts on how and when to predict in criminal justice settings," in *New Directions in the Study of Justice, Law, and Social Control.* School of Justice Studies, Arizona State University. New York: Plenum.

Scull, A. 1984. *Decarceration. Community Treatment and the Deviant—A Radical View.* 2nd ed. New Brunswick NJ: Rutgers University Press.

———. 1989. *Social Order/Mental Disorder: Anglo-American Psychiatry in Historical Perspective.* Berkeley: University of California Press.

———. 1990. "Deinstitutionalization—cycles of despair," *Journal of Mind and Behaviour* 11: 301-312.

Shah, S.A. 1978. "Dangerousness: A paradigm for exploring some issues in law and psychology," *American Psychologist* 33: 224-238.

Smart, C. 1989. *Feminism and the Power of Law.* London: Routledge.

Spelman, E.V. 1988. *Inessential Woman: Problems of Exclusion in Feminist Thought.* Boston: Beacon Press.

Spitzer, S. 1987. "Security and control in capitalist societies: The fetishism of security and the secret thereof," in J. Lowman, R.J. Menzies and T.S. Palys (eds.), *Transcarceration: Essays in the Sociology of Social Control.* Aldershot UK: Gower.

Spruill, C.R. 1983. *Power Paradigms in the Social Sciences.* Lanham MD: University Press of America.

Steadman, H.J. 1973. "Some evidence on the inadequacy of the concept and determination of dangerousness in law and psychiatry," *Journal of Psychiatry and Law* 1: 409-426.

Steadman, H.J. and J.J. Cocozza. 1974. *Careers of the Criminally Insane.* Lexington MA: Heath Lexington.

Steadman, H.J., J.J. Cocozza and M.E. Melick. 1978. "Explaining the increased arrest rate among mental patients: The changing clientele of state hospitals," *American Journal of Psychiatry* 135: 816-820.

Steadman, H.J., P.C. Robbins and J. Monahan. 1991. *Predicting community violence among the mentally ill.* 50th Annual Conference of the American Society of Criminology. San Francisco CA.

Stone, A.A. 1984. *Law, Psychiatry and Morality: Essays and Analysis.* Washington DC: American Psychiatric Press.

Taylor, I. 1981. *Law and Order: Arguments For Socialism.* London: Macmillan.

————. 1983. *Crime, Capitalism and Community: Three Essays in Socialist Criminology.* Toronto: Butterworths.

Thornberry, T.P. and J.E. Jacoby. 1979. *The Criminally Insane: A Community Follow-up of Mentally Ill Offenders.* Chicago: University of Chicago Press.

Toch, H. and K. Adams. 1989. *The Disturbed Violent Offender.* New Haven CT: Yale University Press.

Torrey, E.F. 1988. *Nowhere to Go: The Tragic Odyssey of the Homeless Mentally Ill.* New York: Harper and Row.

Valenstein, E.S. 1986. *Great and Desperate Cures: The Rise and Decline of Psychosurgery and Other Radical Treatments For Mental Illness.* New York: Basic.

Valverde, M. 1991. *The Age of Light, Soap, and Water: Moral Reform in English Canada, 1885-1925.* Toronto: McClelland and Stewart.

Verdun-Jones, S.N. 1991. "The insanity defence in Canada: The Supreme Court of Canada strikes down the system providing for the indefinite incarceration of those acquitted by reason of insanity and the Canadian government proposes an alternative system," *International Bulletin of Law and Mental Health* 3: 19-21.

von Hirsch, A. 1987. *Past or Future Crimes: Deservedness and Dangerousness in the Sentencing of Criminals.* New Brunswick NJ: Rutgers University Press.

Voumvakis, S.E. and R.V. Ericson. 1984. *News Accounts of Attacks on Women: A Comparison of Three Toronto Newspapers.* Toronto: University of Toronto Centre of Criminology.

Walker, N. 1978. "Dangerous people," *International Journal of Law and Psychiatry* 1: 37-51.

Warren, C.A.B. 1982. *The Court of Last Resort: Mental Illness and the Law.* Chicago: University of Chicago Press.

Webster, C.D. 1990. "Prediction of dangerousness polemic," *Canadian Journal of Criminology* 32: 191-196.

Webster, C.D., M.H. Ben-Aron and S.J. Hucker (eds.). 1985. *Dangerousness: Probability and Prediction, Psychiatry and Public Policy.* New York: Cambridge University Press.

Webster, C.D., B. Dickens and S. Addario. 1985. *Constructing Dangerousness: Scientific, Legal and Policy Implications.* Toronto: University of Toronto Centre of Criminology.

Webster, C.D. and R.J. Menzies. 1987. "The clinical prediction of dangerousness," in D.N. Weisstub (ed.), *Law and Mental Health: International Perspectives.* Vol. 3. New York: Pergamon.

Webster, C.D., R.J. Menzies and M.A. Jackson. 1982. *Clinical Assessment Before Trial: Legal Issues and Mental Disorder.* Toronto: Butterworths.

Webster, C.D., D.S. Sepejak, R.J. Menzies, D.J. Slomen, F.A.S. Jensen and B.T. Butler. 1984. "The reliability and validity of dangerous behaviour predictions," *Bulletin of the American Academy of Psychiatry and the Law* 12: 41-50.

Weeks, J. 1989. *Sex, Politics and Society: The Regulation of Sexuality Since 1800.* 2nd ed. London: Longman.

West, D.J. and A. Walk. 1977. *Daniel McNaughton: His Trial and its Aftermath.* London: Gaskell.

Wexler, D.B. 1981. *Mental Health Law: Major Issues.* New York: Plenum.

Whitley, S. 1984. "The lieutenant-governor's advisory boards of review for the supervision of the mentally disordered offender in Canada: A call for change," *International Journal of Law and Psychiatry* 7: 385-394.

Wilson, J.Q. and R.J. Herrnstein. 1985. *Crime and Human Nature.* New York: Simon and Schuster.

Wiltsher, A. 1985. *Most Dangerous Women: Feminist Peace Campaigners of the Great War.* London: Pandora.

Young, J. 1988. "Realist criminology in Britain: The emergence of a competing paradigm," *British Journal of Criminology* 28: 159-183.

Chapter 4

Regional Variation in Sentencing of Young Offenders in Canada[*]

Carl Keane, Paul Maxim and Martha Dow

Introduction

The purpose of this chapter is to examine the implementation of the concept of equality under the law, as it applies to sentencing disparity within the Canadian juvenile justice system. The social goals enveloped in the principle of equality under the law are embedded in the moral doctrines of most democratic nations (Phillips 1979). Many theorists, however, would argue that although Canada's legal system requires equality to be a philosophical imperative, at the operational level "justice objectives often frustrate the pursuit of this mandate" (Cauthen 1987).

The principle of equality under the law, as it applies to young offenders, encompasses both the young offenders' rights to equality with their adult counterparts and equality of treatment with their peers. This chapter will examine the latter of these two issues by identifying some of the inequalities apparently experienced amongst the Canadian young offender population. Before any disparities can be assessed though, a discussion of the Canadian juvenile justice system is in order.

The Canadian Juvenile Justice System

The early development of the Canadian juvenile justice system was closely modelled after the British example which began to take form during the

---

[*] This chapter is based upon earlier research conducted by Dow (1990). Order of authorship does not reflect priority.

sixteenth and seventeenth centuries (Finckenauer 1984). Many of the first legislative reforms were aimed at protecting and caring for orphans and were significant because they were the first steps taken in recognition of the fact that children were not simply "miniature adults" (Leon 1977).

As the Industrial Revolution progressed, the social and cultural climate shifted so that protective reforms, such as the *Factory Acts* of 1847 and 1883, were enacted to restrict the use and abuse of all children within the labour market (West 1984). Unfortunately, the unintended consequence of these pieces of protective legislation was the creation of an "expendable, surplus population" made up of children who had previously been labourers (West 1984: 26), but who were now much more visible and, more importantly, idle. In what conflict theorists would argue was a predictable manipulative response, the government implemented universal compulsory education legislation in order to control this potentially disruptive population (West 1984).

Examination of these early pieces of legislation reveals a commitment to a paternalistic approach, which holds that young people are too immature to exercise any of their civil rights. Therefore, it is the responsibility of the justice system to act in the best interests of the child (Adams 1986). The acknowledgment of the young person's right to the due process accorded adults was not made nor considered essential by those in power (Caputo 1987).

The legal separation of youth and adult criminal proceedings was entrenched during the latter part of the nineteenth century. In 1887, J.J. Kelso, a journalist renowned for his role in the development of the juvenile justice system in Canada, established the Toronto Humane Society (Leon 1977). Kelso's activities prompted the passage of *An Act for the Protection and Reformation of Neglected Children* (1888) and *An Act Respecting the Custody of Juvenile Offenders* (1890). These *Acts* provided for the care and control of neglected children under the age of fourteen and the establishment of separate custody facilities for young offenders (Leschied 1986). The importance of these reforms can best be summarized by recognizing that up until approximately one hundred years ago children could be legally imprisoned alongside their adult counterparts.

In 1908, the *Juvenile Delinquents Act (J.D.A.)* was enacted in Canada, representing the first nationwide, comprehensive legislative attempt aimed at youthful offenders (Stewart 1978). The *J.D.A.* was designed to incorporate the philosophical tenets of "parens patriae" (judgments were to be made on the basis of a paternalistic attitude towards the youth) and the supposition that the offenders were "blameless but guilty"; in other words they were misguided youths (Caputo 1987: 127). Predictably, many of the problems that arose subsequent to the implementation of the *J.D.A.* were the result of the confusion between the "notions of the protection of children and protection from children" (Leon 1977: 74).

The paternalistic approach that had been predominant during the pre-*J.D.A.* period was entrenched in the *J.D.A.*, and perpetuated the avoidance of issues surrounding the young person's rights through indeterminate sentencing practices and the enforcement of status offences. While there were some procedural and organizational amendments made to the *J.D.A.* in 1929, the substantive content of the *Act* remained the same and essentially unchallenged for the next fifty years (Leon 1977).

The 1960s marked the beginnings of reform movements on numerous social fronts including that of juvenile justice. The international focus on civil rights that was facilitated by activities in the United States motivated the children's rights movement in Canada. These activities provided the catalyst for the legislative changes that were to follow by emphasizing the potential, and actual, systemic abuses under the *J.D.A.* (Caputo 1987). The major criticisms levelled at the *Act* included: the absence of any due process or concern for the rights of the young person (Hudson, Hornick and Burrows 1988); the inequalities which arose out of the inter-provincial variations in age limits (Caputo 1987); and, the invalidity of the parental philosophy espoused by proponents of the *Act* when children as young as seven could be prosecuted (MacDonald 1971).

The 1967 draft of the *Children's and Young Person's Act*, which was the result of a study conducted by the Department of Justice (Hudson, Hornick, and Burrows 1988), embodied one hundred recommendations for revisions to the juvenile justice system; however, the *Act* was never formally presented before the House of Commons because of the public and political sentiment that continued to support the paternal approach advocated by the *J.D.A.* (Stewart 1978). This opposition to change could also be interpreted as the collective unwillingness of those in power to afford young persons equal rights with adults within our legal system. As Adams (1986: 114) points out: "...the justice system in general and the custodial sector especially are particularly resistant to change, if change implies any contraction in power or resources."

This institutional (economic, legal and political) opposition to change was evidenced by the rejection in the House of Commons of Bill C-192, *An Act Respecting Young Offenders and To Repeal the Juvenile Delinquent's Act* (Hudson, Hornick and Burrows 1988). In response to that rejection, a committee organized by the Solicitor General of Canada produced a report entitled "Young Persons in Conflict With The Law" which cited several recommendations (Stewart 1978). After two years of surveying political and public opinions regarding the contents of the report, revisions were made, and the report was resubmitted as the "Highlights of Proposed New Legislation for Young Offenders" (Hudson, Hornick and Burrows 1988).

A preliminary draft of the *Young Offenders Act* was introduced to the House of Commons, and after further revisions, was enacted by Parliament (Ward and Weiler 1985). On April 1, 1985, after almost two decades of political opposition, the *Young Offenders Act* (*Y.O.A.*) came into full effect nationwide marking a significant shift in the legal and social philosophy surrounding the rights of youthful criminals.

The Young Offenders Act: Its Declaration of Principle

The philosophy of the *Y.O.A.* is the target of many critics' attacks and the crux of most proponents' arguments (Dow 1990). The goals of the legislation as they are presented in the *Act*'s Declaration of Principle are attacked for being contradictory in their nature and praised for being innovative and comprehensive. These critics do not pretend that any approach to dealing with youthful crime will be simple; however, they argue that the absence of priorities (i.e., rights of the young person versus protection of society versus the "treatment" of the young person) within this piece of legislation has confounded the innovative potential of the *Act*.

To highlight some of these inconsistencies, contradictions and general absence of any substantive or implemental priorities, the eight subsections of the Declaration of Principle have been collapsed into five philosophical mandates.

1. Young persons have special needs, however, they are responsible for their actions.
2. Society has the right to protection from crime perpetrated by youthful offenders.
3. Alternative measures should be used where it is appropriate.
4. Young persons have the right to due process.
5. Young persons have the right to the least possible interference under the law.

Under the *J.D.A.*, judges had a clear mandate during sentencing which was to act in the "best interests" of the young person. The *Y.O.A.* instructs judges to balance the three major considerations which are, (i) the right of society to protection, (ii) the need to make the young person accountable, and (iii) the special needs of the young person. This balancing act has promoted fundamental differences in the judicial interpretations and subsequent applications of the *Act*'s mandates.

Historically, the determination of a person's guilt in a criminal sense rested on two criteria: "actus reus" which was the physical committal of the act and "mens rea" which described the individual's intention (Dalby 1985); therefore, a major shift in emphasis occurred when the *Y.O.A.* recognized the intent and hence the accountability of young offenders. No longer is it an acceptable practice to dismiss the actions of law-breaking youth as misguided and therefore beyond their control; however, it is also obvious that the concerns regarding equal treatment and due process have been tempered by the acknowledgment that young offenders have special characteristics which may be of consequence in any decision. Not only may they have the emotional, psychological and environmental problems that have contributed to their criminal behaviour, they also have the normal developmental issues that confront all teenagers. While this clause (section 3(1)(c) *Y.O.A.*) is reminiscent of the paternalistic approach advocated by the *J.D.A.*, it is not supported by the same superstructure of protection, and therefore does not dictate a similar response by our courts.

The declaration that society must be protected from criminal activity whether it is perpetrated by an adult or a young person supports the claim that with equal rights young persons should also be subject to similar interventions.

The *J.D.A.* encouraged extensive variation in sentencing practices by affording the judiciary carte blanche in their dealings with young offenders; however, this opportunity for innovation often resulted in indeterminate and inconsistent sentences and in the unnecessary removal of the young person from the home. The *Y.O.A.* has attempted to provide the opportunity for innovative sentencing through a highly structured program of alternative measures in addition to the more traditional dispositions. This attempt to divert young offenders away from the juvenile justice system contains elements of an exemptionist philosophy whereby diversionary mechanisms are sought in order to avoid the harms of the formal system.

The *Y.O.A.* has been a reactive piece of legislation in that it has attempted to correct the absence of offender rights under the *J.D.A.* by ensuring that young persons have the same rights as adults (with the exception of the right to a preliminary inquiry and the right to a jury trial). This important shift in philosophy is advocated by those children's rights activists supporting a liberationist perspective; however, many others would argue that:

> ...the legalization of children's rights in juvenile justice is a mixed blessing. The strength of law lies in its capacity to provide positive safeguards and restrictions on violations of personal space. Its weaknesses include the risks of distancing children from the means to exercise their own rights, and through the mystification that tends to accompany the professionalization of an activity.
>
> (Adams 1986: 113)

It should be noted that the principle of least interference deserves a great deal more attention than has been devoted to it. It is this principle that declares that the *Y.O.A.* should not be interpreted as a punitive piece of legislation; instead, dispositions should reflect society's need to be protected and the young person's need to be "treated." Dispositions should not be handed down to compensate for the gravity of the crimes or the suffering of the victims and their families as is the case in the ordinary court system. It is this principle that mandates a complex and innovative approach for dealing with young offenders which would combine the philosophical imperatives of the exemptionist approach, emphasizing alternative measures and treatment, the paternalist or protectionist approach, emphasizing the special needs orientation, and what has been called the liberationist approach, emphasizing due process.

Sentencing: Some Theoretical and Practical Considerations

...the problem of sentencing disparity has been identified as one of the major issues that should be addressed in any contemporary proposals for reform of the Canadian criminal justice system.

(Linden 1986: 3)

The debate regarding the need for sentencing guidelines, the type of guidelines needed, and the extent of disparity in sentencing that exists within the criminal justice system, cannot be adequately explored within the confines of this chapter. The purpose of this section is to introduce some of the more provocative questions surrounding the debate as it relates to the juvenile justice system.

Brodeur (1989) presents two fundamental choices that face legislators when they construct the principles of a piece of legislation which will mandate the purpose of a sentence. The first option is to implement an Integrated Declaration of Principle which is designed to promote consistency by putting priority on a single goal and principles which are compatible with that goal and each other (Brodeur 1989). This approach has been criticized despite its consistency for being too narrow and restricting judges from focussing on different goals depending on the offence committed.

The second option available to law-making bodies is the Integrative Declaration of Principle which combines goals and principles that are often incongruent and does not supply any formula to rank these goals (Brodeur 1989). This very broad approach has been praised for providing a comprehensive sentencing tool and condemned for creating unjustifiable differences in sentences adjudicated. The *Young Offenders Act* fits into the second option with its Integrative Declaration of Principle. In fact, many of the criticisms which have been levelled at the *Act* are based on the inconsistencies in the implementation of the *Act* that have been attributed to the incompatibility of the principles presented in the *Y.O.A.*

Studies focussing on the adult criminal system have indicated that there are significant inter-provincial differences in the types of sentences assigned for similar offence categories (Hann 1983). This trend has been discussed within the realm of juvenile justice because of the tremendous onus put on the provinces to regulate and administer the *Act*.

Despite the absence of specific guidelines (aside from maximum penalties) structuring the delivery of sentences, youth court judges consistently respond to unofficial constraints including resource availability, the needs of the community and public opinion (Brodeur 1989).

In addition, many would argue that personal interpretational issues play an important role in judicial decision-making. Hogarth's (1971) study indicated that over 50 percent of the variation in sentencing patterns could be accounted for by "knowing certain pieces of information about the judge himself" whereas only 9 percent of the variation could be explained by "objectively defined facts" (Griffiths and Verdun-Jones 1989: 339).

Documented patterns of sentencing disparity in the adult system suggest that the decision-making process dictated by the Declaration of Principle of the *Y.O.A.* will inevitably lead to similar unjustifiable differences in sentencing within the juvenile justice system. The youth court judge must first decide which of the goals specified in the *Act* should be given priority. After this decision is made, an inventory of the resources which are available to achieve this goal will need to be constructed (Trepanier 1989). It is important to remember that, because of the nature of the *Act*, decisions regarding the goal which is given priority and the resources available in each province are likely to be affected by public sentiment and regional differences in the political interpretation of the overall philosophy of the *Act*.

It is these factors which will become increasingly more important and more visible as the *Y.O.A.* emerges from its early years of operation. The discussion surrounding equality and the special circumstances involved in juvenile justice supports the contention that looking for national consistency in sentencing is a reasonable and desirable goal.

Objectives of the Study

Previous studies have indicated that there are important differences in sentencing patterns when examining variables such as region (Dow 1990). As stated earlier, the purpose of this chapter is to determine whether or not there are systemic inequalities in Canada's juvenile justice system as they relate to inter-provincial variations in patterns of adjudication. It is acknowledged that there are specific circumstances of individual cases which contribute to the decisions made within the youth court setting; however, the goal of this study is to investigate the inequalities of these processes at a systems-level of analysis, thereby emphasizing the importance of systemic and operational biases.

The empirical portion of this chapter will concentrate on two specific areas. The first area of interest focusses on the characteristics of young offenders entering the youth court system, such as the average age of the offender, types of crimes committed and national and regional rates of young offender crime. In addition, differences between males and females on these same variables will be examined.

The second major area involves the types of dispositions most commonly used by youth courts in Canada. The age of the young offender is also examined in this section to provide additional information on sentencing patterns.

The goal of uniformity under the *Y.O.A.* was to facilitate a more equal system of adjudication of young persons involved with the law. Hence, one of the most energetically debated topics is the potential for inter-provincial differences in the processing of young offenders due to interpretational differences and availability of services and facilities such as alternative measures programs and custody institutions.

Data Set

The primary data used in this study were obtained from the Youth Court Statistics (1984/85-1987/88) which are compiled annually by the Canadian Centre for Justice Statistics (C.C.J.S.). In addition, Census Data (1986) collected by Statistics Canada were used to determine the population breakdown across regions, age groups and sex.

Data for the Youth Court Survey are made available to the C.C.J.S. by Newfoundland, Prince Edward Island (P.E.I.), Nova Scotia, New Brunswick, Quebec, Manitoba, Saskatchewan, Alberta, British Columbia and the Yukon. Ontario does not participate in the survey and, until recently, the Northwest Territories did not take part in the collation of this data bank. The emphasis of the survey is on the examination of the "primary court processes" relating to *Criminal Code* and other federal statute charges, thereby excluding statistics associated with appeals, reviews, provincial statutes and municipal by-law infractions (Youth Court Survey).

A preferable design for this study would have included a comparison of the functioning of the youth court system under the J.D.A. and under the Y.O.A.; however, because of the political manoeuvering of various provinces there has not been complete national reporting of Youth Court statistics since 1972.

The absence of Ontario data impacts upon the results of this study through the elimination of approximately one third of the population of interest

(Canadian youth between the ages of 12 and 17) (Census Data, 1986); therefore, it can be assumed that a significant proportion of the young persons appearing in youth court in Canada are missing from this data set. Despite this obvious exclusion, the regions examined provide important information, regarding sentencing trends, which is unaffected by the exclusion of Ontario and the Northwest Territories.

The emphasis in this study on the regional variation in patterns of adjudication necessitates the use of official statistics as opposed to unofficial statistics. Only data collected from official mechanisms can address the inadequacies of present juvenile justice legislation as an intricate system of social control; however, it is important to acknowledge the problems with official sources.

By collecting data at the adjudication stage of criminal proceedings, young offenders who avoid the formal court process through mechanisms such as police discretion and the reporting habits of citizens in the community (Nettler 1984) are overlooked in explanatory models of crime distribution patterns. As a result of these informal methods of diversion, inaccurate and misleading estimations of the amount, location and types of crime are likely. However, because this study concentrates on systemic inequalities and inconsistencies within our legal system, the post arrest proceedings are the focus of interest.

Method

The specific objectives and design of this study necessitated the re-structuring of the data obtained from the published accounts of the Youth Court Survey.

The variable REGION was constructed by reducing the original ten provinces/territories used by the Youth Court Survey to six regions. The inconsistent representation of the Northwest Territories across variables and time frames made it necessary to eliminate it from the analysis undertaken by this study. The Yukon was dropped from the analysis because of inadequate sample sizes and the East Coast provinces (Newfoundland, Prince Edward Island, Nova Scotia and New Brunswick) were combined to enhance the sample size for those regions. The result of this data transformation was the creation of a variable labelled REGION made up of the following six geographic areas:

1.   Maritimes (M.T.)
2.   Quebec
3.   Manitoba
4.   Saskatchewan
5.   Alberta
6.   British Columbia.

The variable OUTCOME refers to the most significant decision and disposition, and was created by combining the eighteen categories examined by the Youth Court Survey according to theoretical criteria to construct eight categories for the variable OUTCOME as follows:

1. Transfer to Adult Court
2. Not Guilty or Charges Dismissed
3. Secure Custody
4. Detention for Treatment
5. Open Custody
6. Probation
7. Fine/Compensation (includes Community Service Order, Restitution)
8. Other (includes Not Fit to Stand Trial, Stay of Proceedings, Charges Withdrawn, Transfer to Other Jurisdiction, Prohibition, Seizure or Forfeiture, Absolute Discharge).

For comparison purposes, the study also categorizes offence types into violent, property, and other offences. In addition, since yearly comparisons were not a focus for this study, all four fiscal years were combined which enhanced the cell sizes for all of the variables and compensated for any annual fluctuations.

Results

Descriptive Statistics: Nationwide Assessment

Previous research investigating demographic correlates of crime has consistently shown that males are more involved in the juvenile justice system than are females (Nettler 1984). Table 1 indicates that males are charged at a rate 3.2 times greater than that of females and that there are 6.6 times more charges laid against males than females. In addition, the average age of the male young offender is 15.42 years compared to 15.06 years for the female offender.

As shown in Table 2, there is an overall increase in both the rate of persons being charged (except for age 17) and the rate of charges being laid as age increases. In addition, there is a consistent increase in the average number of charges laid against each young offender as he/she gets older with rates ranging from 2.43 charges per young person (age 12) to 3.39 charges per young person (age 17). This finding may be the result of a number of factors including the fact that younger individuals are more likely to be diverted from the court system through the use of informal mechanisms such as police discretion.

Table 1

Decomposition of the Rate of Persons Charged and the Rate of Charges Laid by Sex		
Rate	Sex	
	Male	Female
Persons/100,000	2894 (15.42)*	901 (15.06)*
Charges/100,000	8858	1334

* Average age of the young person charged.

Table 2

Decomposition of the Rate of Persons Charged and the Rate of Charges Laid by Age						
Rate	Age					
	12	13	14	15	16	17
Persons/100,000	864	1515	2253	2698	2915	2835
Charges/100,000	2099	3622	5755	7820	9521	9600
Average Number Charges/Person	2.43	2.39	2.55	2.90	3.27	3.39

The final nationwide assessment of charges (see Table 3) indicates that there are 3.9 times as many persons charged with property offences as are charged with violent offences. There are 7.3 times as many charges laid related to property offences as there are violent offences.

Also shown in Table 3 is that the average number of violent offences committed by each violent offender is 1.64 while the average for each property offender is 3.06 offences. This finding is to be expected based on the supposition that it is more likely that an offender would commit multiple break and enter or theft related offences as opposed to multiple assaults or murders. In addition, the average age of the violent offender is slightly older than that of the property offender.

Table 3

Decomposition of the Rate of Persons Charged and the Rate of Charges Laid by Offence Type			
Rate	Offence		
	Violent	Property	Other
Persons/100,000	862 (15.45)*	3374 (15.19)*	605 (16.05)*
Charges/100,000	1413	10340	2179

* Average age of the young person charged.

Table 4

Decomposition of the Rate of Persons Charged and the Rate of Charges Laid by Region		
Region	Rate	
	Persons/100,000	Charges/100,000
Maritimes	2349	5762
Quebec	1212	6263
Manitoba	3052	9892
Saskatchewan	2935	8617
Alberta	3438	10248
British Columbia	2369	7923

Regional Comparison

A comparison of the six regions shows that the prairie and western provinces have consistently higher rates of persons charged and charges laid than that of the Maritimes and Quebec (Table 4).

Age

Table 5 shows that Quebec has a dramatically lower rate of persons charged than any of the other regions throughout all of the age categories; however, the most prominent differences occur for those persons aged 12, 13 and 14. Quebec's notably lower rate, especially at the younger ages might be attributed to numerous factors including a policing and legal philosophy supportive of diversionary mechanisms.

Table 5 confirms the general trend shown in Table 2 that there is an overall increase in the rate of persons charged and rate of charges laid as the age of young persons increases.

Sex

The differences in involvement in the juvenile justice system between males and females is fairly consistent for the Maritimes, Manitoba, Alberta and British Columbia (Table 6). The rate of females charged is 20 percent to 27 percent that of males charged and the rate of charges laid against females is 13 percent to 16 percent that of the charges laid against males. The most dramatic difference between the sexes is evident in Quebec where the rate of females charged is only 6 percent of the rate of males charged and the rate of charges laid against females is only 4 percent of the rate of charges laid against males. Also shown in Table 6 is that the lowest differential appears in Saskatchewan where females are charged at a rate of 54 percent of the rate at which males are charged.

Offence Type

Table 7 shows that the nationwide trend of property offences being the most common offence category is illustrated across all six of the regions studied. The average rate of persons charged with violent offences is 27 percent of the rate of persons charged with property offences and the average rate of charges laid which are related to violent offences is 13 percent of the rate of charges laid related to property offences. Both Quebec and Manitoba appear to have an above average rate of persons charged with violent offences: persons are charged with violent offences at a rate of 34 percent of the rate of persons charged with property offences.

Disposition Utilization

Table 5

Decomposition of the Rate of Persons Charged and the Rate of Charges Laid by Age and by Region						
Region	Age					
	12	13	14	15	16	17
Maritimes	728	1292	1977	2432	2959	2602
	(4)	(4)	(4)	(5)	(4)	(4)
	1799*	2408*	4291*	5475*	7620*	6671*
	[3]	[5]	[5]	[5]	[5]	[6]
Quebec	81	229	624	1030	1284	1546
	(6)	(6)	(6)	(6)	(6)	(6)
	433*	1084*	3138*	5227*	7160*	7776*
	[6]	[6]	[6]	[6]	[6]	[5]
Manitoba	1175	1820	2723	3093	3688	3442
	(1)	(2)	(2)	(2)	(2)	(3)
	3663*	5723*	8658*	9382*	11700*	11888*
	[1]	[1]	[1]	[2]	[2]	[2]
Saskatchewan	973	1764	2480	2915	3563	3455
	(3)	(3)	(3)	(3)	(3)	(2)
	1712*	2634*	5148*	7540*	10944*	11330*
	[4]	[4]	[4]	[4]	[3]	[3]
Alberta	1034	2024	3072	3732	3888	4063
	(2)	(1)	(1)	(1)	(1)	(1)
	2248*	4814*	7016*	10561*	12450*	12990*
	[2]	[2]	[2]	[1]	[1]	[1]
British Columbia	365	1017	1917	2515	2758	2591
	(5)	(5)	(5)	(4)	(5)	(5)
	1187*	3139*	6321*	8417*	9510*	8565*
	[5]	[3]	[3]	[3]	[4]	[4]

Rate of young persons charged per 100,000 (non-duplicate count).
()Rank among regions assessed by number of young persons charged (1=highest number).
*Rate of charges laid per 100,000 (duplicate count).
[]Rank among regions assessed by number of charges laid (1=highest number of charges laid).

Descriptive Statistics: Nationwide Assessment

Table 6

Decomposition of the Rate of Persons Charged and the Rate of Charges Laid by Sex and by Region		
Region	Sex	
	Male	Female
Maritimes	2624	512
	6317*	907*
	[15.25]	[15.13]
Quebec	1295	84
	6528*	264*
	[15.83]	[15.63]
Manitoba	3587	733
	11233*	1473*
	[15.27]	[15.10]
Saskatchewan	3353	1826
	9931*	1436*
	[15.43]	[14.79]
Alberta	4032	1079
	11751*	1883*
	[15.25]	[14.94]
British Columbia	2744	595
	8917*	1152*
	[15.44]	[15.20]

Rate of young persons charged per 100,000 (non-duplicate count).
* Rate of charges laid per 100,000 (duplicate count).
[] Average age of the young person charged by region by sex.

Table 7

Decomposition of the Rate of Persons Charged and the Rate of Charges Laid by Offence Type and by Region		
Region	Offence		
	Violent	Property	Other
Maritimes	589	2987	438
	763*	7223*	1126*
	[15.33]	[15.10]	[15.94]
Quebec	569	1656	229
	1004*	8108*	1645*
	[15.78]	[15.72]	[16.28]
Manitoba	1403	4085	698
	2521*	12957*	2802*
	[15.28]	[15.06]	[16.01]
Saskatchewan	841	3735	1048
	1204*	11373*	3389*
	[15.44]	[15.04]	[16.08]
Alberta	989	4451	804
	1481*	13100*	2994*
	[15.28]	[15.00]	[15.96]
British Columbia	805	3136	534
	1276*	10292*	1516*
	[15.46]	[15.24]	[16.05]

Rate of young persons charged per 100,000 (non-duplicate count).
* Rate of charges per 100,000 (duplicate count).
[] Average age of young persons charged by region by offence.

Age and Outcome

Findings presented above summarized the relationship between age and the rate of persons charged and the rate of charges laid (Table 2). Table 8 reiterates these findings showing that the rate of cases processed in youth court increases with age nationwide. In addition, Table 9 indicates that the average age of the offender sentenced to the two most serious dispositions examined, transfer to ordinary court and secure custody, is higher than for any of the other categories. Also shown in Table 9 is that dispositions associated with probation and fine or compensation oriented sentences are utilized at a much higher rate, 1,958 per 100,000 and 1,373 per 100,000 respectively, than any of the other dispositions. Interestingly, the rate of young persons transferred to ordinary court is almost nine times that of young persons detained for treatment.

Table 8

Decomposition of the Rate of Cases Processed by Age						
Rate	Age					
	12	13	14	15	16	17
Cases/100,000	450	781	1227	1534	1708	1866

Table 10 shows dramatic increases in the rate of young persons transferred to ordinary court as age increases, especially between 14 and 17 years of age. This result is expected due to the Y.O.A. qualification that an accused youth must be fourteen years of age to be eligible for transfer to ordinary court. In addition, sentencing patterns for secure and open custody dispositions are similar except that the most pronounced increase in the rate occurs a year later for secure custody (age 14) than for open custody. Finally, treatment dispositions remain rare, independent of the age category examined.

Regional Assessment

The results displayed in Table 11 show that Quebec has a dramatically lower rate of cases processed than any of the other regions at a rate of 519 cases per 100,000. Manitoba has the highest rate with 2,239 cases processed per 100,000 compared to 1,224 for the Maritimes, 1,716 for British Columbia, 1,776 for Saskatchewan, and 1,791 for Alberta.

Table 9

Decomposition of the Rate of Cases Processed by Outcome		
Outcome	Average Age	Cases/100,000
Transfer/Ordinary	16.59	105
Not Guilty	15.33	1752
Secure Custody	15.86	554
Treatment	15.66	12
Open	15.41	503
Probation	15.22	1958
Fine/Compensation	15.76	1373
Other	15.44	91

Table 10

Decomposition of the Rate of Cases by Age and Outcome						
Outcome	Age					
	12	13	14	15	16	17
Transfer/Ordinary	0	3	4	34	55	129
Not Guilty	563	829	1223	1646	2006	2381
Secure	24	76	221	393	610	729
Treatment	4	7	11	12	12	12
Open	66	207	342	481	605	628
Probation	490	985	1668	2113	2369	2208
Fine/Compensation	183	471	806	1017	1192	1982
Other	28	42	80	97	86	112

Rate per 100,000

Table 11

Decomposition of the Rate of Cases Processed by Region	
Region	Cases/100,000
Maritimes	1224
Quebec	519
Manitoba	2239
Saskatchewan	1776
Alberta	1791
British Columbia	1716

Cases = Rate of cases per 100,000 people adjudicated in the youth courts.

Age

The pattern of the rate of cases processed increasing with age remains virtually unchanged when each region is examined individually (Table 12). The only exceptions appear to be slight decreases at age 17 for the Maritimes and British Columbia.

Outcome

Table 13 shows the interregional differences in the usage of the eight outcome categories examined in this study. One of the most notable findings appears to be in Manitoba where the rate (per 100,000) of 210 transfers to ordinary court is 2.6 times greater than the next highest rate of 80 found in Alberta. In addition, Saskatchewan appears to be notably more prone to use both of the custody dispositions available to the courts with rates of 831 cases per 100,000 sentenced to secure custody and 820 cases per 100,000 sentenced to open custody.

The Maritimes and Saskatchewan appear to utilize treatment dispositions at a rate approximately 2 to 6 times that of the other four regions; however, the rates of 21 and 18 are still substantially less than for any of the other outcomes assessed. Finally, there are dramatic interregional differences found when examining not guilty decisions. Quebec's rate of 348 is substantially lower than the highest rate which is found in Manitoba at 3,281 persons per 100,000.

Conclusion

Table 12

Decomposition of the Rate of Cases Processed by Age and Region						
Region	Age					
	12	13	14	15	16	17
Maritimes	314	597	924	1171	1516	1498
Quebec	26	89	247	410	541	684
Manitoba	814	1143	1697	2139	2615	2843
Saskatchewan	378	696	1102	1568	2238	2323
Alberta	441	901	1404	1793	1857	2544
British Columbia	246	757	1510	1858	1968	1806

Numbers represent cases per 100,000 adjudicated in Youth Court.

The results of this study indicate that there are significant interregional differences in the extent of youth involvement in the justice system and the types of outcomes adjudicated in Canada's youth courts.

Many of the findings observed nationwide are consistent with trends which have been documented in previous studies. The indication that males and older individuals are charged at a much greater rate than females and younger persons has been documented by numerous studies (Jensen and Rojek 1980). Some of the most common explanations for this trend focus on the socialization of both law enforcement agencies and the individuals brought into the system. Society's expectations regarding appropriate behaviours for young men and young women have impacted our juvenile justice system through police discretion and the nature and severity of the sentences adjudicated.

Older offenders are more likely to receive more severe dispositions than are younger persons processed. This apparent sentencing disparity has been addressed by the Ontario Court of Appeal with respect to the two-tier juvenile justice system in Nova Scotia and Ontario. Among other things, the court found that "if older youths received more severe dispositions, this was rational and not a foundation for a finding of age discrimination" (Platt 1989). A contributing factor to this rise in the utilization of more serious dispositions as age increases could be the fact that older individuals tend to commit more serious offences (Jensen and Rojek 1980). In addition, an older young offender is more likely to have compiled a criminal record which has a direct impact on the

Table 13

Decomposition of the Rate of Cases Processed by Outcome and Region						
Outcome	Region					
	M.T.	Quebec	Manitoba	Sask.	Alberta	B.C.
Transfer/Ordinary	67	36	210	12	80	13
Not Guilty	701	348	3281	1643	1654	1375
Secure	625	378	588	831	627	491
Treatment	21	10	8	18	3	7
Open	394	242	543	820	674	472
Probation	1822	721	1854	2536	2186	2431
Fine/Compensation	663	597	1565	1311	2134	639
Other	84	24	177	114	64	27

Numbers in table represent cases per 100,000.

nature and length of the dispositions handed down.

This study also shows that property offences are processed at a much higher rate than are violent offences which is consistent with many other studies investigating this issue (Nettler 1984).

Finally, examination of two of the most controversial dispositions available, transfers to ordinary court and treatment orders, shows that the former are used at a much greater rate than are treatment orders. This finding, coupled with evidence from previous studies suggesting a greater propensity on the part of judges to utilize custodial dispositions and longer terms of custody under the *Y.O.A.* (Leschied and Jaffe 1988), indicates that the *Young Offenders Act* may be creating a more restrictive approach to juvenile justice than was the intention. While some would argue that this trend is contrary to the idea that punishment is not the aim of the *Y.O.A.*, others maintain that this approach is in keeping with the principle dictating the need for societal protection.

Manitoba, Saskatchewan, the Maritimes and Quebec all show substantial interregional variations at various stages of the analysis. Both Quebec and Manitoba have above average rates of persons charged with violent offences; however, mechanisms used to cope with this clientele appear to be different for each region.

Results of this study show that Manitoba may be dealing with their violent offenders through the use of some of the most restrictive measures available to the courts. Manitoba was found to use custodial dispositions and transfers to ordinary court at a much greater rate than any of the other regions.

The differences between Manitoba and Quebec also serve to highlight the tremendous spectrum available for the interpretation and implementation of the *Y.O.A.*. Even if all jurisdictions agreed on the emphasis of the *Act* there would continue to be discrepancies between regions on the mechanisms used to achieve this emphasis. As an example, there may be a philosophical commitment to accountability as a governing principle; however, there might be wide disagreement regarding the appropriate mechanism to promote accountability (e.g. restitution versus custody).

Proposed partial explanations of this trend include a resounding public outcry in Manitoba for a juvenile justice system which makes accountability its highest priority (Ryant and Heinrich 1988). In Manitoba, it appears that this widely held attitude of accountability may contribute to a high rate of incarceration for young offenders, a trend which was ingrained in the previous system operated under the *Juvenile Delinquents Act* (Ryant and Heinrich 1988). A possible contributor to this strong public sentiment is the fact that Manitoba, as this study indicates, had the highest rate of cases processed compared to the other five regions. Possibly this high level of system utilization has suggested to the Manitoba public that a "get tough" response is in order. An alternate explanation, however, is that this higher than average rate of persons involved in the system is the result and not the catalyst of this emphasis on accountability. Interestingly, Manitoba's neighbour Saskatchewan shows similar trends through the increased use of custodial dispositions and transfers to ordinary court; however, the anomaly in Saskatchewan is the higher use of treatment orders, an attribute it shares with the Maritimes.

As stated above, Quebec also shows an above average rate of persons charged with violent offences but the results do not suggest a restrictive reaction similar to Manitoba's response. With respect to the relatively lower rate of custodial dispositions utilized in Quebec, a partial explanation may be found in the historical use of custody facilities in Quebec before the enactment of the *Young Offenders Act*. Prior to 1984 the "least restrictive measures" mandate encompassed in the *Y.O.A.* was already in effect through a social and legal philosophy supportive of the use of extreme controlling mechanisms such as custody only for chronic offenders who had committed serious offences (LeBlanc and Beaumont 1988).

One of the most interesting findings in this study is the dramatically lower rate of young persons charged in Quebec compared to the other six regions. These substantial differentials in Quebec are apparent for all of the age categories but are most pronounced for those persons aged 12 and 13 years of age.

To promote a better understanding of some of the factors that may have contributed to this relationship it may be helpful to explore the unique nature of Quebec's juvenile justice system prior to the *Y.O.A.*

In 1977, Quebec passed the *Youth Protection Act* which embodied a philosophy which was a complete departure from the *Juvenile Delinquents Act* through its declaration of protection and delinquency as two separate entities (LeBlanc and Beaumont 1988). Over the first three or four years of the *Y.P.A.*'s infancy, numerous debates regarding social and legal interpretational difficulties were heard and by 1982 there was a consensus among the social and legal authorities in Quebec supportive of minimal legal intervention in the cases of young offenders wherever possible (LeBlanc and Beaumont 1988).

Based on the trend analysis pursued in this study, it appears that the early implementation of the philosophical mandate of the *Y.O.A.* through Quebec's *Youth Protection Act* assisted this province in a more successful transition in terms of limiting youth involvement in the formal court system. The pronounced differences for the younger age categories in Quebec may be attributed in part to the 14 to 18 year target group under the *Y.P.A.* It is possible that the already predominant philosophy of diversion which is maintained under the *Y.O.A.* is heightened for those youths who are 12 and 13 years of age due to the mind set created by the *Y.P.A.*'s age restrictions.

> Recognizing that children had a number of rights, particularly the right to be kept in their natural environment insofar as possible, this Act pursued the objective of diversion, by limiting court intervention to cases where such intervention was absolutely necessary and by promoting the use of "voluntary measures.
>
> (LeBlanc and Beaumont 1988: 83)

Although statistics regarding the utilization of Alternative Measures are not incorporated in the Youth Court Survey, perhaps a good indicator of diversion is the rate of cases which result in not guilty verdicts. The dramatically lower rate of not guilty findings evident in Quebec compared to any of the other regions may suggest a more effective interpretation of the role of diversion in our youth courts. In other words, Quebec is apparently successful in using pre-charge mechanisms to divert youths from the formal court process while other regions have a high rate of not guilty findings after the accused has experienced the system to some degree.

This study indicates that there are a number of differences in the operation of the youth court system across the regions examined, including the extent of youth involvement in the system and the types of dispositions utilized. It is these systemic differences which question the validity of our societal emphasis on equality under the law and the achievement of an equitable and uniform system of justice with the enactment of the *Young Offenders Act*. It is these differences that must receive attention in any just society.

References

Adams, R. 1986. "Juvenile Justice and Children's and Young People's Rights." Pp. 97-122 in B. Franklin (ed.), *The Rights of Children*. England: Basil Blackwell Ltd.

Brodeur, J.P. 1989. "Some Comments on Sentencing Guidelines." Pp. 107-117 in L.A. Beaulieu (ed.), *Young Offender Dispositions: Perspectives on Principles and Practice*. Toronto: Wall & Thompson.

Caputo, T.C. 1987. "The Young Offenders Act: Children's Rights, Children's Wrongs." *Canadian Public Policy* 13(2):125-143.

Cauthen, K. 1987. *The Passion for Equality*. New Jersey: Rowman and Littlefield.

Criminal Code. 1989. *Pocket Criminal Code and Miscellaneous Statutes*. Toronto: Carswell.

Dalby, J.T. 1985. "Criminal Liability in Children." *Canadian Journal of Criminology* 27(2): 137-145.

Dow, M.C. 1990. *"Sentencing Disparity and the Young Offenders Act."* Unpublished M.A. Thesis, Department of Sociology, The University of Western Ontario, London, Ontario.

Finckenauer, J.O. 1984. *Juvenile Delinquency and Corrections*. London: Academic Press Inc.

Griffiths, C.T. and S.N. Verdun-Jones. 1989. *Canadian Criminal Justice*. Vancouver: Butterworths.

Hann, R.G. et al. 1983. *Sentencing Practices and Trends in Canada: A Summary of Statistical Information*. Ottawa: Department of Justice, Canada.

Hogarth, J. 1971. *Sentencing as a Human Process*. Toronto: University of Toronto Press.

Hudson, J., Hornick, J.P. and B.B. Burrows. (eds.) 1988. *Justice and the Young Offender in Canada*. Toronto: Wall and Thompson.

Jensen, G.F. and D.G. Rojek. 1980. *Delinquency: A Sociological View*. Toronto: D.C. Heath and Company.

LeBlanc, M. and H. Beaumont. 1988. "The Quebec Perspective on the Young Offenders Act: Implementation Before Adoption." Pp. 81-92 in J. Hudson, B.A. Burrows and J.P. Hornick (eds.), *Justice and the Young Offender in Canada*. Toronto: Wall & Thompson.

Leon, J.S. 1977. "The Development of Canadian Juvenile Justice: A Background for Reform." *Osgoode Hall Law Journal* 15(1): 71-106.

Leschied, A.D.W. 1986. "Whatever Happened to the Child Saver—Reconciling Children's Rights." *The Journal*.

Leschied, A.D.W. and P.G. Jaffe 1988. "Implementing the *Young Offenders Act* in Ontario: Critical Issues and Challenges for the Future." Pp. 65-81 in

J. Hudson, B.A. Burrows and J.P. Hornick (eds.), *Justice and the Young Offender in Canada*. Toronto: Wall & Thompson.

Linden, A.M. 1986. "A Fresh Approach to Sentencing in Canada." *RCMP Gazette* 48:1-7.

MacDonald, J.A. 1971. "A Critique of Bill C-192: The Young Offenders Act." *Canadian Journal of Criminology and Corrections* 13:166-180.

Nettler, G. 1984. *Explaining Crime*. (Third Edition) London: McGraw-Hill.

Phillips, D.L. 1979. *Equality, Justice and Rectification: An Exploration in Normative Sociology*. London: Academic Press.

Platt, P. 1989. *Young Offenders Law in Canada*. Toronto: Butterworths.

Ryant, J.C. and C. Heinrich. 1988. "Youth Court Committees in Manitoba." Pp. 93-104 in J. Hudson, B.A. Burrows and J.P. Hornick (eds.), *Justice and the Young Offender in Canada*. Toronto: Wall & Thompson.

Stewart, V.L. 1978. "The Faces of Juvenile Justice in Canada." Pp. 157-172 in V.L. Stewart (ed.), *The Changing Faces of Juvenile Justice*. New York: New York University Press.

Trepanier, J. 1989. "Principles and Goals Guiding the Choice of Dispositions Under the *Y.O.A.*" Pp 27-66 in L.A. Beaulieu (ed.), *Young Offender Dispositions: Perspectives on Principles and Practice*. Toronto: Wall & Thompson.

Ward, B. and R. Weiler. 1985. "A National Overview of the Implementation of the *Young Offenders Act*: One Year Later." *Perception* 8(5):7-13.

West, W.G. 1984. *Young Offenders and the State: A Canadian Perspective*. Toronto: Butterworths.

Chapter 5

A Closed Security Youth Facility: Rehabilitation or Joyride?

An Exploratory Study of a Murder Case Processed Through the Young Offenders Act

Gary M. O'Bireck

Introduction

On April 2, 1984, the *Young Offenders Act* replaced the *Juvenile Delinquents Act* of 1908 as new legislation designed to attend to and control criminogenic youth in Canada. A year later, a triple murder was committed by a young offender in a quiet middle-class neighbourhood in Southwestern Ontario. Research data presented here are the result of intensive interviews conducted with the youth while incarcerated in a secure custody youth facility in the province of Ontario. Possibly of greater importance is the inclusion of additional interviews upon release during which this individual reflected upon time spent in secure custody, revealed impressions of the *Young Offenders Act* and graphically described details of life after incarceration.

Of primary concern is this offender's impressions of the quality of life within the walls of a secure custody youth facility. However, in order to assess concisely this offender's experience, it is necessary to provide an essence of the quality of life before the murders, during incarceration and upon release. In order to increase accuracy, evidence is presented from a youth worker employed at and familiar with this offender's facility. To conclude this case study, the way in which this particular individual manipulated the *Young Offenders Act* into incentive to commit society's most heinous crime is developed and analysed.

Life Before the Murders

Probings into this offender's early adolescence revealed that constant parental physical and mental abuse resulted in this youth becoming the most consistent deviant troublemaker at the public school attended by this offender. Feared by other students, this youth was ostracized by other students, routinely punished and suspended by teachers and physically punished for these infractions by this offender's parents. A vicious cycle of abuse developed which included this youth's habitual involvement in alcohol and drug use, the practice of Satanism, theft and repeated physical assaults upon other students. The young offender describes life before the murders in this way:

G.O.   You say your Dad used to whip you?

Y.O.   Yeah, with a belt with a Budweiser buckle—that's how I got into Budweiser beer! (Laughs) He used to just crack that across my face..., and I got the telephone book treatment, 'cause he used to have a friend who was a cop—a crooked cop—and he used to come home and if I was bad or something or was suspended from school he'd just pick up the book an' whack me across the face or something like that.

G.O.   That doesn't sound too cool—wow—you feel like talkin' about motive or reasons why you did it?

Y.O.   I guess a little bit. Just that I felt that I'd been rejected more—that I was outcast from the family—I felt that they were against me 'cause they always had an eye on me in school because I was bad. I felt betrayed 'cause they'd always say if you have a problem instead of getting in trouble at school, come an' talk to us, right? So I tried comin' an' talkin' to them twice, so like "I need to talk about it"—you know, it's okay we don't sit down talkin' about it, you know if it's a girl or whatever then they'd start gettin' personal about it an' expressin' their feelings about it—like they'd get angry with me about why I was bein' upset, instead of helping me or comforting me with it, you know, they'd start gettin' mad about whatever it was that was buggin' me—an' comin' down on me for it—which didn't make me feel any easier about comin' to them again.

G.O.   Like takin' the other side?

Y.O.   Right!

G.O.   Sayin' that you were in the wrong?

Y.O.   Right! Rather than help me out..., an' I thought what's the use of comin' an' talkin' with them when they didn't wanna help me.

G.O.   Right.

Y.O.   Even if they didn't say anything..., they offered an' they fucked me up—jus' rejection an' stuff—that was a little bit part of it—just all the emotional strain that they gave me, I just felt like they're..., (pause) I needed to get out "cause their treatment was bad an' I just couldn't handle bein' there—I jus' kept thinkin' what if it gets like when I'm twenty, if I'gonna be alive sorta thing..., you know? I don't like bein' controlled—like to that degree—an' I couldn't handle it.

G.O.   Seems like the little bit I've read about your father..., he sorta lived on the outside himself—he was almost like a rebel.

Y.O.   Sorta..., he was into illegal gambling and cocaine dealing and all sorts o'shit. I never knew about that 'til after I was charged but I knew somethin' was up. There were people after him an' stuff to kill him.

G.O.   Really?

Y.O.   Yeah..., an' he was always after me to get ready to take over an' kept sayin' "If anything happens to me...." I never clicked into any of this shit 'til now, but he used to always say that I want you to learn the ropes of my business so you can take over for me, you know? The fuckin' guy was jus' settin' me up to get wasted, you know? Nice Dad, huh? I only wanted to kill him, I didn't wanna do my Mother or my sister..., my sister was a total accident—that was a..., I never meant it. That was jus' something that fucked up when I went down, I didn't mean to do it at all. It was more my Dad, because my Dad jerked me around an' I needed to get out an' I didn't like him settin' me up.

G.O.   That's an awful lot of pressure on a fourteen-year-old.

Y.O.   Most of it you can't explain 'cause it's all feelings and you just can't get them out.

G.O.   I understand..., it can be rough.

Y.O.   I'm not a person who goes outa my way to bug people an' shit..., I mean..., my crime is a situation that'll never happen again—something that happened because I lived in that environment an' that's the only way at the time I thought I could get out of—by doin' that—I realize now I could a done a lot of other things to get out of that situation but I was just a stupid fourteen-year-old kid who didn't, you know..., see any better than violence an' stuff, because that's what I was used to.

At this juncture, the conversation shifted towards the *Young Offenders Act* to ascertain whether the youth felt that this new legislation facilitated or exacerbated this abusive parental situation. Establishing whether the youth was aware of this new legislation before committing the murders was of initial importance as well as any type of reactions to it.

G.O.   Before all of this went down did you know about this new thing called the *Young Offenders Act*?

Y.O.   Oh yeah..., the police and all..., they had this big thing in our school—the auditorium—in about '84 when they first brought out the *Young Offenders Act*. So everybody was..., we went and sat in the auditorium an' listened to them..., they were all goin' through a list of what you get for whatever charge an' they were talkin' about the *Young Offenders Act* an' how it's s'posed to be better than the *Juvenile Delinquents Act* an' all that stuff. It had only been a month old or not even..., it was the first couple weeks..., they were jus' bringin' it out. I remember sittin' there an' jus' laughin' at it thinkin' fuck, thirty days for shoplifting all this shit! I remember sayin' it to one kid, 'cause I planned to wipe out my teachers 'cause they were always fuckin' me around—I wasn't that serious about it, right? I was jus' sayin', "Fuck..., I'll only get three years!"

Under extreme physical and emotional pressure and accustomed to the deployment of violence in the settling of disputes, this offender shifted the focus from teachers to parents and began to plan the murder of the father. After locating the family hunting rifle and practising repeatedly to effect rapid fire, this offender expanded the plan to include the mother as well as the father:

Y.O.   The day before I stayed home from school, faked I was sick an' they were real cool to me bringin' me tea an' stuff. After he went out my Mom came over an' gave me a hug an' told me she loved me..., I could see the reflection in the microwave..., but my mind was made up..., because she loved him so much..., she'd have to go too.

After executing the parents on the morning of the murders, a bullet accidentally dislodged from the rifle and embedded itself in the lung of a younger sister, the remaining family member. After six hours, the sister died of asphyxiation.

Y.O.   Like I told you before..., I only really wanted to kill him. I didn't really want to do my mother—my sister was a total accident. I was really fucked up when it went down..., I didn't mean to do her at all.

Arrest and Incarceration

Not completely believing that three murders had been committed, this young offender attempted to continue throughout the day as if everything was normal. Peers soon realized that this individual was deeply troubled and they demanded some form of explanation. The youth confessed to the murders and offered to illustrate the carnage to these peers as an explanation for the source of the personal trouble as well as proof to the youth that the murders had actually happened and that it was not a particularly heinous illusion. After a tour of the home this peer group agreed to a pact of silence. However, later that evening a member of that peer group experienced nightmares and complained to his parents. In an effort of reassurance the parents of this peer group member requested that the police verify that all was normal at the murdered family's residence. The police discovered the bodies, then located the remaining family member (who confessed to the crime of premeditated murder) and effected an arrest. The arrest procedure and resulting confinement were executed to the letter of the law as prescribed by the *Young Offenders Act*. This resulted in this young offender being treated in a far better manner than had been previously anticipated:

G.O.   When you were arrested, what was the atmosphere like? Were they jivin' you or giving you a hard time or were they nice to you?
Y.O.   No, nobody ever bugged me.
G.O.   No?
Y.O.   I was treated like a king, actually!
G.O.   Yeah?
Y.O.   Like, when I was in the police station that night in my own cell, they asked if I wanted anything for breakfast—they went out an' brought me breakfast—anything I wanted..., gave me a pack of smokes.
G.O.   Really?
Y.O.   They they... jumped to every command had, sorta. Jus' to make sure I was treated properly....
G.O.   Yeah..., 'cause this was a major test of the *Young Offenders Act* in all of Canada..., I guess they wanted to make sure it went down to the letter of the law..., you know..., not lose out on a technicality.
Y.O.   You got it! That's exactly it.

In total, this young offender served eleven months "dead time" which refers to time that is served in secure custody while the criminal proceedings are prepared by the Crown and defence attorneys. The first month of this "dead time" was served at a smaller congested youth facility in a major Southwestern Ontario metropolis while the remaining ten months were served at a more modern and larger youth facility in a smaller Southwestern Ontario city. This offender explains this procedure and transfer in this way:

Y.O.   I was in the holding cells at the police station for about four hours until they showed up and did all these questions an' stuff an' said they were gonna send me to _____ (smaller youth facility) detention centre to hold me until court which was on Monday, 'cause I was arrested on a Saturday morning 1:24 a.m., I still remember that!

G.O.   Really?

Y.O.   Yeah..., 'cause I remember them sayin' "Time of arrest 1:24 a.m." So I went to _____ an' waited 'til Monday for court an' it was remanded for a couple weeks or something like that..., an' went through the normal routines there in the detention centre, like gym an' stuff like that.

G.O.   What was that like?

Y.O.   It was slow! The way time was goin' I thought a couple weeks after courts over I'd be out, 'cause like every day seemed like a month! So like I thought three years, four years had gone by in only a couple weeks! After a month I was there they said they were gonna transfer me to _____ (larger youth facility) for treatment..., like ah..., assessment treatment. They were gonna check me out an' I was gonna be there for four weeks, I was just there in the OMD, right? Like same as that other place, just detention—then they asked me, "Do you wanna go back?" an' I was just about to start my trial then too, or so I thought, an' I said no..., that I liked it there 'cause you do more there you could play more sports an' stuff. It's a good place..., it's a great place for kids. For someone like me, I mean to be in an environment like that where things are sorta controlled—you don't need to worry about anything on the outside..., it's all right.

Trial and Sentencing

Both the Crown and the defence had agreed to not move this case up to adult court (as per section 4 of the *Young Offenders Act*—Alternative Measures, and section 16-17) but to try this murder case under a plea of not-guilty by reason of insanity. The success of this plea would result in this offender being committed to a mental health facility on an indeterminate sentence. In order to attain this sentence, the Crown is obligated to prove that the defendant was insane at both the actual time of the crime and in the courtroom at the time of the trial. Even though this offender's own psychiatrist testified that three days before the triple slaying he felt the youth was "seriously ill" and "recommended immediate psychiatric treatment" and two Crown-appointed psychiatrists also testified that this youth was "easily frustrated," "a bully" and "was not able to direct the youth's mind toward the consequences of the act," the judge rejected this plea of not-guilty with the explanation that, "he knows what is going on in this courtroom."

Therefore, what remained for this young offender was the maximum disposition available under section 20 of the *Young Offenders Act*, which at that time was three years in a secure custody youth facility. For three counts of first degree murder, this young offender was sentenced to three years. After this sentence was rendered and it's perceived leniency digested by the Crown, the prosecuting attorney applied to have the case re-opened in order to have it re-tried in adult court. The judge rejected this motion as he felt it would "fly in the face of the law." Since guilty verdicts are not appealable and since this offender received the maximum sentence under the *Young Offenders Act* no further movement could be made on this case. The judge also recommended psychiatric treatment, which this individual was allowed to, and did, refuse, and prohibited the youth from possessing any object that could be construed as a weapon for life. On the day the sentence was rendered, the National News Service in Ottawa released this statement to summarize this decision:

> Accepts Opinion—the judge said he accepted the opinion of the two psychiatrists who said the accused had a "disease of the mind" but did not accept that the youth could not appreciate the nature and quality of the act. Both elements are necessary to establish insanity under the criminal code.
>
> Ball said that he "was not unmindful of the concern of the public in this case." However, he said the blame for this sentence lies not with him or the *Young Offenders Act*, but with the Crown's decision not to have the case transferred to adult court in the first place. The *Young Offenders Act* has provisions for serious cases to be transferred to adult court at the outset, "and this was a serious case if there ever was one." The judge reminded the Crown that he had asked him when the psychiatrists were giving evidence whether the case should be transferred to adult court and the Crown had decided that he did not feel it was necessary.

Life Within a Secure Custody Youth Facility

Upon conviction this young offender became a resident of a secure custody facility in a smaller Southwestern Ontario city. Referred to as "the Hilton" of youth correctional facilities by staff and social workers, this youth quickly became accustomed to the quality of life within the walls of this total institution. This individual describes aspects of the three years spent in secure custody in this way:

G.O.   Since you've just been released maybe you could take me through..., uh..., what would a day be like?

Y.O.   A week day you wake up at 7:00 a.m., get showered an' all that an' get ready for breakfast—go to school at 9:20 in the morning..., like go to school..., regular classes....

G.O.   In there?

Y.O.   Yeah..., and then you get out at 11:30 and you sit around in the unit, watch TV, play cards, whatever 'til 1:20—you know, have lunch too—1:20 you go back to school for the rest of the afternoon, different subjects—four periods in the morning, three in the afternoon. I guess from a quarter after three 'til five is your free time—you do whatever you want to sorta thing—do whatever you want in the unit, stereo, TV, play guitar—5:00 is dinner—then from 5:30 to 6:15 you're in your room for quiet time..., give the staff time to do their writing, I guess....

G.0.   Right.

Y.O.   Then the rest of the night you have gym periods or movies or whatever—order pizza, play music—then you go to bed at ten o'clock unless you have a program where you can uh..., then to eleven..., stay up on a weeknight to watch TV or something. At 11:00 everybody is locked in their room..., and it happens again, same thing over....

G.O.   So there is an actual lock on your room?

Y.O.   (nods) Yep!

G.O.   No bars though, eh?

Y.O.   Barred windows.

G.O.   Yeah..., but is it a humane type of thing?

Y.O.   Oh yeah..., for sure! It's more like uh..., it's not even close to bein' like a jail..., I mean..., the only thing that makes you think it's like a jail is that you have to ask for certain things—like, I was the first one to have money, like contraband—it's considered contraband in there—money, gum, stuff like that, right? Not allowed to have that—I was the first one to be allowed to have money—here I am the most dangerous kid in Canada, so they say, and I'm the first trusted with all these contraband things in that place..., like bracelets... these weren't allowed in case I wanted to smack somebody—I was allowed all sorts of things.

G.O. So did they sorta give these things to you as....

Y.O. As I earned them, yeah—I earned them—I earned their trust..., I didn't show any problems that I was gonna use them against anybody or myself—so I earned everything I had (says proudly)—I was the first to earn an extension cord in my room! To play an amplifier and guitar—electric guitar—I was the first one to have cowboy boots with spurs..., to be able to wear them in that place—first one to wear earrings that hang and dangle..., yeah, I did well in there!

G.O. Was it fun?

Y.O. Oh yeah..., for the most part. A whole lot better than what I had before... you know, before all that shit went down. It was a great place to grow up and mature.

G.O. So I guess the ultimate reward would be allowing you to go to work, right?

Y.O. Yeah, but before I went to work I had passes like, once every two weeks with two staff—I'd go out an' see a movie..., or shop whatever.

G.O. Really? Staff people cool?

Y.O. Yeah..., I get to pick who I wanna go with, so I picked the ones I was good with..., friends with.

G.O. So they must've been paying you in there, huh?

Y.O. I worked in the tuck shop in there and made money.

G.O. Yeah, 'cause you had to buy..., a B.C. Rich is an expensive guitar!

Y.O. Six hundred bucks! I made money through that an' home ec. (economics) cooking—I had my own cake business in there! HA! Two murderers in there havin' a cake business! (Laughs) People were buyin' our cakes an' it was great! In there you can't judge somebody by their crime, because everybody's a person..., an' I agree that people that murder to get life, that are nuts like people who don't regret what they do, don't give a shit about it..., you know? I mean, I didn't show any remorse..., I don't cry.

G.O. I see..., *Young Offenders Act* says, "an extensive review process provided to monitor and re-evaluate changing needs of the young offender." Like... as you were growing older, did they sorta monitor what you wanted to do....

Y.O. Yeah, yeah..., they wanted to make sure I had thing for me when I got out, like get me set up..., you know? Get me a place, get me into work, get me used to working so when I got out I can just leave and know what the fuck was goin' on.

G.O.   So they helped you get your temporary job?

Y.O.   Yeah, they helped me get my job—workin' in a fuckin' warehouse—they helped me get in touch with people to get my place..., they helped me to get me out on passes to like check out what the world's like..., budgeting, bank accounts and shit like that.

G.O.   Really?

Y.O.   Like I did my own banking an' stuff..., like I went and opened my own bank account an' stuff..., I didn't need their help for that—like to get out! Just to get outa that place..., go downtown an' see what it's been like in three years..., see what life's like, how expensive it is to live..., what good music is..., what everyone's wearin'..., you know, stuff you don't see when you're locked up. So they helped me with that stuff.

G.O.   So in that regard, they (youth facility and staff) did pretty well then, huh?

Y.O.   Yep!

G.O.   So would you say..., did they offer you what they call rehabilitation?

Y.O.   Yeah..., that place did! But not the act. (Y.O.A.) I guess that place did—'cause the act seems a lot different like in what it says than what that place did—because like I met a lot of staff there doin' their job professionally an' not holdin' against me what I did which most staff in there do—but the staff I'm close to gave me a chance, right? In order to build a friendship an' feel confident enough in myself to go on day to day in that place an' try to make something of myself—deal with what I did an' try an' get on..., so I got that with some staff. But some staff there are just assholes an' they really pissed me off sometimes.

A Youth Worker's View

During the late fall of 1991 a chance encounter resulted in contact with a youth worker who was present and employed at the same secure custody youth facility that this young offender was held. This youth worker revealed that on many occasions occupational time was spent with this individual during the entire length of incarceration. When questioned about this young offender the youth worker readily admitted clear recollection of the youth's behaviour while incarcerated. This was revealed in this way:

Y.W.   Sure I remember! But I can get in deep shit talkin' about it...,
        well..., maybe not now 'cause it's pretty well water under the
        bridge..., what the hell!
G.O.   Well, you don't have to if it'll cause you any heat.
Y.W.   Well..., let's see where we get to..., Yeah..., I remember (*him/her*).
        _____ was a real shit disturber! A grand pain in the ass! Always into
        something..., causing trouble..., even inciting a riot a couple of
        times..., real trouble!
G.O.   Really? You must be kiddin'! That's not what I heard. _____ told me
        that _____ did real well in there. You know, at school, socially...,
        even earned rewards.
Y.W.   You have to understand what it's like in there, like the pecking order
        of importance. This kid killed three people..., murdered them in cold
        blood.... _____ knew this and also knew this was a big deal!
        Everyone in there knew _____ was a murderer, a "teen killer" and
        this kid acted as if it would and could happen again if just the right
        combination of buttons were pressed. Without question, _____ was
        the king of the castle in there, man! _____ ran the joint. Everyone
        stayed clear of _____. If this kid wanted anything from anyone else,
        _____ got it, no questions asked.
G.O.   How about friends..., social adjustment..., good?
Y.W.   Just one or two other murderers—a couple of them had a cake
        business or something—they thought it was pretty funny to be doing
        something good like that when they were supposed to be punished
        for murder. _____ worked in the tuck shop for awhile but we had to
        take him out of there 'cause other residents wouldn't go in there
        when _____ was working. They felt too intimidated, or so they said.
G.O.   Really? Tell me, in your estimation do you thing that _____ was
        rehabilitated in any way?
Y.W.   Not in my mind. Not by a long shot. A real hard case. _____ was
        almost proud of what _____ did, at least that's what it seemed like to
        me.
G.O.   You mean while incarcerated?
Y.W.   No, the murders! You see, with a lot of those kids parents are
        authority figures not friends or pals. When they see commercials that
        show a mother and daughter discussing something like problems with
        school work or boys, or fathers taking their sons to play hockey they
        fuckin' roar with laughter. Parents are authority figures, like cops or
        security guards that stand in the way of adulthood. You know sort of
        impede freedoms to get high, get pissed, skip school and have sex. It
        was very well known that _____ sure didn't like the situation at home
        so did something about it. _____ offed _____ parents. That made _

kind of a hero in the other resident's eyes. You remember that movie where the broadcaster guy says "I'm madder 'n hell an' I'm not gonna take it anymore?" That's how they looked at ____ —like a real superstar celebrity..., and believe you me ____ just lapped it up—I mean revelled in it every day, you know? But ____ was a real smart cookie—knew right under the *Young Offenders Act.*

G.O.   What do you mean?

Y.W.   Like for instance, the act allows for any residents to refuse psychiatric therapy, and ____ did refuse. Nobody could get close enough to figure out what made ____ tick, so everyone kinda just walked on eggshells. In my mind that just prevented ____ from getting any help for these deep seated problems, and believe you me this one really needed help! Like, ____ never showed any remorse for those three murders. That just blew all of us away..., I mean not only was ____ not sorry in any way, really seemed to be proud of it. Nobody could push ____ around—not even the parents. Like I said before Gary, ____ was sharp enough to know that this would gain status in there and ____ certainly used it..., every fucking day. __ _ intimidated everyone in there, including the staff..., a real bad kid for sure.

G.O.   Do you think ____ learned anything while incarcerated?

Y.W.   Learned how to have fun! (Laughs) It was a cakewalk for ____..., absolutely fun and games. ____ figured out exactly how to manipulate the staff to get these rewards you were tellin' me about but at the same time carve out a large helping of fun for ____ self. I bet you thought they were punished in places like that, huh? It looks like punishment but like this kid proves, it can be manoeuvered to be a lot of fun. I don't know what kind of upbringing you had, but I'll tell you I never had some of the comforts these residents have. It's amazing how they abuse them too!

Post Incarceration

Having served the maximum term of incarceration under the *Young Offenders Act* in secure custody, (total time served was three years plus eleven months "dead time") this offender was released from this closed security youth facility. A huge public outcry and swirl of controversy generated by all media sources greeted this youth upon release. To escape the constant harassment of news reporters and cameramen, the youth hitchhiked to the United States for a holiday. After returning to Ontario after ten days during which the youth did little else but drink alcohol and attend rock music venues, we agreed to a further series of interviews. During this time frame of approximately three months, the young offender began a downhill slide into deep depression and anomie characterised by alcohol abuse, vandalism, homelessness and police harassment. Realizing that the celebrity status experienced during incarceration had evaporated upon release, the youth could not steer clear of trouble in any aspect of life.

G.O.   When did you get back?

Y.O.   Oh a little while ago..., I haven't stopped drinkin' since I been out! I haven't been drunk once yet at all..., at least I don't think so. Other people been sayin' I was but I guess I don't feel it as much. Believe me, it's been pretty wild!

(Approximately five weeks later)

G.O.   Hi! How ya been?

Y.O.   Yeah..., (pause)..., I'm just sorta in hiding away from everybody.

G.O.   Why?

Y.O.   Well..., I tried to kill myself on Sunday.

G.O.   What??? Why?

Y.O.   'Cause I'm just not happy with the way things are goin'—it's just hassle after hassle. The cops have been hasslin' me all fuckin' Easter..., ever since we last talked. I've been pulled over so many times I can't count..., on the street. I haven't done nothin' man, just walkin' down the street an' they pull me over an' tell me I'm wanted for theft, wanted for this an' that..., I fit the description of so an' so. Fuck they won't leave me alone man! So I ended up talkin' off on this one guy—I don't know why I did it—I come outa the pool hall, okay..., first this guy pulls me over an' like I say, "I've got nothin' to say to you an' if you got anything to say..., you got no right hasslin' me—I want my lawyer if you're gonna talk to me this way...."

G.O.   This is a cop?

Y.O.   Yeah..., so he says okay, fine..., bye—so I went away, played pool come outa the pool hall an' he comes speedin' over with another car behind him an' both pulled over beside me. Just before they got outa the car I took off—I don't know why I did it, but like I got nervous and I ran—I ran an' got away from them an' shit so now I was goin' to the train station, forgettin' about this happening an' there was cops everywhere all lookin' for me, right, so then I went an' jumped on a bus that was at a stop on the street so I've been in _____ (another small city) ever since sleepin' in a construction site an' it's fuckin' cold!

G.O.   So the cops are lookin' for you in _____?

Y.O.   Yeah for like I haven't done nothin' but I could go back an' get busted for whatever it is they want and after a day or two when it's straightened out and it's over with..., but they're fuckin' hasslin' me man an' I don't know why.

G.O.   Just harassment.

Y.O.   Right on! Like if some staff at _____ (youth facility) has set something up or somebody's settin' me up or something an' it's gettin' to me so I'm just tryin' to get away from it 'cause I'm gonna fuckin' blow a fuse soon an' then just..., I dunno..., I can't handle this shit.

G.O.   So what's this..., you tried to kill yourself on Sunday..., whatdya mean?

Y.O.   Yeah..., (pause)..., I just thought I might as well go out enjoyin' it, right..., so I thought well fuck it I'll just drink an' hope I die so I took two twenty-sixers straight, non-stop..., drank both of 'em an' just fuckin' dropped and passed out, right? I'm still sick from it, throwing up an' I haven't eaten since like Friday—haven't eaten a thing.

G.O.   Where was this now? Where did y'all do this?

Y.O.   Oh, I took a chance an' came home..., I did this at home—I just took it an' drank it passed out an' woke up in puke—I been sick ever since, I can't eat or nothin' man—just livin' on cigarettes..., so it didn't work.

G.O.   Fuck man..., you don't wanna do that!

Y.O.   I thought about today...; if I really wanna do it right I could get an easier way an' pretend I'm pullin' a gun on one of those cops an' like..., (pause)..., like I don't wanna really do it, but I was doin' it like in a way maybe it could happen.

G.O.   C'mon..., get it together!

Y.O.   Yeah..., but life's a drag..., but my record for phone booths is up to seven now!

G.O.   Phone booths? What dya mean?

Y.O.   Pay phones..., I total them—to relieve my frustrations—you know, rip out the wires, smash shit outa them—the last one was the best! All six panes o' glass an' the phone on the ground. I never realized I could be charged a hundred dollars for wreckin' them!

G.O.   Probably a lot more than that if you get caught.

Y.O.   I won't get caught..., I'm too fast for the cops!

G.O.   What happened to all this talk of being a rock an' roll singer? You can't be a rock an' roll singer dead!

Y.O.   Maybe in my next life, I dunno..., I been in a twilight zone since... like I don't have parents an' I don't have a sister and that's my fault—I fucked that up—I regret that like so much because I miss them so bad an' I wanna..., I don't know..., I got no fuckin' friends—nobody I can call up an' just go out an' hang out with an' shit. I don't know how to make friends an' shit like that..., like I been away from that shit for four years right? I don't know about much except what I been doin' for the last four years like goin' to work sometimes an' hangin' out by myself an' shit. I just wanna go off by myself an' meditate for hours—I can never find the time to think—this is the first time I talked to anyone about this shit.

G.O.   I'm honoured you'd call me. Listen..., the world is a fuckin' crazy place sometimes and after you've been locked up for a time the outside never seems to be what you'd think it was when you were inside.

Y.O.   That's not it, man. It's me thinkin' more now about what I did..., I mean when I was in there, like it's still not a shock to be able to do anything. It's a problem yeah with money only because I'm stupid and I go an' spend it on stupid things..., but I mean it's just the problem of being one person.... That's my fuckin' problem! I have a war with myself is what it is.... I'm slowly killing myself because inside I'm fightin' with myself for everything.

G.O.   You feelin' guilty about what you did? Like when you were inside there was so much goin' on and there was such a structure that you didn't really have time to sit back and think of..., you know.

Y.O.   Yeah..., you're right. I also didn't get enough time to realize or see things to realize what I missed. I mean..., everyday I see a fuckin' little girl on the bus that reminds me of my sister and it bums me out....

Conclusion

And doin' time isn't a hassle, it's what you make it to be. I've done well..., I never served time, I made time serve me.

According to this quotation taken from a letter written to this author by this young offender while still incarcerated, life within the walls of the maximum security youth facility was not the least bit unpleasant. Due to the enormity of the crime committed and the resultant media publicity, this offender received high status among other inmates and became clever enough to use this high status to this youth's advantage. Consequently, mandatory skills training resulted in little more than recreational activities and methods by which to exert influence while passing time. None of these skills became transferable to life after release.

Of greater importance, staff attempts at socializing this young offender to life outside of incarceration failed to provide this youth with any acceptable value system. Rudimentary functions of societal life were either ignored or replaced by habitual deviant pursuits. What resulted was the vicious cycle of abuse predominant during adolescence being re-enacted in the form of self-abuse after the passage of four years.

For this young offender what was desired at the age of fourteen, that is the permanent eradication of parental control, was accomplished. The factual evidence presented here inform that very little had changed in the mind set of this youth by the age of eighteen. Personality characteristics possessed before the premeditated murders were nearly identical to those displayed after incarceration. This may be attributed to a type of breakdown in the rehabilitative capabilities of the closed security facility, but although this may be a contributing factor, it is the opinion of this author that it is not the only one.

Of crucial concern is this youth's admission that this new legislation designed to attend to and control criminogenic youth in Canada was employed as an accelerator or facilitation device in the commission of murder. Once informed by police that the *Young Offenders Act* would provide a maximum disposition of three years in a closed security youth facility instead of an indeterminate term in a mental health facility as prescribed under the *Juvenile Delinquents Act*, this youth realized that planning and committing three murders would solve all problems on the homefront. In the initial letter to this author, this feeling is succinctly stated:

> In the way it's worked (the Y.O.A.) and is working for me is that it gave me three years and that helped a lot 'cause fuck man, I was just a stupid fourteen-year-old thinkin' I knew everything and tryin' to prove I was though, well gettin' three years was cool 'cause in that time I was able to get away from ordinary life and get my head together and that's exactly what I did. Fuck, I just needed time to clear my head of the bullshit I was into (Satanism) and grow up and mature which is what really helped me. Just having time to be able to be in a secure setting and not have to worry about ordinary outside life and just mature.

It is truly unfortunate that legislation designed to inhibit and control criminal activity actually resulted in the promotion of criminality.

Chapter 6

The Use of Detention for Aboriginal Offenders in East James Bay Courts

Carol LaPrairie

Introduction

The use of carceral sentences for aboriginal people in Canada has been at the heart of the aboriginal criminal justice discourse for two decades. Clarity, however, about the exact nature of dispositional practices has not been apparent because of the difficulties in controlling for the range of variables which confront judges at the time of sentencing. For this reason, unwarranted disparity in the sentencing of aboriginal and non-aboriginal offenders remains the prevalent explanation for the over-representation phenomenon. The available data, however, are contradictory at best and for every finding that appears to treat aboriginal offenders more severely there is another which suggests the opposite. The research reported here by no means provides a definitive answer to the unwarranted disparity charge but does give some information about the use of detention (incarceration) in one aboriginal region of Canada—James Bay, Quebec.

The data on which this article are based emerged from a larger study of crime and disorder in the east James Bay Cree communities and the response of the criminal justice system, where sentencing was one component. The findings, which run counter to the prevailing thesis that aboriginal accused are given carceral dispositions more frequently than are non-aboriginals for the same offences, suggest that there are no simple answers to the over-representation phenomenon. Moreover, the findings argue for further research in other geographic areas to more clearly delineate which variables are most significant in determining the sentencing of aboriginal accused to terms of detention.

Sentencing Aboriginal Accused

Recent inquiries into the situation of Canadian aboriginal people in relation to the dominant criminal justice system have all commented on the sentencing of aboriginal offenders as this is the single most important criminal justice factor in determining who serves time in correctional institutions. The Manitoba Justice Inquiry (1991) was scathing in its indictment of the over-use of incarceration, in general, and particularly in relation to aboriginal people. The authors of the report attributed this situation, in part, to the lack of pre-sentence reports, which would provide judges with more information about the accused and the propensity of aboriginal accused to plead guilty. They also commented on the dependence of courts on incarceration and noted that judges often consider only two options—incarceration or community service and generally view the latter as too lenient (Manitoba Justice Inquiry 1991: 392-398).

In a similar vein, the Law Reform Commission Report (1991) decried the extensive use of incarceration and argued for alternatives but at the same time recognized the complexities in explaining the "over-representation" phenomenon (LRCC 1991: 68-79). Previous work by the Standing Committee on Justice and the Solicitor General, however, was unequivocal in laying blame for the problem of the numbers of aboriginal people housed in Canada's correctional institutions when it stated: "One reason why Native inmates are disproportionately represented in the prison population is that too many of them are being unnecessarily sentenced to terms of imprisonment (Standing Committee, 1988: 211-12)."

There are, however, many unexplained and often ignored anomalies. There are research studies which have revealed, for example, that for some offences aboriginal accused receive shorter sentences than do non-aboriginals (Canfield and Drinnan, 1981; Moyer, 1987; Morse and Lock 1988). Unfortunately, there has not been a concerted effort to understand the relationship between the type of offence, characteristics of offenders, number and type of priors, and the use of detention. In addition, there have been few attempts to analyse the use of incarceration for certain offences, the disproportionate involvement of aboriginal people in the commission of these same offences, and the over-representation phenomenon. Perhaps, for example, if incarceration was totally eliminated for all but violent offences there would no longer be an over-representation problem in provincial institutions as aboriginal people appear to be disproportionately involved in and incarcerated for liquor act, fine defaults, and administrative failure offences. In these terms, the over-representation "problem" may be more appropriately viewed as a problem with the use of incarceration for certain offences rather than unwarranted disparity in sentencing.

This article has only a limited capacity to deal with fundamental issues of sentencing which require high level policy consideration and which were examined extensively by the Canadian Sentencing Commission (1987). What it can provide is information from one region of the country, James Bay, Quebec, regarding the use of detention (incarceration) in courts in which Cree youth and adult accused appear. It looks at the use of detention over a four-year period of time and, where possible, compares the findings to sentences given non-aboriginals for similar offences in other geographic locations.

Methodology

The research reported here was part of a larger justice study carried out in the James Bay region of Quebec in 1990-91 through the auspices of the Grand Council of the Crees (Quebec) and the Cree Regional Authority, the respective political and administrative arms of the Cree. The study from which these findings are taken examined the nature and extent of crime and disorder in the eight James Bay coastal and inland communities, the role of the communities in generating problems, informal and formal responses to crime and disorder, and what Cree people wanted by way of new justice approaches. Data were collected from police, court, youth protection and probation files and in interviews with Cree people and criminal justice personnel. Information from court files is reported here.

The youth and adult data, from which the findings below were drawn, were coded from four years of court files—1986-89 inclusive. Each file from the Itinerant Courts, which service the Cree communities on circuit and which sits in the urban areas of Val d'Or, Chibougamau, Senneterre and Amos and where Cree accused also appear, was coded using a case as the basic unit of analysis. Each case might involve one or more offences so information on all offences was collected as well as the most serious offence. Accused from James Bay who appeared in courts off-reserve in the same time period (either because of a same day appearance for serious offences or for offences committed in those areas) were included to provide an on-reserve/off-reserve and an urban/rural dimension. The urban court data were aggregated and are identified in the text as "Other" courts.

The data were analysed from three perspectives: Files (offences), Cases (appearances) and unique offenders. A program model that used five groups of offences (based on a scale of seriousness from existing scales in which Group 1 represented the most serious and Group 5 the least serious offences), cases with single and multiple counts and with prior offences, and dispositions based on degree of severity was designed. By using this model it was possible to determine the relationship between seriousness of offence and disposition, between cases with single and multiple offences and dispositions, and finally to determine what an offender walked out of the courtroom with as compared to what was received for each offence in the case. All analyses relating to dispositions are based on cases using severity of offence and a composition of offences comprising each case. All outcome findings refer to real as compared to nominal dispositions. Adult prior records were gathered within the data-set from youth and adult records.

Comparisons between the situation in James Bay and elsewhere were collected piecemeal as there was not readily accessible comparative data. For example, Statistics Canada data were used for youth court comparisons, special information on adult court processing was provided by the Department of Justice, Quebec and the Canadian Centre for Justice Statistics.

Findings

Dispositions given by judges at the conclusion of an appearance or trial were examined over the four-year period. There has been a preoccupation about the use of carceral sentences for aboriginal accused so this issue was one aspect of the analysis. Other issues were: the use of various dispositions; the effect of seriousness of offences on dispositions, urban/rural and community variation in sentencing, and the length and severity of sentences. Adult and youth dispositions were compared, as were dispositional findings from the Itinerant and urban courts in James Bay, to Canada and Quebec.

Dispositions

An analysis of the data revealed that the most common disposition given in adult court was fines (51%), followed by probation, detention and community service, each 13% and other (including concurrent and suspended sentences) at 10%; for youth, the most common disposition was community service (35%), followed by probation (26%), detention (23%), other (8%), and fines (8%) (Figures 1 and 2).

There is variation in the use of dispositions in the community and Other courts for adults and youth. For example, in youth cases in courts in Chisasibi, Great Whale River, Waskaganish and Waswanipi, community service orders are the most frequently used single disposition, whereas courts in Eastmain, Nemaska and Mistissini relied on simple probation, in Wemindji on a combination of both, and Other courts on detention. In adult cases, fines were the single most common disposition in all courts except in Great Whale River and Waswanipi, which relied more on "other" sentences (suspended\concurrent) and probation, respectively (Figures 3 and 4).

Figure 1

Dispositions - Adult Court, 1986-89

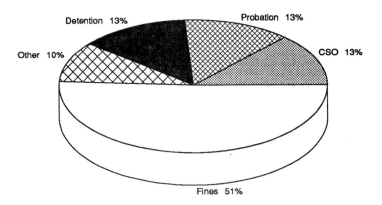

Where there was more than one offence in youth court, concurrent sentences were given in two-thirds of the cases (mostly involving Group 3

Figure 2

**Dispositions - Youth Court
1986-89**

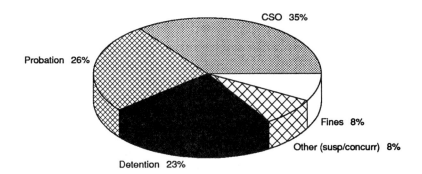

Figure 3

Disposition by Community
Youth Court, 1986-89

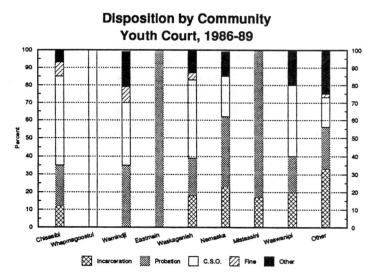

offences); the reverse, however, is true in adult court where consecutive sentences were most often given in cases of multiple offences (68%).

Figure 4

Disposition by Community
Adult Court, 1986-89

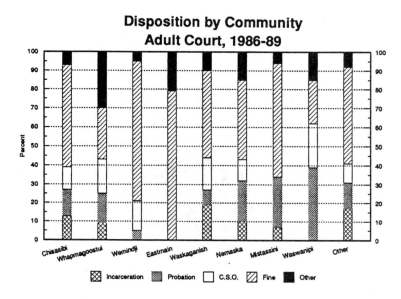

A particularly interesting finding relates to the actual number of Cree offenders who served detention orders. Figure 5 shows that from 1986-89, 106 actual (not concurrent) detention orders were given to 64 people which means that some individuals served more than one sentence; for youth, 62 detention orders were given to 39 youths. This suggests the repetitiveness of offenders and the shortness of sentences as these were given within a four-year period of time. It also demonstrates the importance of distinguishing admissions to correctional institutions from the actual individuals serving sentences. When examining Figure 5, it is important to remember that approximately 40% of accused adults and youths were repeat offenders over the four years and detention may have been only one of several dispositions. Thus, the individuals who actually served time probably also received non-carceral sentences for other offences.

Seriousness and Priors
In examining dispositions on the basis of seriousness, there was, for both adults and youth, a relationship between the seriousness of the offence, the prior record of the offender and detention. For example, 26% of youth and 30% of adult Group 1 offenders received a disposition of detention as compared to 3% (youth) and 6% (adult) for Group 4. Groups 3 and 4 (mainly involving B&Es and Failures, respectively) had higher use of detention than Groups 2 and 4 for both youth and adults probably because of the prior record of offenders (Figures 6 and 7).

Use of Detention in Urban and Rural Courts
When examining youth detention by urban and rural courts, the former use this disposition more frequently than the latter (Figure 8). There are community and urban\rural differences in adult court but these are less pronounced than those for youth (Figure 9). However, when examining the use of detention by seriousness for the courts which hear the most cases (i.e., Chisasibi, Waskaganish and Other), the urban\rural differences are less apparent (Figure 10 and 11). Judges in the urban courts requested psychological and social assessments more frequently than in rural courts (probably because of a lack of resources in the latter), and more often for youth than for adults.

Detention by Type of Offence
Examining the use of detention for adults and youth for particular offences reveals that it is most often used for aggravated assaults and robbery and frauds for adults, and assaults with a weapon (33%), Failures (17%) and B&Es (13%) for youth (Figures 12 and 13). Frauds for which detention was given usually involved multiple offences or offenders who had committed several frauds over time. Only one of the five fraud detention dispositions was for a

Figure 5

**Actual Individuals Detained by Actual
Detention Orders Served**
(not including concurrent orders)

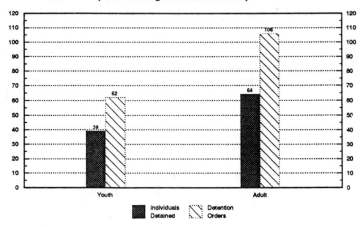

single fraud, and the other cases involved multiple frauds and forgeries.

Figure 6

**Use of Detention by Seriousness
Adult Court, 1986-89**
(% of all dispositions)

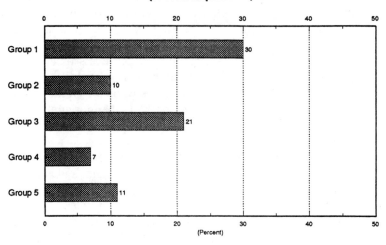

Figure 7

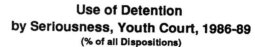

**Use of Detention
by Seriousness, Youth Court, 1986-89**
(% of all Dispositions)

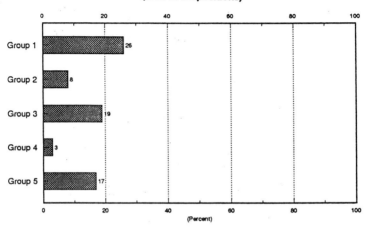

When assault with a weapon was the only offence, probation was the most common disposition. However, when the assault occurred in conjunction with

Figure 8

**Use of Detention by Community Court:
Youth Court, 1986-89**
(% of all dispositions)

Figure 9

Use of Detention by Community Court:
Adult Court, 1986-89
(% of all dispositions)

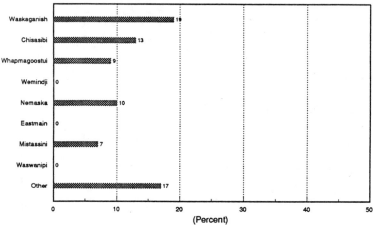

(Percent)

another offence such as a common assault and\or a B&E, a detention order might result. "Other" courts (i.e., urban) gave the majority of the detention orders for B&Es and one-half for assaults with a weapon.

Figure 10

Detention by Seriousness Offences
Urban/Rural, Adult Court, 1986-89

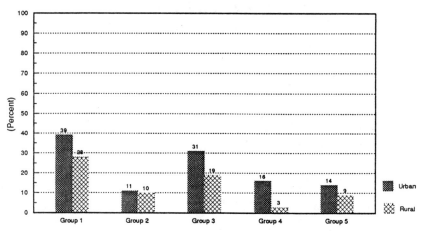

Figure 11

Detention by Seriousness Offences
Chisasibi, Waskaganish, Other Courts
Adult Court, 1986-89

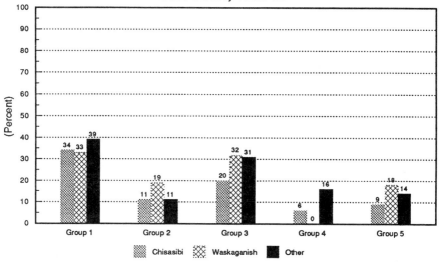

Figure 12

Use of Detention by Specific Offence
Adult Court, 1986-89

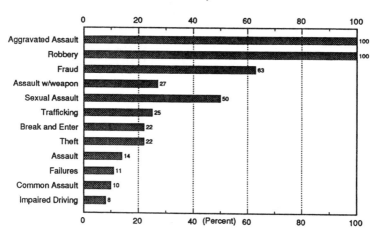

Figure 13

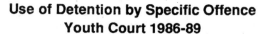

Use of Detention by Specific Offence
Youth Court 1986-89

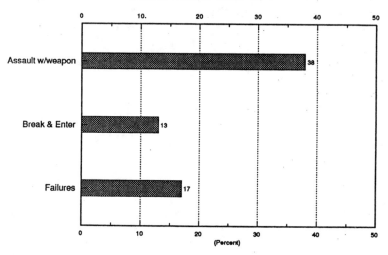

(Percent)

Detention and Priors
In looking at the prior records of accused where these were known (N=222), nearly 60% had prior records and the heaviest concentrations were for Failures to appear (88%), mischief (75%), B&Es (53%) and common assault (50%). In calculating prior records by the seriousness variable, over 60% of Groups 1 and 4, 50% of Groups 2 and 5, and 89% of Group 5 offenders had prior records (Figure 14).

In adult court, only 2% of offenders without a prior record received detention as compared to 19% with a prior record. No Group 3, 4 and 5 offenders without prior records received detention as compared to 9% in those same groups with prior records. The impact of the combination of seriousness and prior record on sentencing is revealed in Figures 15 and 16.

Severity of Detention
There was some similarity in the severity of sentences for adults and youth. The majority of detentions for both groups was three months or less (60% for youth and 79% for adults), and 96% of youth detention orders involved open custody (Figures 17 and 18). More severe dispositions involving longer detention were directly related to the seriousness of offences. For example, 59% of Group 1 adult offenders received more than three months detention as compared to 23% of Group 2, 30% of Group 3, 25% of Group 4, and none of Group 5.

Discussion

The above findings reveal that detention is used more often for youth than for adults, there are some urban\rural differences in the use of detention, and seriousness and prior records are important factors in determining the use of detention. These are discussed in turn below.

There are two issues to be considered in the way detention is used for youth; the first relates to differential use of detention for youth in urban and rural courts, and the second to the differential use of detention for adults and youth.

The variation in use of detention for youth and adults to a lesser degree, in urban as compared to rural courts, cannot be explained on the basis of seriousness of offence or prior record alone as urban courts do not hear the highest proportion of serious offences or repeat offenders, even though they are in the higher range of cases with multiple offences. Neither can it be explained solely on the basis of differences in judges as the same judges sit in most of the urban and rural courts.

Differential use of detention for youth is more likely explained by the reluctance of judges to sentence youth from rural areas to detention because of the distances from home communities, whereas offenders sent to detention from communities close to urban areas are generally more urban in outlook

Figure 14

Prior Record by Seriousness: Adult Court, 1989

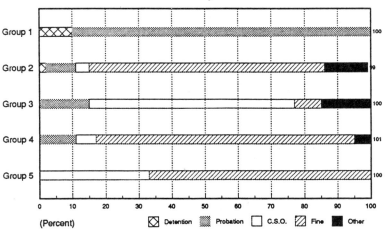

Figure 15

**Disposition by Seriousness with
No Prior Record, Adult Court, 1986-89**

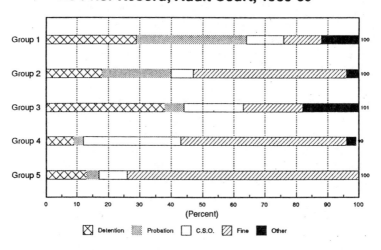

and lifestyle as well as being closer to home. Also, judges sentencing youth in urban courts may be directed by psychological and social investigations because more are ordered in these courts.

Figure 16

**Disposition by Seriousness with
Prior Record, Adult Court, 1986-89**

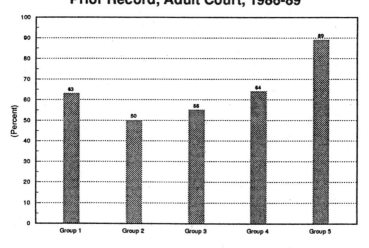

Figure 17

Time of Detention
Youth Court, 1986-89

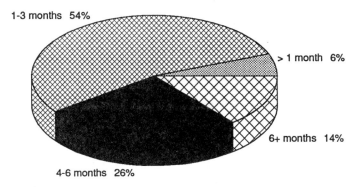

The more prevalent use of psychological and social investigations and detention for youth than for adults, may be attempts by judges to rehabilitate

Figure 18

Time of Detention
Adult Court: 1986-89

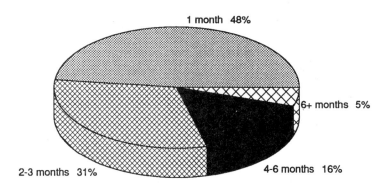

young offenders. The reliance on open custody and short sentences does not suggest punitiveness or severity on the part of judges but a rehabilitative approach. For adult offenders, however, sentencing is different. There is less use of detention and the urban\rural detention dimension is less pronounced. There is greater use of detention for adults in urban as compared to rural courts when the latter are combined but the differences are less when the courts are compared more directly for certain groups of offences. For example, detention is used similarly in Chisasibi, Waskaganish and Other courts for Group 1, 3 and 5 offences.

One explanation for using detention less often for adults than for youth may be that judges do not regard detention as having any particular rehabilitative value for this group. Despite the range of dispositions given offenders, their future offending behaviour does not appear to be dramatically affected. Findings from the larger study suggested that neither adult offenders nor communities regarded any of the dispositions as very useful in changing behaviour.

The other important area to consider in examining the findings is whether or not judges in the east James Bay courts are treating Cree accused more harshly than non-aboriginal accused elsewhere. As mentioned previously, comparable data were not collected during the data collection period primarily because of time and budget constraints so that information from existing sources had to be collected later from other jurisdictions. Because of this comparability is limited so the following provides some rough comparisons only.

Using Statistics Canada 1986-89 youth court data to compare offences and dispositions in James Bay courts to Canada and Quebec, reveals some differences. The proportion of assaults was 12% in James Bay and Canada and 16% in Quebec, but the proportion of B&Es in James Bay courts was almost double that of Canada or Quebec—47%, 21% and 25%, respectively. The use of detention in James Bay youth courts was almost identical to the Canadian figures (26% and 24%, respectively), but somewhat less than the use of detention in Quebec—31%. Considering that urban courts in James Bay use detention most frequently, the use of detention in community youth courts is much less than in Canada or Quebec. Virtually all the detention dispositions in James Bay courts are for open custody (96%) as compared to approximately 50/50 in Canada, and 60/40 (closed-open) in Quebec.

Community service orders are used far more extensively (nearly 6 times), fines approximately the same, and probation one-half as often for youth in the James Bay courts as in Canada or Quebec. Time of detention is the same for James Bay and Canada (60%) but more youth receive 3 months or less in James Bay courts than elsewhere in Quebec—60% and 51%, respectively. There is little variation in amounts of fine or length of probation among the three jurisdictions.

Comparative court data for adults are much more difficult than youth to acquire for Canada and Quebec. One source of comparison was provided, however, in the Val d'Or police occurrence records for 1989. These files systematically contain data on offences, charges and dispositions.

There was little variation in offence types between the Cree and non-Cree groups, except the Cree contained younger offenders and had twice the proportion of "escape from custody" offences for youth, while the non-Cree offenders were somewhat older and had more impaired and theft offences. The Cree received incarceration in 1% of cases as compared to 8% for non-Cree but more Cree cases than non-Cree were pending; Cree received simple fines three times more often than non-Cree who received probation and probation/ fine three times more often than Cree. The same proportion of cases was "not proceeded with" for both groups. These findings, however, are from police and not court files so are problematic because they may not contain the full range of information necessary to make reliable comparisons.

One of the few available studies comparing the sentencing of Cree and non-Cree was undertaken in Val d'Or in 1987 (Racicot:1987). Dispositional data for select offences were collected for a three-year period. The analysis revealed that dispositions for Cree offenders were generally more lenient for failures to comply, B&E with intent, assault, failure to appear offences; were generally the same for mischief, assault police officer, impaired and cause disturbance offences; and were generally more severe for assaults OBH. The difficulty with interpreting these further is the lack of information about prior records, which is the other major factor in sentence decision-making.

More recent dispositions in 10 Quebec provincial courts from January to March 1989, revealed the following: incarceration was given in 23% of the cases, fines 62%, probation 13%, and Other 1.7% (CCJS 1990). As mentioned previously, the comparable dispositions for James Bay courts over a four-year period from 1986-89 were incarceration 13%, fines 51%, probation/CSO 26%, and Other 10%. It should be stressed, however, that the Quebec courts data do not provide information on seriousness of offence or prior record of offender which makes comparisons difficult.

With regard to the available data (as well as police UCR data for 1990 which shows crimes against the person and total offences to be higher in the James Bay communities than in those of comparable size elsewhere in Quebec), sentences in the James Bay adult courts are not more severe and appear to be more lenient than those in other Quebec courts. Taken together, the findings suggest that while seriousness of offence and prior record are very important variables in determining dispositions (as has been found in general studies of sentencing) sentencing is complex in this region and other factors such as age, home community and the availability of resources, also come into play.

Conclusions

This paper has not attempted to deflect the accusation that aboriginal accused are disproportionately subjected to periods of incarceration than are non-aboriginals, but to provide some information about the use of detention in one region of the country. What the findings revealed is that detention appears to be used less in the region in general, and in the Cree communities in particular, than elsewhere in Quebec especially when adult accused are involved. The findings also revealed differences in the use of detention for adults and youth, and in urban and rural settings. These differences seemed to reflect an attempt to rehabilitate youthful offenders particularly if residing in communities close to urban areas. No such attempt was evident in the use of detention for adults.

More than anything else, this research identifies the need for a clearer enunciation and understanding of the over-representation phenomenon and of on-reserve\off-reserve, urban-rural, regional, and non-aboriginal\aboriginal differences in the use of detention. It also suggests the need for clarity about the relationship between the use of detention and the type of offences committed by aboriginal people. It may be that effective and long-lasting solutions to the over-representation problem will not be forthcoming until there is a more complete understanding of the issue.

Notes

1.   Aboriginal people would probably continue to be over-represented in federal institutions where their presence reflects a greater involvement in serious offences against the person.

References

Canadian Sentencing Commission. 1987. *Sentencing Reform: A Canadian Approach.* Ottawa: Supply and Services Canada.

Canfield, Carolyn and Linda Drinnan. 1981. *Comparative Statistics on Native and Non-Native Inmates—A Five Year History.* Ottawa: Correctional Service of Canada.

Law Reform Commission of Canada. 1991. *Report on Aboriginal Peoples and Criminal Justice.* Report 34, Ottawa.

McCaskill, Don. 1985. *Patterns of Criminality and Corrections among Native Offenders in Manitoba: A Longitudinal Analysis.* Ottawa: Correctional Service of Canada.

Morse, Brad and Linda Lock. 1988. *Native Offenders' Perceptions of the Criminal Justice System.* Ottawa: Department of Justice.

Moyer, Sharon. 1987. *Homicides Involving Adult Suspects 1962-1984. A Comparison of Natives and Non-Natives.* Ottawa: Ministry of the Solicitor General.

Muirhead, Gregory. 1983. *An Analysis of Native Over-representation in Correctional Institutions in B.C.* (unpublished) B.C.: Ministry of the Attorney General, Corrections Branch.

Racicot, Jean-Gilles. 1987. *Sentencing in the Cree Communities of James Bay: A Comparison Exercise.* Val d'Or.

Report of the Aboriginal Justice Inquiry of Manitoba. The Justice System and Aboriginal People. 1991. *Public Inquiry into the Administration of Justice and Aboriginal People.* Province of Manitoba.

Standing Committee on Justice and Solicitor General. 1988. *Taking Responsibility (Report on its Review of Sentencing, Conditional Release and Related Aspects of Corrections.* Ottawa.

Task Force on the Criminal Justice System and its Impact on the Indian and Metis People of Alberta. 1991. *Justice on Trial.* Edmonton, Alberta, March.

Chapter 7

Confronting Individual & Structural Barriers to Employment: The Employment and Skills Enhancement (EASE) Program for Prisoners

Denis C. Bracken and Russell J. Loewen

It is tempting to link unemployment to crime. The idea is a compelling one that if someone is not involved in some kind of "productive" labour, they are up to no good. In his historical study of unemployment, Garraty suggests that the unemployed have always been considered as potential criminals, and that proposed methods to ameliorate the problem of unemployment have been around almost as long as the problem itself.

> Unemployed persons have been treated as criminals who must be isolated from society or driven to hard labour, and as sinners to be regenerated by exhortation and prayer.... Nearly every scheme for both improving their lot and sustaining them in their misery that is currently in vogue, along with many no longer considered workable, was known and debated at least as far back as the 16th century. What actually has been done for the unemployed and about unemployment has depended upon the interaction of moral and religious attitudes, the sense of what is economically possible, the locus of political power in society, and the extent to which those who possess the power are aware of how unemployment affects both its victims and their own interests (Garraty, 1978 p. 9).

Conversely, one might say that if someone is, in fact, involved in productive labour, then chances are that he or she is quite unlikely to be participating in criminal activity. Indeed, the image of the criminal as someone who is not "working," in the traditional sense of the term, is an enduring one (Chambliss, 1964). Some would argue that the development of the prison in the 19th century was strongly influenced by the need to reinforce the routines of industrial discipline necessary for emerging industrial societies (cf. Rothman,

1990). As such, finding employment for people "at risk" of being involved in crime (particularly if they have been convicted of criminal activity before) has been a major part of efforts to keep people out of jail for over 100 years. As Rothman pointed out in the American context of the last century:

> The commitment to a daily routine of hard and constant labour...pointed to the close correspondence between the ideas on the causes of crime and the structure of the penitentiary. Idleness was part symptom and part cause of deviant behaviour. Those unwilling to work were prone to commit all types of offences; idleness gave time for the corrupted to encourage and instruct one another in a life of crime (Rothman, 1990, p. 103).

What we attempt to do in this chapter is to examine a program in place in two provincial prisons in Manitoba which tries to address directly a prisoner's chances of finding employment upon release in the context of looking at both structural barriers to employment, and personal ones. We consider this first within a context of some summary research on the relationship between unemployment and imprisonment, particularly with respect to the notion of recidivism, i.e., the likelihood of prisoners committing new offences following release from custody.

The idea that crime is likely to increase as unemployment increases is one initially considered by Rusche (1933). The needs of a labour market are thought to have an impact on the number of crimes committed, and, concomitantly, the number of people receiving convictions and prison sentences. Direct correlations between crime rates and unemployment rates, however, have not been well established.

In a review of the literature, Box and Hale (1986) found that "The best available evidence...does not provide unambiguous support for the hypothesis that unemployment causes more crime..." (p. 77). A subsequent review of the literature came to essentially the same conclusion (Crow, Richardson, Riddington & Simon, 1989, p. 11). What Box and Hale do suggest, however is the importance of the enduring perception:

> ...it is clear that many people believe that unemployment causes crime and this belief has real consequences, particularly when it affects decisions taken by state officials processing suspected and convicted persons (p. 72).

Indeed, they suggest that the evidence supporting this conclusion is easier to find. Reviewing several studies on factors employed in sentencing, they find that the employment status of the offender at time of sentencing will influence the likelihood of a custodial sentence. They believe that although research suggests no simple relationship between incarceration and crime rates, it "fails to dissuade the judiciary from using their commonsense notions of crime/causation to guide them in sentencing unemployed males" (p. 83).

In an extensive study of the relationship between unemployment and criminal offenders in the United Kingdom, Crow, Richardson, Riddington & Simon (1989) point out that what happens to an offender at various stages of the criminal justice process (e.g., bail, sentencing, parole) is quite likely to be influenced by whether or not the offender is employed or has a chance at employment. When one considers, as they do, that offenders by and large come from those segments of the population most often unemployed, the issue becomes an important one. They found that employment-related approaches to "rehabilitation" often neglect the situation of the labour market, and instead focussed on the perceived needs of the offender population for some type of training with the dual hope of getting these people employed and reducing the likelihood of their return to prison. There was very much a linkage, in the minds of these authors, between the presumed individual shortcomings of offenders and employment-related rehabilitation programs.

>...people convicted of offences tend to come from sectors of the population who are most at risk of unemployment or are disadvantaged in the labour market because they have few qualifications. One consequence of this was that in the past schemes for unemployed offenders were seen as rehabilitative, in the sense that their aim was to compensate for these deficiencies and to re-integrate offenders into what was taken to be normal working life.... Another feature of such schemes was that the emphasis was very much on the individual offender, rather than the needs of the labour market (p. 76).

Someone interested in working with prisoners on the issue of employment and unemployment, then, is faced with a daunting task. The "normal" correctional approach, as Crow et al. outline above, has been to assume that unemployment and its attendant problems are the result of deficiencies within the prisoner population, and the segment of society from whence they have come. As they point out, the larger issues related to social and economic causes of unemployment have largely been considered marginal to criminal justice. Bringing these issues back from the margins, so to speak, as part of a program of working with prisoners on the issue of unemployment, might be one approach. As such, it might involve a lessening of the goal of most employment programs for offenders of simply finding a job and not returning to prison. It might include an awareness of the personal impact of one's position in society on how one communicates, deals with stress, and looks for some meaningful and constructive relationship to one's community, be it through employment or something else. The endeavour here is to attempt to utilise an approach similar to the "social analysis of penality" described by Garland and Young (1983). More specifically, working with prisoners on problems like employment can possibly allow for bridging the gap between those "...institutions which 'deal with offenders'...[and] those which can intervene to transform the offenders' social conditions" (Garland and Young, 1983, p. 34). The EASE Program of the John Howard Society of Manitoba has attempted to address a small segment of these much larger concerns.

During the summer of 1990, the John Howard Society of Manitoba evaluated the services it provided to the Headingly Correctional Institution, the largest provincial prison in Manitoba. A number of institutional staff and agency service providers were interviewed to determine, in part, those areas of greatest need experienced by prisoners. The Employment and Skills Enhancement (EASE) pilot project was developed and implemented as a result of the 1990 agency evaluation. It was intended for prisoners who, for a variety of reasons, had not experienced successful employment in the community. It has since been offered in a modified form at the Brandon Correctional Institution by the John Howard Society in Brandon.

Adult institutional corrections in Manitoba are centred largely around the two main provincial prisons, Headingly (just west of Winnipeg) and Brandon, although there are smaller institutions in Dauphin, The Pas and Milner Ridge near the town of Beausejour. Headingly and Brandon are the most secure institutions with the largest percentage of the prison population. To put this in perspective, it is worth noting the following information about adult corrections in the province. Total sentenced admissions in 1990 to Manitoba correctional facilities were 5148, of whom 49% were native. The median sentence was 90 days and the median age on admission was 28 (Canadian Centre for Justice Statistics, 1991). Institutional programming is limited.

The EASE program begins with the assumption that obtaining and maintaining employment is a major factor in preventing prisoners from receiving a custodial sentence should they be rearrested after release. Underlying assumptions about individual employment skills include the need for self-esteem, motivation, and courage building. EASE attempts to address issues such as street support, conflict resolution (anger and stress management), literacy, résumé writing, and self-presentation—all barriers to individuals finding and maintaining employment. In addition, EASE also focusses on the structural barriers to employment that prisoners often face on release.

EASE also serves as a way to enhance other employment-related programs on the outside, by providing an entry level program on employment issues. The John Howard Society of Manitoba operates a six week pre-employment course entitled the Social Skills Orientation Course (SSOC). Part of one EASE session is devoted to a description of SSOC. Those individuals who would like to attend the community-based program may discuss that with the SSOC presenter. The John Howard Society of Manitoba also provides a community-based Employment Assistance Service (EAS). The EASE worker discusses this service and thus serves as a community link. Additionally, C.E.I.C. presenters discuss U.I. benefits and eligibility. This linkage to the community through outside agency participation provides an avenue for breaking down of stereotypes, awareness raising, and the sense that the community may have something to offer in terms of the welfare of people in prison.

The EASE program is open to virtually any prisoner at Headingly or Brandon, although it is primarily geared for individuals who have some job skills but have failed to maintain regular employment while on the street. Prisoners are informed about the program through their Unit Counsellors, members of the inmate counsel, or John Howard Society workers at the institution, and given the opportunity to participate if they wish. Selection is undertaken by the EASE co-facilitators; participants are asked to indicate a willingness to participate actively in the program, attend the nine sessions over three weeks, and to be prepared to address personal barriers to employment. A total of 50 prisoners have participated in the program over three sessions at the two institutions. The sessions are described in the chart given below:

Session 1: Introduction	Program co-facilitators	Intro to program. Discussions on anger and implications for work setting
Session 2: Stress	Program co-facilitators	Stress in the workplace and problem solving
Session 3: Communication and Conflict	Program co-facilitators	Discussion on communication and conflict
Session 4: Community programs	Program co-facilitators and two staff from local literacy program	How to make use of community programming, discussion on available literacy resources in the community
Session 5: Logistical aspects of employment	JHS worker	Résumés, SIN, birth certificates, bonding, application forms, etc.

Session 6: Conflict resolution 1	Worker from the Community Dispute Centre	Role plays dealing with non-violent conflict resolution in the workplace
Session 7: Government sponsored programs	Canada Employment and Immigration Commission worker	Information on unemployment insurance, employment opportunities and programs through CEIC
Session 8: Job searching and pre-employment programs	JHS Employment counsellor, and two members of the business community; SSOC staff member.	Discussion on looking for a job, and comments from business people on who they hire, and why
Session 9: Closing session .	Program co-facilitators	Review of the previous sessions, feedback and completion of feedback instruments, diplomas & applause

The program has been under way for a short time, and the total number of participants has been small. Resources have not been available to date for any extensive review of the program, nor for post-release follow-up with participants. However, information has been gathered at the end of each session to assist in planning for additional sessions. This has involved asking participants to complete questionnaires related to the content of the sessions, using scales to focus answers across a range from most helpful/beneficial to least. As well, other questions provide for more open-ended answers concerning the sessions. This data, rudimentary though it is, would tend to suggest that virtually all participants found the sessions to be useful, particularly those in stress management and the practical aspects of employment.

Much of current correctional programming involves keeping people within the walls of the prison until either an early departure has been earned, or the expiry of the penal sentence. Freedom in the sense of release from prison means a "return" to the society from which the individual came, but likely that individual will be no better equipped to deal with the challenges that one is confronted with in society each day. One challenge of the released prisoner probably will be the prospect of participating in some productive manner in an economy which increasingly requires more than the ex-prisoner has to offer in the way of skills. It is beyond the scope of the EASE program to overcome this challenge. However, it is important that prisoners have some ability both to cope with these challenges, and to understand why these challenges are arising. To do this, the EASE Program attempts to promote values like self-determination and the view that freedom is strongly dependent on economic and political equality. The participants of the EASE program are encouraged to consider personal and structural barriers to employment. Blame is not placed on the individual who, perhaps for reasons related to race or socio-economic class, finds himself unable to secure employment. Participants are encouraged to consider those structures in society (political, racial, economic) which prevent equal access to employment. This perspective elevates the participant to take responsibility for those things which he can change while locating responsibility for structural barriers to employment where they belong—not within him.

The four goals of incarceration—deterrence, punishment, protection and rehabilitation—are inherently value laden. Persons who enter prison become keenly aware that if they are to survive the system, they must construct their lives according to these system goals. These sentencing goals are ignored within the EASE program because they are in fact incompatible with the program's overall objectives. The goals of sentencing imply that autonomy is taken away from the prisoner for the prisoner's own good, the system then dictating what is right or wrong for the prisoner. This is not a climate under which anyone is willing to address barriers to employment.

A fundamental assumption of the program is that people have the capacity to change certain aspects about themselves, including those which may seem incompatible with employers or co-workers. For many, this change does not occur due to a lack of self-confidence. The EASE program attempts to value individuals for who they are, and without blaming people for where they have come from. The hoped-for result is that there is less reason for participants to remain defensive about personal barriers to employment. As well, there is then an attempt to differentiate between structural and personal barriers. Skills in conflict resolution and problem solving may prove helpful in resolving certain interpersonal relationship issues, but such skills are not recognized as necessarily the solution to more structural issues like inadequate education. For these, the group discussions in EASE encourage consideration of appropriate social action, not self-blame. With this, a greater sense of control over one's life may be developed among participants.

Group discussions within the EASE program also encourage participants to recount their barriers to employment, not necessarily for the purpose only of changing those barriers, but primarily for the value of identifying a common experience. When an individual discusses how anger or conflict has impeded successful employment, he has a great deal in common with other group members. Further group discussion encourages the discovery of the causes of that anger and also how it can be expressed as a positive emotional expression. The participant's anger is affirmed with the group as a natural and healthy emotion which he can take responsibility for and learn to focus.

The goal of EASE is not to rehabilitate. The temptation, however, is to make it fit within current correctional programming in order to fulfil the demands of that system. That elusive carrot of early release dangles ever so closely when one can say that the faults of the individual (i.e., his unemployment) are responsible for imprisonment in the first place. Prison shelters prisoners from life's realities, teaches them to cope by manipulation and coercion, and fails to foster a sense of control over one's own life. Prison employment programs have traditionally been self-serving. Prison "crews" pick garbage, cut trees, clean parks, and harvest vegetables. Inherent is a hierarchical model which maintains a philosophy of divisions between us and them.

Will programs for prisoners such as the Employment and Skills Enhancement meet the real needs of people taking the programs? Whether prison programming can achieve any short term goals without compromising a longer term goal of radically reducing prison populations is questionable. However, there is some argument for suggesting that the traditional measures of success, i.e., reducing recidivism among released prisoner populations, ought not to be the only measure of assessing what a program does. If one goal of EASE is to foster an awareness of the personal impact of one's position in society on how one communicates, deals with stress, and looks for some meaningful and constructive relationship to one's community, then how well this is accomplished might provide a better indication of a program's value or worth. Stan Cohen (1985) suggests that there are issues to be considered when assessing the value of some initiatives other than simply the question of does a given policy or program reduce crime. He states his view that

> ...moral values which are cherished as ends in themselves, should not be relabelled as 'means' for the instrumental enterprise of crime control. Doing so would only be to devalue these values, and to lead to their abandonment if the official purposes of the system are then not achieved (p. 265).

Our belief is that the EASE program addresses the issue that the imprisonment of people is inextricably linked to politics and economics. The strength of the program lies in the participation of the prisoners, where people are not judged or blamed on the basis of their individual race or economic status, but where they have the opportunity to find strength as a group of people with common barriers to employment.

References

Box, S. & Hale, C. 1986. "Unemployment, crime and imprisonment, and the enduring problem of prison overcrowding" in Maths, R. & Young, J. *Confronting Crime*. London: Sage.

Canadian Centre for Justice Statistics. 1991. *Adult Correctional Services in Canada 1990-1991* Ottawa: Statistics Canada.

Chambliss, W. 1964. "NA Sociological Analysis of the Law of Vagrancy," reprinted in Carson, W.G. & Wiles, P. 1971. *The Sociology of Crime & Delinquency in Britain* Volume 1. London: Martin Robertson.

Cohen, S. 1985. *Visions of Social Control.* Cambridge: Polity Press.

Crow, I., Richardson, P., Riddington, C., & Simon, F. 1989. *Unemployment. Crime and Offenders.* London: Routledge.

Garland, D. & Young, P. 1983. "Towards a Social Analysis of Penality" in Garland, D. & Young, P. *The Power to Punish*. London: Heineman.

Garraty, J. 1978. *Unemployment in History: Economic Thought and Public Policy*. New York: Harper & Row.

Rothman, D. 1990. *The Discovery of the Asylum*, 2nd edition. Boston: Little, Brown & Co.

Rusche, G. 1933. "Labour Markets and Criminal Sanction," reprinted in *Crime & Social Justice* 10, Fall-Winter 1978.

Thomas, J. & Boehlefeld, S. 1991. "Rethinking Abolitionism: 'What do we do with Henry?' Review of de Haan, *The Politics of Redress*." *Social Justice.* 18, 3, Fall p. 238-251.

Chapter 8

Reforming Reform Institutions*

Peter Oliver

Allan Grossman was outstanding as the minister responsible for corrections. He fought for, and achieved, numerous reforms, and gave the department a momentum it maintained for years after his departure. Old facilities were closed and new ones opened; new, highly trained personnel, including many professionals, were brought into the department and placed in senior positions; veteran staff were offered unprecedented encouragement and support; and the department proved willing to embark on a striking array of progressive programs. Whether these efforts succeeded—whether, for example, recidivism rates were reduced, individuals rehabilitated, and the crime rate reduced—is not clear; indeed, Grossman and his officials were uncertain about the success of their reforms. They had no doubt at all, however, that by giving a more progressive and humane face to corrections in Ontario, they were assisting those who found themselves in trouble with the law. Grossman and his colleagues were making an important contribution to social betterment in Ontario.

This chapter is about the contribution to that process that can be made by aggressive and determined political leadership. Cabinet ministers come and go, and, for the most part, leave relatively little impact on their departments, to say nothing of the larger society. Even when the opportunity for constructive leadership does exist, the overwhelming weight of the habits, values, and structures of society narrows the possibilities for constructive change. Certainly one would expect this to be true with respect to the way society deals with its so-called criminal element. In Ontario, as in most other jurisdictions, governments spent as little as possible to provide facilities to house or programs to treat the offender. In 1946, the province had established a separate Department of Reform Institutions, but there was not much progress

---

* From Peter Oliver, *Unlikely Tory: The Life and Politics of Allan Grossman,* Toronto: Lester & Orpen Denys, 1985.

in the next decade and a half. Before 1946, the province's principal institutions were the old Mercer Reformatory for Women in Toronto, which dated back to the nineteenth century; the Guelph Reformatory for Men, which opened in 1910; the Industrial Farm, in Burwash, near Sudbury, which opened in 1914; and a facility in Mimico, which opened in 1913, where brick and tile were manufactured. The first sign of reform after World War Two was the opening, in 1947, of a training centre in Brampton for young first offenders who could benefit from educational and vocational training. In 1952 there was a riot at Guelph, and so in 1956 the department established an efficient but impersonal maximum-security facility at Millbrook, intended principally for trouble-makers and recidivists. The department also operated a system of training schools for juveniles. Many of the guards were farmers trying to pick up a little extra cash; they were underpaid and under-trained, and the turnover was high. There were few professionals on staff; little was done to provide treatment for prisoners; and after-care facilities were few. The system also included thirty-five county and two district jails. The province administered the district jails; the county jails were controlled locally. Many of them had been built in the nineteenth century; some were a disgrace to the province.

Anyone who had any contact with the system knew that conditions were bad, but no one was able to do much about it. Colonel John Foote, the former military chaplain who was minister during the 1950s, points out:

> I don't think there was one person within Cabinet that was enthusiastic about the Department. They had no use for the people who were committed to prison and they didn't think society owed them a great deal. They liked to see people reformed and changed and so on but they weren't very hopeful about it and they didn't want to spend very much money on it. We were short of money and the Cabinet just felt that the less they heard of the prisons the better.[1]

His fellow ministers, Foote reflects, were humane enough and willing to see him effect improvements, as long as they were done "with a minimum of expenditures." Their priorities, Foote believed, reflected those of most members of the legislature, and public opinion across the province. Foote's attempts to hire professional staff were often rebuffed by Premier Frost, who firmly believed that criminals were less likely to return to a life of crime if they found their incarceration thoroughly unpleasant. As well, since the province was responsible only for offenders sentenced to less than two years, there seemed little need to deploy substantial resources for treatment and care.

In these circumstances, the various ministers of reform institutions (and, except for Foote, they changed rapidly) were helpless when CCF leader Donald

MacDonald rose in the legislature to denounce the sins of the department. These occasions made a great impact on back-bencher Allan Grossman and he sympathized with the helpless ministers. But when Foote asked the premier to appoint Grossman as his assistant, Frost refused.[2]

In the early 1960s, the progressive new premier, John Robarts, decided the situation could be tolerated no longer. Allan Grossman was nagging Robarts almost weekly to move him out of the Liquor Commission, yet he was not happy when Robarts asked him to take on Reform Institutions. Grossman told himself, however, that "anything is better than Liquor."

> I said to myself, there is only one way to go in Reform Institutions and that is up. Robarts told me the same sort of thing he had told me when I went to the Liquor Board. He said, "You've heard the debates in the House. It's obvious that the department needs a good overhaul." Well, that may have been the case, and I did have an interest in correctional matters, but I wondered why I was being asked to take over a department that was at the bottom of the barrel.

Grossman was not exaggerating the department's lack of status. Doctor Tadeusz Grygier, a criminologist and a teacher at the University of Toronto who would be brought into the department by Grossman to head a new research branch, has recalled that "The speed of the Department was zero. There was nothing. It was a joke. People knew it was a dead-end Department."

On his first visit to the department's head office, located near the corner of University Avenue and Dundas Street, Grossman found it:

> a decrepit old building, just a terrible place. You could hardly breathe in it in the summer. I was appalled at the equipment; there were filing cabinets that would not close and looked like relics of the nineteenth century. In the minister's office there was a desk made at one of the institutions and most of the drawers wouldn't open. Obviously they were short of money and when you looked at it from that point of view, that not even the minister's desk was operative, it was no wonder that the same thing occurred throughout the entire system.

Poor conditions were reflected in poor morale. "They had been hammered in the press almost weekly for years and were not getting anywhere. In some cases staff members were ashamed to admit they worked for the department." One of his first priorities, he decided, would be to change the department's image. "The morale of the civil servants usually reflects the image the public has of them and in turn reflects the way in which the minister is able to project that image to the public and back to the staff." In his years in Corrections, Grossman would go to perhaps excessive lengths to defend his department and its employees against attacks in the House and the press.

Grossman aggressively told the department's staff of his intentions. Leo Hackl, who became deputy minister in 1965, described the impact of Grossman's announcement on the department. "At the very first meeting, the [outgoing] Minister called some of the senior staff into his office and introduced us to Mr. Grossman, and I think Mr. Grossman made a terrible error. He said...there were going to be a number of changes in the Department, and that was our introduction to him."[3] One of the first to go was the deputy minister, Archie Graham, who had worked his way up in the old system and had run the department with little interference from the minister. One senior staff member has recalled that an earlier minister was known as "Mr. Thursday" because "he would come in Wednesday late, usually around five o'clock or so, and sometimes later than that, when everybody was gone, and then he would come in again on Thursday morning about 9:00 and Cabinet was at 10:00 so he'd leave at about a quarter to and we didn't see him again until next week." This was typical, and under those conditions, the deputy ran the department. Not surprisingly, Grossman found that Graham "was reluctant to give up the authority he had assumed under previous ministers, nor was he able to accept new ideas or policies, especially those suggested by the minister." There was a showdown, and the position was assumed by Leo Hackl.

The Archie Graham crisis was symptomatic of larger problems. Here was a much-despised and in many ways reactionary department, staffed by underpaid and often indifferent veterans, many of them old-timers who, although shell-shocked from numerous attacks in the press and from opposition politicians, remained stubbornly committed to old and familiar ways. And here was a tough, aggressive minister determined to effect sweeping changes, a progressive Tory and a social activist who intended to put in long hours to impose his own vision on the department. That Grossman was a Jew was also a cause for resentment among some employees, who let their sentiments be known. Even with Robarts's strong backing, the new minister had his work cut out for him. It would have surprised no one if the task had turned out to be too much for him.

W.E. Mann, an academic who in 1967 published a controversial study, *Society Behind Bars, A Sociological Scrutiny of Guelph Reformatory*, offered some astute observations on that score. It was well known, Professor Mann pointed out, that Allan Grossman "has tried hard to update the Department," but Mann was not optimistic about the prospects. The initial obstacle, he argued, was "the provincial Cabinet's long-standing disinterest in the subject." Secondly, "the Department of Reform Institutions is low in the status hierarchy of departments partly because it is believed that a policy of aggressive prison reform is hardly calculated to gain votes." As well, the department was sometimes viewed as "a potential powder keg": serious changes might lead to riots. The department rarely had a strong leader; the typical minister was "usually not prepared to experiment extensively nor [was] he kept in the post long enough to become deeply acquainted with or committed to the basic programs involved in an effective reform policy." Finally, the minister was forced to rely on the deputy minister, usually someone who had risen through the hierarchy; should he fire the deputy, "he must simultaneously or shortly fire many of the other top administrators." Mann believed such firings would cause unfavourable publicity and appear, in the Cabinet, as a serious political threat. Although Mann saw Grossman as a "recent exception" to the usual type of minister, he regarded Grossman's task as almost impossible.[4] Grossman understood the formidable nature of the challenge he faced. But he was a realist as well as a reformer, and the prospects for success were greater than Mann recognized.

The difference between Grossman's approach and one a theorist might have taken was personified by the new deputy minister, Leo Hackl. Hackl had risen through the ranks: he had served as head teacher at Brampton and as superintendent there and elsewhere. A tall, lean, bespectacled man, serious in mien and possessed of great integrity, he was a painstaking administrator. Naturally cautious, he balanced an inherently humane approach to correctional work with a strong sense of the job's limitations. Here, it seemed, was another roadblock to change. Allan Grossman might well have clashed with Hackl as furiously as he had with Graham. But Hackl and Grossman understood the nature of the minister-deputy relationship. Each learned to trust the other, and each was committed to the best interests of the department. Many of Grossman's brainstorms sent Hackl into barely subdued rages; some of the innovations the two agreed to must have been a source of enormous concern to Hackl, who as administrative head was responsible for safety and security. Almost every day, Grossman's brusque impatience and sometimes unreasonable demands might have caused a blow-up and led to resignations. None of this happened. On his desk, Hackl kept a memorandum, prepared by a federal bureaucrat, on the correct constitutional relationship between deputy and minister. He found that frequent reading of the document helped him keep his temper, and reminded him that his responsibility was to set out all the possibilities but, finally, to follow orders or get out.

Fortunately for the future of Corrections in Ontario, it did not come to that. Grossman had the highest regard for Hackl's experience and good judgment; Hackl proved open to new ideas, and anxious to implement changes; and, perhaps most important, Hackl was able to tell Grossman what could go and what couldn't. To an action-oriented man like Grossman, who wanted to implement a dozen new ideas a day, Hackl's presence was invaluable. As Tad Grygier put it, Hackl's "integrity was beyond question. When he would tell me that I couldn't do certain things that I wanted to do, there was no point in arguing or suspecting him to be an obstructionist. It had to be true."[5] With Hackl as a loyal and supportive deputy, Grossman had won his most important battle. Now it became possible to prod, nudge, and guide the rest of the department into line.

Even so, there would have to be major infusions of new blood at the senior levels. New positions were needed, and different kinds of people were sought to fill them. But before Grossman felt confident enough to engage in such changes, he immersed himself in the department's work so he would know enough to make critical decisions. Grossman became the opposite of those earlier ministers who had been content to let the deputy run things.

The first need was for basic knowledge. Grossman understood that no crash course in criminology could give him the expert skills acquired only after years of study; still, he needed a feeling for the field, something to help him assess the recommendations of his officials and supplement his native shrewdness. As he told the legislature in his 1965 estimates speech, he "read literally hundreds of briefs, brochures, books, theses, yes, and every word from Hansard for the past ten years relating to corrections, and from all of these I have sought guidance for the future." Tad Grygier recalls: "I met him immediately after his appointment. His desk was relatively clear, he was reading a book. The book was written by my former professor, Hermann Mannheim, probably the greatest criminologist in the world. Mr. Grossman started at the basics right away, then from there he started changing things."[6]

He needed no knowledge of criminology to build morale among the demoralized staff. Don Sinclair, who had left the department in disgust in 1963 and was later persuaded by Grossman to return, has commented on Grossman's visits to institutions and his attempts to give staff a sense that head office cared about what was happening to them.

> I have worked in several fields, and can think of no area of human endeavour in which the man directly responsible for operations feels such a sense of isolation as the Superintendent of a prison. Allan Grossman, because he's such an acute observer or the human scene, quickly latched onto the fact that the people running a prison...require a tremendous amount of support and encouragement.... When I left the Department in 1963 it was the practice, whenever there was a conference relating to corrections...to send perhaps two people, more likely one. I think only a month after Mr. Grossman was appointed, there was a correctional conference held in Montreal. I was in Montreal for

a different meeting but it so happened that the headquarters for the corrections conference was in my hotel. I went downstairs for dinner and to my astonishment was greeted by about forty members of the Department of Reform Institutions staff. And I said, "What on earth are all you people doing here, have they suddenly transferred you all to Montreal?" And they just said, "No, we've got a new Minister who believes in involving us in what's going on and in showing Ontario's face on the correctional map." I thought that was a most significant thing.[7]

Hackl recalls: "We had a dinner there in Montreal, just for our staff. Not only was that one of the greatest morale builders we ever had, but people learned something by rubbing shoulders with people in other jurisdictions."[8]

Grossman went out to meet the superintendents and other personnel. He hoped to head off some of the resentment he anticipated from long-time staffers as they learned about the changes he planned. The superintendents were important, and Grossman acknowledged this by instituting regular superintendents' conferences. His concern to give staff a sense of involvement extended to all levels. "He was acutely aware," Don Sinclair has noted, "that all the ramifications of something could not be examined thoroughly unless one looked at the perspective of those at the bottom of the pile."[9] Although there was resentment from time to time, most old-timers, who might have dragged their feet at every step, proved reasonably co-operative.

In a few months, Grossman gained sufficient grasp of correctional fundamentals to enunciate the principles that would serve as a basis for reshaping the Ontario system. He started with broad objectives; details could be developed later, to give shape to general goals. He began with two simple precepts. First, he accepted, as the basis of all he intended to do, a truism of correctional work that much of the public, and indeed many who work in the field, never really comprehend:

The basis on which we worked was that a person was sent to a correctional institution not *for* punishment but as punishment. In other words, incarceration with its loss of liberty was the punishment, nothing else. A lot of people can't understand that, so you have to say to them, "You think we are mollycoddling the inmates, well, how would you like to be mollycoddled to the extent that you had to sleep in that cell every night, you couldn't choose your friends, you couldn't phone anybody when you like, you couldn't eat something you especially like, and be subjected to this routine month after month. You really think that isn't punishment?"

"Inherent in all our operations," Grossman suggested next, "was the principle that what serves no useful purpose should be discarded." In seeking to apply this rule, Grossman was the bane of departmental employees. To his seemingly bland question, "Why do we do it that way?" they replied, equally blandly, "Because it's always been done that way." Innumerable hoary rules and repressive regulations were swept out of existence as the minister ruthlessly applied his second maxim.

Grossman emphasized, too, the essential dilemma facing those in correctional work. He frequently expressed this dilemma in a maxim familiar to correctional workers: "At one and the same time we have to be both jailer and doctor." Unlike some theorists, Grossman knew that correctional work must come to terms with both opportunities and limitations. "We are in the difficult position," he told the House in 1965, "of attempting to gain the confidence and trust of an offender while at the same time restricting his freedom." There were, he argued, no simple answers. It would be easier "to obtain a therapeutic atmosphere without incarceration. Nevertheless, no one has, as yet, produced an effective substitute for it." Lawbreakers were punished; the only variant was the way in which society chose to rationalize that punishment. "It may be rationalized as punishment for wrongdoing, for security purposes, as a deterrent, or for corrective purposes. Whatever the reason, society insists that the offender be restricted in his movements." That restriction might take the form of probation outside an institution or restriction with an institution. But even probation "pre-supposes that at some stage repeating offenders will have to be imprisoned." The dilemma remained: society was jailer and doctor, and therein lay the challenge. Grossman was persuaded that the interest of society and of the offender lay, finally, in treatment and rehabilitation. And the key was the promotion of attitudinal changes and self-respect.

In his view, these were interrelated. Corporal punishment, which Grossman denounced as barbaric, might achieve an element of deterrence, but it would do nothing to increase the self-respect that was necessary to rehabilitation. Up to the early 1970s, when Criminal Code amendments formally ended court-imposed physical punishments, administrators were obliged to administer such punishments. Grossman went so far as to state publicly that punishments might not be carried out, and he informed administrators that they had no obligation to strap prisoners. He wanted to focus entirely on positive reinforcement. To Grossman, all rules and practices in the institutions not directed to this goal were counter-productive.

Changes in policy and practice demanded an infusion of reform-minded personnel and the expenditure of large sums of money on staff and on new facilities. In the 1960s, money was available for large-scale social programs; this made Grossman's task easier. Even so, Corrections did not suddenly become a government priority; Grossman fought hard to persuade his Cabinet colleagues and the Treasury Board that the large sums he was requesting were justified. Don Sinclair points out that fundamental to Grossman's achievement was that "he recognized that the department could not possibly do the job...without having a sound funding base, something it had never had before. It did not take him very long to achieve that."[10] Yet he had to persuade his colleagues that his very costly policy, of closing many old institutions and replacing large old prisons with smaller facilities, was justified. Tad Grygier recalls one story. He had developed an instrument he called "the measure of treatment potential," which Grossman used to justify some of his requests for funds.

> Grossman was really excited and said, "This is what I felt but everybody has been saying to me I didn't have the data. Now I have the data and I'm going to Treasury Board in an hour." Within two weeks the Minister announced in the Legislature that no training schools would be built with a capacity of more than 125 and no institutions for adults larger than 200 and that some existing institutions would be reduced in size.[11]

The commitment to smaller institutions became a cornerstone of the department's policy. Some correctional workers had long held that smaller facilities were a key to rehabilitation, and were overjoyed at this breakthrough. Later some of Grossman's institutional solutions would become problematic, but the kinds of institutions Grossman was promoting were different from the massive facilities built by earlier generations. Regrettably, they were also so costly that governments would later choose to ignore that commitment.

With funding usually available, reorganization could proceed. Grossman and Hackl were in agreement, as Hackl puts it, that "the department needed a real overhauling" and that the process required extensive reorganization. In the 1950s, the head office structure had consisted of the minister, the deputy, and secretaries. Hackl prepared an organization chart, Grossman won Treasury Board approval, and the search was on, recalls Hackl, "to hire a lot of professionals."[12] The new positions included director of training schools, directors of adult male and adult female institutions, a research section with its own head, and several other positions lower in the hierarchy, including director of education. Most of these positions were filled by newcomers.

In 1964 Tadeusz Grygier came to head the research section. Grygier was "not just a director of Research but a policy adviser." Often, he suggests, research in criminology "doesn't seem to have any influence on policy but the research that I was doing was implemented."[13] He made important studies in the juvenile field, which contributed substantially to the Training Schools Act of 1965; other studies helped establish the temporary-absence program, one of the most important innovations of the Grossman years. Grygier's work on treatment effectiveness helped demonstrate a direct correlation between staff numbers and treatment success. "The more treatment staff you have," Grygier argued, "the better are the results," especially with juveniles, who assume the value system of the staff. Grygier's information helped Grossman justify the expense of some of the new training schools opened in the 1960s, including Hagersville, which operated on a cottage system. There, the staff-pupil ratio was one to one.

Other new employees were Doctor Harry Hutchison, director of adult male institutions, and Aideen Nicholson, director of adult female institutions. These appointments were unorthodox, but the opportunity to import fresh thinking more than compensated for the occasional problems they created. Hutchison, a psychologist, had worked at the Toronto Psychiatric Hospital, with the department of psychiatry at the University of Toronto, and with the department of health. He recognized that his appointment represented "a risk on their part," and he saw it as part of Grossman's effort "to turn the department around from an old custodial set-up to one which really exemplified modern corrections."[14]

Aideen Nicholson, a psychiatric social worker, had been employed at the forensic clinic of the Toronto Psychiatric Hospital for Sick Children. When the position at the department opened, she relates, "I would never have thought of applying." However, the department "had started an effort to bring in...people who had some background in the behavioural sciences." She had been critical of the department, and when she was offered the job she felt obliged to try to improve things from within. She encountered "a lot of entrenched people with entrenched ideas who were opposed to change." She understood their attitude because "there's a fair amount of evidence that riots and disturbances are more likely to happen when things are being loosened and improved," but she was confident that she and her allies would be able to deal with practical matters and anticipate difficulties.[15] Nicholson helped to plan the new women's facility, the Vanier Centre, which would replace the Mercer; she also planned new treatment programs, and helped in the push towards community programming.

From within, Harry Garraway, a training-school superintendent, was promoted to director of training schools. An administrator in the Hackl mould, Garraway was cautious yet believed in moderate reform. Former newspaperman Don Kerr was appointed director of information, an expanded and upgraded position. Kerr was privy to all major decisions, and helped to ensure that the department's work was understood by the media.

The roster of principal players was completed in 1968, when the minister persuaded the bright and independent-minded Don Sinclair to return to the department as executive director of the institutions branch. Sinclair's iconoclastic ways did not hinder his mobility in the department: he later became deputy minister.

With the money on tap and the team in place, the time had arrived for decisions. Many of these emerged naturally from policy discussions, which Grossman encouraged as part of the daily administrative routine. Aideen Nicholson explains:

> Grossman was not your "correct" administrator who wanted a gap between him [and line personnel]. He needled people, he provoked, he tolerated a lot of fiercely emotional discussions. Where Mr. Grossman is you don't necessarily have the greatest order in the sense that you prepare a submission and make an appointment to discuss it. Often it was a matter of informal discussions, often very heated, but if as a result of that he got a frank opinion.... I think it was a fairly good thing for a department which had been run along military lines.[16]

Don Sinclair describes Grossman's technique:

> He would always pretend to be far more ignorant than he really was of the situation. After I got to know him, I got wise to the fact that if he ever called you in and asked you a question, you'd better be well prepared because, although it was always asked under a mask of bland innocence, that man is never innocent and doesn't ask questions unless he's at least halfway to the answer to begin with. He used sessions in his office of four or five people as a means of digging out all aspects of a problem and getting a pretty shrewd idea of exactly who was on solid ground in stating an opinion and who was trying to bluff. He was always the devil's advocate but he'd never preface what he was doing, as most others do, by saying, "I'll play the devil's advocate." He was a pretty shrewd actor and you were never too sure whether he actually believed what he was saying.[17]

The people at the meetings did not constitute a regular policy group; says Sinclair, "You never knew who would be in there." Usually Don Kerr, Harry Garraway, and Tad Grygier went; Leo Hackl always attended. Unlike the more customary relationship between a minister and his deputy, Grossman developed policy ideas and Hackl assessed their implications. Hackl recalls,

> Mr. Grossman would never sign anything or agree with anything
> unless he really understood it. And in order to understand it, he
> wanted to discuss it.... He wanted you to bring up counter-
> arguments and argue points with him, the same way as he would
> argue with the opposition in the Legislature. I never had another
> minister who wanted that and most of them would probably
> throw you out of their office if you attempted such a thing.

Grossman preferred to talk about things because he suspected his advisers would be reluctant to present some of their innovative ideas on paper. "Although memoranda outlining new ideas were sometimes necessary," says Hackl, "as a general rule we found them to be time-consuming and often a waste of time. Instead we had frequent free-wheeling discussions and after we gained a consensus the ideas would be committed to paper for final editing and approval by the minister."[18]

These sessions achieved results. Policy changes came with such speed that even Grossman began to wonder whether it was wise to do so much so quickly. New institutions were being constructed and old ones closed, but ministry officials agreed that the key to rehabilitation lay less in modern facilities than in a sensitive, progressive staff. Pay scales increased substantially; a new emphasis was placed on staff training and a new training college was opened in Mimico. A major thrust was the effort to lessen the perennial tensions between custodial officers and treatment personnel. The old-style staff training, which had focussed on security and custody, was replaced by a new system. Correctional officers (no longer called guards) were trained by professionals, who emphasized the behavioural sciences.

The Grossman regime rejected many old practices; existing practices were justified or ended. Grossman reacted angrily when he learned that an inmate in one institution had been strapped into a chair so his hair could be cut short. "When this came to my attention it seemed to me another example of destroying someone's self-respect. Why shouldn't a guy keep his hair or beard long? The problem was that it could be done to excess or become a matter of hygiene, so I put in the rule that hair and beard could be kept at the length they were when the inmate came in unless it was creating a hygienic problem." Self-respect was also the issue when Grossman visited the Brampton Training Centre:

> Whenever I visited an institution I tried to speak with as many
> inmates and staff as possible. On one visit to Brampton, when I
> met with the student council, they said they'd like to get some
> deodorant.

That's one of the things that used to hit you right in the nostrils when you went into the institutions, body odour. It was a surprise to me that they'd never had deodorant and when I asked the officials why not, nobody could give me any reason. This was the sort of change you dare not talk about in public. Can you picture the headlines, "Government orders deodorant so inmates will smell sweeter." The most important aspect of the process of rehabilitation is self-respect. I ordered deodorant to be supplied but not publicly announced.

Two innovations, canteens and pay for prisoners, caused much grumbling among prison staff, who objected to the additional work; perhaps they also felt Grossman was "mollycoddling" the inmates. Grossman viewed pay and canteens as rehabilitative tools. The pay was small—it was really an incentive allowance—and did not compete with rates paid to workers outside the institutions. The inmates could save part of their pay to supplement what they were given when they were released. They could also spend some of it at the canteen. "We insisted," says Hackl, "that [a canteen] be set up in each institution and run like a little store so the prisoner could look across the counter and order what he wanted. As well, we insisted that each inmate be interviewed on a regular basis and told how much he had earned."[19]

Until the 1960s, no one had bothered with such humanizing moves. Hackl relates:

Take a small thing such as mattresses. We didn't get mattresses in the institutions until I became deputy minister. Then I spoke to Mr. Grossman about it and said "Look, we haven't got the money. It's going to cost $40,000 to put them throughout the institutions, not including jails." So he said, "We'll put them in and I'll get the money," and that was the first time I had ever heard a minister speak like that. Finally we had a minister who was willing to fight for what we needed.[20]

Public opinion continued to impose restraints. When the Vanier Centre was being planned, someone suggested that it include a swimming pool. Grossman agreed: he viewed recreation as part of the rehabilitative process. But he feared that "the public would be up in arms about providing a luxury for inmates." Grossman wanted to keep public opinion behind him as he made changes, so the idea was dropped. There was a similar problem about food and medical facilities, which some of the public regarded as being better than they themselves were able to afford. Grossman insisted that proper food was important to the safety and security of the institution. Other people were concerned about former inmates who postponed dental treatment until they were again on the inside, and then demanded expensive treatment. The minister did not take these problems very seriously. He made arrangements with a well-known plastic surgeon to operate on disfigured inmates—particularly women—free of charge, if it could be demonstrated that plastic surgery would be a useful part of the rehabilitative process.

To promote self-respect, Grossman gave each inmate a copy of the "Inmate Information Booklet," which set out the range of legal and other rights in the institution. As well, notices were posted, in several languages, that explained legal aid and bail procedures. In Leo Hackl's view, Grossman's main purpose, when he joined the department, "was to humanize things."[21] In this he succeeded: because of Grossman, Ontario's correctional facilities wore a human—and a humane—face.

To emphasize its determination, the department committed itself to a "Statement of Purpose," published in each annual report beginning in 1965. Grossman says:

> I was very much surprised that a simple statement of purpose would create so much favourable comment. We were just saying what we were going to do. Of course I realized subsequently why that was important. Correctional institutions all over the world generally never liked to lay their intentions on the line. They knew they weren't going to be able to carry through with their programs because they were so low on the priorities of their governments. We were sticking our necks out. We could always be criticized by someone pointing to our statement and saying, "Why haven't you done this?"

Hackl was proudest of the commitment that "in planning new institutions we will aim for units with a maximum capacity of 200 for adults, and schools with a maximum capacity of 125." "I don't think there's a jurisdiction in the world that laid down numbers as small as those we mentioned."[22] As well, the statement maintained the commitment to rehabilitative goals, communication between residents and staff, and reintegration of the residents into the community. The statement of purpose, a proud beacon of progressive intentions, was a product of the collective thinking of the department under Grossman's leadership.

Many of the reforms were internal, and relatively inexpensive; others were costly indeed. A provincial takeover of the jails had been discussed, from time to time, for more than a century; for various reasons it had never been done. Shortly before Grossman's appointment, the John Howard Society presented a persuasive indictment of the condition of the jails and urged a provincial takeover; a ministry committee reached similar conclusions at about the time Grossman became minister. But local sensitivities and political pitfalls seemed likely to block effective provincial action once again.

Grossman was appalled at conditions in some of the jails he visited. He thought the best way to ensure improvements was through aggressive provincial action, and decided to begin the process and see it through. To Grossman the jails were important because, as he described them in one address, they were "the front door for corrections." In 1963 about sixty thousand people passed through them—four times the number handled by provincial institutions—and a good number of these were later found not guilty. Yet they were subjected to facilities that often imposed physical hardships and to personnel who lacked training, were underpaid, and were not interested in the work. The facilities did not always allow for segregation of prisoners or provide space for lawyers to confer with their clients in private. Since many people housed in the jails were charged with serious offences and would ultimately be sentenced to federal penitentiaries, provisions for maximum security were required.

Although the counties owned the jails, the province paid some costs and was responsible for inspecting them. Yet the province seemed unable to move the local authorities to effect much-needed reforms. The counties were not entirely to blame, and responsibility tended to shift back and forth in perpetual deadlock. No one did anything about it until Grossman and Hackl took the situation in hand. Robarts was supportive. In 1964, Grossman reminded him that a plan had been presented "some three years ago" to replace county jails with units that served several counties. That plan had not been approved. "I feel the time is appropriate," said Grossman, "for the Government to take such action." Since there was local opposition because of cost, Grossman proposed that the province establish a pilot regional detention centre in an existing jail, and suggested a Northern Ontario district jail which was already under provincial control. He would have preferred to begin with a southern county but, as he said, "I am not too hopeful because of the multiplicity of complex problems which must be dealt with in order to institute such a plan. In other words, we must consider taking over the system ourselves."[23]

Although the premier was sympathetic, such a radical and expensive departure as a complete provincial take-over was not yet possible. But the Treasury Board agreed that the province would pay fifty percent of the cost of a new facility established along approved lines by any county willing to band together with at least one other county. Grossman announced this agreement late in 1964; in 1965, he presented legislation. The cost of each unit was expected to be between one million and two and a half million dollars. Negotiations, Grossman told the House on 12 May, were already underway with Kingston, Belleville, Hamilton, and Peterborough. A Planning committee was established to advise on and plan all aspects of setting up the new centres, and the department offered to help the counties with planning. The new jails, to be called "regional detention centres," would include therapeutic programs, staff training, treatment personnel, segregation units, improved facilities, work programs, fuller information on prisoners, better security, and a host of other advantages. If several counties co-operated on each centre, they would save thirty percent on operation and twenty-five to fifty percent on construction. The department would encourage the counties to develop regional units by offering them help in organizing the facilities and in administration. Finally, he promised "by means of grants [to] ensure that the building and operation of the Regional Unit is to the financial advantage of each county co-operating."[24]

Accompanied by Leo Hackl and Don Kerr, Grossman made the rounds of the country councils. A number of counties were reluctant to act because they felt the province should take over the jails. Grossman agreed, but noted, somewhat disingenuously, that this subject had been discussed for many years; he urged them not to "waste any of our valuable time prolonging fruitless arguments." Although Grossman did not bully, he knew when to be blunt. In July 1967, for example, he toured the Renfrew Jail, and told the press that its facilities "don't belong to this century. If the only purpose of a jail is to punish people, then this jail is fine."[25] Hackl recalls: "We did a lot of travelling, and it was a real chore, actually a very difficult time. You'd get all kinds of antagonistic people."[26]

The first agreement was signed on 23 November 1965, between the province and the counties of Frontenac, Hastings, Lennox and Addington, and Prince Edward, to build the Quinte Regional Detention Centre. This was a good beginning, Grossman recalls, because four counties were involved, which would effect some major savings. Some of the jails closed down were among the worst in the province. "Kingston," says Grossman, "had a horrible jail. The cell was hewn out of solid rock and there was barely enough room for the guy to lie down. There wasn't even a light except out in the corridor." During the next two years, agreements were reached with the Kawartha region; the United Counties of Durham and Northumberland and the counties of Victoria and Peterborough; Peel and Halton; the Niagara Region, Lincoln, and Welland; the City of Hamilton and the county of Wentworth; and the county of Carleton and the City of Ottawa.

Then in 1968, in response to the Smith Committee on Taxation, the province announced that it was assuming the full cost of the administration of justice in Ontario. This was something Grossman had long favoured; he and his officials were delighted. County and city jails would be under their authority and could be integrated into the provincial correctional system. The department was given nine hundred new employees, and encountered a host of new problems; despite the problems, the province could establish its own priorities and replace those institutions deemed worst. Because of the costs involved, there was no substantial speed-up in the replacement program; the province continued to try to open and/or renovate one centre a year, and to complete this program over the next decade and a half. In the meantime, however, provincial standards and programs could be put in place, and short-term changes could be made in jails not scheduled for replacement.

The provincial take-over, as Grossman anticipated, also presented dangers. Almost immediately, Stephen Lewis and other MPPs began to criticize "those horrible old jails" that were now part of the provincial system. Municipal politicians, especially in Toronto, demanded that the province immediately replace the disgraceful jails in their area, although local governments had been unwilling to spend the money when the responsibility rested with them. In May 1968, Grossman promised that the old wing of Toronto's Don Jail would be replaced as part of the provincial program. At a Jail Governors' conference in February 1968, he emphasized that jails were now "rehabilitation units," and that staff would face new demands. Rehabilitation officers would be provided; workshops would be established; and treatment would become an important part of jail programs. The governors must rethink their roles, and must be prepared to take advantage of the opportunities the new system provided.

The opening of the Quinte Regional Detention Centre in Napanee, in May 1971, was a proud day for Allan Grossman. Although it was the first of the new centres to open, Grossman's long tenure as minister was already over, and it was at the request of his successor that he occupied a position of honour at the ceremony. The Quinte Centre began a new era in corrections in Ontario, and in Canada. As Grossman told his audience, "as the first of its kind this Regional Detention Centre has tremendous potential as an innovating and an experimental institution...a testing ground, a pilot project in which new approaches and techniques can be utilized and evaluated." He cited the trend towards community-oriented programming—the regional detention centre was an example—as the development of which he was most proud. "The days of locking offenders completely away from society, of building walls around correctional institutions to keep the prisoner in and the public out, are gradually fading away." Regional detention centres opened "broad horizons for the introduction of intelligent and humane methods of meeting the needs of those who enter this door."[27]

Throughout Grossman's tenure in Corrections, the most important barrier to reform had been the federal government. Leo Hackl found the department's efforts "continually hampered" by federal legislation, indifference, and intransigence.[28] In juvenile corrections, provincial efforts were restricted by the outmoded Juvenile Delinquents Act of 1908. In adult corrections, the provinces were responsible for the incarceration of all those sentenced to less than two years, but they had to abide by the federal Prisons and Reformatories Act. For example, without federal legislation, it was impossible to utilize such a common rehabilitative tool as a temporary-absence scheme. The most serious problems, however, were remissions and paroles. The remissions situation was dangerous and ludicrous. For example, without federal legislation, it was impossible to utilize such a common rehabilitative tool as a temporary-absence scheme. By a 1960-61 amendment to the Penitentiaries Act, prisoners in federal institutions were given statutory remission for good behaviour that equalled one quarter of their sentence. As well, prisoners received three days of earned remission each month for industrious application to work. Thus a person sentenced to a penitentiary for two years might serve only one year and four months while someone sent to a reformatory for two years less a day served one year and nine months. "This was done," Hackl related, "without consulting the provinces. All of a sudden we saw the legislation and there it was."[29] Ontario officials believed it was done because federal institutions were overcrowded (a situation caused by the low priority given to corrections by the minister of justice). The situation, a classic example of legal stupidity, was disastrous. There were many escapes and some serious disturbances. As Hackl describes the situation:

> The usual sentence for escaping was nine months. The prisoner often would be transferred to a federal institution and even with the additional nine months, he'd probably get out months sooner. We took this up with each successive minister, always ending up with the same frustrating results.[30]

Finally, in 1969, Ottawa provided for equalization of good conduct remission and Ontario also was authorized to carry out a temporary absence program. This was a program Grossman and Hackl had wanted for years. The TAP, as it was called, was part of an omnibus bill Grossman marshalled through the House in 1968. It consolidated eighteen acts into one, and embodied, as well, a good deal of progressive new thinking. Included in the legislation was a provision that changed the department's name from "Reform Institutions" to "Correctional Services." The new Correctional Services Act was written in clear, concise English and could be easily understood by the general public, and by the department's clients.

The most innovative part of the new act was the creation of the TAP, and, with the passage of the 1969 Criminal Law Amendment Act in Ottawa, the province at last had the authority to begin the program. Under the temporary-absence program, inmates were allowed to be absent from a provincial institution for an unlimited period of time for medical reasons, and for up to fifteen days for humanitarian or rehabilitative purposes. As well, prisoners might be permitted to accept employment or attend educational institutions during the day; they would return to the institution at night. The omnibus bill received great attention in the press, and the temporary-absence program, in particular, caught the imagination of the media. The *Toronto Star* described it as a hopeful and humane reform, and urged Ottawa to amend its legislation at once. The *Telegram* saw it as an important step towards "the compassionate society."[31] The federal amendment was passed, and the program came into effect on 26 August 1969. The department regarded it as one of the most significant correctional innovations of the post-war era.

Temporary absence was late in coming to Ontario. The most famous example of a prisoner-leave program, Wisconsin's Huber Law, dated back to 1913. In Ontario, before World War One, a program had permitted convicts to work outside prison under supervision, but this was more a convict-labour device than a rehabilitative tool, and had long since lapsed. By the 1960s, convicts in Ontario could be released on a "ticket of leave" only under supervision, and only for such events as family funerals, while at the federal level a very limited "gradual-release program" had been instituted in the mid 1950s. For TAP, as for many of the reforms of the 1960s, Grossman's role was to push through and implement projects that had been in the air for some time, and to do so within the context of a coherent correctional ideology.

The Ontario scheme had its origins in Grossman's desire to incorporate into the Ontario system the best ideas for penal reform from foreign jurisdictions. Grossman and Don Kerr went to Wisconsin to study that state's scheme; Leo Hackl visited Mississippi to examine its system of conjugal visits. In some jurisdictions, conjugal visits were regarded as an alternative to temporary absences. In February 1969, Morton Shulman had introduced a private member's bill, in the Ontario House, to permit wives to have sexual relations with their husbands in jail "to reduce the amount of homosexuality in our prisons." But Hackl was not convinced that the Mississippi scheme was fair and practical. In a letter to Grossman, A.M. Kirkpatrick of the John Howard Society said a system of temporary leaves was vastly preferable to conjugal visits to address the problem "of maintaining family and community relationships at a level which recognizes human dignity."[32] Grossman made the same argument in the House.

There were many other advantages to the temporary-absence scheme. By working outside the prison, prisoners might be able to keep a job held at the time of conviction, or they might find a new position and be well established in it by the date of release. Through educational leave, Grossman pointed out, prisoners could pursue trade, technical, or academic training not offered in the institution. Most important, prisoners could maintain or re-establish close family and community relations. As well, the program saved the province a considerable sum of money. Inmates on work release were required to pay part of their salary to the institution and part to help maintain their families.

Grossman and his officials emphasized that the program was not a substitute for parole; it was, rather, an additional rehabilitative tool. One academic critic argued that a person who can be trusted to leave jail to go to work or school can be trusted on probation or parole; the critic was wide of the mark.[33] Probation and parole continued to exist, but TAP allowed prisoners a limited degree of freedom when they were not ready for parole. It helped them to cope with the transition to the community with the assistance of professional staff. It was especially useful at the provincial level, Grossman stressed, where prisoners were sentenced to a maximum of two years less a day and would be back on the streets and "likely to commit other offences unless [their] attitudes and anti-social behaviour have changed" in prison. And TAP also forced correctional officers to become more closely aware of the strengths and shortcomings of all prisoners. It thus reinforced the trend in the late 1960s to fuller inmate/staff involvement and to closer relations between the department and the community.

As Leo Hackl puts it, TAP was simply "a marvellous rehabilitative tool."[34] To head the program, the department created a new position: Administrator of Community Programs. This official would also work with citizen volunteers, group homes, and halfway houses. The program was an important step in the department's transition from an institutional bias to a new emphasis on community programming.

By the late 1960s, the department's changes in policy, personnel, and structure were irreversible. Modernization had been achieved. Whatever problems the future might bring, the bad old days were gone for ever.

Notes

1. Interview, John Foote.
2. At that time there were no parliamentary assistants to ministers. Frost was considering the establishment of such a system but rejected it, evidently on grounds of expense.
3. Interview, Leo Hackl.
4. W.E. Mann, *Society Behind Bars, A Sociological Scrutiny of Guelph Reformatory* (Toronto: Copp Clark, 1967), Chapter 8.
5. Interview, Tadeusz Grygier.
6. Ibid.
7. Interview, Don Sinclair.
8. Interview, Leo Hackl.
9. Interview, Don Sinclair.
10. Ibid.
11. Interview, Tadeusz Grygier.
12. Interview, Leo Hackl.
13. Interview, Tadeusz Grygier.
14. Interview, Harry Hutchison.
15. Interview, Aideen Nicholson.
16. Ibid.
17. Interview, Don Sinclair.
18. Interview, Leo Hackl.
19. Ibid.
20. Ibid. According to the Public Accounts of Ontario, the department's net expenditures increased from $12,623,996 in 1960-61 to $49,600,237 in 1970-71. Despite Grossman's achievements this remained a low-spending department and its expansion was not out of line with other departments in the same period; it could not be accused of "mollycoddling" inmates.
21. Interview, Leo Hackl.
22. Ibid.
23. G.P., Grossman to Robarts, June 2, 1964.
24. See G.P., address to John Howard Society, Kingston, February 17, 1964; address to Huron County Council, November 14, 1964; statements to legislature, February 23, May 12, 1965; speeches to Ontario Association of Mayors and Reeves, June 24, 1965 and to John Howard Society, London, February 14, 1966.
25. G.P., unidentified press clipping, July 1967.
26. Interview, Leo Hackl.
27. G.P., "Remarks.... The Opening of the Quinte Regional Detention Centre," May 15, 1971.

28. Interview, Leo Hackl.
29. Ibid.
30. Ibid.
31. *Toronto Star* and *Toronto Telegram,* May 29, 1968.
32. On conjugal visits see G.P., A.M. Kirkpatrick, Executive Director, John Howard Society, to Grossman, March 3, 1969; and Department of Correctional Services Position Paper, "Conjugal Visiting."
33. See Richard G. Fox, "Temporary Absence, Work-Release and Community Corrections in Ontario," Centre of Criminology, University of Toronto, n.d.
34. Interview, Leo Hackl.

Chapter 9

The Great Repression: Criminal Punishment in the Nineteen-Eighties[*]

Michael Mandel[**]

Introduction

Even before the stock market plummeted in October of 1987, parallels were being drawn between our era and the years just before the Great Crash of 1929. According to the experts, in each era an extraordinarily narrow concentration of wealth was aided and abetted by governments that were strikingly similar in their non-doctrinaire support for big business, combining handsome subsidies on the one hand with a laissez-faire approach to regulation and taxes on the other. Each era was seized by a takeover/merger mania financed by spiralling debt and fragile credit devices such as "margin buying" (in the 1920s) and "junk bonds" (in the 1980s). The stock market was widely believed, in each era, to be completely out of touch with the strength of the economy, and based instead on pure speculation (Davis 1987; Thomas 1987; Galbraith 1987), the whole thing resembling a mass game of chicken. Both periods saw quantum leaps in Canada's integration into the American economic orbit: the twenties was the decade in which U.S. capital bought out Canadian manufacturing and extraction industries, and the eighties was the decade of the Free Trade Agreement. Each decade started with a severe recession and the

[*] From L. Samuelson and B. Schissel (eds.), 1991. *Criminal Justice: Sentencing Issues and Reform.* Halifax, N.S.: Garamond Press.

[**] The author wishes to thank William Evans and Elain Bright for their help compiling tables and graphs, Caroll Barrett and Maggie Stockton for their stenographic work, and Harry Glasbeek, as always, for his friendly advice. For reasons of space, several sections of this paper had to be omitted, which may account for (some of) the disjointedness.

second half of each saw a boom which created unheard-of wealth, but also unheard-of inequality; spectacular profits were made amid falling wages and farm incomes. Even the moral crusade of the late eighties, the "War on Drugs," seemed like a replay of Prohibition, complete with its hypocrisy, international adventurism, official and unofficial violence, and, naturally, the fortunes being made from it (Thompson 1985: 63-69, 77-96, 138-157, 193-195; Granatstein et al. 1986: 197-203).

Conventional wisdom holds that a crash of 1929 dimensions would be very different this time around, what with social "safety nets" and the "general cushioning effect" of Keynesian fiscal policies (Galbraith 1987: 64). But there is reason to believe that the results of the next crash will be much *worse* than they were after 1929 because, on at least one very important index, the appropriate comparison for our times is not with the period just before the Great Depression but with its very depths. This is the index of *repression*. In criminal punishment terms, the Great Depression was more repressive than any period before, and as repressive as any period since, *except our era*.

As far as criminal punishment is concerned, the 1980s was the most repressive decade in Canada's history. During that decade, the *per capita* prison population reached and sustained an all-time post-confederation high. This occurred at a time when the official philosophy of corrections emphasized "community" above all else. The emphasis on community was due to the fact that in *relative* terms—but only in relative terms—imprisonment is a declining form of punishment. Since the 1960s, imprisonment has been greatly outstripped by the growth of penal measures that operate outside of the traditional prison setting. The most prominent of these is the probation order, a device of infinite variety: from the occasional meeting with a probation officer, through unpaid work ("community service"), to conditions identical to imprisonment ("Probation hostels"). On any given day, there are now three times as many people serving sentences of probation as there are in prison. Of course, this should not be allowed to obscure the fact that our imprisonment rate is higher than it has ever been. And this is *in addition to* a probation population never before seen in Canada's history.

Canada's Most Repressive Decade

The prison population

In determining the relative repressiveness of various periods in Canadian history, we are at the disadvantage of lacking consistent, comprehensive data. Comparable adult imprisonment figures covering all of Canada are only available since 1955. However, the method of reporting has changed significantly in two major respects. In the first place, since 1979 a distinction has been made between those "on register" and those "actually in" a given prison. This reflects the growth in the 1970s and 1980s of lawful absences from prison, especially "day parole." Since these mechanisms are part of the new "community" form of punishment, it would be misleading to include them in a comparison of *prison* populations in the past, especially since there were no comparable forms of lawful absences during the periods of high prison populations prior to the current one (e.g., 1961-1965 and 1931-1935). Consequently, I have tried to stick to the "actual in" counts, though sometimes these have had to be estimated. The second major change affecting comparability of data is the Young Offenders Act (YOA), which came into force in April 1985. The effect of this was to transfer a large number of offenders from adult court and adult punishment to youth court and youth punishment because it raised the age of majority for criminal law purposes from between 16 and 18, depending on the province, to a uniform national age of 18. This, *and this alone*, is responsible for the apparent fall-off in the adult prison population after 1985. However, to adopt the new definitions for comparison purposes would also be misleading, because 16- and 17-year olds are still being imprisoned; in fact they are being imprisoned in greater numbers than they were before YOA. The only real difference is that they are being imprisoned under different legislative mandates. To merely accept the reclassification as determinative would make long-term historical comparisons impossible. I have tried, therefore, to adjust the figures to counteract this "Young Offenders Act effect."

Ontario keeps separate figures for 16- and 17-year olds sentenced under the YOA and I have used these to project a national effect (based on Ontario's share of the relevant measures). I have then simply added these projected national figures to the conventionally reported adult imprisonment figures.[1] It turns out that, even apart from the YOA, the 1980s were the most prison-prone decade in Canada's history, but not to take account of the YOA effect would be to unnecessarily minimize the trends of the decade. Furthermore, excluding these numbers gives the completely misleading impression that the prison population started to fall drastically in the late 1980s.

Appendix Table I shows that in each of the years 1983 through to 1988 the per capita prison population exceeded the previous record high (for the period covered by the table) of 1963 by between 2.7 percent and 9.5 percent. The average prison population per 100,000 Canadian population for the five-year period 1984-1988 exceeded the five-year period 1961-1965 (the previous five-year high) by 111.3 to 103.6 (a difference of 7.4 percent). The decade average for 1980-1988 exceeded the 1960s average by 105.6 to 99.7.[2] The average prison rate for the 1970s was only 89.3 per 100,000, with a high of 96.4 in 1977.

Since 1955, therefore, the current period is clearly the most repressive in terms of the proportion of the Canadian population in prison on any given day.

To reach back farther, we have to use proxy figures. The "total institutional population" (Appendix Table II) has the advantage of going back to 1916; but it has the considerable disadvantage of not distinguishing between adult and juvenile detention. This table shows that the high imprisonment period of 1961-1965 was also higher, on average (123.2 per 100,000), than any other period since 1916, including 1930-1934 (117.3), though the rate for its highest year in total institutional terms (1964: 125.9) was slightly lower than the rate for 1932 (126.1), the depths of the Depression. To estimate the adult rate for the Depression so that it can be compared with the 1980s requires deflating the Depression figures to remove the element of juvenile imprisonment. This results in an average adult imprisonment rate for 1934 of between 98.6 and 105.3 per 100,000 (depending on the assumptions one makes),[3] putting the Depression's worst years well below the levels reached in the 1980s. The most repressive year of the Depression era, 1932 (0.2 percentage points above the most repressive year of the early 1960s), would, on this calculation, be assigned an adult imprisonment rate of between 105.7 and 113.2[4] per 100,000 Canadian population, still below the 1987 level of 114. If the entire decade of the 1930s is considered, the relative severity of our era becomes even more obvious. The average total (including juvenile) imprisonment rate for the 1960s was 118.7 per 100,000; it was 99.7 for adult institutions. For the 1930s as a whole, the average total institutional population was 113.1 per 100,000, from which can be estimated an adult population of between 95 and 101.5 adult prisoners per 100,000 population, compared to the 1980s adult institution average of 105.6.[5]

The only figures we have going back all the way to 1867 are for the *penitentiary* population (Appendix Table III; Figure 1). In Canada, "penitentiary" has a specialized meaning: prisons administered by the federal government. Consequently, these figures leave out of account those prisoners serving sentences in provincially administered institutions, a varying percentage of the prison population which has always constituted more than half of the total prisoners. The penitentiary population has varied as a percentage of the total prison population from a low of 26.7 percent in 1937 to a high of 43.5 percent in 1974. On the other hand, while "penitentiary," is a purely jurisdictional term and does not designate any particular type of prison, Canadian criminal law has always reserved "penitentiaries" (i.e., federally-administered prisons) for prisoners serving sentences of two years or more, i.e., the longest sentences. So the penitentiary population can serve as an index of penal severity: at any given time, what proportion of the Canadian population are serving prison sentences of two years or more? Here, too, the current era takes the prize. The average penitentiary population for 1984-1988 was 42.9 per 100,000, while for 1931-1935 it was only 38.2.

Table 1

Penitentiary Population Per 100,000 Total Population		
Decade	Decade Average	Decade High
1980-88	40	44.2 (1986)
1970-79	38	41.3 (1973)
1960-69	37	39.7 (1964)
1950-59	34	36.0 (1959)
1940-49	29	33.1 (1940)
1930-39	35	43.1 (1933)
1920-29	26	29.6 (1922)
1910-19	24	26.6 (1910)
1900-09	24	26.9 (1900)
1890-99	26	27.9 (1898)
1880-89	26	28.5 (1880)
1870-79	22	28.7 (1879)
1867-69	25	28.1 (1867)

[From Appendix Table III]

So, in terms of imprisonment, the 1980s were the most repressive years in Canada's history, including the years of the Great Depression.[6] Of course, imprisonment is not the only form of state repression and certain other forms were more typical of the Great Depression than of our own era. One such form was the death penalty (Appendix Table IV). There were 83 executions for murder in the years 1931-1935, almost twice as many as during the five-year period either preceding or following, and over one-third more than any other period in Canada's history (the next blood thirstiest period was 1946-1950, with 62 executions). The Depression was more violent in terms of the death penalty than any era before or since. There have been no judicial executions in Canada since 1962. In purely quantitative terms, these numbers are very insignificant:

adding them to the prison population does not change the rounded per 100,000 population rate at all. But state-sanctioned killing cannot just be ignored. On the other hand, our era has no right to be complacent about its lack of capital punishment. Deaths "by legal intervention" (that is, killings by police or prison guards), judicially sanctioned, were far from unknown in the 1980s. In the years 1980-1986 (the latest for which figures are available), such deaths numbered 63, or 9 per year (Statistics Canada 1980-86). Furthermore, deaths of prisoners averaged 77 a year for the last ten years for which information is available (1979-1988); of these, 33 per year were suicides—about 6.5 times the Canadian rate (Statistics Canada 1987-1988: Table 31; 1980-86). There are no readily available figures with which to compare our era and the 1930s in this respect.[7]

In quantitative terms, far more significant than deaths were the great number of deportations that took place during the Depression (Appendix Table V). The deportations for the years 1930-1933 were almost triple the per capita rate for any four years in the nineteen-eighties. Adding deportations to imprisonment changes the picture considerably, making the 1980s at most only slightly more repressive than the 1930s (122.7 to 121.3), and perhaps even less repressive (122.7 to 127.8), depending on the formula used. Whatever the formula, adding deportations to imprisonment means that the period 1930-1934 was substantially worse than 1984-1988 (146.4/153.1 to 124.7); it also means that the high rate of repression for 1932 far outweighed the rate for the fiscal period 1982-1983 (178.7/186 to 130.4).

It is important to determine whether the number of persons deported should be added to the number of persons imprisoned. Should deportation be regarded as on the same level of repression as imprisonment? There is no question that a large number of Depression deportations were meant to supplement the criminal law system. In the first place, there are many documented cases of the use of deportation to rid the country of political radicals, some of whom had been convicted of crimes and had already served terms of imprisonment (Roberts 1988: 48-52). Secondly, deportation was used "as an alternative to relief," an explicit means of "'shovelling out' the unemployed" (Roberts 1988: 162,169). On the other hand, there are a number of documented cases of people who *wanted* to be deported, especially to the British Isles (where most of the deportees wound up) because of the desperate situation in Canada (Roberts 1988: 185). Things could be substantially better at home and deportation meant a free, if uncomfortable, passage. While the government's claim of 90 percent voluntary deportees was certainly exaggerated (Roberts 1988: 181-82), it is hard to know where the truth lies. More importantly, there is a great difference between imprisonment and deportation to one's home country (assuming one is not claiming to be a refugee). For one thing, the state's concern with the deportee ends at the border; the deportee, as such, is under no sentence of any sort in the home country. For another thing, the element of enforced isolation is lacking; in the 1930s, whole families were deported along with the breadwinner (Roberts 1988).

Of course, the point is not to minimize deportation, or even the desperate conditions of working people neither deported nor imprisoned. What we are trying to grasp, and what distinguishes certain periods in our history, especially our own, is the level of *state* repression, the repression of the public sphere as opposed to the private sphere. In this regard, deportation seems much more like probation than imprisonment. Imprisonment localizes punishment and surveillance in an isolated institution. Probation and related measures, such as parole, extend punishment and surveillance beyond the walls of the prison into the community, where, at various levels of restraint, the offender is kept under surveillance and required to carry out certain duties, more or less onerous depending on the circumstances of the case. Some probation can certainly be more repressive than deportation. Deportation, where involuntary, follows the offender to the border and then says goodbye; probation and related measures follow the offender into the community and keep an eye on him or her for years.

Whether or not the correct analogy for deportation is probation, it is clear that probation must be taken into account in any quantification of repression. If that is so, then the Depression, deportations and all, is not a match for the current era in terms of repression.

The Probation Population

In comparison to the prison population, the probation population has grown not only steadily but spectacularly. This is almost entirely a post-World War II development. There was some probation before the War, but it was on a tiny scale. Ontario appointed the first two adult probation officers in 1922, but progress was slow and there were only eight of them altogether in Ontario between 1930 and World War II (McFarlane 1966: 31-32). These were the only adult probation officers in the entire country (Canada 1956: 13-14; Sheridan and Konrad 1976: 254). Only 14 officers in all had been appointed in Ontario by 1951 (McFarlane 1966: 62). Then, suddenly, between 1952 and 1956, the complement grew from 15 to 94 (McFarlane 1966: 67). By 1965 there were 167 (McFarlane 1966: 96-97). Subsequent developments in admissions can be seen from Appendix Table VI. While jail admissions outnumbered probation admissions by 9:1 in 1965, this ratio had dropped to under 7:1 by 1972, to under 3:1 by 1976, down to just over 2:1 in 1979, where it has hovered since. At the same time, the rate of probation admissions grew from about 98 per 100,000 population in 1965 to 367 per in its peak year of 1982. Another indication of the rate of growth is that between 1951 and 1979 Ontario's adult probation officer complement went from 15 to 429 (including supervisors) (Hatt 1985: 300).

Other provinces shared this experience. Alberta was the second province with adult probation services in 1940 and British Columbia followed in 1946 (Sheridan and Konrad 1976: 254). The number of probation officers in British Columbia just about doubled every five years from 1950 through 1975, from 6 officers to 266, an increase in rate from about .5 per 100,000 British Columbia population to 11 per 100,000 (Sheridan and Konrad 1976: 254-255). The adult probation system in British Columbia employed 350 officers in 1979-1980 (13.5 per 100,000 population) (Hatt 1985: 300). National probation figures do not exist for earlier than 1978-1979, and since that time they have remained fairly stable, with probation accounting for roughly one in every four admissions to the correctional system (Appendix Table VIII) (Ontario's roughly one in three is high on the national scale.)

But *admission* rates are nothing compared to *average daily population* rates (Figure 2). Somewhere between 1965 and 1972, the number of adults on probation in Ontario, which had been insignificant, indeed verging on non-existent prior to 1950, surpassed the number of adults in prison. By 1975 the figure, which had more than doubled in relation to Ontario's total population, was also more than twice as high as the prison population. By 1979 it was more than three times as high, and by 1983 Ontario's adult probation population was more than four times its adult prison population (Appendix Table VII).[8] Once again the national dimensions are similar, if slightly more modest, with the adult probation population at approximately three times the prison population (Appendix Tables IX).

We can now return to our comparison with the Great Depression. During the 1980s (1980-1988), the average daily adult population under judicially ordered control and supervision, including prison, probation, parole and mandatory supervision, was 429.8 per 100,000 (422.4 for 1979-1988), with a high of 462 in 1987. If deportations are added to this, the total "repression rate" can be calculated at 446.8 per 100,000 for 1980-1988 with a high of 471.6 in 1986-1987. This is 3.5 *times* our best estimate for the 1930s, a rate of between 121.3 and 127.8. The particularly repressive years of 1984-1988 had an average rate of 465.8 per 100,000, more than 3 *times* the most repressive Depression years of 1930-1934, with an estimated rate of between 146.4 and 153.1. The peak year of 1987, with a rate of 471.6, was more than 2.5 *times* the Depression high rate of between 178.7 and 186 in 1932.

It is true that there was some minor Depression probation activity which probably should be added to the figures we have already calculated, if only for the sake of completeness. They do not change the picture at all, however. There were only 8 probation officers operating in Ontario during the Depression compared to 429 in 1979. Ontario accounted for all of the

Depression probation for adults, but only about 52 percent of probation in the 1980s (Statistics Canada 1987-1988: 125). There was also a form of parole in the pre-War period, but it was entirely lacking in enforceable conditions, or the parole officers to enforce them. This means that probation/parole levels during the Depression could be no more than about 1 percent of what they are now, even assuming constant caseloads, which seems very unlikely, as caseloads appear to have more than doubled between 1965 and 1979 alone.[9] But even assuming constant caseloads, this would mean a maximum of about 900 cases in total during the Depression, or about 9 per 100,000; adding this to the figures for the 1930s does not change things at all. The 1980s remain more than 3 times as repressive as the 1930s, the late 1980s 2.9 times as repressive as the early 1930s (the worst years of the Depression), and 1987 2.4 times as repressive as 1932, which, until the 1980s had been Canada's worst year for repression.[10] In other words, the 1980s were easily the most repressive years in Canada's history.[11]

Understanding Decarceration

Official ideologists have described the community corrections movement in the most glowing terms imaginable:

> Diversion is a promise!
> It is a promise that the poor, the uneducated, the disadvantaged and the abandoned who come in conflict with the law will receive the support and compassion of their communities (Canada 1978: 10).

Even among left-wing criminologists it is possible to find the rising rate of repression and the proliferation of community corrections treated as "contradictory" or as "a momentous liberal compromise" (Taylor 1985: 331). It is obvious that community corrections is neither promise nor compromise. The level of imprisonment has not only not abated, but has actually increased with community corrections, which have added to the arsenal of the state techniques of repression that are sometimes as intrusive as the traditional forms—indeed indistinguishable from them in some cases—and often more insidious. One thinks, for example, of the electronic bracelet to keep the probationer or parolee under constant Orwellian surveillance; or of the "probation hostel," minimum security prisons where persons under sentence of probation mix with persons under sentence of imprisonment (*R. v Degan* 1985). The community corrections phenomenon has expanded the power of the state's repressive apparatus, and has been predictably employed to increase enormously the proportion of the population under criminal sentence and surveillance, with no observable impact on the level of crime. It is hard to imagine a more important object of criminal law reform than the reversal of this trend. In Foucault's words:

> If there is an overall political issue around the prison, it is not therefore whether it is corrective or not; whether the judges, the psychiatrists or the sociologists are to exercise more power in it than the administrators or the supervisors; it is not even whether we should have prison or something other than prison. At present, the problem lies rather in the steep rise in the use of these mechanisms of normalization and the wide-ranging powers which, through the proliferation of new disciplines, they bring with them (1977: 306).

In order to stop something, though, you usually have to know why it is happening in the first place. Do we know what is causing all of this repression? Do we know anything about what causes variations in the repression rate?

What strikes even the casual student of the history of punishment in the twentieth century is how closely changes in the repressive rate seem to parallel changes in economic conditions or what is often called the "business cycle." The Great Depression of the 1930s, and the recessions of the late 1950s and the early 1980s have all been accompanied by a steep rise in the rate of repression. The recovery periods of the late 1930s and the mid-1960s were both periods of falling repression. During the sustained period of rising repression that Canada has experienced since the Second World War, there has been an "upward drift" of unemployment rates; in other words "the unemployment floor has been at a successively higher level" (Ostry and Zaidi 1979: 146).

Greenberg (1977) has shown a striking correlation between oscillations in the annual unemployment rate for ages 16 and over and annual admissions to Canadian penitentiaries during the years 1945-1959, a correlation of 92 percent with only a slight time lag of imprisonment behind unemployment. U.S. data are reported to be remarkably similar. In fact, the relationship between unemployment and repression is fairly well-established in the criminological literature (Crow et al. 1989). What is not so well-established is the mechanism at work. Most conventional explanations of the connection between repression and unemployment are via an assumed relationship between *crime* and unemployment. The conventional explanation is that economic recession causes crime, and this rather predictably brings forth more repression. For example, Ehrlich argues that high unemployment and an otherwise contracting economy create greater material incentives for property crime and diminish disincentives such as the loss of earning capacity one might experience from a sentence of imprisonment (1973: 529-30, 538-39, 555). Tepperman has provided a more subtle analysis of the Great Depression in Canada along similar lines: severe conditions resulted in crimes of protest, crimes of "day-to-day survival" and crimes of just plain "craziness" (1977: 176-79).

The problem with the conventional explanation is the persistently weak relationship shown between the crime rate and the unemployment rate. In Greenberg's (1977) study, the rate of penitentiary admissions had nothing to do with the criminal conviction rate and little to do with the crime rate itself. The relation between the homicide rate and the unemployment rate, though substantial (.22), was too weak to support the changes in penitentiary admissions. Greenberg concluded that:

> It thus appears that in both Canada and the United States, changes in commitments to prison can be explained almost entirely by changes in the unemployment rate. Changes in the number of cases entering the criminal justice system and potentially available for imprisonment seem to be unimportant, as does the crime rate (1977: 650).

Like American rates, Canadian rates of reported crime since 1960 bear no apparent relation to the oscillations of the prison population over the same period. Crime rates have risen more or less steadily, while repression rates have fluctuated with the business cycle. The same was true during the Great Depression: conviction rates had been rising steadily from the beginning of the century and merely continued to rise through the Depression, albeit at an accelerated rate in some categories (Tepperman 1977: 181, 216).

Such observations have led to more complicated hypotheses. Some studies have emphasized the sentencing system. For example, one study found that when controls for average prison sentences were imposed, the amount of variation in U.S. federal prison population explained by the unemployment rate dropped from 70 percent to 54 percent. Thus, a little more than one-fifth of the connection between prison population and unemployment was explained by sentencing, with nothing explained by the conviction rate (Yeager 1979). Greenberg, too, concluded that the answer lay in the sentencing system. Though he doubted that judges consciously "orient their sentencing policies to the requirements of the labour market and that they agree on how this can best be done" (1977: 650), he was willing to "speculate" along two lines: either that "judges are less willing to grant probation to offenders when they are unemployed, or that unemployment affects levels of community tolerance toward offenders, to which judges respond in sentencing" (Greenberg 1977:650).

Both hypotheses have their adherents. A recent study of English courts emphasized the way "unemployment restricts options" in sentencing (Crow et al. 1989: 27). Controlling for offence and record, the authors found that an offender's employment status made a significant contribution to the severity of the sentence: an unemployed offender was less likely to be fined and was more likely to get probation, a community service order, or prison. The effect varied from community to community. It was most pronounced in traditionally low unemployment areas, in punitive courts, and in areas where unemployment was increasing from low to high (Crow et al. 1989: 47). Even where unemployment was high, it made a difference in a negative way: judges felt it important to keep an employed person out of jail so as not to jeopardize employment status (Crow et al. 1989: 61-62).

In Canada, employment status is both an empirically observable and legally accepted factor in determining a sentence, despite the lack of any plausible philosophical justification (Mandel 1984). On the other hand, employment status is not considered by judges as an end in itself, but rather as a part of the assessment of the offender's "character." "Fault," even in matters of unemployment, is an important part of this. It seems far too legalistic—especially since sentencing is the most "unlegal" aspect of criminal law—to let the courts off the hook by assuming that they would *inadvertently* ignore the general economic climate in assessing the offender's character.

The hardening of official, including judicial, attitudes seems a more likely explanation of increased repression. Tepperman makes a strong case for an increase in "official punitiveness," as well as in real crime during the Depression, with sentencing severity and conviction rates rising to unheard-of heights in the early thirties and then falling back again (1977:62-65). The most striking evidence is the execution rate. As Appendix Table IV shows, the years 1931-1935 had the most executions for any five year period before or since, but they had fewer homicides and murder charges than the prior five year period. What they had was an 89 percent higher conviction-to-charge rate for murder charges, and a 50 percent higher likelihood of a death sentence being carried out. In other words, despite the lower homicide rate, a person charged with murder was almost twice as likely to be executed during 1931-1935 than during 1926-1930.

The Depression was a period not only of severe deprivation but of extremely high working class militancy. The Communist Party achieved its greatest popularity and influence, the Co-operative Commonwealth Federation was founded, and the real fear of revolution led to severely repressive actions on the part of the government. This included the outlawing of the Communist Party, the imprisonment of its leaders, and violent confrontations between workers and police, such as during the "On-to-Ottawa Trek" (Thompson and Seager 1985: 222-35):

With mounting discontent with the way Canada was being run during the Depression, the government, police and courts may have organized more tightly to punish and control the discontent throughout the country (Tepperman 1977: 176).

Tepperman's general hypothesis is that "the worse socioeconomic conditions become, the more punitive judges and juries become" (1977: 63). Stephen Box has advanced a version of this to explain a similar rise of repression in the 1980s in the United Kingdom, where prison sentence admissions rose from 117 per 100,000 population in 1956 to 187 in 1983, and the average prison population went from 64 to 87 per 100,000 during the same period (1987: 12). Box demonstrates that increases in the official crime rate, while reflecting real increases in crime (as shown by victimization studies) greatly exaggerate them.[12] One United Kingdom study showed that about 85 percent of the increase in burglary between 1972 and 1983 was attributable to increased reporting (Box 1987: 18-21). Box argues that some of this is due to increased willingness to report crime on behalf of victims and better record keeping by police, but that it also reflects greater official punitiveness and fear of rebellion:

As unemployment rises, so the surplus labour force becomes a body viewed more suspiciously by the governing elite, not because it actually does become disruptive and rebellious, but because it *might* (1987: 62).

Nevertheless, even those advancing a "punitiveness" hypothesis have attributed at least *some* of the increase in repression to real increases in crime. Recent studies have suggested that it may be stronger than we have thought and that the problem with the studies so far is that they have not been sufficiently sensitive to different *types* of crime. When crime rates are "disaggregated" into different types, a much closer relationship between repression and crime can be observed. A sophisticated cross-national study has found that prison rates correlate with serious crimes (homicide, robbery, aggravated assault, fraud) but not with minor ones (theft, burglary) (Moitra 1987: 71, 86). This difference is something we should expect from the changing roles of prison and probation mentioned above. Furthermore, disaggregated unemployment data has shown a closer relationship between unemployment and crime: certain age groups are more vulnerable than others to being affected by unemployment, and their situation is better grasped by certain measures of unemployment (e.g., participation rates) rather than others (Crow et al. 1989: 6-10). Once again, there is clearly an exaggeration effect: for example, unemployed people are searched more often by police (Crow et al. 1989: 10-11).

There is much scepticism among eminent criminologists about the reality of the increase in crime. Chan and Ericson have shown that most of the post-war increase in minor crime can be accounted for by increases in per capita policing alone (Chan and Ericson 1981: 51-53). Furthermore, the steady rise in official U.S. crime rates has not been matched by victimization surveys which show the crime rate stable through the 1970s and actually falling through the 1980s (Hagan 1986: 59; Siegel 1989: 62-63; Chambliss 1988: 32-35). On the other hand, victimization surveys exclude the homicide rate, which has also increased substantially. This increase is extremely unlikely to be artificial because of the difficulty in manufacturing homicides that have not really occurred and the high likelihood that those that occur will come to official attention. There is very little doubt, even among statistic sceptics, about the reality of the homicide increase (Chambliss 1988: 40-41; Hagan 1986: 175). Indeed, the homicide rate during the late 1920s and the early years of the Depression, though a historical high water mark until the mid 1960s, was far below the averages Canada has experienced for the last two decades. Homicide averaged 1.1 per 100,000 between 1936 and 1966, while for the 1930s, the average was 1.4 per 100,000. The worst five years for homicide in the Depression era (1928 to 1932) averaged 1.7 per 100,000; since the 1970s, the homicide rate has averaged 2.6 per 100,000 population, and the murder rate (only the most serious homicides), 2.4. The worst year for homicide during the Depression was 1930, with a rate of 2.1 per 100,000; since 1972, the *murder* rate in Canada has *never fallen below* 2.1, and the homicide rate, never below 2.3 (Reed 1983: 21-27). Indeed, it has been argued that homicide rates *underestimate* the increase in the rate of lethal violence:

> Faster ambulances, better communications, transportation, and emergency room service meant better treatment for seriously injured persons, so that many who previously would have been homicide statistics were surviving (Hagan 1986: 177).

It is worth noting that the *attempted* murder rate increased more than four times as rapidly as the murder rate between 1962 and 1987 (Dominion Bureau of Statistics 1962a, 1965, 1968; Statistics Canada 1971b, 1975a, 1980, 1983a, 1984, 1985a, 1986, 1987b).

If murder has genuinely increased, there is good reason to believe that violence in general has as well, even if some part of the official increase is a reporting phenomenon. On the other hand, it is also clear that violent offenders make up a small part of the clientele of the total population under sentence, and can in no way account for either the increase in prison populations or, for the explosion in probation. This it is clear from the sheer numbers that many of those in community corrections would never have gone to prison.

Furthermore, with what we know about the increasing punitiveness and intrusiveness of community corrections, it is also clear that those who would not have gone to prison would not have been subject to anything like the supervisory regime they now experience. This also lends support, indirectly, to the notion that much of the conduct now attracting probation would not even have reached the level of official notice before. It is hard to see the incentive for the police bothering to take notice of things about which nothing or virtually nothing is going to be done.

None of the alternatives—increased crime, increased repression, or both—is very appetizing, of course. Either we are more repressed because we are more victimized or we are merely more victimized by being more repressed. But on the best evidence, we seem to be left with this: downturns in the business cycle cause real crime to rise, and this is met by increased repression, but in a way that exaggerates, sometimes to a great extent, the real increase in crime. How is it though, that we are now more punitive than during the Depression? If unemployment is responsible, then the Depression should have been far more repressive than our own era. The Depression was a "total and massive disruption of the economy" with unemployment rates reaching more than 19 percent, almost twice the worst post-Depression rate of 11.8 percent in 1983.

It is possible to dispute the comparability of unemployment figures. Modern statistics clearly underestimate unemployment by excluding "discouraged workers," those who have given up actively looking for work because there are no jobs (Chen and Regan 1985: 20-21). Also, unemployment rates do not take into account the growing substitution of part-time for full-time jobs. Between 1975 and 1985 part-time workers as a percentage for all workers increased from 10.6 percent to 15.2 percent (Rinehart 1987: 165-66; van Cleef 1985). On the other hand, it is clear that there was nothing in the 1980s to match the severity or abruptness of the economic downturn of the early 1930s, when unemployment, however measured, increased threefold between 1929 and 1930 and sixfold between 1929 and 1933, and when average per capita income was cut in half between 1928 and 1933 (Thompson and Seager 1985: 350-51). Furthermore:

> The unemployed of that period were mainly adult males—the sole family earner—and there was no "safety net" of unemployment insurance or other income-support measures which today greatly reduce the disastrous economic effects of unemployment on the working population (Ostry and Zaidi 1979: 145).

In other words, the reasons for the greater repressiveness of our era must be sought outside of the short-term economic fluctuations, which have been the object of most studies of crime and unemployment. The reasons must have something to do with long-term differences between our era and the Depression.

Several theorists have postulated a kind of self-perpetuating expansion of the repressive capacity of the state, which is supposed to have an inbuilt tendency to spread from the enclosed institutions and to penetrate society ever more deeply. The foremost proponent of this thesis was Foucault. Foucault argued that the disciplinary technique, which first flourished in factories, schools, hospitals, and prisons, from very early on exhibited a "swarming" tendency, a "tendency to become 'deinstitutionalized,' to emerge from the closed fortresses in which they once functioned and to circulate in a 'free' state" (1977: 211). At the beginning of the penitentiary system in the late eighteenth century one already sees the use of disciplinary mechanisms, not in the form of enclosed institutions, but "as centres of observation disseminated throughout society." Foucault gave the example of the Paris charity associations that sent our their missionaries on regular family visits for the purpose of reforming proletarian life (1977: 212):

> On the whole, therefore, one can speak of the formation of a disciplinary society in this movement that stretches from the enclosed disciplines, a sort of social "quarantine," to an indefinitely generalizable mechanism of "panopticism" (1977: 216).

For Foucault the prison held a special place in the disciplinary design. It was the mechanism which fashioned the "delinquent" (the dangerous individual—whose dangerousness does not reside solely in the offence—needing supervision) from the "offender" (the mere violator of laws needing no supervision). Delinquency, "with the generalized policing that it authorizes, constitutes a means of perpetual surveillance of the population: an apparatus that makes it possible to supervise, through the delinquents themselves, the whole social field." Foucault argued that this surveillance was at first "able to function only in conjunction with the prison" because of the powers of surveillance it authorized over the prisoner and ex-prisoner population (1977: 281). But soon there began to develop a "carceral archipelago," a series of institutions "beyond the frontiers of criminal law" (Foucault 1977: 298). The frontiers of criminal law:

> tended to disappear and to constitute a great carceral continuum that diffused penitentiary techniques into the most innocent disciplines, transmitting disciplinary norms into the very heart of the penal system and placing over the slightest illegality, the

smallest irregularity, deviation or anomaly, the threat of delinquency. A subtle, graduated carceral net, with compact institutions, but also separate and diffuse methods, assumed responsibility for the arbitrary, widespread, badly integrated confinement of the classical age (1977: 297).

The formation of this "archipelago" had for Foucault some important implications. One of these was the tendency to dissolve the distinction between crime and abnormality. Instead:

A certain significant generality moved between the least irregularity and the greatest crime; it was no longer the offence, the attack on the common interest, it was the departure from the norm, the anomaly; it was this that haunted the school, the court, the asylum or the prison.... You will end up in the convict-ship, the slightest indiscipline seems to say; and the harshest of prisons says to the prisoners condemned to life: I shall note the slightest irregularity in your conduct (Foucault 1977: 299).

Extending the carceral system beyond legal imprisonment succeeded "in making the power to punish natural and legitimate, in lowering at least the threshold of tolerance to penalty" (Foucault 1977: 301). It did this by giving legal legitimacy to all of the disciplines through their connection with the law (Foucault 1977: 302) and by freeing legal punishment from the appearance of excess and violence:

Between the latest institution of "rehabilitation," where one is taken to avoid prison, and the prison where one is sent after a definable offence, the difference is (and must be) scarcely perceptible. There is a strict economy that has the effect of rendering as discreet as possible the singular power to punish, the carceral "naturalizes" the legal power to punish, as it "legalizes" the technical power to discipline. By operating at every level of the social body and by mingling ceaselessly the art of rectifying and the right to punish, the universality of the carceral lowers the level from which it becomes natural and acceptable to be punished. (Foucault 1977: 302-03)

The spread of disciplinary power involved its fragmentation and dispersal to ubiquitous practitioners:

> The judges of normality are present everywhere. We are in the society of the teacher-judge, the educator-judge, the "social worker"-judge; it is on them that the universal reign of the normative is based.... The carceral network...has been the greatest support, in modern society, of the normalizing power (Foucault 1977: 304).

Foucault's vision of the localized penitentiary mechanism inexorably dissolving into the invisibly carceral city is obviously a profoundly disturbing one. An ever larger section of the population comes under the sway of an increasingly superior means of exercising power, superior because it is more subtle, more finely tuned, less visible and, therefore, more acceptable. The central locus of Bentham's "Panopticon" turns out to have limited its ability to "see without being seen." Most disturbing of all is the implication that the growth of this power is inevitable and completely detached from the history of political struggle that (even on Foucault's account) gives rise to it. It represents an inevitable technological impulse which, once set in motion, we are powerless to stop. Though Foucault did counsel opposition, nothing in his work provides any theoretical foundation for it actually to occur. Indeed, in his view, if discipline had not already eliminated politics altogether, it eventually would.

There are a number of reasons, however, to doubt this bleak view. If there are really no political forces driving these mechanisms, how is it that the decarceration boom had to await the aftermath of the cataclysmic events of the mid-twentieth century? Why does repression rise and fall with the business cycle? How is it that these community measures are compatible with a great expansion in the traditional overt, "compact" repression of the penitentiary? Why has the growth of the carceral city not seen the decline of the penitentiary? Has Foucault unduly neglected the purely repressive features of imprisonment, of the penitentiary as an institution for punishment, in his concern with the disciplinary "addition"? Repression implies resistance, or at least a lack of discipline. How can an increasingly "disciplinary society" also be an increasingly chaotic one where resort must increasingly be had to undisguised repression?

A useful contribution to a resolution of these contradictions has been made by Santos who argues that there is a "structural combination" between the community therapy of decarceration and the retributive renaissance in punishment (1980: 386). Both, he argues, are ways of replicating the social status quo while appealing to symbols of autonomy. Santos relies on the notion of "chaosmic power" to describe the repressive aspects of decarceration and other forms of informal or community justice. By leaving people to their own devices, these reforms *replicate* and therefore reinforce social power. They "integrate the sanctioning power in the ongoing social relationships connecting cosmic power to the chaosmic power which up until now had been outside its reach" (Santos 1980: 391). Where retribution legitimizes the status quo through the fiction of free will, community therapy does so by prescribing the status quo (the "community") as therapy. In other words, it is the "community" not the "therapy" that is the key to the concept.

In using the community, the state *"is expanding through a process which on the surface appears to be a process of retraction"* (emphasis in original):

> In other words, the state is expanding in the form of civil society and that is why the dichotomy of state/civil society is theoretically not useful anymore if ever it was. And because the state expands in the form of civil society, social control may be exercised in the form of social participation, violence in the form of consensus, class domination in the form of community action. In other words, the state power expands in a kind of indirect rule. (Foucault 1980: 391)

The community corrections movement fits this description very well. Whereas the prison was meant to be the egalitarian penalty (Foucault 1977: 232), probation represents the fruition of the penitentiary technique's replication of the inegalitarianism of the private sector. Probation is an infinitely *flexible* instrument for the distribution of offenders. It can use the entire community, with its diversity, to situate the offender in the proper designated role. The desired power relations can be enforced (or not enforced as in the case of privileged offenders) *in situ*, where and when they are supposed to take place, not, as with prison, after some period of preparation. One not only teaches the delinquent habits of industry, one actually puts the delinquent to work.

Apart from the enormous growth in the *dimensions* of the penal system which can be credited to the advent of community measures—"net widening," et cetera—this added flexibility itself represents a net increase in power. Indeed, flexibility is what unites the developments in probation with the expansion and elaboration of the prison itself. Increases in the use of both probation and imprisonment have been accompanied by further changes in the nature of both imprisonment and probation. Both have become more fungible, in the sense that each measure contains such great variety in levels of intrusiveness that imprisonment can be very much like probation and probation very much like imprisonment. Flexibility means that the differences within the notions of prison and community become as important as the differences between them. The specific designation of the sanction is increasingly irrelevant. Even the conviction itself is of decreasing importance as the conviction melts into the discharge which melts into the diversion program with no admission of guilt. All of these form a great continuum along which offences and offenders can be subtly distributed, according to their prescribed role in the structure of social power relations.

Thus, while in the case of *R. v Malboeuf* (1982), in which the defendant was a young Native in need of "stabilization," probation meant the equivalent of a minimum security prison for his breaking and entering, for businessman A. (*R. v A.* 1974), it meant a $1000 payment as "restitution" to the employee he tried to rape; and while for thousands of Ontario offenders, probation meant menial tasks such as snow-shovelling, for Keith Richards, caught in Toronto with 22 grams of heroin, it meant two free concerts for the blind at the earliest convenience of the Rolling Stones (*R. v Richards* 1979).

Accepting that we have a new, insidious form of power to contend with, we are still left trying to explain why this should be happening now. One attempted explanation comes from the frequently heard official defence of community corrections in terms of economics, i.e., that they constitute a great money savings over imprisonment. The embrace of community measures coincided with the "fiscal crisis" of deficit financing that hit Western governments in the nineteen-seventies, so many commentators have sought to explain community corrections this way. Santos himself favours a fiscal crisis explanation, supplemented by the ideological appeal of notions of "community" in an era in which real community is disappearing. Legitimacy in a time of economic contraction is more a matter of symbols than of "goods and services," thus the appeal to "transcendental values" (Santos 1980: 391) such as "community" and "responsibility" (Law Reform Commission of Canada 1976a, 1976b; Canada 1977: Chapter 4). Santos believes that "state sponsored community organization will be the specific form of disorganization [of the oppressed classes] in late capitalism" (Santos 1980: 390). Like Foucault, Santos foresees:

> A dislocation of power from formal institutions to informal networks. Social networks will then become the dominant unit of power production and reproduction, a source of power which is diffuse and interstitial and which as a consequence is as familiar as it is remote (1980: 392).

The fiscal crisis explanation has also been adopted by Scull (1977, 1984) who treats "decarceration" as a form of carceral "privatization."

Privatization has both fiscal and correctional aspects. It is the ideal-term designation of the 1980s movement by right-wing provincial and federal governments, following the example of the United Kingdom, to raise billions of dollars by selling off large chunks of the public sector, often at bargain-basement prices (Corcoran 1990); at the same time, the private sector itself has been turned over to the free play of market forces, through such deregulation initiatives as the Canada-U.S. Free Trade Agreement. The movement has many counterparts in the correctional system. One of these is the delivery of correctional services by private enterprise.

In the United States privatization of prison services, indeed of entire prisons in some states, has been a way governments have attempted to solve the problem of the costs of building new prisons to cope with overcrowding (Wilson 1989: 175ff.; *Globe and Mail*, July 24, 1986: A11, July 25, 1986: A8). In Canada, privatization has so far been restricted to community corrections, but that has meant that most of the expansion of such services has come in non-governmental form, through agencies of both the "not-for-profit" and, increasingly, the "for-profit" form (Griffiths and Verdun-Jones 1989: 592-93). In Ontario, all community residential centres and agencies are privately run on contract with the government, as are two-thirds of the community service order programs (Ontario 1985: 46). In the mid-eighties, the federal government also began to contract agencies run privately for profit to provide parole supervision and half-way houses (*Globe and Mail*, December 9, 1986: A19).

When public services are privatized by right-wing governments under a free market ideology, they generally operate more in accordance with market principles, which means a deterioration in those services delivered primarily to poor people. Even when the government is the main consumer in privatized service, the quality is reduced, because the government is seeking to reduce costs (often in wages to skilled, unionized employees), and because the private service exists to make profit. But the prison is not just another social service; besides meeting the needs of its clientele, it must also control and discipline them. Thus, we should not be surprised to learn that in the context of prison, privatization can mean something quite different from what it means in the context of other social services; in fact, prison privatization means quite the opposite of neglect. When a major privatization initiative in parole supervision was announced in 1986, the government reassured the public by promising that the reporting requirements for parolees had been *doubled* (*Globe and Mail*, September 20, 1986: A11). So privatization in corrections does not entail a loosening of the grip on offenders; on the contrary, it gives the government "more bang for its buck" and thus becomes a form of expansion and intensification of penal discipline.

Privatization takes other forms. The rather sudden concern by the penal system for "the victim" can be seen in this light. Victims and their grievances are obviously not new; what is, is the attention paid to them by the penal system. Practically, this has meant making restitution an important part of punishment, usually as part of a probation order. In Ontario, restitution orders are included in 15 percent of all probation orders, amounting to $5 million worth for adult offenders and another half million dollars for young offenders in 1987 alone (Ontario 1987: 12, 16). Restitution orders seem to function both as an alternative to prison for respectable offenders with the ability to pay

(Jackson 1982: 23-24), and as a means of toughening up an otherwise non-incarcerative sentence, in either case placating actual and potential victims. Both the community service order and the restitution order appeared with the denunciatory rationale of punishment (Law Reform Commission of Canada 1974a, 1974b, 1975, 1976a), and were conceived as *punitive*, not therapeutic, devices. A greater role in sentencing is also being given to the victim through "victim-impact" statements (*Criminal Code*, section 735 (1.1) in force January 1, 1989) and mediation alternatives (Baskin 1988). As with community service orders and other community measures, it appears that the offenders sentenced to restitution are drawn primarily from offenders who would not have gone to prison in the first place. The authors of one study of a popular Ontario restitution/mediation program concluded:

> On the whole VORP [Victim/Offender Reconciliation Program] has contributed little to sparing offenders imprisonment. Instead of avoiding problems created by the use of the prison system, another sentencing option has been implemented which pulls a different set of offenders deeper into the system of social control and inevitably increases cost (Dittenhoffer and Ericson 1983: 346).

The net result of the restitution initiative is to leave the punishment increasingly to a negotiation between victim and offender. No less than in the case of economic privatization, the private sphere is not an equal one; negotiation is inevitably influenced by the bargaining strength of the parties. The availability and onerousness of a restitution order depends on the financial status of the offender (*R. v Hudson* 1981; *R. v Sugg* 1986; *R. v Collard* 1987; *R. v Wilcox* 1988). The more the offender can pay, the more likely the offender will be able to buy off a more intrusive sentence. Furthermore, the more the offender can pay, the more likely it is that the victim can be persuaded to ask the court to make a restitution order instead of ordering a prison sentence (*R. v A.* 1974; *R. v Davies* 1988). If the offender cannot pay, then the offender works, either for the victim, or more often, under a community service order. The latest development combines restitution and community service through fines. Increasingly, offenders without money are given the choice of working off their fines instead of serving the time in prison (Ontario 1986: 13; *R. v Hebb* 1989; *Globe and Mail*, February 10, 1989: A11). These fines in turn are being earmarked for victim-assistance programs, as in the 1989 "victim-fine surcharge" amendment to the *Criminal Code* or the 1985 "fine-option" amendment (*Criminal Code*, ss. 718.1; 727.9). Of course, people who can afford their fines (which are still not set according to ability to pay) just pay them.

This seems rather appropriate for our economic system: those without property must work while those with property need not bother.

We have been examining the "fiscal crisis" explanation of community measures. The problem with *purely* fiscal explanations of this phenomenon, however, is that it has not resulted in a diminution of traditional repressive measures; it is part of the expansion, not the contraction, of the state's repressive capacity. In other words, though community measures clearly cost less than prisons, when both are expanding, the explanation cannot be restricted to governments trying to save money (Chan and Ericson 1981).

In their important work on the origins of the penitentiary system, Melossi and Pavarini (1981) have also offered a plausible interpretation of the developments we have been examining. Their main point is to show how changing productive relations can account for the rise of the penitentiary as the specific form of social control in competitive capitalism; but they also argue that the radical changes which have since taken place in productive relations in the twentieth century can similarly account for the nature of modern social control. They point to the concentration, centralization and changing organic composition of capital, the rise of unions, state involvement in the economy and the disintegrating effect this has all had on the once firm lines between public and private spheres. In late capitalism the market place becomes more and more the object of organization by business, union, and state:

> The sphere of circulation and consumption were subjected to the direct rule of capital: decisions on prices, the organization of the market and at the same time of a consensus, all became part of one and the same thing. Not only were the traditional instruments of social control strengthened—those areas of "the sphere of production" outside the factory from capitalism's inception—but also new instruments were created. The new strategy was towards dispersion, towards the extension and pervasion of control. Individuals are no longer locked up; they are got at where they are normally locked up: outside the factory, in society as a whole. Propaganda, the mass media, a new and more efficient network of police and social assistance, these are the bearers of a new kind of social control (Melossi and Pavarini 1981: 6).

More control of the marketplace is necessitated by ever more severe market dislocations, such as that of the Great Depression itself; inefficiency and unemployment abound and capital can no longer afford to follow its own logic. Rising unemployment even diminishes the need to prepare people for the factory; more and more what they have to be prepared for is idleness in the community. Community measures become part of this attempt to organize the community coercively when it can no longer be relied upon to regulate itself efficiently. This was, in fact, the express rationale of those who advocated an increased role for probation in the 1940s in Canada. Blaming rising prison populations on the breakdown of "proper home training during the past quarter century," the call went out for better funding, co-ordination and "legal authority" for the state's efforts to "step in and apply the necessary remedy where parents are failing in their duties" (Ontario 1943: 6):

> Parents who have failed are rather likely to fail again unless they are sufficiently strengthened and helped by probation officers and others who are capable. Very often that support and help are non-existent. In much of this province there are no regular probation officers, and where there are their time and energies are spread over too many cases (Ontario 1945: 6-7).

Not for one moment was probation to be confused with leniency in punishment; it was *more* and not less intervention that was being called for:

> Probation without proper supervision is dangerous. Too frequently it is worse.... Akin to the abuse of probation is the practice of suspending sentences without a proper follow-through. Generally there is no follow-through. Delinquents and criminals are well aware of that fact. The chance that they will be brought back and sentenced for breach of recognizance or the offence on which sentence is suspended is so small that they boldly ignore it and pursue their way (Ontario 1945: 6-7).

Thus the ideology underpinning the rapid expansion of the Ontario probation system in the early 1950s was an explicitly *disciplinary* one. The increase in prison population was blamed on a lack of proper supervision *in situ*, which could only be solved by state intervention in the form of probation supervision. Probation was advocated as a kind of penal Keynesianism, a state intervention into a malfunctioning private sphere. It is thus no coincidence that the great post-war increases in the proportion of economic activity taking place through the state and the increase in public sector employment coincide with the dramatic increase in community measures. But, rather than one causing the other, they turn out both to be products of the same underlying contradiction, the increasing inability of an economy structured upon private profit to (a) reproduce itself without violence, and (b) meet our basic economic needs. Instead of the full development and use of the energy and talent of the entire population, improved standards of living, and decreasing inequality, we have precisely the opposite: ever higher levels of unemployment (Ostry and Zaidi

1979), a stagnating economy (Statistics Canada 1988: 21-22, 28) and increasing inequality (Ross and Shillington 1989: 34; CALURA 1988: 28-29, 56; Davis 1987: 36; *Globe and Mail*, December 30, 1989: E11).

This leads to a much different assessment than the one offered by Foucault (1977), who saw "decarceration" as a purely technological movement detached from politics and bound to fix humanity in a seamless web of inescapable discipline. Instead of an invincible movement, decarceration becomes merely a strategy for holding on to an increasingly unstable social situation, a strategy which seems, furthermore, to be fraught with its own contradictions, such as escalating costs and the debasement of the coinage of punishment through overuse (Matthews 1979). The community measures phenomenon can be seen as the late capitalist breakdown in the separation between public and private spheres as applied to the penitentiary system: an attempt to expand state discipline ever more deeply into the community as capitalism becomes ever less capable of "standing on its own two feet" and traditional penal measures and levels of punishment become ever less capable of holding things together.

Notes

1. As adult and juvenile regimes become more alike, the justification for considering adult repression separately, as the present study does, diminishes; however, for most of Canada's history adults and children have been subjected to very different legal punishment regimes.

2. If we leave out the low year of 1969 to make the comparison more symmetrical, the difference is slightly less: 105.6 to 100.4.

3. If we assume that the relationship between adult imprisonment and juvenile imprisonment was more or less constant between 1930-34 and 1961-1965, an adult rate for 1930-1934 can be estimated by applying the known adult-total ratio of 1961-1965 to the figures for 1930-1934. This would give an adult rate of ($103.6/123.2 \times 117.3 = 98.6$).

    But was the relationship constant? There seems no statistical way of knowing this for sure. The relative use of training school as a disposition for those found delinquent was similar for the periods 1930-1934 ($3464/38815$ or 8.9 percent) and 1961-65 ($9771/87096$ or 11.2 percent), but not identical (Reed 1983: Z238-291). On the other hand, the per capita use of training school as a disposition was 6.6 per 100,000 in 1930-1934, while it was 10.3 in 1961-1965. Per capita use of a disposition is a far cry from institution population per capita, but these figures still suggest that a higher proportion of the later than of the earlier total institutional population involved training schools, which means that the assumption of constant ratios *underestimates* the severity of the repression of adults in the 1930s.

    To attempt to correct for this, we can apply the 1930-1934/1961-1965 disposition ratio of 6.6/10.3 to the proportion of the population during the 1961-1965 period that we know constituted juvenile detention: $123.2 - 103.6 = 19.6$, or 15.9 percent of the total institutional population for 1961-1965. At most training school seems to have been used 6.6/10.3 less in 1930-1934 than in 1961-1965, so the juvenile component of the 1930-1934 population can be reckoned at $6.6/10.3 \times 15.9$ percent $= 10.2$ percent. Therefore, to estimate the 1930-1934 adult population, the period's total population should be deflated by only 10.2 percent $= .898 \times 117.3 = 105.3$ per 100,000 population. This is well below the average for the worst five-year period of the 1980s which was 111.3 per 100,000.

4. On the assumption of a constant ratio between adult and juvenile imprisonment: $126.1/125.9 \times 105.5 = 105.7$; on the more generous deflator outlined in the prior footnote: $126.1 \times .898 = 113.2$.

5. On the assumption of a constant ratio between adult and juvenile imprisonment: $99.7/118.7 \times 113/1 = 95.0$; deflated by the formula of endnote 3 (which works out to .897 in this case): $.897 \times 113.1 = 101.5$.

6. Imprisonment figures just released show a rise in the per capita adult prison population for the fiscal year 1988-1989; it had fallen slightly in 1987-1988. The rise, not adjusted for the effect of the Young Offenders Act, was 1.9 percent for all institutions and 3.2 percent for penitentiaries (Statistics Canada 1988-89).

7. A study recently reported in the press, but not yet available to me, claims that prisoner deaths are at an all-time historical high (*Globe and Mail*, May 3, 1990: A8).

8. The reason for the difference between admission and daily population ratios is the fact that probation terms are generally so much longer than prison terms, meaning that fewer admissions result in high average daily populations. The median prison sentence for provincial admissions (more than 90 percent of all admissions) in 1984-1985 was 32 days, whereas the median probation term was 12 *months* (Statistics Canada 1984-1985: 165,173).

9. McFarlane reports 244 probation officers in Ontario in 1965 with an adult probation population of 5225 (McFarlane 1966: 90), while the 429 Ontario probation officers reported by Hatt for 1979 had to take care of at least 26,362 adult probationers (Hatt 1985: 300; Appendix Table VII).

10. It is possible that the early 1960s surpassed the Depression, or at least equalled it, but lacking better figures on probation it is difficult to be sure.

11. Probation figures just released show a rise in the per capita adult probation population for the fiscal year 1988-1989; it had fallen slightly for the two prior years. The rise, not adjusted for the effect of the Young Offenders Act, was 1.1 percent. However, a simultaneous fall in the parole population kept the total non-custodial supervised population at a constant per capita level (Statistics Canada 1988-1989).

12. There are parallel Canadian data on crime rates and social class area. It appears that the higher reported crime rates of lower social class areas are accounted for partly, but only partly, by higher rates of victimization. Another important contributing factor is the level of policing which, in effect, exaggerates the higher level of crime (Hagan, Gillis and Chan 1978).

References

Bala, N. 1988. "The Young Offenders Act: A Legal Framework," in Joe Hudson, Joseph P. Hornick and Barbara A. Burrows (eds.), *Justice and the Young Offender in Canada*. Toronto: Wall and Thompson.

Baskin, D. 1988. "Community Mediation and the Public/Private Problem," *Social Justice* 15: 98.

Beattie, J.M. 1986. *Crime and the Criminal Courts in England 1660-1800*. Princeton University Press.

Blumstein, A. 1988. "Prison Populations: A System Out of Control?" in Michael Tonry and Norval Morris (eds.), *Crime and Justice: A Review of Research*, Volume 10.

Bochel, D. 1976. *Probation and After-care, Its Development in England and Wales*. Edinburgh: Scottish Academic Press.

Box, S. 1987. *Recession, Crime and Punishment*. Totowa, New Jersey: Barnes and Noble Books.

Braithwaite, J. 1979. *Crime, Inequality and Public Policy*. London: Routledge and Kegan Paul.

CALURA. 1988. *Annual Report of the Minister of Supply and Services Canada under the Corporations and Labour Unions Returns Act. Part I—Corporations 1986.*

Canada. 1938. *Report of the Royal Commission to Investigate the Penal System of Canada*. Ottawa: King's Printer.

————. 1956. *Report of a Committee Appointed to Inquire Into the Principles and Procedures Followed in the Remission Service of the Department of Justice of Canada*. Ottawa: Queen's Printer.

————. 1969. *Report of the Canadian Committee on Corrections. Toward Unity: Criminal Justice and Corrections*. Ottawa: Queen's Printer.

————. 1977. *Third Report of the Sub-Committee on the Penal System in Canada, House of Commons Standing Committee on Justice and Legal Affairs*. Ottawa: Queen's Printer.

————. 1978. *Diversion: A Canadian Concept and Practice. A Report of the First National Conference on Diversion* October 23-26, 1977, Quebec City. Ottawa: Solicitor General of Canada. 1979/80 to 1987/88.

————. 1982. *The Criminal Law in Canadian Society*. Ottawa: Government of Canada.

————. 1983. *Sentencing Practices and Trends in Canada: A Summary of Statistical Information*. Ottawa: Department of Justice Canada.

————. 1984. *Sentencing*. Ottawa: Government of Canada.

————. 1987. *Sentencing Reform: A Canadian Approach. Report of The Canadian Sentencing Commission*. Ottawa: Minister of Supply and Services Canada.

————. 1988. *Taking Responsibility*. *Report of the Standing Committee on Justice and Solicitor General on its Review of Sentencing, Conditional Release and Related Aspects of Corrections*. Ottawa: Minister of Supply and Services Canada.

Canadian Bar Association. 1988. "Imprisonment and Release," *Justice Report* 5, 4: 9.

Caputo, T. and D.C. Bracken. 1988. "Custodial Dispositions and The Young Offenders Act," in Joe Hudson, Joseph P. Hornick and Barbara A. Burrows (eds.), *Justice and the Young Offender in Canada*. Toronto: Wall and Thompson.

Chambliss, William J. 1988. *Exploring Criminology*. New York: Macmillan Publishing Company.

Chan, Janet B.L. and R.V. Ericson. 1981. *Decarceration and the Economy of Penal Reform*. Toronto: University of Toronto Centre of Criminology.

Chen, Mervin Y.T. and T.G. Regan. 1985. *Work in the Changing Canadian Society*. Toronto: Butterworths.

Clement, W. 1975. *The Canadian Corporate Elite: An Analysis of Economic Power*. Toronto: McClelland and Stewart.

Collier, P. and R. Tarling. 1987. "International Comparisons of Prison Populations," *Home Office Research and Planning Unit Research Bulletin* 23: 51.

Conklin, J.E. 1989. *Criminology*. 3rd edition. New York: Macmillan Publishing Company.

Corcoran, T. 1990. "The Big Sell-Off," *Globe and Mail Report on Business Magazine*, January 1990: 25.

Correctional Service of Canada. 1983. *Directory of Community-Based Residential Centres in Canada 1983-84*. Ottawa: Minister of Supply and Services Canada.

Crow, I., P. Richardson, C. Riddington and F. Simon. 1989. *Unemployment, Crime, and Offenders*. London: Routledge.

Culhane, C. 1985. *Still Barred from Prison: Social Injustice in Canada*. Montreal: Black Rose Books.

Davis, L.J. 1987. "The Next Panic: Fear and Trembling on Wall Street," *Harper's Magazine* 274: 35, (May).

Dittenhoffer, T. and R.V. Ericson. 1983. "The Victim/Offender Reconciliation Program: A message to correctional reformers," *University of Toronto Law Journal* 33: 315.

Dominion Bureau of Statistics. 1940. *The Canada Year Book 1940*. Ottawa: King's Printer.

————. 1957-59 to 1970. *Crime Statistics, 1962, 1965, 1968*. Ottawa: Queen's Printer.

_____. 1962a. *Correctional Services 1957-59; 1960-61; 1962; 1963; to 1964; 1965-65; 1965-66; 1966-67; 1967-68; 1968-69; 1969-70, 1969-70; 1970.*
_____. 1968. Ottawa: Queen's Printer.
Ehrlich, I. 1973. "Participation in Illegitimate Activities: A Theoretical and Empirical Investigation," *Journal of Political Economy* 51: 521.
Ekstedt, J.W. and C.T. Griffiths. 1984*Corrections in Canada: Policy and Practice.* Toronto: Butterworths.
Foucault, M. 1977. *Discipline and Punish: The Birth of the Prison.* Alan Sheridan, trans. New York: Pantheon.
Galbraith, J.K. 1987. "The 1929 Parallel," *The Atlantic Monthly* 62: 259 (Jan).
Glasbeek, H.J. 1988. "The Corporate Social Responsibility Movement--The Latest in Maginot Lines to Save Capitalism," *Dalhousie Law Journal* 11: 363.
Granatstein, J.L. I.M. Abella, D.J. Bercuson, R.C. Brown and B.J. Neatby. 1986. *Twentieth Century Canada.* Second Edition. Toronto: McGraw-Hill Ryerson Limited.
Greenberg, David F. 1977. "The Dynamics of Oscillatory Punishment Processes," *The Journal of Criminal Law and Criminology* 68: 643-51.
Griffiths, C.T. and S. Verdun-Jones. 1989. *Canadian Criminal Justice.* Toronto: Butterworths.
Hagan, F.E. 1986. *Introduction to Criminology: Theories, Methods, and Criminal Behaviour.* Chicago: Nelson-Hall.
Hagan, J., A.R. Gillis and J. Chan. 1978. "Explaining Official Delinquency: A Spatial Study of Class, Conflict and Control," *The Sociological Quarterly* 19: 386.
Hatt, K. 1985. "Probation and Community Corrections in a Neo-Correctional Era," *Canadian Journal of Criminology* 27: 299.
Hay, D. 1975. "Property, Authority and the Criminal Law," in D. Hay, et al. (eds.), *Albion's Fatal Tree: Crime and Society in Eighteenth-Century England.* London: Allen Lane.
Hornick, J.P., B.A. Burrows, J. Hudson and H. Sapers. 1988. "Summary and Future Directions," in Joe Hudson, Joseph P. Hornick and Barbara A. Burrows (eds.), *Justice and the Young Offender in Canada.* Toronto: Wall and Thompson.
Hunter, Alfred A. 1981. *Class Tells: On Social Inequality in Canada.* Toronto: Butterworths.
Jackson, M.A. 1982. *Judicial Attitudes Towards Sentencing Options.* Toronto: Ontario Ministry of Correctional Services.
Jaffe P. 1985. "Young Offenders System Tougher than Adult Court," *Ontario Lawyers' Weekly* 7: 4.
Kulig, P. 1990. "Lawyers Knock Report Suggesting Counsel to Blame for Increase in YOA Custody Rate," *Law Times,* April 9-15: 8.

Landerville, P., M. Hamelin and S. Gagnier. 1988. *Opinions of Quebec Inmates Regarding Questions Raised by the Mandate of the Canadian Sentencing Commission*. Ottawa: Department of Justice Canada. Research Reports of the Canadian Sentencing Commission.

Law Reform Commission of Canada. 1974a. *Working Paper No. 3: the principles of sentencing and dispositions*. Ottawa: Information Canada.

————. 1974b. *Working Papers 5 and 6: restitution and compensation; fines*. Ottawa: Information Canada.

————. 1975. *Working Paper 7: Diversion*. Ottawa: Information Canada.

————. 1976a. *Community Participation in Sentencing*. Ottawa: Information Canada.

————. 1976b. *Report: Our Criminal Law*. Ottawa: Information Canada.

Leacy, F.H., ed. 1983. *Historical Statistics of Canada*. 2nd ed. Ottawa: Minister of Supply and Services Canada.

Leschied, A.W. and P.G. Jaffe. 1988. "Implementing the Young Offenders Act in Ontario: Critical Issues and Challenges for the Future," in Joe Judson, Joseph P. Hornick and Barbara A. Burrows (eds.), *Justice and the Young Offender in Canada*. Toronto: Wall and Thompson.

Lynch, J.P. 1988. "A Comparison of Prison Use in England, Canada, West Germany and the United States: A Limited Test of the Punitive Hypothesis," *The Journal of Criminal Law and Criminology* 79: 180.

Madden P.G. and C.A. Carey. 1982. *Bail Verification and Supervision in Ontario*. Toronto: Ontario Ministry of Correctional Services.

Madden P.G. and S. Hermann. 1983. *The Utilization of Community Resource Centres*. Toronto: Ontario Ministry of Correctional Services.

Mandel, M. 1975. "Rethinking Parole," *Osgoode Hall Law Journal* 13: 501.

————. 1983. "McDonald and the R.C.M.P.," in *The Canadian Broadcasting Corporation Ideas: Law and Social Order*. Toronto: CBC Transcripts. Part I: 1.

————. 1984. "Democracy, Class and Canadian Sentencing Law," *Crime and Social Justice* 21-23: 163, also in Stephen Brickey and Elizabeth Comack (eds.), *The Social Basis of Law in Canada: Critical Readings in the Sociology of Law*. Toronto: Garamond Press, 1986.

————. 1985. "Democracy, Class and the National Parole Board," *Criminal Law Quarterly* 27: 159.

————. 1986. "The Legalization of Prison Discipline in Canada," *Crime and Social Justice* 26: 79.

————. 1987. "'Relative Autonomy' and the Criminal Justice Apparatus," in R.S. Ratner and John L. McMullan (eds.), *State Control: Criminal Justice Politics in Canada*. Vancouver: University of British Columbia Press.

————. 1989. *The Charter of Rights and the Legalization of Politics in Canada*. Toronto: Wall and Thompson.

Marx, K. 1853. "Capital Punishment," in Maureen Cain and Alan Hunt (eds.), *Marx and Engels on Law*. London: Academic Press.

Mason, B. 1988. "Implementing the Young Offenders Act: An Alberta Perspective," in Joe Hudson, Joseph P. Hornick and Barbara A. Burrows (eds.), *Justice and the Young Offender in Canada*. Toronto: Wall and Thompson.

Matthews, R. 1979. "'Decarceration' and the fiscal crisis," in Bob Fine et al. (eds.), *Capitalism and the Rule of Law: From Deviancy Theory to Marxism*. London: Hutchinson & Co.

McFarlane, G.G. 1966. *The Development of Probation Services in Ontario*. Toronto: Queen's Printer.

Melossi, D. and M. Pavarini. 1981. *The Prison and the Factory: Origins of the Penitentiary System*. G. Cousin, trans. London: The Macmillan Press Ltd.

Moitra, S.D. 1987. *Crimes and Punishments: A Comparative Study of Temporal Variations*. Freiburg i. Br.: Max Planck Institute for Foreign and International Penal Law.

Nettler, G. 1982. *Killing One Another*. Cincinnati: Anderson Publishing Company.

Niosi, J. 1985. "Continental Nationalism: The Strategy of the Canadian Bourgeoisie," in Robert J. Brym (ed.), *The Structure of the Canadian Capitalist Class*. Toronto: Garamond Press.

Ontario

————. 1891. *Report of the Commissioners Appointed to Inquire into the Prison and Reformatory System of Ontario*. Toronto: Legislative Assembly of Ontario.

————. 1941-45. *Annual Reports 1941, 1942, 1943, 1945*. Department of Reform Institutions of Ontario.

————. 1968-70. *Annual Report of the Minister 1968, 1969, 1970*. Department of Correctional Services of Ontario.

————. 1981-88. *Annual Reports of the Minister 1981-1988*. Ministry of Correctional Services.

————. 1987. *Corrections in Ontario: Everyone's Business*. Toronto: Ontario Ministry of Correctional Services.

Osberg, L. 1981. *Economic Inequality in Canada*. Toronto: Butterworths.

Ostry, S. and M.A. Zaidi. 1979. *Labour Economics in Canada*. Third Edition. Toronto: Macmillan of Canada.

Pate, K.J. and D.E. Peachey. 1988. "Face-to-Face: Victim-Offender Mediation Under the Young Offenders Act," in Joe Hudson, Joseph P. Hornick and Barbara A. Burrows (eds.), *Justice and the Young Offender in Canada*. Toronto: Wall and Thompson.

Pease, K. 1980. "Community Service Orders," in *International Conference on Alternatives to Imprisonment Report* Solicitor General of Canada (Workshop 6: 41). Ottawa: Minister of Supply and Services Canada.

Polonski, M.L. 1981. *The Community Service Order Program in Ontario. 4. Summary.* Toronto: Ontario Ministry of Correctional Services.

Powell, C.M. 1976. *Arrest and Bail in Canada.* 2nd ed. Toronto: Butterworths.

Reed, P. 1983. "Section Z: Justice," in F.H. Leacy (ed.), *Historical Statistics of Canada*, 2nd ed. Ottawa: Minister of Supply and Services Canada.

Rinehart, J.W. 1987. *The Tyranny of Work: Alienation and the Labour Process.* 2nd ed. Toronto: Harcourt Brace Jovanovich.

Roberts, B.A. 1988. *Whence They Came: Deportation from Canada 1900-1935.* Ottawa: University of Ottawa Press.

Roberts, J. 1988. "Early Release From Prison: What Do the Canadian Public Really Think?" *Canadian Journal of Criminology* 30: 231.

Ross, D.P. 1980. *The Canadian Fact Book on Income Distribution.* Ottawa: The Canadian Council on Social Development.

Ross, D.P. and E.R. Shillington. 1989. *The Canadian Fact Book on Poverty—1989.* Ottawa: The Canadian Council on Social Development.

Rusche G. and O. Kirchheimer. 1938. *Punishment and Social Structure.* New York: Russell and Russell.

Santos, B. 1980. "Law and Community: The Changing Nature of the State Power in Late Capitalism," *International Journal of the Sociology of Law* 8: 379-397.

Schwendinger, J. and H. Schwendinger. 1981. "Rape, Sexual Inequality and Levels of Violence," *Crime and Social Justice* Winter: 3.

Scull, A.T. 1977. *Decarceration: community treatment and the deviant: a radical view.* Englewood Cliffs, N.J.: Prentice-Hall.

————. 1984. *Decarceration: community treatment and the deviant: a radical view.* 2nd ed. New Brunswick, N.J.: Rutgers University Press.

Sheridan A.K.B., and J. Konrad. 1976. "Probation," in W.T. McGrath (ed.), *Crime and Its Treatment in Canada*, 2nd edition. Toronto: Macmillan.

Siegel, L.J. 1989. *Criminology.* 3rd edition. St. Paul, Minnesota: West Publishing Company.

Solicitor General of Canada. 1979. *National Inventory of Diversion Projects.* Ottawa: Solicitor General of Canada.

————. 1980. *International Conference on Alternatives to Imprisonment Report.* Ottawa: Minister of Supply and Services Canada.

————. 1981-85. *Annual Reports 1981-82, 1982-83, 1983-84, 1984-85.* Ottawa: Minister of Supply and Services Canada.

————. 1983. "Victims of Crime," *Canadian Urban Victimization Survey,* Bulletin No. 1.

————. 1984. *Long Term Imprisonment in Canada. Working Paper No. 1: An Overview of the Long Term Prisoner Population and Suggested Directions for Further Research*. Ottawa: Ministry of the Solicitor General of Canada.

————. 1985. *Ministry Facts*. Ottawa: Minister of Supply and Services Canada.

————. 1987. "Patterns in Violent Crime," *Canadian Urban Victimization Survey*, Bulletin No. 8.

————. 1988. "Patterns in Property Crime," *Canadian Urban Victimization Survey*, Bulletin No. 9.

Statistics Canada (listed by title date, no publication date)

————. 1971a. *Correctional Institutions Statistics 1971; 1972; 1973; 1974; 1976; 1977; 1978; 1979*. Ottawa: Information Canada (1974-75); no publisher (1976, 1979); Minister 1974 of Supply and Services Canada (1979-81).

————. 1971b. *Crime Statistics*. Ottawa: Information Canada (1973).

————. 1971c. *Traffic Enforcement Statistics*. Ottawa: Information Canada (1973).

————. 1973b. *Statistics of Criminal and Other Offences* 1973. Ottawa: no publisher (1978).

————. 1975a & 1980. *Crime and Traffic Enforcement Statistics*. Ottawa: Information Canada (1977); Minister of Supply and Services Canada (1982).

————. 1975b. *Penitentiary Statistics 1975*. Ottawa: no publisher (1978).

————. 1980-86. *Vital Statistics, Part IV: Causes of Death*. Ottawa, Minister of Supply and Services Canada.

————. 1980-88. *Adult Correctional Services in Canada 1980-81; 1981-82; 1982-83; 1983-84; 1984-85; 1985-86; 1986-87; 1987-88. Canadian Centre for Justice Statistics*. Ottawa: Minister of Supply and Services Canada (1982, 1983, 1984, 1986, 1986, 1987, 1988).

————. 1983a, 1984 and 1985a. *Canadian Crime Statistics 1983-1987*. Ottawa: Minister of Supply and Services Canada (1985, 1986).

————. 1983b. *Homicide Statistics 1983*. Ottawa: Minister of Supply and Services Canada (1984).

————. 1985b. *Historical Labour Force Statistics—Actual Data, Seasonal Factors, Seasonably Adjusted Data, 1985*. Household Surveys Division. Ottawa: Minister of Supply and Services Canada (1986), 205, 228.

————. 1986. *A Description of Bail: Verification and Bail Supervision Programs in Western Canada*.

————. 1986a. *Criminal Injuries Compensation 1986*. Canadian Centre for Justice Statistics. Ottawa: Minister of Supply and Services Canada.

————. 1986b. *Juristat Service Bulletin*. Vol. 6, No. 1.

————. 1986c. *Policing in Canada 1986*. Ottawa: Minister of Supply and Services Canada.

_____. 1986d. *A One-Day Snapshot Profile of all Persons in Provincial Adult Correctional Institutions*. Ottawa: Canadian Centre for Justice Statistics. May, 1986.

_____. 1987. *Income after tax, distributions by size in Canada 1987*. Household Surveys Division. Ottawa: Minister of Supply and Services Canada, 1989.

_____. 1987a. *Homicide in Canada 1987: A Statistical Perspective*. Ottawa: Minister of Supply and Services Canada.

_____. 1988. *Income Distributions by Size in Canada 1988*. Household Surveys Division. Ottawa: Minister of Supply and Services Canada.

_____. 1989a. *Income Distributions by Size in Canada 1988*. Household Surveys Division. Ottawa: Minister of Supply and Services Canada.

_____. 1989b. *Labour Force Annual Averages 1981-1988*. Household Surveys Division. Ottawa: Minister of Supply and Services Canada.

Taylor, I. 1985. "Criminology, the Unemployment Crisis, and the Liberal Tradition in Canada. The Need for Socialist Analysis and Policy," in Thomas Fleming (ed.), *The New Criminologies in Canada: State, Crime and Control*. Toronto: Oxford University Press.

Tepperman, L. 1977. *Crime Control: The Urge Toward Authority*. Toronto: McGraw-Hill Ryerson.

Thomas, M. 1987. "Why This Is 1929 All Over Again," *The Nation* 244: 641 (May 16).

Thompson, J.H. with A. Seager. 1985. *Canada 1922-1939: Decades of Discord*. Toronto: McClelland and Stewart.

Tonry, M.H. 1987. *Sentencing Reform Impacts*. Washington: U.S. Department of Justice National Institute of Justice.

Urquhart, M.C. and K.A.H. Buckley, eds. 1965. *Historical Statistics of Canada*. Cambridge: University Press.

van Cleef, D. 1985. "Persons Working Long Hours," in Statistics Canada, *The Labour Force*, May.

West, W.G. 1984. *Young Offenders and the Canadian State: A Canadian Perspective on Delinquency*. Toronto: Butterworths.

Wilson, D.G. 1989. "The Impact of Federal Sentencing Guidelines on Community Corrections and Privatization," in Dean J. Champion (ed.), *The U.S. Sentencing Guidelines: Implications for Criminal Justice*. New York: Praeger.

Yeager, M. 1979. "Research Note: Unemployment and Imprisonment," *The Journal of Criminal Law and Criminology* 70, 586-88.

Zay, N. 1965. "Section Y: Justice," in M.C. Urquhart and K.A.H. Buckley (eds.), *Historical Statistics of Canada*. Cambridge: University Press.

Statutes

An Act for the More Speedy Trial and Punishment of Juvenile Offenders 20 Victoria, c. 29 (1857).

An Act to Permit the Conditional Release of First Offenders in Certain Cases, S.C. 1889, c. 44.

The *Bail Reform Act 1972*, R.S.C. 1970 (2nd Supp.), c. 2.

The *Criminal Code*, R.S.C. 1970, c. C-34.

The *Criminal Records Act*, R.S.C. 1970, C. 12 (1st Supp.).

The *Juvenile Delinquents Act*, R.S.C. 1970, Chap. J-3 (originally, 7-8 Edward VII, c. 40, 1908).

The *Narcotic Control Act*, R.S.C. 1970, c. N-1.

The *Opium and Narcotic Drug Act, S.C. 1929, c. 49.*

The *Parole Act*, R.S.C. 1970, c. P-2.

The *Young Offenders Act*, R.S.C. 1985, c. Y-1.

Cases

R. v A (1974), 26 C.C.C. (2d) 474 (Ontario High Court of Justice).
R. v Collard (1987), 39 C.C.C. (3d) 471 (Manitoba Court of Appeal).
R. v Davies (1988), 26 O.A.C. 382 (Ontario Court of Appeal).
R. v Degan (1985), 20 C.C.C. (3d) 293 (Saskatchewan Court of Appeal).
R. v Drew (1978), 45 C.C.C. (2d) 212 (British Columbia Court of Appeal).
R. v Hebb (1989), 47 C.C.C. (3d) 193 (Nova Scotia Supreme Court).
R. v Hudson (1981), 65 C.C.C. (2d) 171 (Ontario Court of Appeal).
R. v Jones (1975), 25 C.C.C. (2d) 256 (Ontario County Court).
R. v Kergan (1985), 21 C.C.C. (3d) 549 (Alberta Court of Appeal).
R. v Malboeuf (1982), 68 C.C.C. (2d) 544 (Saskatchewan Court of Appeal).
R. v Richards (1979), 11 C.R. (3d) 193 (Ontario Court of Appeal).
R. v Sidley (Le Roy versus Sr. Charles Sidley) (1675), 82 E.R. 1036.
R. v Sugg (1986), 28 C.C.C. (3d) 569 (Nova Scotia Supreme Court, Appeal Division).
R. v Wilcox (1988), 43 C.C.C. (3d) 432 (Northwest Territories Supreme Court).

Appendix

Figure 1
Per Capita Prison Population
1867-1988 (Canada)

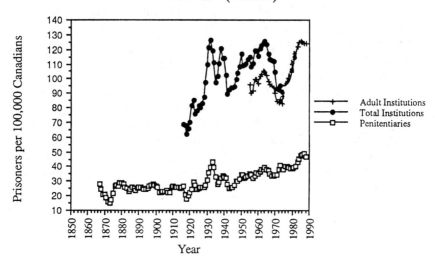

Figure 2
Per Capita Prison Population
1867-1988 (Canada)

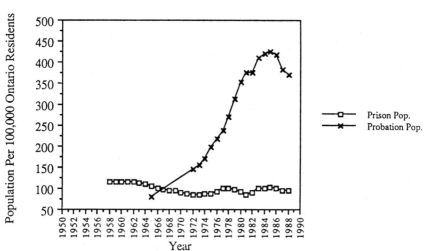

Appendix I

	Adult Institution Population 1955-1988					
	Daily Adult Institution Population Population On Register (Actual Count)		Rate per 100,000 Canadian		Actual Count Adjusted for YOA Effect*	
1988	31,750(e)	(26,634)	123.9	(103.9)	(28,873e)	(112.7)
1987	31,378(e)	(26,893)	124.0	(106.2)	(28,864e)	(114.0)
1986	31,647(e)	(27,392)	124.8	(108.0)	(28,277e)	(111.5)
1985	31,540(e)	(27,634)	125.5	(110.0)		
1984	30,992(e)	(26,980)	124.5	(108.4)		
1983	30,044(e)	(26,924)	122.0	(109.3)		
1982	27,484(e)	(24,064)	112.9	(98.9)		
1981	25,678(e)	(22,502)	106.8	(93.6)		
1980	24,539(e)	(21,936)	103.3	(92.4)		
1979a	25,201(e)	(21,956e)	107.2	(93.4)		
1979b	22,076		92.9			
1978	22,034		93.7			
1977	22,337		96.4			
1976	21,821		94.9			
1975	20,009		88.2			
1974	18,484		82.7			
1973	18,913		85.8			
1972	18,259		83.7			
1971	18,165		84.2			
1970	19,218		90.2			
1969	19,655		93.6			
1968	19,712		95.2			
1967	19,506		95.7			
1966	19,695		98.4			
1965	20,141		102.5			
1964	20,210		104.8			
1963	19,974		105.5			
1962	19,222		103.4			
1961	18,559		101.8			
1960	17,240		96.5			
1959	17,461		99.9			
1958	16,962		99.3			
1957	15,171		91.3			
1956	14,503		90.2			
1955	15,053		95.9			

Sources: Statistics Canada, 1979, 1982-1983, 1983-1984, 1984-1985, 1985-1986, 1986-1987, 1987-1988; Reed, 1983:Z292-304; Chan and Ericson, 1981:77.

"On register"
includes prisoners temporarily out of the institution, whereas "actual custody" does not. The on-register figures are estimates based on figures for the federal government and all provinces excluding: B.C. for the whole period, NWT for the whole period except 1982, Ontario for 1979a-1985 and the Yukon for 1988. It includes day paroles (69 percent of those on register but not in custody in the federal system for 1987-88: Statistics Canada, 1987-1988: 91), unlawfully at large (12 percent), in hospital (5 percent), at court (7 percent), out on bail (2 percent), temporary absence (1 percent) and unspecified (4 percent). Figures in the table prior to 1979 are from a different series of publications which purport to be based on the same principle, viz., "on register" whether or not in actual custody, but notice the similarity between "actual count" of 1979a (new series) and "on register" of 1979b (old series). On the other hand, the same does not hold for penitentiary statistics where there is a divergence between the on-register population of the old series and the actual count of the new (see Table III).

(e)
both sets of figures for 1979a-1988 are average daily or less frequent count for the fiscal year ending March 31st of the year named. In 1972-1979b the prison population is as of December 31st of the year named. For 1971 it is December 31st for federal and Quebec institutions and March 31st for all other provincial institutions. For 1955-1970 it is March 31st. The Canadian population bases for the rates are as of June 1st of year named 1955-1979b and as June 1st of the year before the year named 1979a-1988.

The "YOA effect"
is the effect on the prison population of changing (as of April 1, 1985) the age of adulthood so far as the penal system is concerned: 16- and 17-year-olds, who were classified as adults before that date, now became young offenders. An adjustment has been made to correct for the fact that 16- and 17-year-olds are still being imprisoned, but under a different label. The adjustment is not a projection; it is based on the number of 16- and 17-year-olds actually imprisoned during the years mentioned. The difference is that they are now imprisoned under the authority of the Young Offenders Act. On the other hand the figures are only estimates based on data pertaining to the Ontario system only. These figures have undergone complicated calculations in order to derive a national figure. One perhaps controversial move is to treat "open custody" as part of the institutional population. There are good legal and practical grounds for doing this, though the differences are not great. If open custody had been treated as non-institutional, the figures for 1986-88 would have been: 1988: 28,009 (109.3); 1987: 28,168 (111.3); 1986: 28,277 (110.9).

Appendix II

	Total Institutional Population 1916-1974				
	Daily Population of All Penal Institutions Including Training Schools	Rate per 100,000 Canadian Population		Daily Population of all Penal Institutions Including Training Schools	Rate per 100,000 Canadian Population
1974	20,407	91.2	1944	11,212	93.9
1973	20,966	95.1	1943	10,862	92.1
1972	20,136	92.4	1942	10,451	89.7
1971	20,124	93.3	1941	11,763	102.2
1970	22,329	104.8	1940	12,951	113.8
1969	23,448	111.7	1939	12,874	114.3
1968	23,368	112.9	1938	13,348	120.5
1967	23,111	113.4	1937	12,208	110.5
1966	23,455	117.2	1936	11,154	101.9
1965	24,179	123.1	1935	10,550	97.3
1964	24,288	125.9	1934	11,899	110.8
1963	23,512	124.2	1933	12,657	119.0
1962	22,747	122.4	1932	13,255	126.1
1961	21,960	120.4	1931	12,549	120.9
1960	20,628	115.4	1930	11,223	109.9
1959	20,790	118.9	1929	9,796	97.7
1958	20,382	119.3	1928	8,561	87.0
1957	18,301	110.2	1927	7,964	82.6
1956	17,352	107.9	1926	7,593	80.3
1955	18,048	115.0	1925	7,543	81.2
1954	17,369	113.6	1924	7,126	77.9
1953	16,383	110.4	1923	6,849	76.0
1952	15,846	109.6	1922	7,601	85.2
1951	15,295	109.2	1921	7,191	81.8
1950	16,012	116.8	1920	6,004	70.2
1949	14,573	108.4	1919	5,442	65.5
1948	13,454	104.0	1918	5,026	61.7
1947	12,481	99.4	1917	5,468	67.8
1946	11,651	94.8	1916	5,459	68.2
1945	11,334	93.9			

Sources: Reed, 1983:Z198-208; Z292-304; A1-14.

Figures are for the last day of the fiscal year: for 1916-1948 this is September 30th, excepting Ontario (March 31st), Nova Scotia (November 30th) and Quebec (December 31st); for 1949-1970 it is March 31st except for Quebec (December 31st); for 1971 it is March 31st excepting training schools, federal penitentiaries and Quebec (all December 31st); for 1972-1974 it is December 31st with no exceptions.

Appendix III

Penitentiary Population 1867-1988				
	Daily Penitentiary Population on Register (Actual Count)		Rate per 100,000 Canadian Population	
1988	11,969	(10,557)	46.7	(41.2)
1987	12,318	(11,106)	48.7	(43.9)
1986	12,281	(11,214)	48.4	(44.2)
1985	11,872	(10,857)	47.2	(43.2)
1984	11,359	(10,438)	45.6	(41.9)
1983	10,638	(9,775)	43.2	(39.7)
1982	9,765	(8,938)	40.1	(36.7)
1981	9,452	(8,651)	39.3	(36.0)
1980	9,305	(9,465)	39.2	(35.6)
1979a	9,219	(8,370)	39.2	(35.6)
1979b	9,290		39.1	
1978	9,309		39.6	
1977	9,335		40.1	
1976	9,285		40.4	
1975	8,700		38.3	
1974	8,499		38.0	
1973	9,111		41.3	
1972	8,253		37.9	
1971	7,483		34.7	
1970	7,337		34.5	
1969	7,117		33.9	
1968	7,026		33.9	
1967	7,167		35.1	
1966	7,438		37.2	
1965	7,514		38.2	
1964	7,651		39.7	
1963	7,219		38.1	
1962	7,156		38.5	
1961	6,738		36.9	
1960	6,344		35.5	
1959	6,295		36.0	
1958	5,770		33.8	
1957	5,432		32.7	
1956	5,508		34.3	
1955	5,507		35.1	
1954	5,120		33.5	
1953	4,934		33.2	

Appendix III

Penitentiary Population 1867-1988		
	Daily Penitentiary Population on Register (Actual Count)	Rate per 100,000 Canadian Population
1952	4,686	32.4
1951	4,817	34.4
1950	4,740	34.6
1949	4,260	31.7
1948	3,851	30.0
1947	3,752	29.9
1946	3,362	27.4
1945	3,129	25.9
1944	3,078	25.8
1943	2,969	25.2
1942	3,232	27.7
1941	3,688	32.1
1940	3,772	33.1
1939	3,803	33.8
1938	3,580	32.1
1937	3,264	29.6
1936	3,098	28.3
1935	3,586	33.1
1934	4,220	39.3
1933	4,587	43.1
1932	4,164	39.6
1931	3,714	35.8
1930	3,187	31.2
1929	2,769	27.6
1928	2,560	26.0
1927	2,480	25.7
1926	2,474	26.2
1925	2,345	25.2
1924	2,225	24.3
1923	2,486	27.6
1922	2,640	29.6
1921	2,150	24.5
1920	1,931	22.6
1919	1,689	20.3
1918	1,468	18.0
1917	1,694	21.0
1916	2,118	26.5

Appendix III

	Penitentiary Population 1867-1988	
	Daily Penitentiary Population on Register (Actual Count)	Rate per 100,000 Canadian Population
1915	2,064	25.9
1914	2,003	25.4
1913	1,970	25.8
1912	1,895	25.6
1911	1,865	25.9
1910	1,859	26.6
1909	1,765	26.0
1908	1,476	22.3
1907	1,423	22.2
1906	1,439	23.6
1905	1,367	22.8
1904	1,328	22.8
1903	1,250	22.1
1902	1,214	22.1
1901	1,382	25.7
1900	1,424	26.9
1899	1,445	27.6
1898	1,446	27.9
1897	1,383	27.0
1896	1,361	26.8
1895	1,277	25.4
1894	1,223	24.6
1893	1,194	24.2
1892	1,228	25.1
1891	1,249	25.8
1890	1,251	26.2
1889	1,195	25.3
1888	1,094	23.4
1887	1,159	25.1
1886	1,200	26.2
1885	1,112	24.5
1884	1,039	23.2
1883	1,113	25.1
1882	1,127	25.8
1881	1,218	28.2
1880	1,213	28.5
1879	1,200	28.7

Appendix III

	Penitentiary Population 1867-1988	
	Daily Penitentiary Population on Register (Actual Count)	Rate per 100,000 Canadian Population
1878	1,110	26.9
1877	1,108	27.3
1876	1,069	26.7
1875	848	21.4
1874	679	17.4
1873	567	14.8
1872	605	16.1
1871	692	18.8
1870	756	20.9
1869	745	20.9
1868	861	24.5
1867	972	28.1

Sources: Statistics Canada, 1979, 1982-83, 1983-84, 1984-85, 1985-86, 1986-87, 1987-88; Reed 1983:Z173-174; A1-14; Z-292-304. The 1980-88 figures are average daily counts for the fiscal year ending March 31st of the year named; they are in all respects like the figures in Table 1; the 1979a figures are estimates derived from a census figure reduced by the proportion of average population to census given in the 1982-83 report for the year 1980 for which we have both figures (Actual Count: 8465/8627 x 8530 = 8370; On Register: 9305/9519 x 9431 = 9219); the 1960-1979b figures are a single census taken on December 31st; the 1906-1959 figures are as of March 31st; 1877-1905 figures are as of June 30th; 1867-1876 figures are as of December 31st. Canadian population bases for the rates are as of April 1st from 1867-1901 and as of June 1st from 1902-1987.

Appendix IV

Execution Statistics				
	Number of Executions	Per Death Sentences	Per Murder Charges	Per Homicides
1879-80	11	.579 (19)	.180 (61)	———
1881-85	30	.508 (59)	.216 (139)	———
1886-90	23	.535 (43)	.198 (116)	———
1891-95	14	.412 (34)	.135 (104)	———
1896-1900	26	.591 (44)	.234 (111)	———
1901-05	29	.580 (50)	.206 (141)	———
1906-10	42	.656 (64)	.204 (206)	———
1911-15	51	.405 (126)	.166 (308)	———
1916-20	47	.420 (112)	.162 (290)	———
1921-25	49	.538 (91)	.166 (295)	———
1926-30	46	.523 (88)	.190 (242)	.058 (796)
1931-35	83	.783 (106)	.359 (231)	.108 (772)
1936-40	42	.477 (88)	.205 (205)	.062 (674)
1941-45	34	.523 (65)	.198 (172)	.054 (626)
1946-50	62	.544 (114)	.232 (267)	.085 (731)
1951-55	41	.554 (74)	.198 (207)	.056 (735)
1956-60	10	.159 (63)	.053 (190)	.019 (945)
Average (excluding 1956-58)		.539	.203	.071

Source: Zay, 1965: 649 (Y61-67); Reed, 1983: Z21.

Appendix V

Deportation and Imprisonment 1929/1939-1980/1988				
	Deportation		Prison	Total of Deportation and Prison
Year	Number	Rate per 100,000 Population	Average Daily Population per 100,000	
			(Adult Institutions)	
1929	1,964	19.6	97.7	
1930	3,963	38.8	109.9	
1931	6,583	63.4	120.9	
1932	7,647	72.8	126.1	
1933	5,138	48.3	119.0	
1934	1,701	15.8	110.8	
1935	675	6.2	97.3	
1936	605	5.5	101.9	
1937	421	3.8	110.5	
1938	439	3.9	120.5	
1939	413	3.7	114.3	
			(Adult Institutions)	
1979-80	5,107	21.5	92.4	
1980-81	5,376	22.4	93.6	
1981-82	5,191	21.3	98.9	
1982-83	5,197	21.1	109.3	
1983-84	5,099	20.6	108.4	
1984-85	3,950	15.8	110.0	
1985-86	2,467	9.8	111.5	
1986-87	2,446	9.6	114.0	
1987-88	2,809	11.0	112.7	
Average	1930-39	26.2	95.1*	121.3*
		26.2	101.6**	127.8**
	1930-34	47.8	98.6*	146.4*
		47.8	105.3**	153.1**
	1932	72.8	105.9*	178.7*
		72.8	113.2**	186.0**
Average	1980-88	17	105.6	122.7
	1984-88	13.4	111.3	124.7
	1983			130.4

The figures with asterisks have been adjusted to make them comparable with figures for adult institutions only as per footnote 3 in the text

* denotes deflator of 99.7/118.7
** denotes deflator of .898

Sources: Roberts, 1988: 38; Dominion Bureau of Statistics, 1940: 160; Employment and Immigration Canada, Annual Reports 1979/80-1987/88.

Appendix VI

	Prison	Probation	(Rate)	Ratio	Prison	Probation	(Rate)	Ratio
			Adult Prison and Probation Admissions in Ontario 1964-1988					
1987-88	66,170	24,168	(261)	2.7:1	72,093	30,266	(326)	2.4:1
1986-87	64,311	23,237	(255)	2.8:1	69,719	29,296	(322)	2.4:1
1985-86	64,466	24,555	(271)	2.6:1	68,166	28,999	(320)	2.4:1
1984-85	67,785	30,053	(336)	2.3:1				
1983-84	68,138	28,997	(329)	2.3:1				
1982-83	71,090	29,500	(338)	2.4:1				
1981-82	65,576	31,665	(376)	2.1:1				
1980-81	65,776	31,107	(361)	2.1:1				
1979-80	60,701	29,775	(350)	2.0:1				
1978-79	61,834	27,822	(329)	2.2:1				
1977-78	59,072	21,413	(256)	2.8:1				
1976-77	59,362	18,851	(228)	3.1:1				
1975-76	54,791	19,323	(235)	2.8:1				
1974-75	54,721	17,386	(215)	3.1:1				
1973-74	56,072	13,691	(172)	4.1:1				
1972-73	56,754	11,225	(143)	5.1:1				
1971-72	65,664	10,270	(133)	6.4:1				
1970-71	76,284							
1969-70	66,595							
1968-69	62,097							
1967-68	61,120							
1966-67	61,343							
1965-66	58,230	6,547	(97)	8.9:1				
1964-65	58,431							

Sources: Ontario, 1967, 1968, 1969, 1970, 1981, 1982, 1983, 1984, 1985; Statistics Canada, 1976, 1977, 1978, 1979, 1982-1983 through 1987-1988; McFarlane, 1966: 89 (for 1965); Reed, 1983: Z175-197.

All admissions save probation admissions for 1965-1966 are for the fiscal year ending March 31st. Probation admissions for 1965-66 are for the calendar year 1965. The Canadian population bases for the rates are as of June 1st of the fiscal year comprehended by the admissions.

The YOA effect is calculated as in Table I, with "open custody" treated as imprisonment. Had it not been so treated, the differences would again be small, with the ratios for 1986-1988 each being 2.3:1 instead of 2.4:1.

Appendix VII

	Average Daily Adult Prison and Probation Population—Ontario 1957-1988					
	Prison (Rate)	Probation (Rate)	Ratio	Adjusted for YOA		
1987-88	8,701 (94)	34,493 (371)	1:4.0	9809 (106)	40853 (e) (441)	1:4.2
1986-87	8,610 (95)	34,868 (383)	1:4.0	9575 (105)	41,187 (453)	1:4.3
1985-86	8,927 (99)	37,771 (417)	1:4.2	9372 (103)	39,915 (441)	1:4.3
1984-85	9,090 (102)	37,974 (425)	1:4.2			
83-84	8,741 (99)	36,902 (419)	1:4.2			
82-83	8,739 (100)	35,666 (409)	1:4.1			
81-82	7,864 (91)	2,406 (376)	1:4.1			
80-81	7,334 (86)	32,011 (374)	1:4.4			
79-80	7,779 (92)	29,941 (352)	1:3.8			
78-79	8,236 (98)	26,362 (312)	1:3.2			
77-78	8,437 (101)	22,631 (271)	1:2.7			
76-77	8,254 (100)	19,672 (238)	1:2.4			
75-76	7,538 (92)	17,838 (218)	1:2.4			
74-75	7,010 (87)	15,832 (197)	1:2.3			
73-74	6,899 (87)	13,561 (171)	1:2.0			
72-73	6,567 (84)	12,044 (154)	1:1.8			
71-72	6,464 (84)	11,237 (146)	1:1.7			
70-71	6,669 (88)					
69-70	6,746 (91)					
68-69	6,811 (94)					
67-68	6,812 (96)					
66-67	6,749 (97)					
65-66	6,748 (99)					
64-65	6,934 (105)	5,225 (79)	1:3.1			
63-64	7,157 (110)					
62-63	7,205 (113)					
61-62	7,232 (116)					
60-61	7,072 (116)					
59-60	6,791 (114)					
58-59	6,712 (115)					
57-58	6,475 (115)					

The prison data are a combination of the population of Ontario correctional institutions and federal penitentiaries located in Ontario. For 1978/9-1987/8 they consist of average daily counts for the fiscal year ending March 31st; for 1957-1958 to 1969-1970 they are the average of the counts for March 31 of each year; for 1970-1971 to 1977-1978 they are the average of the counts for March 31st of each year for the provincial prisons only, while for the federal penitentiaries they are the count for December 31st of the first year mentioned. The probation data are the average daily counts for 1978-1979 to 1984-1985; for 1970-1971 to 1977-1978 they are the average of the counts for March 31 of each year; for 1964-65 they are the population under supervision for January 1, 1965; Rates are per 100,000 Ontario population as of June 1st comprehended by the fiscal year.

    The YOA effect is calculated as in Table 1, with open custody assigned to prison and not to probation. If it were assigned to probation, the ratios for 1986, 1987 and 1988 would be 1:4.3, 4.5 and 4.4 respectively.

Sources: Dominion Bureau of Statistics, 1957-1959, 1960-1961, 1962, 1963, 1964, 1964-1965, 1965-1966, 1966-1967, 1967-1968, 1968-1969, 1969-1970, 1970; Statistics Canada, 1971a, 1972, 1973a, 1974, 1975, 1976, 1977, 1978, 1982-1983 through 1987-1988; Ontario, 1985; McFarlane, 1966: 89.

Appendix VIII

Yearly Admissions to Custodial and Supervised Population—Canada 1978-1988					
	Provincial Custody	Probation	Total	Rate Per 100,000 Canadian	Custody as % of Total
1987-88	196,552 (e)	53,521	250,073	976	78.6
	(208,607)(e)	(64,408)	(273,015)	(1,065)	(76.4)
1986-87	190,108	52,749	242,857	960	78.3
	(200,973)	(63,954)	(264,927)	(1,047)	(75.9)
1985-86	190,286	54,838	245,124	967	77.6
	(197,729)	(63,034)	(260,763)	(1,028)	(75.8)
1984-85	193,602	62,986	257,714	1,026	75.2
1983-84	199,852	63,567	263,419	1,058	75.9
1982-83	201,690	65,550	267,240	1,085	75.5
1981-82	183,450	66,245	249,695	1,026	73.5
1980-81	170,874	62,875	233,749	972	73.1
1979-80	160,078	58,631	18,709	921	73.2
1978-79	158,428	56,342	214,770	913	73.8

Admissions are "from liberty" not including transfers.
Figures in brackets are adjusted for YOA, assuming as in Table I that open custody should be assigned to prison and not to probation. If it were assigned to probation, the percentage custody for 1986, 1987 and 1988 would be 75.7 percent, 75.3 percent and 75.7 percent respectively.
Sources: Statistics Canada, 1982-83 through 1987-88, Ontario, 1985.

Appendix IX

Average Daily Custodial and Supervised Population — Canada 1978-1988					
	Average Daily Probation	Parole and Mandatory	Total Non-Custodial	Custodial and Non-Custodial	Total Custodial
1987-88	66,405	11,526	77,931	26,634	104,565
	(76,291)		(87,817)	(28,873)	(116,690)
1986-87	67,133	10,887	78,020	26,893	104,913
	(77,078)		(87,965)	(28,864)	(116,829)
1985-86	72,249	9,994	82,243	27,392	109,635
	(75,646)		(85,640)	(28,277)	(113,917)
1984-85	74,707	10,191	84,898	27,634	112,532
1983-84	74,386	10,042	84,428	26,980	111,408
1982-83	71,880	9,032	80,912	26,924	107,836
1981-82	65,123	9,182	74,305	24,064	98,369
1980-81	62,656	8,131	70,787	22,502	93,289
1979-80	59,248	8,037	67,285	21,936	89,221
1978-79	53,937	7,801	61,738	21,956	83,694

Rates Per 100,000 Canadian Population				
	Custodial	Non-Custodial	Total	Non-Custodial as % of Total
1987-88	104 (112.7)	304 (343)	408 (455)	74.5 (75.3)
1986-87	106 (114.0)	308 (348)	415 (462)	74.4 (75.3)
1985-86	108 (111.5)	324 (338)	432 (449)	75.0 (75.2)
1984-85	110	338	448	75.4
1983-84	108	339	448	75.8
1982-83	109	328	438	75.0
1981-82	99	305	404	75.5
1980-81	94	294	388	75.9
1979-80	92	283	376	75.4
1978-79	93	263	356	73.8

Figures in brackets are adjusted for YOA effect, assuming as in Table I that open custody should be assigned to prison and not to probation. If it were assigned to probation, the percentage non-custodial for 1986, 1987 and 1988 would be 75.3 percent, 75.9 percent and 76.0 percent respectively.

Sources: Statistics Canada, 1982-1983 through 1987-1988, Ontario, 1985.

Note: The 1987-1988 Statistics Canada report excludes lock-up data for the first time. In the interests of comparability they have been included in the table nevertheless. This required an estimate to be made for 1987-1988, based on the Statistics Canada report for 1986-1987 where lock-ups for 1986-1987 are included and the report for 1987-1988 where lock-ups for 1986-1987 are not included. It was assumed that the proportion of lock-ups to ordinary imprisonment was the same for both years. Therefore the 1987-1988 figure of 190,141 without lock-ups was multiplied by 190,108/183,907 to get the total of 196,552. The same reasoning applies to daily population figures, but the numbers in this case are tiny due to the short duration of lock-up imprisonment, so no attempt has been made to include them in the tables on population.

Appendix X

Reported Crime per 100,000 Population 1962-1987

Year	Murder	Attempted Murder (Wounding)	Manslaughter	Sexual Assault	Aggravated Assault	Other Assault	Robbery	Break and Enter	Theft	NCA/FDA	Total Driving*	Impaired Driving**
1987	2.3	3.6	.19	87	10.5	650	88	1,421	3,712	241	1,584	570
1986	2.1	3.5	.17	81	11.4	603	92	1,440	3,656	222	1,599	565***
1985	2.6	3.4	.19	73	11.0	558	90	1,418	3,593	227	1,630	609
1984	2.5	3.7	.17	99	12.5	529	93	1,429	3,622	220	1,648	652
1983***	2.5	3.6	.21	48	14.6	507	98	1,462	3,700	221	1,662	671
1982	2.5	3.8	.17	57	10.5	502	111	1,505	3,876	263	1,769	681
1981	2.5	3.7	.18	55	11.1	486	101	1,509	3,797	309	1,689	721
1980	2.1	3.3	.40	53	10.0	477	102	1,454	3,569	309	1,694	704
1979	2.5	3.2	.16	52	9.7	466	88	1,248	3,274	273	1,643	692
1978	2.5	3.2	.24	49	9.2	443	84	1,184	3,021	258	1,723	663
1977	2.7	2.9	.33	47	8.9	438	84	1,163	2,944	283	1,655	666
1976	2.7	3.0	.21	46	8.7	448	87	1,167	3,004	274	1,657	645
1975	2.8	2.8	.28	48	9.4	440	94	1,148	2,988	245	1,622	649
1974	2.4	2.3	.24	50	9.5	424	76	1,043	2,782	262	1,579	651
1973	2.2	2.2	.30	54	8.5	407	60	898	2,493	239	1,410	585
1972	2.2	1.9	.18	50	7.8	391	54	876	2,449	132	1,217	499
1971	2.0	1.6	.22	52	8.6	385	52	874	2,468	111	1,082	449
1970	2.0	1.2	.16	52	7.7	363	55	834	2,308	88	979	379***
1969	1.6	1.0	.21	51	7.8	343	48	770	2,026	50	856	259
1968	1.5	.9	.29	51	6.2	322	40	700	1,854	26	785	218
1967	1.4	.7	.27	48	5.1	290	35	586	1,662	14	714	202
1966	1.1	.7	.14	44	4.9	267	29	510	1,529	7	680	198
1965	1.2	.6	.17	38	4.2	227	28	491	1,405	4	N/A	191
1964	1.1	.6	.18	39	4.3	210	29	504	1,459	3	N/A	180
1963	1.1	.6	.18	37	6.7	173	31	498	1,359	5	N/A	172
1962	1.2	.4	.26	36	6.8	150	27	442	1,263	5	N/A	176
Factor by which 1987 figure exceeds 1962 figure:	1.9	9	(.7)	2.7 (est)	1.5	4.3	3.3	3.2	2.9	48.2	2.3 (66.87)	3.2 (est)

*   Total Driving includes the offences of criminal negligence causing death, criminal negligence causing bodily harm, criminal negligence in the operation of a motor vehicle, driving while impaired or with more than the allowed alcohol/blood ratio (Criminal Code), failure to remain at the scene of an accident, dangerous driving, and driving while disqualified (Criminal Code and provincial statute).

**   Driving while impaired or with more than the allowed alcohol/blood ratio and refusal to provide a breath sample.

***   Commencing 1986, changes were made to the Criminal Code, which affect the comparability of driving offence statistics. Offences were expanded to include boats and aircraft as well as motor vehicles. In 1986 and 1987 such offences constituted less than one percent of the total but, the way statistics are reported makes it impossible to determine the precise numbers. The figures in the table attempt to exclude offences committed with boats and aircraft. Including them would change the figures to 1589 and 572 for 1987, and 1604 and 587 for 1986. Also, as of 1986 the offences of impaired operation of a motor vehicle et cetera causing bodily harm or causing death were added. Theoretically these should be included in the impaired offences because they would have constituted such offences before the change. But most certainly some of these offences, perhaps all of them, would have been prosecuted under other charges (criminal negligence causing death or bodily harm) before and to include them now would suggest more of an increase or less of a decrease in the impaired category than has actually occurred. I have therefore excluded them. If they were included, the figures for 1987 would be 579 (with boats and aircraft) or 577 (without) and for 1986: 594 (with) and 591 (without).

Calculations for 1986: Total driving: 406,635 (1604); without boats: 405,333 (1599); impaired driving: 150,571 (594); without harm: 148,794 (587); impaired driving without boats: 149,932 (591); impaired driving without boats and without harm: 148,316 (585).

Calculations for 1987: Total driving: 407,087 (1589); without boats: 405,836 (1584); impaired driving: 148,320 (579); without harm: 146,586 (572); impaired driving without boats: 147,741 (577); impaired driving without boats and without harm: 146,107 (570).

****   In 1983 several changes in the Criminal Code came into effect which affect comparability. For the category of "sexual assault": the offences of "rate" and "indecent assault" were replaced by three categories of "sexual assault" in 1983; while the figures under "sexual assault" for 1962-1982 include not only rape and indecent assault but also various forms of sexual intercourse with minors, seduction, as well as the offences of "gross indecency" and "buggery and bestiality," the figures for 1983 and afterwards are restricted to pure sexual assault. For the category "Aggravated Assault (Wounding)": Wounding was redefined in 1983 and partially replaced by "aggravated assault." The figures under "Aggravated Assault (Wounding) for 1962-1982 include all offences under the former section 228 of the Criminal Code, including discharging a firearm; but the 1983 offence of aggravated assault is somewhat narrower. However, separate statistics are now kept on discharging firearms and I have included these in the category for 1983 and following to maintain rough comparability. "Other Assault": this category excludes wounding before 1983 and aggravated assault after 1982; it includes unlawfully causing bodily harm in all years.

***** In 1969, the offence of driving while intoxicated was repealed and the offences of driving with a higher than permitted alcohol to blood ratio and of refusing to provide a breath sample were created. This appears to have led to an immediate increase in the reported offence rate.

Sources: Dominion Bureau of Statistics, 1962a, 1962b, 1965a, 1965b, 1968a, 1968b and Statistics Canada, 1971a, 1971c, 1975a, 1980, 1984, 1987a, *Juristat Service Bulletin*, Volume 7, No. 4 (September, 1987); for driving offences in 1986 and 1987: unpublished statistics kindly provided to me by the Canadian Centre for Justice Statistics of Statistics Canada.

Chapter 10

From Big House to Big Brother: Confinement in the Future

Ian M. Gomme

...the poster with the enormous face gazed from the wall. It was one of those pictures which are so contrived that the eyes follow you about when you move. BIG BROTHER IS WATCHING YOU, the caption beneath it ran (George Orwell, *Nineteen Eighty-Four*).[1]

Introduction

The big houses[2] are full to overflowing. Canada's jails and prisons are generally filled to capacity or, depending upon the season, stretched beyond their limits (Canadian Centre for Justice Statistics, 1991a). By comparison, penal facilities in the United States are holding convicted criminals in numbers far in excess of what their designs humanely and safely permit (Inciardi, 1987). The big houses are expensive to build and to maintain and they cost a king's ransom to operate and to staff. For Canada in 1990-91, the bills for operating the corrections system were $862 million federally and $938 million provincially for a grand total slightly in excess of $1.8 billion. Over the five year period from 1986-87 to 1990-91, there was an increase of 26% in government operating costs. The increase in the single year from 1989-90 to 1990-91 was 8%.[3] For provincial corrections in 1990-91, the operation of custodial services accounted for 82% of costs. In comparison, community corrections programs[4] generated about 11% of the operating expenditures. During 1990-91, the average daily cost of housing an inmate in a provincial institution was $114.76. Staff salaries accounted for 75% of the total provincial expenditures (Canadian Centre for Justice Statistics, 1991a).

When it comes to financing corrections, taxpayers tend to subscribe to the "principle of less eligibility." The less eligibility postulate holds that persons convicted of crimes ought to benefit less from society's bounties than the worst off of law abiding citizens. Those who have broken society's laws should experience more pain and deprivation than any of those who have adhered to the rules. Given the pain and deprivation routinely endured by the law abiding poverty stricken and homeless across North America, the principle of less eligibility does not bode well for those convicted of criminal offences. At any rate, the maintenance and expansion of high quality corrections facilities and programs are unpopular targets for the expenditure of tax dollars. The reticence to expend scarce resources to ensure that law breakers are contained under any more than the most minimal of conditions is especially true at times when the standards of essential services to the law abiding such as education and health care appear threatened.

From all appearances, North Americans find themselves on the horns of a rather thorny dilemma. On one hand, official data indicate that crime is rising. On the other hand, government revenues are severely stretched. Violent crime increased 56% over the decade from 1980 to 1990. The rate for violent offences rose from 947 per 100,000 in 1989 to 1,013 per 100,000 in 1990 for a single year increase of 7%. Nationally, property crime also increased 7% from 1989 to 1990. The 1990 national rate for the Criminal Code category "other crimes" was 31% higher than the 1980 rate and 8% above the 1989 rate[5] (Canadian Centre for Justice Statistics, 1991b).

By no means have reported increases in crime escaped the public eye. The General Social Survey conducted by Statistics Canada in 1988 showed that 25% of all Canadians felt unsafe walking alone in their own neighbourhoods at night. For women, the percentage rose to 40%. The survey also revealed that the majority of Canadians (65%) believes that sentences handed down by the criminal courts are insufficiently severe. Significantly, older Canadians (over the age of 25) and Canadians in higher income brackets are among those most likely to express concern over the soft sanctions meted out by Canadian courts.

At the same time as they have experienced the problems associated with rising levels of crime, Canadians are faced with tough economic times brought on by a troubled global economy. Canadians, and Americans for that matter, must cope with growing budget deficits, with increasing corporate disinvestment, with rising unemployment rates, with shrinking tax bases, and with the mushrooming costs of social services. Significant expansion of prison systems in an effort to deal with apparent rises in crime across North America would cost Canadian and especially American governments millions upon millions of dollars. Plainly speaking, citizens want a more punitive system to address increasing crime but they and their governments are reluctant to foot the bill for it. Alternatives, less expensive but nonetheless punitive, would appear to be the order of the day.

While 1984 may be fading into memory, Big Brother most certainly is not. More than alive and well, he continues to leap from the pages of science fiction into the realm of everyday life. In the progression toward a presumably better world, captains of technological wizardry continue to transform yesterday's fantasies into today's reality with a dizzying array of machinery in a host of disparate contexts. The crime control industry has by no means been left untouched by the high tech revolution. Ever more highly specialized and increasingly sophisticated equipment continues to be introduced in the campaign to win the war against crime as it unfolds in the brave new world of the next century.

It is becoming increasingly common to employ state of the art technological devices and procedures in the pursuit, apprehension, conviction, and containment of society's outlaws. The impacts of modern scientific developments on the control of crime have been enormous. The automobile, the shortwave radio, and finger printing were early technological developments that transformed the face of crime control during the early decades of the twentieth century. By the 1990s, the use of high powered technology has become routine and taken for granted. The radar trap and the breathalyzer have enabled traffic officers to catch and convict speeders and impaired drivers with much improved efficiency. On the less mundane level, police with electronic bugs listen in on the private conversations of organized crime figures (Rhodes, 1984). They use video cameras to build cases against participants in "indecent" sexual exchanges in public rest rooms (Desroches, 1990). Forensic experts gather physical evidence at the scenes of murders and later accused persons are convicted in part because fibres found under the victim's fingernails match the textiles used to manufacture a garment worn by the accused. Scientists use semen samples taken from sexual assault victims to construct genetic profiles of rapists. The genetic prints can subsequently be used to confirm whether or not an accused person is the attacker (Zonderman, 1990).

The use of technology is not confined solely to detection, apprehension, and conviction. It is also making its mark in the area of penology. Various jurisdictions in North America are now using or considering the use of electronic monitors. These devices are highly sophisticated miniature radio transmitters attached to an offender's wrist, ankle, or neck. The transmitter monitors the detainee's presence in a given location thereby restricting his or her geographical mobility. Should a detainee move beyond a specified range, a signal is triggered alerting authorities who then investigate to determine whether or not a breach has occurred (Friel and Vaughn, 1986). In essence, electronic monitoring is a means of detecting curfew violation.

Our analysis of the movement toward electronic monitoring begins with a discussion of the context in which the need for an intermediate sentencing option has arisen in the United States. Transformations in the field of corrections south of the border have historically affected the nature and pace of innovation in Canadian correctional policy. Developments in the United

States are by no means irrelevant to the evolution of corrections initiatives north of the 49th parallel and this fact makes it necessary for us to consider carefully American conditions and circumstances. The policies adopted by Canada with respect to electronic monitoring will be in part a consequence of the outcomes of the American experience.

Following a discussion of intermediate sentencing, the history of electronic monitoring is documented and the operation of the most popular of the active and passive systems is described. The advantages articulated by electronic monitoring's proponents are catalogued and the applications of this technology in Canada to date are outlined. The problems that arise from the implementation of electronic monitoring are examined in some detail. The paper concludes with an assessment of the prospects and implications associated with the application and deployment of this technology in the future.

The Need for an Intermediate Sentence

The recent growth in enthusiasm surrounding electronic monitoring has arisen out of the fact that the sentencing options available to courts over the last few decades have been bi-polar in nature (Currie, 1985). Either those convicted have been sentenced to unnecessarily lengthy prison terms or, in the public eye especially, they have been effectively "let off easy" through their relegation to non-custodial community-based corrections programs with low intensity supervision. Community-based corrections are alternatives to incarceration that reflect the conviction that rehabilitation and reintegration can be more effectively achieved in the community as opposed to the institutional context (Ekstedt and Griffiths, 1988). The objectives of community corrections programs are to divert people out of the corrections system entirely, to provide offenders with temporary relief from the pains of imprisonment, and to reduce the period of an offender's incarceration. Probation and parole are two well known traditional community corrections strategies[6]. In the 1960s and 1970s, new programs were added and expanded (Menzies, 1986). Among these initiatives were diversion, community service orders, and restitution.[7]

The bi-polar extremes represented by imprisonment on one hand and by community corrections on the other have fuelled desires for a penal sanction that falls somewhere between the two ends of the continuum. Home confinement with intensive supervision, supplied either through frequent face-to-face checks or through electronic monitoring, is a non-custodial measure with a very high degree of supervision that on the face of it would appear to assure considerable security. Compared to traditional non-custodial community corrections, house arrest is a more intrusive means of controlling detainees. On the other hand, home confinement is less intrusive than imprisonment. For these reasons, house arrest in conjunction with the intensive supervision afforded by electronic monitoring is considered an intermediate or mid-range sentence (Berry and Matthews, 1989).

Several factors warrant consideration in understanding the popularity of the movement toward home confinement with electronic monitoring. Prisons in Canada are filled to, and occasionally beyond, their capacities. In the United States, however, they are packed to the proverbial rafters. Overcrowding is a very serious problem that, for a number of reasons, became particularly acute during the 1970s and early 1980s. It was during these years that the baby boomers reached the critical age for participation in violent and property crime.[8] It was also during this period that the creation and enforcement of laws prohibiting the use, trafficking, and smuggling of psychoactive illicit drugs took on the epic proportions of an all out war. Enormous numbers of people are currently in jail in the United States for criminal activity related to the manufacture, distribution, sale, or purchase of prohibited substances (Inciardi, 1986). Concern over the illicit drug trade and growing fears of violent and property crime have merged to fuel the development and implementation of a more punitive set of correctional policies. These policies were first, to make imprisonment a mandatory sentence for an expanded list of crimes, second, to increase the probability that convicted offenders would indeed be incarcerated, third, to stiffen jail sentences by lengthening prison terms, and fourth, to reduce or eliminate the early release of prisoners by restricting parole or abolishing it altogether (Friel and Vaughn, 1986). To say the least, these tactics have fused to mushroom the numbers of offenders behind bars in American penal facilities. Furthermore, many of these measures were implemented during a period of fiscal turmoil, government spending restraint, and the general political conservatism of the Reagan years.

Between 1980 and 1988, the corrections population in the United States increased 90% (Maxfield and Baumer, 1990). State expenditures on corrections did not keep pace with the need for more facilities and as a result massive overcrowding has occurred in many jurisdictions. Indeed, in several of the United States, prisoners have successfully undertaken class action litigation against the government claiming that overcrowded conditions represent cruel and unusual treatment. In some cases, entire states have been placed under court order to reduce prison populations one way or another by simply turning offenders loose, by expanding community corrections programs, or by developing other viable alternatives (Vaughn, 1987). Indeed, a United States court in 1980 declared the entire Texas prison system unconstitutional. Moreover, the decision was upheld upon its appeal in 1982 (Inciardi, 1987).

Community-based corrections arose as a partial solution to a combination of problems associated first with incarceration and later with prison crowding. Prison reformers have always been cognizant of the potential evils of imprisonment. Among the more serious of these perils are subcultural socialization into a life of crime and the material and physical victimization suffered by relatively powerless inmates at the hands of their more powerful comrades (Sykes, 1958). For reasons such as these, reformers have sought to limit the prison experience in terms of who is jailed in the first place and for how long. Diverting offenders out of the prison system altogether and providing early release to those who have remained satisfactory institutional citizens throughout their sentences are not initiatives that have enjoyed universal popularity, however.[9] In conservative political times especially, non-custodial programs are seen as soft and their effectiveness in rehabilitating offenders is considered suspect. There is, in short, a certain disillusionment with community-based corrections initiatives (Friel and Vaughn, 1986) and there is a desire to replace them with stronger medicine (Berry, 1985).

In sum, apparent rises in crime rates, growing fear of crime among citizens, and disillusionment with the rehabilitative potential first of prisons and more recently of community corrections programs have combined with an air of general political conservatism to increase the public's desire for an ever more punitive regimen of criminal sanctions. One of the most tangible results of the shift toward greater punitiveness, especially in the United States, has been institutional overcrowding. In some states more than others, crowding itself has been profoundly exacerbated by crippling economic constraints.

Three fundamental questions emerge in this context. First, how can society contain as many of its burgeoning numbers of undesirables as possible? Second, how can this containment be accomplished while preserving the legal and constitutional rights of prisoners? Third, how can the dual and frequently conflicting objectives of crime control on one hand and the preservation of due process on the other be met as economically as possible? The answers are found with a crime fighting super-hero and a Harvard psychologist. To their stories, we now turn.

Spiderman and Dr. Schwitzgebel

The solution came to a district court judge in Albuquerque, New Mexico in 1977 in what is one of the most unusual accounts in the field of crime control. According to the story, Judge Jack Love was reading a comic at the time of his remarkable flash of insight. The hero of the piece, Spiderman, had confronted an especially ingenious villain who had placed around the super-hero's wrist an electronic device that allowed the blackguard to monitor the web-slinging crime-fighter's every move. Keeping tabs on Spiderman's whereabouts proved to be a distinct advantage for the villainous scoundrel bent on the perpetration of a series of dastardly deeds. The enterprising judge was struck by the possibilities for the creation of a similar device but one that would turn the tables by allowing champions of truth and justice to monitor the whereabouts of those embodying the forces of evil.

Love approached a variety of computer manufactures with his idea for the design of a mechanism that would enable law enforcement agents to verify electronically the location of a given convicted offender at a specified point in time. He was unable to interest the communications industry initially but the employee of one corporation, Michael Goss, eventually left his employer to develop the product through his own company newly formed for just this purpose. In April of 1983, Judge Love became the first to sentence an offender to electronically monitored house arrest. The detainee, a probation violator, was sentenced to home confinement and required to wear the GOSSlink device for the duration of a month (Fox, 1987).

Judge Love's idea for the practical development of an electronic monitoring device was not the first, however. These honours go to a Harvard psychologist, Ralph K. Schwitzgebel, who in the early 1960s foresaw the utility of an electronic devise capable of tracking wearers' locations, transmitting back information about their conditions, communicating with them, and perhaps even modifying their behaviours. The prototype of such a device, not surprisingly referred to as "Dr. Schwitzgebel's Machine," was created and tested in the mid 1960s.

In the initial experiments, Dr. Schwitzgebel strapped his machine onto his research subjects and turned them loose. The prototype device consisted of a transmitter and battery pack weighing in excess of one kilogram and capable of emitting a signal that could be picked up by a receiver located within a quarter mile range. The information from the receiver was fed into a missile tracking device and the subject's location was displayed on a computer screen (Schwitzgebel, 1969).

The results of these early experiments were greeted with considerable enthusiasm as Dr. Schwitzgebel and his colleagues contemplated the modifications to the technology that they thought might be possible in the future. They speculated that the device could be adapted to gather and transmit data on a subject's physiological condition (pulse, blood alcohol level, brain-waves) and, through a listening device, on the content of his or her conversations. Researchers also foresaw the potential for incorporating into the contrivance the means whereby stimuli could be administered to subjects from afar. Dr. Schwitzgebel patented his machine in 1969 (Fox, 1987).

The potential applications to corrections of more refined versions of his device were by no means lost on the good doctor. Noting the limitations of custodial restraint, Schwitzgebel advocated the use of more humane non-custodial measures wherein offenders could remain in the community and yet still be closely controlled through the intensive supervision afforded by his technological marvel. The claims for the potential utility of the machine were by no means modest. First, future models would provide a continuous record of the offender's location throughout his or her sentence. Second, because future offending would be detected by the machine, it would reduce recidivism by serving as a deterrent. Third, by tracking the offender's whereabouts the device would also discourage both commiseration with undesirables and the hatching of new nefarious plots in the company of other known criminals.

But the possibilities did not stop there. Schwitzgebel mused that the day might come when science would catalogue the physiological precursors to a criminal act. When this occurred, he speculated that it would be possible to use the machine first to identify the crime-related physiological changes occurring in the offender immediately prior to his or her law breaking, second, to transmit this information back to the base station, and third, to intervene from the base station with an appropriately noxious stimulus (Schwitzgebel, 1970).

The good doctor's musings aside, we proceed with an examination of the monitoring systems that have been developed in the wake of the pioneering efforts of Judge Love and his associate Michael Goss in the early 1980s.

The Device

The devices currently being used in electronic monitoring programs in North America, thanks to micro-chip technology, are considerably more compact and lighter than Dr. Schwitzgebel's one kilogram prototype. Despite the existence of the technologies that could offer the level of surveillance Schwitzgebel envisaged, the extent of supervision afforded by contemporary monitoring systems is in practice much less. Monitors in use neither track offenders over extended distances nor do they gather and transmit data on the wearer's conversations and physiological conditions. The devices most certainly do not permit the application from afar of noxious anti-crime stimuli.

Contemporary monitoring systems can be either active or passive in their functioning. Active systems consist of three parts—a transmitter worn by the offender, a receiver-dialler located in the detainee's home, and a central monitoring computer connected via the phone line to the receiver-dialler. With active systems, controllees wear a miniature battery operated radio transmitter that weighs about 110 grams and is shock resistant, waterproof, and provides indication when power is running low. The monitor is usually attached to offenders' ankles or wrists by means of a tamper proof strap. Under normal conditions, the transmitter broadcasts radio signals to the receiver-dialler at regular intervals ranging from several seconds to a few minutes. The electrically powered receiver-dialler detects radio impulses from the transmitter worn by the offender, automatically dials the central computer, and reports over the phone line the status of the signal. Should the wearer move outside the sixty or so metre range beyond which the signal can be picked up by the receiver-dialler, a violation will be recorded. The severing or stretching of the transmitter strap breaks a circuit and also signals a violation.

Through messages sent from the receiver-dialler, the central computer records the existence of the signal, its loss, and if lost, the time of its subsequent return. The computer compares the times of signal receipt against the offender's curfew schedule and records discrepancies. The computer also keeps track of phone disconnections, power failures, and any equipment tampering in the offender's home. Printed reports generated by the central computer are reviewed on a regular basis by corrections personnel who investigate any apparent violations of curfew conditions.

Most modern electronic monitoring systems are relatively free of major technical problems. Nonetheless, some conditions do occasionally interfere with the transmission of signals. Radio interference can be a problem as can the creation of dead space in the wearer's home. Sleeping in certain positions and walking behind major metal appliances such as furnaces, freezers, and shower stalls can disrupt transmission and indicate a violation where none has occurred. Some offenders have complained about chafing and skin irritation caused by the transmitter strap (Fox, 1987; McCarthy, 1987; Blomberg et al., 1987).

Passive systems differ from their active counterparts in that with passive monitoring it is the corrections office that initiates contact. On this dimension, passive monitoring resembles regular probation wherein corrections authorities check on offenders at various points in time. As with active systems, the connection is usually made by phone. Offenders are automatically dialled during periods when they are required to be home but the exact times of the calls are randomized in order that detainees will not know precisely when to expect them. When contacted, offenders must reply to a series of inquiries. They are asked to respond with their names, with the time of day, and with answers to random questions. Their verbal acknowledgements facilitate manual or mechanical voice confirmation. Some state of the art systems are fully automated and make use of voice verification boxes (Erwin, 1989). As with active systems, controllees wear watch-sized sealed modules. The circuitry of these monitors contains a code unique to the individual offender. When called upon to do so, controllees must insert the module into a verifier that signals their presence to the central computer via the phone lines.

The passive system is rather more simple to operate than the active system and the chances of false violation signals are smaller. The major disadvantage of this particular system is that it usually involves making calls to offenders during their curfews. Calling controllees in the evenings and on the weekends presents few problems. However, it is necessary for obvious reasons to contact detainees at various times during the middle of the night. For offenders, being awakened at three in the morning can be both disruptive and annoying. Nonetheless, advocates maintain that being called at home in the dead of the night is better than being awakened at the same time in prison with a flashlight check (Fox, 1987; McCarthy, 1987; Friel and Vaughn, 1986).

Another passive system in limited use does not require a phone connection. With this system, a corrections officer patrols designated areas in a vehicle equipped with a special radio receiver capable of picking up signals from the wrist or ankle module worn by a controllee. The officer drives to within about a block of where an offender is supposed to be located and checks that he or she is present. This system is particularly useful in monitoring an offender's presence at a treatment session, at school, or at work (Vaughn, 1987).

Whether active or passive, the central monitoring computer station is usually staffed only for the standard eight hour work day. Records of a controllee's presence or absence during the evenings, at night, and on weekends are reviewed by corrections personnel when they come to work and indications of violations are pursued at that time. Some programs have telephone answering machines available in order that offenders can call to explain the reasons for apparent after hours violations. The delay in investigation is justified by noting that those who are eligible for enrolment in electronic monitoring programs have committed very minor offences and do not represent a danger to the community. Face-to-face inspections represent a component of some passive monitoring programs. As with regular probation and parole, officers responsible for electronic monitoring with both active and passive techniques exercise considerable discretion in recommending incarceration for violators. Penalties for absconding typically involve being charged with the theft of the transmitter and being required to serve the original sentence behind bars (Fox, 1987; Nellis, 1991; Friel and Vaughn, 1986).

Uses and Offender Types

Electronic monitoring is designed for use either at the "front end" or at the "back door" of the corrections system as a means of limiting the size of the population behind bars (Walker, 1990; Nellis, 1991). The initiative involves placing *those who would otherwise be incarcerated* in non-custodial programs with more intensive supervision than is provided by less intrusive community corrections programs such as probation or parole. The goal is to reduce the numbers imprisoned without sacrificing the safety and protection of the public that is provided through incarceration. The heightened security afforded by the electronic monitoring of home confinement makes it an intermediate sentence falling between imprisonment on one hand and diversion, probation, community service, and parole on the other (McCarthy, 1987).

Electronic monitoring can be used at the front end of the correctional system in two ways. First, home confinement with electronic monitoring is employed as a condition of probation for some of those low risk offenders who have committed minor offences but who nonetheless are destined to be incarcerated. Second, electronic monitoring can be used to place under house arrest some of those being held on remand in municipal lock-ups.[10] The number of people held on remand in the United States is increasing making local gaols, the most dilapidated confinement facilities in the American system, even more crowded than in the past. Furthermore, accused persons held under these less than desirable conditions are just that—accused. Many so confined are never found guilty of an offence (Berry and Matthews, 1989). In Canada in 1990-91, the provinces recorded over 92,000 remand admissions. The average count of those held on remand at any one time during the year was 4711. In Canada, most people on remand (71%) are released within a week. Fewer than 10% are held more than a month (Canadian Centre for Justice Statistics, 1991a). At the back door, house arrest with electronic monitoring is presumably intended to provide early release to a broader range of correctional clientele than would normally meet the requirements for ordinary parole.

To be eligible for electronic monitoring, offenders must be classified as low risk. Low risk offenders are those who have committed relatively minor property offences such as petty theft, break and enter, and fraud. Another quality that defines detainees as low risk involves their having few if any prior criminal convictions and generally being of "good character." Typically, candidates for the program must have a home, possess a phone, and be able to pay, in full or in part, for the rental of the monitoring equipment (McCarthy, 1987; Friel and Vaughn, 1986; Berry and Matthews, 1989). In many jurisdictions, the rule in this regard is "No home and no phone, no program" (Vaughn, 1987).

The time served under home confinement with electronic monitoring often ranges from three to four times as long as the mandated period of incarceration. Therefore, a jail sentence of two months could translate into six to eight months of electronically monitored house arrest (Fox, 1987).

One of the offences for which electronic monitor has proved a popular option is impaired driving (Schmidt and Curtis, 1987). Across Canada and the United States, drunk driving statutes increasingly make mandatory, especially for repeat offenders, some period of incarceration. In some jurisdictions, compulsory jail time has placed a considerable strain on facilities that are already overburdened. Another reason for the popularity of this option for drunk drivers is that so many of those convicted of this offence are ideal candidates for success in the program. In comparison to those convicted of many other offences, impaired drivers are older, better educated, more affluent, more mature, and have families (Baumer et al., 1990). These same traits, incidently, are possessed by many of those contained in another offender group considered a prime candidate for electronic monitoring—those convicted of white collar crime.

Advantages of Electronic Monitoring

The catalogue of positive outcomes that its advocates attribute to electronic monitoring is similar to the list put forward by proponents of community-based corrections more generally with one important addition—the luxury of the added level of security. First and foremost, home confinement with electronic monitoring is touted as an effective means of limiting the size of burgeoning jail and prison populations. Furthermore, since the offenders involved have committed relatively minor offences, the level of security is considered sufficient to meet the citizenry's demand both for public safety and for punitiveness. The privilege of being monitored as opposed to jailed is easily revoked should a particular controllee violate the conditions of the program. Finally, because electronic monitoring is typically offered as a condition of release, its use does not require special legislation (Fox, 1987).

Proponents maintain that while it is more expensive than traditional community corrections programs, home confinement with electronic monitoring is much less expensive than incarceration. The primary reason for the lower cost is that electronic monitoring is considerably less labour intensive (Schmidt and Curtis, 1987). The technology eliminates the need for the large numbers of custodial personnel essential for the operation of prison facilities.

Like other forms of community-based corrections, house arrest with electronic monitoring provides a means by which those convicted of comparatively minor offences can avoid the deleterious impacts of life behind bars. Criminologists have long observed that prisons provide a pivotal training ground wherein an initiate can learn from his or her more seasoned colleagues the skills and motivations conducive to more serious offending (Thomas and Peterson, 1977). Therefore, they argue, it is better to reduce as much as possible the extent to which young first time offenders are exposed to the subculture of more hardened criminals.

Containing offenders in their own homes also avoids two other problems central to the prison experience. First, advocates maintain that those kept out of jail, whether they are awaiting trial or whether they have already been convicted, experience less in the way of negative social stigma (Berry and Matthews, 1989). There is evidence that those who are held on remand awaiting trial are more likely to be found guilty of their offences and to experience harsher sanctions upon conviction than those who are not held in custody prior to trial (Berry, 1985). Research also indicates that ex-inmates are discriminated against in a variety of ways when they attempt to resume the straight life upon release. Jobs are more difficult to find and housing is harder to come by (Kratcoski and Walker, 1984).

Second, doing time behind bars is intended to represent punishment through the deprivation of liberty. The pains of imprisonment actually experienced, however, are routinely in excess of those engendered by captivity alone. Prisons are settings where physical violence and sexual assaults are matters of routine. The strong prey on the weak and in prisons the most vulnerable are often first time offenders jailed for comparatively minor crimes (Jayewardene and Doherty, 1985). Confinement of such offenders in non-institutional contexts is considered far more humane in that it protects them against personal victimization (McCarthy, 1987).

Advocates maintain that home confinement facilitates rehabilitation and reintegration into society because it allows offenders to participate in treatment programs, to attend school, and to hold a job (Nellis, 1991). It also permits those who are employed to continue to work thereby supporting their families and paying taxes (Clarkson and Weakland, 1991; Schumacher, 1987). Furthermore, by ensuring that curfews are observed, electronic monitoring reduces crime. For all intents and purposes, the program effectively incapacitates controllees because they are isolated from fellow miscreants and they are kept away from high risk locations such as street corners, pool halls, and bars during prime crime times such as evenings and weekends (Nellis, 1991).

Finally, proponents point out that house arrest with electronic monitoring is extremely flexible. It is an ideal strategy for dealing with the special needs of detainees who are disabled, who require specialized medical treatment or psychological counselling and, in the case of women, who are pregnant. Perhaps the major problem facing the prison system in the 1990s, particularly in the United States, is a large scale outbreak of full blown AIDS among the institutionalized population. Electronic monitoring is seen as one means by which the special requirements of this inmate group may be more effectively and more humanely met while simultaneously maintaining surveillance and control (Berry and Matthews, 1989).

The second point about flexibility concerns the pairing of electronic monitoring with other correctional strategies. Electronic monitoring can be used alone or in concert with other programs. It can also be tailored to provide security at different times of the day as required. Electronic monitoring can be twinned with incarceration in such a way that the offender is institutionalized at some times and confined in the home at others. Electronic monitoring can be applied at different stages in the processing of prisoners from pre-trial through parole and it can be administered by a variety of different agencies in both the public and the private spheres (Berry and Matthews, 1989).

Electronic Monitoring in Practice

Electronic monitoring is well on the road to becoming the latest fashion on the corrections scene (Fox, 1987). While programs are most numerous in the United States, they are also being implemented or seriously considered in the United Kingdom, Australia, and Canada. Program evaluation reports issued by the jurisdictions in which home confinement with electronic monitoring has been undertaken have by and large cast the program in a favourable light (Schmidt and Curtis, 1987).

In the United States in 1988, estimates of electronically monitored controllees numbered between 3,000 and 4,000 (Ball et al., 1988). By 1990, the number of detainees was estimated at about 7,000 (Nellis, 1991). Approximately forty of the United States have implemented the strategy (Renzema, 1989). More than a half a dozen companies in that nation are currently manufacturing and distributing the necessary hardware under such trade names as "Supervisor" and "On Guard" (Griffiths and Verdun-Jones, 1989). While the idea of electronic monitoring has been aggressively marketed and has been greeted with enthusiasm by politicians and corrections personnel eager to diminish prison crowding and to cut costs, there has been very little in the way of rigorous and independent empirical research investigating the implementation and operation of these programs and evaluating their success (Berry and Matthews, 1989).

Given that eligibility for electronic monitoring to date has been for the most part confined to less serious offenders, it seems likely that the technique is most suited in Canada for those facing incarceration in provincial institutions. Provincial facilities, with a few exceptions, hold offenders convicted of crimes for which the maximum sentence is less than two years. Of those contained in provincially operated prisons across the country, 74% have been convicted of Criminal Code offences. This figure includes impaired driving offences. Seventeen percent of inmates have been convicted of violating provincial statutes. The majority of these convictions is alcohol related. Eight percent of prisoners have broken federal laws and the lion's share of these violations is drug related. Only 1% of those incarcerated in provincial institutions has been jailed for infractions of municipal bylaws.

There are 162 provincial facilities in operation from coast to coast with a total regular bed space of 18,537. Over the five years prior to 1990-91, the average provincial inmate population has increased 14% to its current level of 17,944. In addition to this figure, there were on average approximately 2,400 provincial inmates who were "on register" but not in custody at the time of the enumeration upon which these figures are based. The median sentence length on admission to provincial facilities in 1990-91 was 31 days. By comparison, the equivalent figure for inmates incarcerated in federal facilities was just under four years. The differences in these medians reflect the fact that the offences qualifying an offender for federal prison tend to be much more serious.

Sentenced inmates admitted to provincial custody are typically 28-year-old males. Twenty seven percent of all admissions are for fine default. Provincial facilities on average run at 97% of capacity but do experience problems of overcrowding due to seasonal variations in intake (Canadian Centre for Justice Statistics, 1991a).

The Canadian experience with electronic monitoring is quite limited. In 1983, the Corrections Service of Canada and several of the provinces undertook feasibility studies and designed experimental electronic monitoring programs. In 1987, the Corrections Service of Canada abandoned its plans to test electronic monitoring on a trial basis citing as its reason the threat of legal action from concerned civil liberties groups (Griffiths and Verdun-Jones, 1989).

The only province to proceed with electronic monitoring trials is British Columbia. In 1987, the British Columbia Corrections Branch implemented a 9 month program involving the house arrest with electronic surveillance of 25 offenders serving intermittent sentences many of which were for impaired driving. Meeting several conditions were necessary for a participant's inclusion. Participation could not undermine the intent of the offender's sentence. Public safety had to be assured. Candidates were required either to hold a job or to be attending an educational institution. The monitoring system employed was active as opposed to passive and participation in the program was entirely voluntary. An evaluation centred upon the following dimensions: cost, safety, the affect on offenders and members of their families, the type of offender most suited to participation, and the reactions of the public, the professional corrections community, and various interest groups (Solicitor General of Canada, 1987). The evaluation deemed the program a success (Griffiths and Verdun-Jones, 1989).

A report in 1989 on a 12 month project undertaken by the Vancouver Court Adult Probation Office emphasizes the success of electronic monitoring and underlines the enthusiasm for this corrections strategy. According to the report, the 12 month test program involved 92 violent offenders anticipating sentences of 90 days or less and who were considered likely to serve their time intermittently. The assessment indicated that electronic monitoring worked well with all but one participant. The evaluation report stated that "the cases accounted for 1533 days of EMS residential confinement or the equivalent of 4.2 jail beds per day on an annualized basis." Based upon these results, program assessors estimate that the demand for beds for those sentenced to 90 days or less can be reduced by 11% province wide. The report recommends that all defendants potentially sentenced to intermittent terms be screened to determine their suitability for electronic monitoring (Neville, 1989).

An Evaluation of Electronic Monitoring

Electronic monitoring has four fundamental and interconnected goals: 1) to reduce the population in custody, 2) to reduce the costs of corrections that are generated by custodial sentences, 3) to provide humane punishment while promoting rehabilitation and reintegration, and 4) to maintain the security and the safety of the public. The ability of electronically monitored house arrest to meet successfully each of these objectives appears highly suspect. In the absence of rigorous program evaluations, the extent to which goals are attained cannot be definitively discerned. Nonetheless, there is justification for scepticism on logical, historical, and empirical grounds. The concern over the rapid proliferation of these programs in the absence of independent, meticulous, and methodologically sound research is well founded. In this section, we assess the extent to which each of the stated aims of electronic monitoring are (or can be) achieved.

1.   Reduction of the Population in Custody.

Recent years have been characterized by economic recession, political conservatism, ever increasing concerns about apparent rises in crime, growing desires for punitiveness in corrections, and heightening perceptions of an inefficient criminal justice system gone soft on hardened criminals. Among other developments, rehabilitation has increasingly come to be seen as a goal beyond the capability of prisons to provide. Rehabilitative programs are being scaled down or eliminated in favour of a purely punishment oriented approach to more serious offenders (Ekstedt and Griffiths, 1988). Disenchantment with the rehabilitative potential of community corrections is also mounting (Friel and Vaughn, 1986).

In keeping with trends toward greater punitiveness, it is conceivable that the intermediate sentence of electronic monitoring will be used not as an alternative to incarceration but rather as a tougher alternative to other less intrusive forms of community corrections. Those convicted of minor offences who might formerly have been either released altogether or channelled into existing non-custodial programs may well be sentenced to house arrest with electronic monitoring largely because the more restrictive and secure option is available. Evidence suggests that there would be little in the way of return on the added insurance, however. Because candidates for these programs are low risk minor offenders in the first place, non-custodial low intensity supervision programs such as probation, community service orders, and parole are successful in approximately 85% of cases (Berry and Matthews, 1989; Muncie, 1990; Griffiths and Verdun-Jones, 1989).

It must be remembered as well that electronic monitoring does not successfully contain all controllees. In the United States, despite comparatively stringent eligibility requirements, failure rates run between 10% and 20% on average (Berry and Matthews, 1989). Where serious violations occur, the non-custodial sentence is revoked and jail sentences are invoked. As the numbers of electronically monitored offenders grow, the numbers of violations warranting incarceration will increase commensurately.

It is unlikely that electronic monitoring can significantly reduce the numbers of persons incarcerated unless more serious personal and property offenders are made eligible in reasonably large numbers. Inclusion of higher risk offenders in electronic monitoring programs, however, increases the likelihood of security breaches. More serious offenders with less desirable socio-biographical attributes are more likely to abscond and to re-offend (Schmidt and Curtis, 1987). Higher failure rates necessitate efforts to recapture those who abscond. If those who escape also re-offend, police forces are called upon to devote their time and their resources to deal effectively with the new crimes committed (N.E.E., 1990). The public's confidence in the corrections system would hardly be bolstered if higher risk offenders on electronic monitoring were to breach security in anything resembling large numbers (Schmidt and Curtis, 1987). In addition, higher failure rates and the eventual return of offenders to prison would limit any overall reductions in numbers produced by electronic monitoring.

The lessons of history should not be ignored. During the 1960s and the 1970s, community corrections were substantially expanded as an alternative to incarceration. Their stated purposes have an all too familiar ring. Their aims were to reduce the numbers of offenders imprisoned, to offer a more humane alternative to incarceration, to promote rehabilitation and reintegration, and to lower corrections costs. Evidence suggests that the numbers in community corrections programs increased as predicted. However, the numbers incarcerated did not decrease (Chan and Ericson, 1981). Indeed, the numbers behind bars also grew (Hylton, 1982). On the whole, more people found themselves under the supervision and control of the state than had been the case before these alternatives to incarceration were expanded (Blomberg, 1987; Lowman and Menzies, 1986). What was in theory intended as a substitute for incarceration was in practice transformed into a supplement to incarceration (Rothman, 1980).

Should history come close to repeating itself, a new intermediate sanction program confined to non-serious offenders with acceptable socio-biographic traits will simply expand the social control net. With added numbers of minor offenders on electronic monitoring, space may be created to expand the ranks of those eligible for less intrusive measures such as probation. The danger is that increasing numbers of non-serious offenders will be "netted" while at the same time serious offenders will continue to be incarcerated at the previous rate.

2. Cost Cutting.

If in practice electronic monitoring is confined to low risk offenders and added as insurance to the less intrusive community corrections provisions already in existence, overall costs cannot help but increase since electronic monitoring is more expensive than other forms of non-custodial supervision (Fox, 1987). American data suggest that this danger is real. In some programs, it is estimated that at least 25% of those currently being monitored electronically were probably not destined for prison (Berry and Matthews, 1989). Presumably these offenders should have qualified for non-custodial options with less intensive surveillance.

Where violations result in revocations, the cost of imprisonment is simply deferred. The state must ultimately assume financial responsibility not only for offenders' electronic monitoring but for their jail terms as well since these offenders eventually wind up serving their time behind bars after all. For offenders who abscond, expenditures are incurred for their initial monitoring, for their re-apprehension, re-trying, and re-sentencing, for damage to or loss of monitoring equipment, and for their eventual incarceration (Fox, 1987). Where those who abscond commit additional offences, the cost of these new crimes must also be added to the tally. The failure rate for low risk offenders on electronic monitoring ranges between 10% and 20% on average. If higher risk offenders are eventually included in these programs, failure rates and associated costs will grow commensurately.

The costs engendered by program failures are rather difficult to determine with precision and they are seldom calculated when the economic advantages of electronic monitoring are being assessed (McCarthy, 1987). Typically, the degree of benefit is measured by comparing the average daily cost of an offender's incarceration with the average daily cost of maintaining a controllee under house arrest with electronic supervision. Using this simple formula, most estimates suggest that the expense of electronic monitoring is between 33% (Ball et al., 1988) and 45% (Fox, 1987) of the costs of incarceration. The comparison is misleading, however, because the electronically monitored are low risk offenders and consequently would cost less than the average dollar sum for incarceration. Moreover, if one day in prison translates into more than one day of electronically monitored house arrest, the savings decline substantially (Berry and Matthews, 1989). For example, if one day in prison translates into three or four days of home confinement with electronic monitoring, the latter could become more expensive than the former.

Cutting the costs of corrections by a simple reduction in the numbers confined in institutions is not as straightforward an undertaking as it might seem at first glance. First, if only the excess "crowd" were eliminated, no meaningful staffing reductions could be realized because institutions would still be operating at or near capacity (Vaughn, 1987). Second, it is estimated that about 85% of institutional costs are fixed (Berry and Matthews, 1989). The lion's share of operating expenses is devoted to staff salaries (75% in Canadian provincial institutions (Canadian Centre for Justice Statistics, 1991a)) and certain minimum staffing requirements are necessary for these institutions to function regardless of the numbers incarcerated. Researchers estimate that the inmate population would have to be cut by 50% before significant staff cuts could be made and the associated savings realized (Berry and Matthews, 1989). It seems unlikely that a reduction of that magnitude would be feasible. Third, observers note the historical tendency for any available corrections space to be filled by one means or another (Inciardi, 1987). For these reasons, it seems improbable that meaningful savings can be achieved by limiting institutional populations and cutting costs through the expansion of electronic monitoring.

3.   Humanity, Rehabilitation, and Justice.
Some observers have suggested that the cost savings from electronic monitoring are far from the most important consideration (Nellis, 1991; McCarthy, 1987; Vaughn, 1989). They suggest that home confinement with electronic monitoring is superior to incarceration because it is more humane and because it increases the likelihood of rehabilitation.

The humaneness of electronic monitoring can be challenged on a number of dimensions. Confinement, whether in an institution or in one's own home, represents a deprivation of liberty. North American jurisprudence views deprivation of liberty as a serious sanction to be used only as a last resort. More restrictive measures should not be the preferred option if less restrictive measures are equally effective. If, however, electronic monitoring is added to community corrections options as insurance, punishment will become more punitive than necessary (Fox, 1987; Berry, 1985). Where the duration of time in confinement is increased two, three, or four times by virtue of the fact that people are being detained in their homes as opposed to in jail, the time for which liberty is deprived is dramatically extended (Berry and Matthews, 1989). Furthermore, few jurisdictions have guidelines in place to govern the application of electronic monitoring at the sentencing stage. This lack of direction may well exacerbate sentencing disparity (Fox, 1987; Berry and Matthews, 1989).

Home confinement for obvious reasons frequently involves offenders' families and where this is the case a number of problems can arise. First, a family can be stigmatized as it becomes common knowledge that one of its members is a state detainee. Second, a home containing a monitored offender is subject to ongoing intrusion around the clock by corrections officials. Such invasions of privacy can be stressful for the kin of detainees who, after all, have themselves not been convicted of an offence (Friel and Vaughn, 1986). Third, being cooped up at home for lengthy periods of time may result in offenders suffering varying degrees of cabin fever (Friel and Vaughn, 1986). Life in close quarters for lengthy periods under less than ideal conditions can easily create friction within the home (Nellis, 1991). Fourth, families may have contributed to the offender's problems with the law in the first place. Dysfunctional families can be criminogenic. Finally, the offender's kin may aid and abet such licentious diversions as alcohol consumption and illicit drug use.

Another point of contention regarding the humaneness of electronic monitoring concerns the issues of consent and privacy (Blomberg et al., 1987). The question raised about consent pertains to whether or not it is freely volunteered or, given the threat of jail as an alternative, whether or not it is coerced. The other issue is the extent to which the intrusive supervision entailed in electronic monitoring represents an undue invasion of privacy. The very few American test cases to date are instructive. The courts would appear to consider as unfounded concerns about coerced consent and invasion of privacy. Rather, they view electronic monitoring as less of an infringement of human rights than the alternative of incarceration (Del Carmen and Vaughn, 1986). Nonetheless, should a case be made in future that the alternative being replaced by electronic monitoring is not incarceration but rather that the alternative being replaced is a less intrusive form of community corrections, the courts might well take a different view. Among the legal rights that might be at issue under such circumstances would be freedom of speech and association as well as protection from unreasonable search and seizure, from self incrimination, and from cruel and unusual punishment (U.S. Bureau of Justice, 1989).

The degree to which electronic monitoring facilitates rehabilitation has also been questioned. First, rehabilitation entails the development of trusting and supportive relationships between controllees and community corrections counsellors. The surveillance and control functions served by the electronic monitoring device are not conducive to the development of these sorts of bonds (Fox, 1987).

Second, to the extent that electronic monitoring is fully automated, personal contact between offenders and trained personnel is greatly curtailed. Some critics have pointed out that to be economically viable and cost effective it may prove necessary for very large numbers of electronically monitored controllees to comprise the caseload of a single corrections officer (Fox, 1987). If electronic monitoring is widely available but limited to use with low risk offenders convicted of non-serious crimes, the likelihood that electronic monitoring will be overused is by no means far fetched. Should electronic monitoring services be privatized, the tendency for abuse may be further exacerbated. It is by no means inconceivable that market forces might fuel an expansion in the numbers of "clients" especially given the importance to profits of economies of scale (Nellis, 1991).

Third, compared to less secure community corrections initiatives such as probation and parole, levels of community contact are less. Living under house arrest diminishes normal socialization and erodes the re-integrative functions promoted by the nurturing of strong ties to the community (Fox, 1987; Berry and Matthews, 1989). Finally, because the devices cannot be removed and are often visible, there is concern that wearers will experience stigmatization when they are at work, at school, in treatment, or in a public place (Fox, 1987). The visibility of the device is a problem that more frequently confronts women because of their feminine attire. Women's dresses do not conceal ankles with nearly the effectiveness of men's pants (Vaughn, 1987). One observer goes so far as to suggest that for many monitored females the device may become the equivalent of an electronic scarlet letter (Friel and Vaughn, 1986).

The justice of electronic monitoring programs has been challenged on the equity dimension. To be eligible for electronic monitoring requires, at the very least, a home and a phone. "No home and no phone, no program." Sometimes admission to the program also requires the ability to pay both for equipment rentals and for administration fees. Each of these requirements necessitates some degree of material well being. Those without resources can be denied the right to participate (Berry, 1985). Programs that allow the more affluent to avoid institutionalization while relegating the poor to imprisonment are inequitable and discriminatory.

At present, the most suitable candidates for electronic monitoring are those convicted of minor offences for which traditional community corrections programs cannot be used because the minor offences have attached to them mandatory jail terms. The classic example in this regard is a repeat conviction for impaired driving. With respect to impaired driving, however, it is worth remembering that the rationale for the mandatory jail term was to demonstrate to the offender and to the public at large the seriousness of this crime. Confining convicted drunk drivers at home with electronic monitoring mitigates the gravity of the offence because house arrest is perceived as a soft sanction. This is particularly true where offenders come from the middle or upper classes. According to critics, house arrest as a punishment trivializes the crime and in so doing defeats the original purpose of the law (Fox, 1987).

4.   Protection of the Public.

Existing electronic monitoring programs contain low risk offenders. Since the risk to the community posed by controllees who violate their curfews is negligible, the reaction time separating violation from response can stretch from several hours to a couple of days. Most monitoring stations operate only during standard working times—eight hours per day five days per week. If higher risk offenders are placed in electronic monitoring programs, maintenance of security will demand immediate responses. Immediate responses in turn will necessitate the staffing of facilities around the clock seven days a week. Failure to do so might place the citizenry at some risk and it would certainly undermine public confidence in the program (Schmidt and Curtis, 1987). Nevertheless, even an immediate response would be insufficient to protect the public if a serious offender were to violate a curfew and be at large in the community. The inability to guarantee such a high level of protection will likely be sufficient to preclude the inclusion in electronic monitoring programs of higher risk offenders who have committed truly serious crimes.

Conclusions

Electronic monitoring has four fundamental and interconnected goals: a) to reduce the population in custody, b) to decrease the costs of corrections that are generated by custodial sentences, c) to provide humane punishment with the potential for rehabilitation and reintegration, and d) to maintain the security and the safety of the public. There are several points that require emphasis in evaluating the extent to which electronic monitoring meets its specified objectives. These points concern the nature of the offence and the eligibility requirements that make the intermediate sentence a judicious option.

First, for electronic monitoring to be an acceptable alternative to incarceration, the offence must be comparatively minor and worthy only of a short jail term. Many existing electronic monitoring programs automatically exclude from participation offenders who have been convicted of violent offences such as common assault, wife battering, child abuse, sexual assault, and other sex offences. Many programs also rule out the participation of offenders who have committed serious property offences (judged by the value of loss created by the theft or fraud). Also excluded are those guilty of drug offences such as trafficking and smuggling (Palm Beach, 1987; Fox, 1987; Nellis, 1991; Friel and Vaughn, 1986; Berry and Matthews, 1989). With these exclusions, the offences rendering someone eligible for electronic monitoring are pared down to minor property crimes such as break and enter, to white collar crimes such as fraud and income tax evasion where dollar amounts are relatively low, and to impaired driving offences. It is not an insignificant point that convictions for impaired driving and for tax evasion have mandatory sentences attached to them. People convicted must go to jail.

Second, to qualify for electronic monitoring instead of incarceration, offenders must meet certain eligibility requirements in addition to having committed only minor offences. They must, in short, possess the requisite socio-biographical traits. Typically, they must be of good character, they must not be drug addicted, they must have a home and a phone, they must have a job or be going to school, and they must have no prior record for serious criminality. If they have minor criminal records, offenders must have no history of absconding (Fox, 1987; Nellis, 1991; Solicitor General of Canada, 1987).

Third, offenders placed upon electronic monitoring must be destined for incarceration. They must, therefore, be ineligible for less intrusive community corrections programs such as probation and parole. Herein lies the proverbial Shakespearean rub. Home confinement with electronic monitoring is an intermediate sentence falling between incarceration on one hand and a non-custodial option with low intensity supervision on the other. As an intermediate sanction, proponents claim that it has many of the advantages of less intrusive non-custodial corrections programs along with the added benefit of heightened security. Presumably, the intermediate sentence is tailored for the intermediate offender. It is designed for those whose law breaking is sufficiently non-serious that incarceration is essential neither as punishment nor as protection for the public. On the other hand, offenders receiving intermediate sentences must be ineligible for existing less intrusive community corrections programs such as probation and parole either because of the seriousness of their offences or because they possess certain socio-biographical attributes that designate them as high risk candidates for escape and re-offending.

Given current eligibility requirements, the line separating the offender who requires the intermediate level of security afforded by electronic monitoring from the offender who requires the maximum level of security afforded by imprisonment is reasonably clear. Those who have committed serious crime and whose socio-biographical traits indicate high risk of escape and re-offending go to jail. Alternatively, offenders who have committed comparatively non-serious crimes and whose socio-biographical characteristics are considered low risk are confined at home under electronic surveillance.

Not nearly so clear, however, is the line that separates the non-serious and low risk offender who nonetheless requires electronic monitoring from the non-serious and low risk offender who qualifies for less intrusive measures such as probation and parole. Except for minor offences with mandatory jail sentences, it is difficult to imagine that persons with the characteristics necessary to qualify for electronic monitoring would not also qualify for non-custodial measures with less intensive supervision. In other words, the qualifications for electronic monitoring (non-serious offence, employment, a home etc.) and for other less intrusive forms of community corrections are essentially the same. It seems all too likely that if the application of electronic monitoring extends much beyond offenders convicted of minor crimes with mandatory jail sentences (impaired driving) that it will become in practice not an alternative to incarceration as claimed but an alternative to non-custodial sanctions involving less intensive and less intrusive supervision. Sentencing judges must keep an extremely sharp eye to ensure that they avoid misclassification and inconsistency.

Electronic monitoring as a substitute for or condition of probation or parole is problematic on several dimensions. First, such applications represent an escalation of penalties in cases where those placed on electronic monitors do indeed qualify for less punitive non-custodial sentences with low intensity supervision. Second, there is considerable danger that more people will become enmeshed in the criminal justice net as the use of this intermediate sanction expands. Greater numbers of offenders will be accommodated in non-custodial sentences with various levels of supervision. Third, given the stringency of the eligibility requirements for non-custodial sentencing (minor offences and good character), it will be impossible to reduce prison populations to any meaningful extent. Too few of those presently in jail meet the conditions. With crime rates, especially violent crime, reportedly on the rise, it seems reasonable to assume that there will be no shortage in the near future of candidates for incarceration. It seems more reasonable to expect that electronic monitoring on a larger scale will expand the scope of state control by escalating penalties and by increasing the size of the pool of non-custodial controllees. At the same time, the number of offenders incarcerated will remain constant or continue to rise. Such a widening of the net would of course also drive up the overall costs of corrections.

The invention and refinement of electronic monitoring equipment is accelerating at a rapid pace while the legal standards governing the application of these technologies lag behind. The development and proliferation of electronic monitoring systems provides yet another example of corrections policy being implemented either in the absence of sound research or in the face of solid data suggesting that its virtues are at best overstated and at worst non-existent. Despite uncertainty regarding the efficacy of this control strategy, enthusiastic advocates remain undeterred. Proponents continue to call not only for the continued use of the technology but for the exploration and development of its potential promise for controlling a broader range of client groups and for intruding further into the lives of those monitored (Erwin, 1989).

As a number of critics have pointed out, community corrections generally and electronic monitoring and surveillance in particular represent a decentralization of state control and an expansion of penal space (Muncie, 1990; Cohen, 1979). The potential for the abuse of electronic monitoring and surveillance techniques is considerable and caution is warranted. Today's practices may substantially influence the legal standards governing tomorrow's applications and tomorrow's applications will be executed with increasingly more accurate, powerful, and intrusive equipment. Even now, the Japanese, who themselves have neither a major crime problem nor any interest in using electronic monitoring domestically, are developing for the export market camera systems specially designed for installation in offenders' homes (Nellis, 1991). Big Brother may be watching soon.

Endnotes

1. George Orwell's *Nineteen Eighty-Four* was published in June of 1949. Its images of double think, the Thought Police, the all seeing, all hearing telescreen, the Party, and of course, Big Brother have made "1984" the classic fictional exemplar of the evils associated with political authoritarianism, state control, and the total domination and indoctrination of the individual.

2. "The big house" is a slang term used to refer to such old, large, and infamous American prisons as Alcatraz, San Quentin, and Sing Sing. The term was immortalized through its use in early gangster films starring the likes of Humphrey Bogart, George Raft, Edward G. Robinson, and Paul Muni.

3. These percentage increases are computed on the basis of constant dollars.

4. Community-based corrections are non-custodial programs situated in the community. Operated both by the Correctional Service of Canada and by the provinces and territories, they are intended to serve as alternatives to imprisonment. Their principle goals are to promote offender rehabilitation and, for offenders who have been incarcerated, to facilitate reintegration into society.

5. Crimes of violence consist of six categories of offences—homicide, attempted murder, assault, sexual offences, robbery, and abduction. Property crime also consists of six categories—breaking and entering, motor vehicle theft, theft of $1000 and under, theft over $1000, possession of stolen goods, and fraud. Drinking and driving offences include impaired operation of a motor vehicle, vessel, or aircraft (i) impaired driving with over 80 mgs., ii) impaired driving causing bodily harm, or iii) impaired driving causing death, and failure or refusal to provide a breath or blood sample. The "other crimes" category includes all offences within the Criminal Code that are neither violent nor property crimes.

6. Probation is a type of court disposition that is served in the community under conditions of supervision. A probation order may be issued in conjunction with a suspended sentence, conditional sentence, or fine. In most but not all cases, probation is a substitute for a jail term.

the National Parole Board. Provinces have the option of establishing parole boards to oversee early release from provincial facilities. At present, only Quebec, Ontario, and British Columbia have established parole boards (Ekstedt and Griffiths, 1988).

7. Diversion is a mechanism through which accused persons who are charged with minor crimes and who do not have long criminal records are "diverted" out of the criminal justice system into an appropriate resource program. Normally, alleged offenders are given the choice of either participating in the resource program or facing prosecution on the charge. A community service order is usually granted as a condition of probation. It requires offenders to perform community services for an individual or non-profit organization in lieu of serving time in jail. Attempts are often made to have offenders perform services for the victims of their criminal activities. Restitution is a program available to those on probation wherein the offender agrees to partially or fully compensate the victim for damages.

8. The most crime prone age group for property and violent offences contains those in their late teens and early twenties. In circumstances where this age category represents the largest age cohort in the population, it is not surprising that crime rates increase. Birth rates in the post-war years from 1948 until 1960 were unusually high. A person born in 1954 (the mid point of the range) was twenty one, a prime crime age, in 1975. The same person in 1990 was thirty-six, an age at which involvement in violent and property crime is much less likely. A factor such as society's age structure is a significant consideration in understanding the production and distribution of criminal activity.

9. Mandatory supervision is a form of early release based upon earned remission. Eligibility requirements dictate that inmates serve two thirds of their sentences. Released inmates are supervised in the community for the duration of their sentences. Failure rates have been higher for mandatory supervision than for parole primarily because parole requires the meeting of criteria beyond good institutional behaviour. Mandatory supervision, because it is administered by the National Parole Board, has often been confused with parole. The media frequently report that offenders out on parole have committed crimes when in fact these offenders have been released on mandatory supervision. Dissatisfaction with this program has resulted in the National Parole Board being given (in 1986) the power to deny mandatory supervision to an offender whom it considers might pose a threat to the community.

10. Accused persons confined on remand are people who have been charged with offences but not convicted. They are held in jail as opposed to being released on their own recognizance or on bail either because

the court believes that they will not appear for trial or because it fears that they will tamper with or intimidate witnesses for the prosecution.

Bibliography

Ball, R., C. Huff, and R. Lilly. 1988. *House Arrest and Correctional Policy*. Beverly Hills: Sage.

Baumer, T.L., R. Mendelsohn, and C. Rhine. 1990. *Final Report: The Electronic Monitoring of Non-Violent Convict Felons: An Experiment in Home Detention*. Indianapolis, IN: School of Public and Environmental Affairs, Indiana University.

Berry, B. 1985. "Electronic Jails: A New Criminal Justice Concern," *Justice Quarterly* 2: 1-24.

Berry, B. and R. Matthews. 1989. "Electronic Monitoring and House Arrest: Making the Right Connections," in R. Matthews. (ed.) *Privatizing Criminal Justice*. Beverly Hills: Sage.

Blomberg, T.G. 1987. "Criminal Justice Reform and Social Control: Are We Becoming a Minimum Security Society?" in J. Lowman, R.J. Menzies, and T.S. Palys. (eds.). *Transcarceration: Essays in the Sociology of Social Control*. Aldershot, U.K.: Gower Publishers.

Blomberg, T.G., G.P. Waldo, and L.C. Burcoff. 1987. "Home Confinement and Electronic Surveillance," in B.R. McCarthy. (ed.). *Intermediate Punishments: Intensive Supervision, Home Confinement and Electronic Surveillance*. Monsey, New York: Criminal Justice Press.

Canadian Centre for Justice Statistics. 1991a. *Adult Correctional Services in Canada 1990-91*. Ottawa: Supply and Services.

Canadian Centre for Justice Statistics. 1991b. *Canadian Crime Statistics 1990*. Ottawa: Supply and Services.

Chan, J.B.L. and R.V. Ericson. 1981. *Decarceration and the Economy of Penal Reform*. Toronto: Centre of Criminology, University of Toronto.

Clarkson, J.S. and J.J. Weakland. 1991. "A Transitional Aftercare Model for Juveniles: Adapting Electronic Monitoring and Home Confinement," *Journal of Offender Monitoring* 4: 1-15.

Cohen, S. 1979. "The Punitive City: Notes on the Dispersal of Social Control," *Contemporary Crises* 3: 339-363.

Currie, E. 1985. *Confronting Crime: An American Challenge*. New York: Pantheon.

Del Carman, R. and J. Vaughn. 1986. "Legal Issues in the Use of Electronic Surveillance in Probation," *Federal Probation* 50: 60-69.

Desroches, F.J. 1990. "Tearoom Trade: A Research Update," *Qualitative Sociology* 13: 39-61.

Ekstedt, John W. and Curt T. Griffiths. 1988. *Corrections in Canada: Policy and Practice* (2nd. ed.). Toronto: Butterworths.

Erwin, B.S. 1989. *Intensive Probation Supervision with an Electronic Monitoring Option*. Atlanta, GA.: Georgia Department of Corrections.

Fox, Richard G. 1987. "Dr. Schwitzgebel's Machine Revisited: Electronic Monitoring of Offenders," *Australian and New Zealand Journal of Criminology* 20: 131-147.

Friel, C.M. and J.B. Vaughn. 1986. "A Consumer's Guide to the Electronic Monitoring of Probationers," *Federal Probation* 50: 3-14.

Griffiths, Curt T. and Simon N. Verdun-Jones. 1989. *Canadian Criminal Justice.* Toronto: Butterworths.

Hylton, J.H. 1982. "Rhetoric and Reality: A Critical Appraisal of Community Corrections Programs," *Crime and Delinquency* 28: 341-373.

Inciardi, J.A. 1986. *The War on Drugs: Heroin, Cocaine, and Public Policy.* Mountainview, CA.: Mayfield.

Inciardi, J.A. 1987. *Criminal Justice* (2nd. ed.). New York: Harcourt Brace Jovanovich.

Jayewardene, C.H. and D. Doherty. 1985. "Individual Violence in Canadian Penitentiaries," *Canadian Journal of Criminology* 27: 429-439.

Kratcoski, P. and D. Walker. 1984. *Criminal Justice in America: Processes and Issues.* New York: Random House.

Lilly, J.R., R.A. Ball, and J. Wright. 1987. "Home Incarceration with Electronic Monitoring in Kenton County, Kentucky: An Evaluation," in B.R. McCarthy (ed.). *Intermediate Punishments: Intensive Supervision, Home Confinement and Electronic Surveillance.* Monsey, New York: Criminal Justice Press.

Lowman, J. and R.J. Menzies. 1986. "Out of the Fiscal Shadow: Carceral Trends in Canada and the United States," *Crime and Social Justice* 26: 95-115.

Maxfield, M.G. and T. Baumer. 1990. "Home Detention with Electronic Monitoring: Comparing Pre-trial and Post-conviction Programs," *Crime and Delinquency* 36: 521-536.

McCarthy, B.R. 1987. "Introduction," in B.R. McCarthy (ed.). *Intermediate Punishments: Intensive Supervision, Home Confinement and Electronic Surveillance.* Monsey, New York: Criminal Justice Press.

Menzies, K. 1986. "The Rapid Spread of Community Service Orders in Ontario," *Canadian Journal of Criminology* 28: 157-169.

Muncie, J. 1990. "A Prisoner in My Own Home: The Politics and Practice of Electronic Monitoring," *Probation Journal* 37: 72-77.

N.E.E. Corrections Research and Planning Unit. 1990. *Home Office Research and Statistics Department Research Bulletin.* 29: 28-31. London: British Home Office.

Nellis, M. 1991. "The Electronic Monitoring of Offenders in England and Wales," *British Journal of Criminology* 31:*-*.

Neville, Linda. 1989. *Electronic Monitoring Systems for Offender Supervision: Pilot Project and Evaluation.* Ottawa, Canada: Corrections Branch, Minister of the Solicitor General.

Orwell, G. 1949. *Nineteen Eighty-Four.* London: Secker and Warburg.

Palm Beach County, Florida Sheriff's Department. 1987. "Palm Beach County's In-House Arrest Work Release Program," in B.R. McCarthy (ed.). *Intermediate Punishments: Intensive Supervision, Home Confinement and Electronic Surveillance.* Monsey, New York: Criminal Justice Press.

Renzema, M. 1989. "Annual Monitoring Census: Progress Report," *Journal of Offender Monitoring* 2: 20-21.

Rhodes, R.P. 1984. *Organized Crime: Crime Control Vs. Civil Liberties.* New York: Random House.

Rothman, D. 1980. *Conscience and Convenience: The Asylum and Its Alternatives in Progressive America.* Toronto: Little Brown and Co.

Samaha, J. 1988. *Criminal Justice.* New York: West Publishing.

Schmidt, A.K. and C.E. Curtis. 1987. "Electronic Monitors," in B.R. McCarthy (ed.). *Intermediate Punishments: Intensive Supervision, Home Confinement and Electronic Surveillance.* Monsey, New York: Criminal Justice Press.

Schumacher, M. 1987. *Supervised Electronic Confinement Pilot Program.* Santa Ana, CA.: Orange County Probation Department.

Schwitzgebel, R.K. 1969. "Issues in the Use of an Electronic Rehabilitation System with Chronic Recidivists," *Law and Society Review* 3: 597-611.

Schwitzgebel, R.K. 1970. "Behavioural Electronics Could Empty the World's Prisons," *The Futurist* 4: 59-62.

Scull, A.T. 1977. *Decarceration: Community Treatment and the Deviant—A Radical View.* Englewood Cliffs, N.J.: Prentice Hall.

Scull, A.T. 1983. "Community Corrections: Panacea, Progress, or Pretence?" in R.A. Abel (ed.). *The Politics of Informal Justice: The American Experience.* New York: Academic Press.

Smith, M.E. 1984. "Will the Real Alternatives Please Stand Up?" *New York University Review of Law and Social Change* 12: 171-197.

Solicitor General of Canada. 1987. "Electronic Surveillance: Turning Homes into Jails," *Liaison* 13-10: 4-8.

Sykes, G.M. 1958. *Society of Captives: A Study of Maximum Security Institutions.* Princeton, N.J.: Princeton University Press.

Thomas, C.W. and D.M. Peterson. 1977. *Prison Organization and Inmate Subcultures.* Indianapolis, IN.: Bobbs Merrill.

United States Bureau of Justice Assistance. 1989. *Electronic Monitoring in Intensive Probation and Parole Programs.* Washington, D.C.: United States Bureau of Justice Assistance.

Vaughn, J.B. 1987. "Planning for Change: The Use of Electronic Monitoring as a Correctional Alternative," in B.R. McCarthy (ed.). *Intermediate*

Punishments: Intensive Supervision, Home Confinement and Electronic Surveillance. Monsey, New York: Criminal Justice Press.

Vaughn, J.B. 1989. "A Survey of Juvenile Electronic Monitoring and Home Confinement Programs," *Juvenile and Family Court Journal* 40: 1-36.

Walker, J.L. 1990. "Sharing the Credit, Sharing the Blame: Managing Political Risks in Electronically Monitored House Arrest," *Federal Probation* 54: 16-20.

Zonderman, Jon. 1990. *Beyond the Crime Lab: The New Science of Investigation.* New York: John Wiley and Sons.

Chapter 11

Corrections and Community (In)action

K.R.E. McCormick and L.A. Visano

"Propaganda begins when dialogue ends"
Jacques Ellul

Introduction

The concept of community pervades all levels of the criminal justice system. Throughout the last few decades we have witnessed a proliferation of programs, strategies and policies ostensibly designed to encourage a greater degree of "community" participation (Boostrom and Henderson, 1983; Visano, 1983). This passionate rediscovery of viable alternatives in the community has been sought to supplement traditional and more formal methods of control. To elaborate, such ideological manipulations of this concept in community policing, criminal trials, sentencing and corrections has attained a heightened significance within the criminological "chatter" of control (Foucault, 1977: 304) This shift towards community crime prevention, compensation, restitution, victimization and the simple return of the bad or the mad (Scull, 1977: 41) to the community echo a lingering pastoral nostalgia.

The corrections industry has been busy in promoting a community argument in ensuring greater degrees of co-operation and input. As Commissioner of Corrections Ingstrup celebrates:

> Accepting that the community is the only environment in which the offender can fully demonstrate the ability to function as a law-abiding citizen, gradual release to the community, and quality community supervision and support are essential to achieve our Mission of protecting society by facilitating the timely reintegration of offenders (1987: 7).

Moreover, as Ingstrup elucidates:

> We will also strive to enhance public understanding and acceptance of our role through active, responsive and honest communication with the public (1987, 9).

Likewise, provincial counterparts continue to highlight in their annual reports their respective government's commitment to community service orders. Typically, community alternatives are singled out in terms of their effectiveness, that is, in responding to such criteria as the protection of society and the rehabilitation of offenders. Ontario's 1984 *Annual Report of the Ministry of Correctional Services*, which virtually remains unchanged currently, cites the following goals:

> "To encourage and develop community—based work programs" and "To facilitate the participation of both individual citizens and the community at large in the criminal justice system." (Ontario, *Annual Report*: Correctional Services, 1984: 5)

What emerges from the plethora of government documents is the theme that the community plays an incredibly vital role in the overall corrections process, a critical element in forging new relationships with offenders and state agencies. The general public concurs, as indicated by Doob and Roberts (1988) who report that 70% of Canadians indicate that they would rather put money into the development of community sanctions than in building more prisons. Admittedly, the government sanctions directly and symbolically the processes of community participation. The notion of community in these contexts, however, remains poorly operationalized within an normatively illusory framework that masks any connotations of politics and struggle.

The purposes of this paper are to evaluate critically the concept of community in corrections, provide a case study of a much celebrated exercise in federal corrections—the Citizens' Advisory Committee—and to focus attention on the need to transform community inaction into communities-in - action.

Within the correctional marketplace of rhetoric, jargon and clichés, the concept of community has become a negotiable commodity the value of which is conveniently determined by the state. The community concept provides more than ideological legitimacy. Rather as currently manipulated by sophisticated cadres of state bureaucrats committed to public relations campaigns, the community concept is designed to discipline "outside" participation, pre-empt criticism and discourage much needed critical dialogue. How then does the public participate in corrections? Much is known about the efforts of the state in infiltrating, penetrating and getting connected to local initiatives. Yet, relatively little information exists documenting the extent to which the community actually participates in its own right in government activities. That is, a paradox is apparent regarding non-governmental community initiatives. What happens when, for example, representatives of community-based organizations, who are all carefully appointed according to bureaucratic criteria, demand an agenda that departs from state-filtered priorities?

Citizens' Advisory Committee: Maintaining An Inactive Community

According to Correctional Service of Canada (1984), the Citizens' Advisory Committee (C.A.C.) benefits from a rich heritage of citizen participation. C.A.C.s have not only helped wardens become more aware of community concerns but have also encouraged citizens in a free society to make valuable educational, cultural and employment opportunities to offenders (Correctional Service of Canada, 1981). C.A.C.s open the operation of federal corrections to the public and are influential in bringing the offender and the community in work projects which benefit both (Correctional Service of Canada, 1981). In 1965 there were at least three formal committees—Saskatchewan Penitentiary, Matsqui in British Columbia and Beaver Creek Correctional Camp in Ontario. Throughout the 1970s as federal corrections expanded centralized control, the C.A.C. evolved to become a more objective check on corrections within a "watchdog" orientation (Thorne and Detlefsen, 1986: 6). In 1977 the Solicitor General accepted the recommendations of the MacGuigan Parliamentary Sub-committee which fully supported the value of C.A.C.s. Recommendation 25 of the MacGuigan Report clearly stated that the Penitentiary Service should be open and accountable to the public. Recommendation 49 further declares that C.A.C.s should be established in all penal institutions; members should be recruited from a cross-section of society representing a wide variety of interests as well as ethno-cultural diversity; C.A.C.s should advise directors of local attitudes towards the institution and programs; C.A.C.s should inform and educate the public—to name but a few recommendations (MacGuigan, 1977). Correctional Service of Canada (C.S.C.) requires these committees in every correctional institution and district parole office (Commissioner's Directive 600-4-08.1). C.A.C.s have the following roles:

1.   — to promote communication between inmates, C.S.C. staff and the public;
2.   — to participate in the overall development of the institution or district parole office;

3.   — to improve the local population's knowledge and understanding of these activities;
4.   — to provide conditions that will encourage public participation in correctional activities;
5.   — to participate in developing community resources designed to support correctional programs.

(Correctional Service of Canada, 1984)

Responsibilities include: advising the responsible local administrator or regional deputy commissioner on the overall development of the institution or district parole office and its programs, assisting in developing community resources, educating the local community, providing continuing advice to the local administrator or regional deputy commissioner regarding the sensitivities, problems, needs, and pulse of the community (Correctional Service of Canada, 1984). Commissioner LeBlanc's Directive (#023; January 1, 1987) details the policy objective:

> To contribute to the functioning of the Service and humane treatment of offenders by involving citizens in the overall development of Service installations and by strengthening the ties between the field units and the local communities through the establishment of Citizen Advisory Committees.

This directive stipulates that members are appointed by the local Director with the consent of the Deputy Commissioner of the Region. C.A.C.s would consist of no less than five members, appointed for no less than two years. Disagreements about the role and responsibilities of the C.A.C. which cannot be resolved locally may be referred to the Deputy Commissioner of the Region, or if necessary to the Commissioner (Correctional Service of Canada, 1984). In *Taking Responsibility*, the Report of the Standing Committee on Justice and Solicitor General recommends that the C.S.C. allocate more resources to the C.A.C. "so that community participation in their activities may be more widespread" (Daubney, 1988: 205).

In light of the above context of governmental support for the C.A.C., the following examination of the treatment of one of the largest C.A.C.s in Canada—Central Ontario Citizens Advisory Committee, is extremely illustrative of institutional manipulations, the politics of corrections and the culture of contradictions that characterize corrections in Canada.

The Central Ontario C.A.C. which operated in Metropolitan Toronto was unilaterally disbanded on October 7, 1988 (*Globe and Mail*, October 19, 1988; *The Toronto Star*, October 18, 1988; *The Toronto Sun*, October 19, 1988). The District Director of the C.S.C., the most senior official in the Toronto area, sent letters to committee members informing them that as a result of "emotional crises," the current C.A.C. was disbanded and indicated that new members would be appointed. The Toronto area had been a hotbed of controversy since the C.S.C. began to issue contracts to private agencies. The matter surfaced in early 1988 with the murder of Tema Conter. For months the local C.A.C. had been critical of the government's move to privatize halfway houses. Although the monthly meetings were congenial, the Chair and the Vice-Chair echoed numerous concerns about the levels of supervision, the "for profit" contracts and the failure of local officials to keep committee members informed of pressing cases. On several occasions, for example, the acting chair, like many other committee members learned much about events not from local C.S.C. officials but from the media. Despite his contacts as a former parole officer in the region, the C.S.C. was often not forthcoming. More importantly, his presence on the committee was endorsed by the well-respected Social Planning Council of Metropolitan Toronto and the Access Action Council of which he was a representative. As result of too many thorny questions about privatization asked by the chair, vice-chair, the secretary and several members, the District Director moved quickly to muzzle any complaints.

Just hours after disbanding this public advisory group, the C.S.C. reversed its decision and restored the committee. In a news release the Deputy Commissioner noted that the dismissal was the result of a "misunderstanding" (*Globe and Mail*, October 20, 1988: A21). According to this senior official:

> The real problem arises when you are into the land of policy.... There are ambiguities here and there..[they] are not a watchdog or an ombudsman. They do not have authority to legislate change in the service. Their role is an advisory one, nudging here and there, or pushing here and there.

The chair of this C.A.C. commented:

> We should be part of the fabric of the correctional service. The role we have played in the past is a very important one.... We have no vested interests. We are not paid...(*Globe and Mail*, October 20, 1988: A21).

In the above example, members of the C.A.C. had been working productively for years. But they mistakenly believed that the C.A.C. was a legitimate mechanism for genuine public input into the operations of the C.S.C.

This illustration demonstrates clearly the consequences of assuming one's responsibility as a community representative. State authorities define the appropriateness of conduct, the parameters of a "partnership" and the levels of accountability. Although the C.A.C. was committed to its advisory mandate, members were often ill-informed of the activities of local parole offices. Material was often screened or edited by the local director.

The C.A.C. is a persuasive ideological device that conceals state coercion by projecting images of community participation and public accountability. When dissent could no longer be trivialized, state agents exaggerated the threat ("emotional crisis") and subsequently sought to remove the trouble. But, to the surprise of many officials, the media—television newscasts, newspapers and interview shows—demonstrated considerable interest in carrying the story of a disbanded governmental advisory committee. The political embarrassment resulted in a series of damage control manoeuvres. Although the Deputy Commissioner re-instated the local C.A.C., none of the key actors on the committee accepted the invitation. The community was treated like a contained colony. Administrators avoided dangerous collisions with community members, defined as meddlesome, by segregation and banishment. The firing of the entire C.A.C. was a vulgar expression of the politics of containment that emerges whenever accommodation fails. Committed to social justice, integrity and a uncompromising rapport with diverse interests in the community, the C.A.C. was "permitted" to function as long as the rhetoric of public consultation was maintained. Once members took their mandate more seriously, authorities were increasingly uncomfortable. By attributing this rebuke to a misunderstanding, the Deputy Commissioner destroyed what little confidence in the C.S.C. existed among the leadership of the C.A.C. The failure to silence criticism, however quiet and in-house, resulted in de-authenticating, de-valuing and negating the C.A.C. altogether. That is, as long as compliance with the ethos of secrecy was secured; as long as the appointed members were well disciplined to reproduce the official ideologies; and as long as the C.A.C. served as an instrument for public relations and not advocacy; the concept of community was distorted for self-serving governmental schemes. Essentially, the community was ideologically incarcerated. The ethics of membership and the concomitant oath of office prevented disclosures.

Community participation as a viable and complex script involves more than reading and rehearsing well prepared government roles. Participation occurs within wider interactive contexts and articulates discourses of power and privilege. The appropriation of community resources by the state to legitimate programs, re-socialize volunteers and to discredit discordance subverts any meaningful dialogue. The C.S.C. seeks a banal accommodation to bureaucratic propaganda—image building, rather than the capacity of the community to "advise." Remedial palliatives like re-instating the C.A.C. are shallow gestures and bankrupt slogans that fail to confront structural deficiencies oriented towards the maintenance of dependency relations. An advisory committee truly independent of the discretionary whims of the C.S.C. holds the prospect of restoring community confidence. Within the former's calculus, the community has limited options since the C.A.C. is a creation of the state. Organizational analyses clearly suggest that bureaucracies are designed to maintain stability while concurrently generating limited outside input. Centralization protects the distribution of power. Controls in decision making and policy formulations are deliberately complex and blurred thereby defying facile access to and understanding of the vagaries of administrative privileges. A characteristic feature of the C.S.C. is to shift from goal-oriented mission statements to procedural priorities. Thus, professionalism not voluntarism overwhelms. In unmasking authority structures it is evident that the work in corrections is clouded in secrecy. Decisions, policies and strategies are effectively insulated and immune from general inspection. Secrecy is rationalized, in turn, as organizational imperatives. The norm of secrecy or the cowardice of anonymous committees is a valuable tool in controlling information and avoiding accountability. Secrecy is a screen behind which incompetence is protected. Keeping secret its expertise and motives, organizations treat knowledge as a very powerful commodity which is differentially distributed even within the bureaucracy. Experts are assigned exclusive tasks. Mysteries are perpetuated. Specialization dislocates and subordinates public input. Once the public has succeeded in participating in formal discussions, a further institutional layer surfaces—informal occupational cultures that do not necessarily share the political enthusiasm of community involvement. Within corrections, the rank and file seeks to protect its own control, self-interests and immunities from the incumbrances of management. The occupational culture arguably has reasons to suspect management-driven initiatives such as citizens advisory committees. Labour is seldom consulted in the wholesale array of impression management schemes that promote the progress and success of administrative plans. The C.A.C. operated much as an appendage of the administration. Alternatives that depart from co-optation are needed despite the resistance from bureaucrats who continue to act with impunity in disregarding the interests of constituencies in favour of their own organizational and political exigencies. As Doob (1990: 420) admonishes: "we often do little to ensure that alternatives work as alternatives rather than as mere supplements to imprisonment." Likewise, Cohen (1985: 44) suggests: "community control has supplemented rather than replaced traditional methods."

An examination of advocacy and community-based empowerment provides a conceptually more comprehensive appreciation of community action in corrections. From a public policy perspective, however, a focus on "communities-in-action" is threatening. This commitment to meaningful action does not suffer from the vagueness and vulnerability of state-sponsored "community" constructions. Changes in legislation, administrative rules and regulations that protect independent community input are long overdue. Moreover, vigilance on the part of community groups in reclaiming that which more appropriately belongs to them.

The unilateral dismissal of the local C.A.C. because on occasion it echoed sentiments that were inconsistent with the practices or views of the local director or the deputy commissioner, smacks of institutional arrogance. The subsequent re-instatement, especially after the media were notified, qualifies as a transparent politically motivated exercise in damage control.

Clearly, the C.A.C. can provide a valuable contribution to the C.S.C. But, long- and short-term inter-related changes at the organizational, inter-organizational, systemic and societal levels are warranted. Immediately, the C.S.C. at the local level must confront numerous barriers that include, for example:

1.   — the denial of a problem, the refusal to recognize the significance of community input;
2.   — a self-arrogated sense of professionalism that fears change and is suspicious of critical inquiry;
3.   — a lack of commitment to change;
4.   — a dysfunctional public accountability;
5.   — a displacement of responsibility.

The following changes could easily be implemented; the C.S.C., for instance, needs to:

1.   — develop an understanding of community interests that moves beyond trite public statements;
2.   — increase the flow of information;
3.   — permit the C.A.C. to distance itself from the C.S.C.;
4.   — field questions from *all* community groups;
5.   — encourage the proactive consultation of the C.A.C.;
6.   — utilize community resources;
7.   — invite participation in the program planning and development stages;
8.   — select C.A.C. members from a cross-section of the community who will articulate issues of inequality, rampant in the criminal justice system, such as the treatment of the First Nation People, race, gender, class, homophobia, biases against the differentially abled;
9.   — use volunteers effectively.

If the C.S.C. is serious about improving access, it needs to take concrete steps in eradicating barriers. In other words, it is now necessary to move from a posture of reflection to one of action. Individual C.A.C.s need to implement initiatives that confront traditional barriers. During the initial stages of involving community groups the C.A.C. would be well advised to:

1. — provide information to prospective volunteers from labour, police, business, tenant/ ratepayers associations, advocacy groups, academics, service providers, inmate committees;
2. — develop a brokerage role that would help volunteers become aware of the responsibilities of senior administrative officials;
3. — publicize in a culturally sensitive manner the activities of the C.S.C. and the C.A.C.;
4. — reach out to identify and encourage community- or neighbourhood-based organizations;
5. — develop a capacity for inter-organizational collaboration not just with the police alone but a wider representation of perspectives;
6. — organize resources so that they have the maximum impact on volunteers;
7. — evaluate the services of the C.A.C. and adjust policies to accommodate to the community rather than strictly to the C.S.C.;
8. — develop and implement explicit policies to improve community participation with appropriate protections against unilateral dismissals;
9. — emphasize more modern management approaches with an emphasis on human resource development and human relations skills especially;
10. — co-ordinate community events and workshops with other agencies to avoid confusion and enhance resource sharing;
11. — encourage joint ventures with other voluntary organizations;
12. — integrate linkages with service providers in health, education, employment, social assistance, etc.;
13. — assist in joint funding, joint personnel exchanges, joint planning and support services;
14. — collaborate with service providers and advocacy groups that work with the socially disadvantaged;
15. — monitor the activities of the local C.S.C.;
16. — evaluate the objectives of the Mission Statement;
17. — provide referrals to community agencies.

According to Warren (1977: 251), even when organizations are transformed into something closer to the heart's desire, they may still remain as islands in a very hostile sea. The need for change directed at the societal level is crucial. As Galper (1975: 46) argues in reference to reform:

> They express concern for individual and social welfare, but they do so in a form shaped to limited and distorted values and structures, and thus ultimately undermine the pursuit of human welfare. They are established within a political and economic context. This context, we believe, acts to subvert.

Figure one illustrates that access is a central dynamic that influences interplay between the community and the state agencies. Access is not limited only to voluntary participation at the local level of community relations. But more significantly, access refers to the level of involvement in policy formulation, advising senior bureaucrats, setting directions for change in the C.S.C. and C.A.C., ongoing consultations with both community leaders and C.S.C. officials.

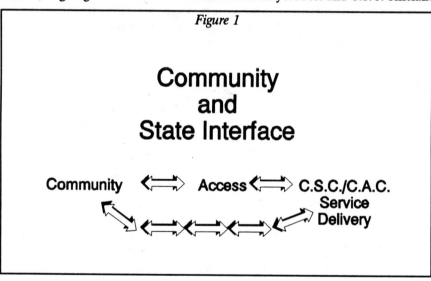

Figure 1

**Community
and
State Interface**

Community ⟷ Access ⟷ C.S.C./C.A.C.
Service
Delivery

Access is not just the enjoyment of a few opportunities made available by the government; access refers to the ownership of the agenda that to date has been exclusively controlled by the C.S.C.

Communities-In-Action: Responding to Barriers

The struggle for change is a challenge, a political process that cannot be left to the "benevolent" gestures of authority agents. By defying the defining authoritative gaze of the C.S.C., alternative formulations are required. In the previous section we detailed the responsibilities of the C.A.C. and the C.S.C.; in the following discussion we highlight the responsibilities of communities.

Briefly, problem solving is a *collective* accomplishment despite the rancorous cacophony of authorities denouncing the involvement of volunteers. Authorities will designate as deviant or subversive the objections of participants. Despite attenuated ties with state officials, public input and pressure ought to continue. Ameliorative action, dispute settlements or the management of grievances may be handled by applying existing practices, rules and policies (Lyman and Scott, 1970). Alternatively, radically more compelling measures are required to secure even a modicum of social justice. The C.S.C., as evident in the case study of the Toronto C.A.C., is institutionally deficient in enhancing community confidence. The norms and values displayed during this episode were inappropriate, confusing and woefully insufficient. Frustration characterized the response of the C.A.C. members. Structural barriers such as the rigid bureaucratic framework, inadequate legislation, systemic bias against any challenge to authority and ineffective accountability prevailed. Mobilization of outside support, therefore, is justified. But, efforts to mobilize a large number of people to bring about change (Clarke et al., 1975: 1; Stone, 1986) are determined by several contingencies.

Mobilization, "the activation of human resources for collective participation" (Clarke et al., 1975: 12) is shaped by the following factors: ideology, an able leadership, and channels of communication or networks of co-operative relationships.

Ideology sustains participation by providing a litany of invaluable rationalizations. This set of interrelated values re-socializes volunteers or activists to become receptive to new competing definitions. Additionally, ideology is a reflexive process that is directed at the self and recasts present troubles through past experiences. Ideological challenges invite, as Lofland (1985) suggests, ongoing conversions in social and personal identities. A change in consciousness emerges as long as alternative visions are explored and a distance from official accounts is maintained. Logically, this quasi-resistance is, in effect, an expression of agency, autonomy and accountability. Gradually, the self becomes oriented towards unlearning the conventions of corrections and increasingly familiar with more compelling, albeit more unorthodox, explanations of power and the consequences of non-compliance. By moving beyond convenience and self-serving rationales, community representatives ideologically situate themselves as committed participants.

Ideology does not alone ensure a successful protest. The potential for mobilization is determined by the cohesiveness of the group, strengths of opposing control agents and the resources available. For Tilly (1978), mobilization is the process of creating commitments that generate a willingness to contribute resources. Group cohesiveness with its attendant collaborative orientations towards advocacy constitutes a pressure to change the state's approach to community interests. This emphasis on cojoint activities will undoubtedly empower any C.A.C. to demand accessibility. Also, coalition building with the socially disadvantaged, economically deprived, community-based organizations, feminist, anti-racist action groups, labour, Aboriginal associations, open and well established communication networks with the media, opposition party members of the legislatures, civil liberties, etc. is a formidable force. Attempts by the state to promote inter- and intra-group conflicts in an effort to construct "the community" in its own image and likeness will falter.

Figure 2

CONTINUUM
OF
COMMUNITY INVOLVEMENTS:
Volunteers in Corrections

STATE SPONSORED (N.P.B.)	PUBLIC/PRIVATE (C.A.C. J.H.S)	COMMUNITY NEIGHBOURHOOD-BASED (Black Action Defence Committee Inmate Councils)
ADVISORY COMMITTEES	SERVICE PROVIDERS	ADVOCACY/ACTION COUNCILS
ROYAL COMMISSIONS	GOVERNMENT CONTRACTS	INFORMATION REFERRALS
GOVERNMENT APPOINTEES	UNITED WAY	DONATIONS
DIRECTORS		UNDER-RESOURCED POORLY-FUNDED

Conclusions

The "community" is an elusive concept that has been too easily appropriated by the state to engineer support for limited initiatives that fail to grapple with fundamental inequalities in corrections. This term is contextually determined and discursively constructed to satisfy organizational interests. Without reference to the context of power, the community concept has become a pretext for intervention and exclusion. A commitment to local contests, for example, is perceived as counter hegemonic and subject to coercive measures. This sponge-like term enables the state to celebrate and parade representations that it has effectively screened—to appoint those individuals and organizations who subscribe deferentially to authority/subject relations and enjoy the benefits of such complicity and deception that something is being done "for" the community.

Admittedly, the case study of the C.A.C. suffers from anecdotal oversimplification and remains suspiciously idiosyncratic. Nevertheless, there are generic principles that are readily applicable to other research sites that demand a more rigorous investigation. This brief discussion urges students of penology to juxtapose the rhetoric inviting community input with actual content and structure of community involvement, the imposed limitations that silence the voices of the concerned. Given the proliferation of chatter about increased community participation, students are further asked to problematize the relationship between the state and democratic accountability. Interestingly, one wonders curiously what price is paid by those who dare to question authority not from the outside community but from behind bars.

Community inaction is rewarded by the exaggerated privilege of being permitted to sit on committees struck by state functionaries. Communities-in-action, however, mobilize, advocate and articulate an agenda that provides an ongoing critique of power. Inequalities in corrections are ubiquitous. Victims feel ignored by an alienating system of justice; inmates, parolees and their families suffer deprivation; correctional officers complain about the insensitivities of management, stress and poor working conditions; and the general public remains ignorant and fearful of "alarming" crime rates, statistics that are often advanced to secure support for state practices.

References

Boostrom, R. and J. Henderson. 1983. "Community Action and Crime Prevention: Some Unresolved Issues," *Crime and Social Justice* 19 (summer): 24-30.

Clarke, H. et al. 1975. *Prophecy and Protest*. Toronto: Gage.

Cohen, S. 1985. *Visions of Social Control.* Cambridge: Polity.

Commissioner's Directive, "Citizens' Advisory Committee," #023, January 01, 1987.

Correctional Service of Canada. 1981. *Citizens' Advisory Committee: Aid to Corrections.*

_____, 1984. *Working Together: Citizens' Advisory Committees and the Correctional Service of Canada.*

Daubney, 1988. "Report of the Standing Committee on Justice and Solicitor General on its review of the sentencing, correctional release and related aspects of corrections," *Taking Responsibility*. Ottawa.

Doob, A. 1990. "Community Sanctions and Imprisonment: Hoping for a miracle but not bothering even to pray for it," *Canadian Journal of Criminology*, 32, 3: 415-428.

Doob, A. and J. Roberts. 1988. "Public Punitiveness and Public Knowledge of the Facts: Some Canadian Surveys," in N. Walker and M. Hough (eds.), *Public Attitudes to Sentencing: Surveys From Five Counties*. Aldershot, U.K.: Gower.

Foucault, M. 1977. *Discipline and Power*. N.Y.: Pantheon.

Galper, J. 1975. *The Politics of Social Services*. Englewood Cliffs, N.J.: Prentice-Hall.

Ingstrup, O. 1987. *Mission Statement of the National Parole Board*. National Parole Board, Communications Division.

Lofland, J. 1985. *Protest.* New Brunswick, N.J.: Transaction.

Lyman, S. and M. Scott. 1970. *Revolt of the Students*. Columbus: Charles E. Merrill.

MacGuigan, M. 1977. *Report: The Penitentiary System In Canada*. Ottawa: Supplies and Services.

Ontario, 1984. *Annual Report*, Ministry of Correctional Services, Toronto: Government Services.

Scull, A. 1977. *Decarceration*. Englewood Cliffs, N.J.: Prentice-Hall.

Stone, S. 1986. "The Lesbian Mothers' Defence Fund," paper presented at the Qualitative Research Conference, Univ. of Waterloo, May 13-16.

Thorne, B. and M. Detlefsen. 1986. "Advisory Citizen Participation in the Correctional Systems of Canada, the United Kingdom and Ireland," unpublished monograph

Tilly, C. 1978. *From Mobilization to Revolution*. Reading: Addison-Wesley.

Turner, R. 1978. "The Public Perception of Protest," in J. Manis and B. Meltzer (eds.) *Symbolic Interaction*. Boston: Allyn and Bacon.

Visano, L. 1983. "Tramps, Tricks and Troubles: Street Transients and Their Controls," in T. Fleming and L. Visano (eds.) *Deviant Designations* Toronto: Butterworth.

Warren, R. 1977. *Social Change and Human Purpose*. Chicago: Rand McNally.

Webber, D. 1987. *Community-Based Corrections and Community Consultation — A How to Manual*. Solicitor General: Ontario Region.

Newspapers, *Globe and Mail*, October 19, 1988: "Ottawa Fires Watchdog Group Critical of Halfway House Plans."

_____ , *Toronto Sun*, October 19, 1988: "Feds Can Watchdog."

_____ , *Toronto Star*, October 18, 1988: "Critics Dumped By Government."

Chapter 12

"The Dark Workshop": Life Sentences, Prison Conditions and the Politics of Punishment[*]

Thomas O'Reilly-Fleming

Introduction

> The complex relationship between power and knowledge is well illustrated in the prison: the state needs us to know that people are being sent to prison and it needs to know everything about its prisoners. But neither we nor the prisoners must know what is really happening to them.
>
> Cohen and Taylor (1976: 1)

The prison is the central mechanism of the control apparatus of the modern state (Foucault, 1979). It functions both symbolically and in reality to reinforce the pervasive nature of the power to punish. Though it is *a part* of society, prison is often perceived as being *apart*. This either reflects a form of cultural amnesia that assuages the feelings of guilt that might afflict citizenry confronted with the violence of the total institution, or alternatively signals a lack of compassion for the fate of offenders. The voices of prisoners are rarely heard outside the walls that ensure their confinement. Those, then, that are subject to a regime widely acknowledged to be inhumane and violent are the silent witnesses to its failings and its system of control. The totality of the prison is further reinforced by their seclusion in rural areas of the country where they provide generations of employment where unemployment would otherwise be the lot of the citizenry. Politicians in an era of conservatism and right wing politics have pursued law and order campaigns into office (Ratner and

---

[*] The author wishes to express his thanks to Mary Lou Dietz, Terrence Morris, Richard Ericson, Bob Ratner and Ron Hinch for various discussions which have influenced the argument presented.

McMullan, 1985) while legislation and criminal justice system policy continues to refocus rehabilitational efforts into a return to the crime-responsibility-punishment framework. The prison, despite all of this remains one of the central contradictions of our society. Since its inception the prison has remained at the core of our control and punishment industry, while its value in that position is questionable at best.

In Canada, there are currently a significant and growing number of prisoners who are serving life sentences without eligibility of parole for 25 years. Canada has one of the highest rates of imprisonment in the Western world lagging only behind the USA in this dubious achievement. Canada, in concert with other western civilizations, overwhelmingly reserves long prison terms for those convicted of first degree murder, armed robbery, and sexual assault that are accompanied by serious bodily injury.

This paper examines the issue of life sentences and the fifteen year review of parole eligibility. First, an analysis of prison conditions and the effects of long-term regimes on prisoners is presented to provide a framework for comprehending the effect of the fifteen year review. Second, an examination of the fifteen year review is undertaken which explores the origins, inadequacies and arbitrariness of the legislation. This is addressed through a comparative analysis of three cases which have been subject to this review. The political context of parole eligibility is reviewed and its connections to wider control efforts are traced. Finally, suggestions for providing a fair system of review and for revision of existing penalties are developed.

The Abolition of Death and the Imposition of Death in Life

When there is no death penalty, banishment or physical torture,
to lock a person away for life or a long period of his life is the
most severe form of punishment which a society uses.

Cohen and Taylor (1981: 9)

In 1976, under the government of Pierre Elliott Trudeau, himself a former Minister of Justice, Canada abolished the death penalty. Trudeau was well acquainted with the case of Coffin, wrongly convicted of the murder of three American hunters who was executed an innocent man. This case had an important impact on Canadian legislators who realized that death was a final penalty that could not be reversed, and so, following the British example that was fuelled by the work of Morris and Blom-Cooper (1963), Canada established new penalties for the most serious of offences. Following 1976, mandatory life sentences were instituted which carried with them an ineligibility for parole until after 25 years had been served in cases of first degree murder.

First degree murder, under Canadian law, requires that an element of planning or deliberation be present, or that the victim is a police officer, prison officer or other person who is employed to keep the public peace. Persons convicted of second degree murder are also given a sentence of life imprisonment, with one proviso; parole eligibility occurs following 10 years of imprisonment or up to a maximum of 25 years as set by the trial judge.

While the 1976 amendments and the abolishment of the capital punishment were sensible and humanitarian efforts, the prison sentences which replaced the death penalty created a new form of cruel and unusual punishment for a large number of inmates. Zubrycki (1984) has traced the evolution of Canadian approaches to those convicted of first and second degree murder. His overview of the evolution of legislation between 1961 and 1976 (and beyond) is instructive for it demonstrates the fundamental inequity in the approach of legislators to the question of an appropriate question. Historically, this evolution is significant, for it predates the concept of the serial murderer in academic literature (Lunde, 1976; Fox and Levin, 1985; Leyton, 1985) and especially the criminal career of Clifford Olson whose name and deeds are often associated with debates on the death penalty in this country. From 1961 to 1976 Zubrycki's research indicates that the parole eligibility for those convicted of first degree murder varied between 7 and 10 years, with 10 years predominating as the usual period of time served before parole eligibility. Eligibility for parole must not however be confused with release. Release on parole is a process that may take several years for the prisoner to attain, and has been described by several experts on Canadian prisons (Culhane, 1985, 1989) and ex-prisoners (Caron, 1985) as a "kangaroo court" where it is virtually impossible to gain a fair hearing. Indeed, ex-inmates often describe the role playing that is necessary to gain parole in vivid detail.

It is also important to note that Zubrycki's work also informs us that after 1961 death sentences were "often commuted" and following 1967 "all" sentences of death in Canada were commuted to life imprisonment. In 1967, when in practice, if not in fact, the death penalty had for all intents and purposes been abolished, parole eligibility occurred 10 years after commutation of sentence.

In amendments that followed a judicial review of parole eligibility was created that allowed for a review after fifteen years had been served. This review is conducted by a judge and jury in the original province in which the offence occurred. The court after this hearing can reduce the eligibility period before parole is considered. Later in this chapter we will explore in detail the implications and limitations of judicial review, but at present it should suffice to indicate that judicial reviews provide a rather arbitrary form of justice. In fact, judicial review, it will be argued later in this chapter, represents no more than a form of indeterminate sentencing calculated to ensure immiseration in many of those falling under its power. Indeterminate sentencing provides that an offender can be held indefinitely, in reality at the pleasure of correctional authorities. The effects of such sentences which have been amply criticized as inhuman do not have to be rehearsed here again, for they transfer absolute authority over an individual to the state (Mitford, 1973).

Marking Time: The Effects of Long-Term Imprisonment

A sentence of 10, 15, 20 or 25 years is difficult for anyone sentenced to it to imagine. Cohen and Taylor (1981) in their classic work, *Psychological Survival* described the phenomenon and reported that inmates constantly repeated the length of their sentence as if this would allow them to gain some measure of its meaning. While ordinarily life is marked by significant events which measure out time for us, births, marriages, divorce, death, the world of long-term prisoners is more of a limbo to which there is no foreseeable end. Even prisoners who are serving only relatively short sentences start to show a marked deterioration in personality, attitudes, and motivation according to the observations of Morris and Morris (1963) in their work at Pentonville. It is important to remember that these prisoners were serving short sentences with an end in sight, and yet still were bound on a downward spiral of despair. Their stay was buttressed both by the limitations of the duration of stay and the support of, and contact with, relatives, friends and others on the outside.

The predicament of long-term prisoners is that this support network is bound to change dramatically over the length of their stay. While initially wives, children and family members may visit and write, more often than not this contact fades with time. Wives get on with life outside and marriages dissolve. Children are ambivalent about a father who is seen as someone who may never return to them and who is conspicuously absent during their childhood. Parents, friends, brothers and sisters may move away or die. After long periods of time the inmate is more dependent upon the letters and visits of those outside, than they are in terms of making them. Their interest in the role generally diminishes greatly over time. So it is that adaptations within the environment of long-term imprisonment are dependent upon whether the individual decides to attempt to keep up their liaison with the outside (if it exists); or refuse all contacts. While in the initial stages of confinement the first form of adaptation may have a very positive impact on the inmate, it can also represent a source of worry, anxiety and depression. Trapped within the prison, long-term inmates are powerless to intervene in the lives of their loved ones. They can share successes and tragedies of the family only vicariously through letters and visits. Like living Rip Van Winkles they experience life outside the prison as rather like a dream in which they can imagine, but frustratingly, not play a real part.

This dream, as I have noted, may soon turn into a nightmare as the lifer sees family and friends fall away, visits slow down or stop, and letters become more infrequent as time passes. Their lifeline to the outside can easily be transformed into the source of great psychological stresses on the inside. In research conducted in Canadian prisons Burtch and Ericson (1979) found that suicide occurred more frequently amongst those serving life sentences than in those serving terms with a limited duration. Although life prisoners represented some 6% of inmates they accounted for 16% of suicides. Alternatively, some inmates deliberately choose to ignore outside contacts during their stay. They reason that the time they will do will be easier if they have no one to worry about. Their mind is then focussed on "doing" and "getting through" their time. The life of the prison, the present, becomes the overwhelming force in their lives. With no markers of the future in sight, life is marked only by the passage of each day (Cohen and Taylor, 1976).

Zubrycki (1984: 401) has questioned the serious effects of long-term imprisonment along with his contemporaries in a now infamous edition of *The Canadian Journal of Criminology* (Gaucher, 1988). In addressing the issue of 25 year sentences his ideological bias is evident, "*Some* foresee the new sentences creating a growing core of inmates who will feel hopeless and desperate." What other feelings would we anticipate them having? Joy and exhilaration perhaps? He suggests that there are those who anticipated violent reactions by those who have nothing to lose. Secondly, he suggests that there are critics who maintain that the effects of long-term incarceration will be experienced as "severely debilitating in human terms emotionally, psychologically, and even physically." There is, I think, reasonable evidence that imprisonment produces not only significant numbers of suicides (Burtch and Ericson, 1979) but also mental disorders amongst a substantial number of prisoners. Amongst those serving life sentences, these effects are doubtless significantly amplified. While Zubrycki argued in 1984 that the effect of these sentence was only "at best speculative" his argument means that the results of decades of prison research and writing on this subject have been strictly ignored. One would only have to be cognizant of Cohen and Taylor's (1981) contribution, or the Montbatten Report (Home Office, 1966) to be able to form a clear idea of the effects of the long-term prison regime without ever referring to the excellent studies that have been conducted of the American prison system (Irwin, 1980, Mitford, 1973). It is interesting to note that Zubrycki's concerns seem to focus on the potential for violence on the part of inmates held under these conditions. Considering the fact that this is the central reason that researchers are routinely barred from conducting research in the Canadian system, it would seem that management of violence is a preoccupation of the system, an observation that Goffman (1961) rendered concerning total institutions some 30 years ago!

The contradictions inherent in the prison system are apparent when one considers the regime that prisoners must endure on a daily basis. First of all we are aware as Mitford (1973) amongst others has pointed out that the loss of liberty is in itself a considerable punishment for any human being. When this is translated in to a sentence of twenty or more years this is a significant, unfathomable penalty. Violence, in a variety of forms, is a feature of the everyday world of life in Canadian prisons. Violent assaults against inmates are common and often go unreported (MacLean, 1983). Like any society, the closed world of the inmate produces its share of dark figure crimes, offences against the person that go unreported for a variety of important reasons. When one considers that a prime rule of prison life is to "do one's own time" and not collaborate with authorities, then one is cognizant that complaints against fellow prisoners who have victimized one often are not acted upon. Just as victims in wider society fear reprisals from the perpetrator, and lack of response from those charged with administering justice, so the prisoner in the contained world of the institution is less likely to report victimization when the assailant is only a few steps away.

While we recognize that life for long-term prisoners is harsh and may be marked by violence, assault, mental disorder, isolation, deprivation, ill health and in an unacceptable number of cases, suicide, there is some evidence which seems to indicate that such effects *may be* largely reversible (Coker and Martin, 1985). However, studies in this area have been few in number. We do require some immediate research on the after prison life of lifers to examine the lasting effects of long-term imprisonment in terms of psychological, emotional and social impairments. However, there is no doubt that these conditions, and the sheer length of these sentences for the vast majority of lifers, should not be tolerated in a civil society.

Prison Conditions in Canada

Despite this, the Correctional Investigator, R.L. Stewart who is independent from Corrections Canada was able to record a large number of complaints from prisoners held in Canada during 1989-90. In the report which covers the period June 1989 to May 1990 he recorded 3,246 complaints from prisoners covering issues as divergent as health care, diet, visits and education. The most significant areas for complaint were: health care (303), case preparation (274), parole board decisions (269), processing (238), transfers involuntary (132), transfers denial (127), staff (122), administrative segregation placement (115) and visits (115). In total complaints were received in 31 categories. The decision of the parole board, one of the top items in terms of inmate complaints, lies outside of the terms of reference of the correctional investigator's powers.

During the period the report covers, Mr. Stewart or his associates were able to interview 1,337 of the complainants. What is more interesting is the disposition of the complaints. Of the 3,422 complaints received, 474 were still pending by the time of the report (15 February 1991), 1,408 were declined as either a) not within his mandate (75); (b) premature (916); or (c) not justified (417). Some 416 complaints were withdrawn; in 915 cases assistance, advice or referral was given, 153 were resolved and some 56 were declared not amenable to resolution (Stewart, 1991: 4-11).

The office of the Correctional Investigator has criticized the correctional service in a number of areas. Specifically, it has opposed the high maximum security units citing a lack of specific rationale for their existence. Secondly, the quality of internal investigations has been the subject of harsh criticism. Stewart writes, ". . . it was my opinion that the Service's investigations were far too often incomplete and lacking in objectivity, with the subsequent reviews of the investigative reports conducted by Regional and National Headquarters authorities being nothing more than a rubber stamp" (Stewart, 1991: 21). Stewart also comments on another aspect of prison life, the national policy of double bunking in our prisons. He states, "there is a serious overcrowding problem within federal institutions, with in excess of 1,000 offenders currently double bunked" (Stewart, 1991: 26). This double bunking coincidentally occurs amongst the non-general population offenders rather than general population and really amounts to one more form of deprivation and punishment.

Finally, Stewart levelled serious criticisms at the grievance process which "at the front end does very little to encourage offender participation" thus effectively rendering it both devoid of objectivity and lacking in thoroughness of the investigation (Lauzon, 1989).

Prisons and Politics

The Ministry of the Solicitor General over a decade ago began to collect data on lifers as part of the mandate of its Ministry-wide Committee on Long-Term Imprisonment. Primarily their emphasis has been upon the collection of statistical data, in contrast to the praxis work of criminologists like Bob Gaucher who is a regular participant in the Infinity Lifers Group at Collins Bay. The perspective of the most widely regarded studies in the field of penology reflected in the work of Cohen and Taylor (1976); Cohen and Taylor (1981); Morris and Morris (1963); Serge (1970); and Irwin (1980) is that it is the prisoners themselves who are subject to the daily regime of a prison who are most qualified to speak on its effects upon them. The interests of correctional researchers who are employed by agencies of correction is unlikely to be upon the presentation of the stark, unpalatable realities of prison effects. We can see this contradiction when we compare the work of correctional researchers like Porporino and Zamble (1984) and Zubrycki (1984) with works that arise from the prison floor. It is also educational to note that Cohen and Taylor, like the Morrises before them, were eventually banned from prisons in Britain due to the "disruptive" character of their research. In essence, such research has a side effect of empowering individuals by a process of consciousness raising. In talking about the pains of imprisonment and trying to make sense of their situations, prisoners are often "awakened" from the lassitude that often accompanies long bouts of confinement. One must further inquire as to why Caron's (1985) vivid account of a life spent behind bars contrasts so sharply to the rhetoric developed by correctional "authorities." Finally, one should also be cognizant that attempts to work on behalf of prisoners' rights by activists like Claire Culhane (1985, 1989), a senior citizen, resulted in such a threat to the prison system that she was barred from being a prison visitor!

These questions are best answered by a reformulation of our basic ideas concerning the penological enterprise. The modern prison is bound upon the path of failure. Contemporary analysts of prison such as Ericson (1976) and MacLean (1989) have clearly articulated the duality of prison work. First, the prison must fail in its task for to succeed would mean the closing of prisons and the loss of long-term employment in many areas of the country where few alternatives for gainful, well-paid work exist in the community. However, at the popular level, the prison must appear to be "doing something" working against overwhelming odds to deal with ever increasing numbers of lawbreakers. The fact that between 66% (Hogarth, 1966) and 80% (MacGuigan, 1977: 35) of offenders recidivate is some measure not of the failure of any rehabilitative effort but rather a lack of imagination in developing alternatives to prison and investing in them, and secondly, the paucity of programs within the prison system. Stewart (1991: 33-35) found that in the Ontario region, for example, that inmates who wanted treatment for sexual problems were often unable to receive it. This raises the spectre of the right to treatment. Sex offenders in particular, are of some central concern to the community; yet as Stewart reported there exists no Canada Correctional Services national strategy for the treatment of sexual offenders, nor even a single office which has been set aside to monitor this work.

Data presented by MacLean (1989: 62-66) is also instructive in that he found that "penitentiary sentences are getting longer during a period when the seriousness of offences is declining." Moreover, he argues that the number of correctional workers has increased to a level approaching 1 staff to 1 prisoner. MacLean concludes that the successes of the prison must be viewed in political terms as a matter of will and manipulation of the public:

...the prison system has been successful in creating more prisoners, not unsuccessful in reducing their numbers. It has been successful in creating more staff and more kinds of staff not unsuccessful in reducing their numbers. It has been successful in professional development of staff not unsuccessful in rehabilitation of prisoners.

Lifers Talk

Although few accounts exist of the effects of life sentences on inmates (See Bolton et al., 1976; Sapsford, 1983; Coker and Martin, 1985; Richards, 1978; McKay et al., 1979; and Caron, 1985) there are sufficient research reports and other forms of accounts available to us from our analysis. Cohen and Taylor's (1981) account of their research and work with the men of E-Wing at Durham prison persists as the only view of long-term prison life conducted as research collaboratively with life prisoners. The themes that dominate life sentences which emerge from their work are (1) survival, (2) coping with the emotional world of a closed society, (3) time and deterioration, and (4) struggles with authority. All of these themes are worthy of some closer analysis.

Survival

For inmates serving life sentences the ever present issue which dominates life inside is survival. Prisoners must quickly come to grips with a complete transformation of their lives. Every routine of life outside will be replaced with new routines. For those who have previously served sentences the acclimation will not be so radical a process, though the devastating effect of the sentence should not be diminished. John Irwin (1980: 49) a sociologist and former prisoner at Soledad has argued that those who have not served prison sentences before will suffer more, "In general, the ill-prepared suffer more in prison; they become more disorganized and they are more likely to withdraw." A 1981 study of persons serving sentences for first degree murder in Canadian penitentiaries found that 33% had served no previous jail or prison time, and 67% had served no previous penitentiary term. The authors also noted that 24% had no record of any kind of criminal activity, and 50% had never been convicted of committing a crime of violence (Zubrycki, 1984: 402). Our records of prison and concentration camp survival also instruct us that it is those who withdraw who are most likely to perish (Bettelheim, 1960). Confinement in long-term conditions carries with it the problems of sensory and perceptual deprivation. Although amenities are available for prisoners, those who endure life sentences in protective custody suffer at a different level of deprivation. Those in protective custody are only able to exit their cells for two hours in any twenty-four hour period, to shower three times a week, or to go to chapel. The prisoners in Cohen and Taylor's study as well as in Victor Serge's 1970 *Men in Prison* compared their feelings of isolation from the world to that experienced by explorers seeking the pole in extreme weather conditions and in close confinement with their fellows. The only difference, of course, is that prisoners did not choose to challenge themselves, and there is no end in sight to their "adventure."

Coping with the Emotional World of a Closed Society

Life in long-term confinement is taxing upon the emotions and psychological well-being of the inmate. Words such as "lifeless" and "claustrophobic" are used to describe the world of the prison for lifers. While most of us are free to change and explore various environments, inmates are trapped within a world that changes little and offers little in the way of variation. The Infinity Lifers Group at Collins Bay Penitentiary (ILG, 1989: 46) described the effects of the 25 year sentence on the psychological well being of inmates in the following way:

> When the noose was abolished in 1976 in its place we were provided a mirror with which to watch ourselves fade away. We most often ask ourselves if we survive this sentence physically, can we survive it psychologically? We have watched as others with this sentence realize that they can no longer handle it and take their own lives, while others give up and go mad; and always that mirror is there. Will the face in it be the next to go?

Relationships are strained in such an environment, and although the lifers are regarded throughout the correctional system as the most co-operative of all prisoner groups, part of this attitude must surely arise from the realization that one will be residing with the same staff and prisoners for the majority of one's life.

Certainly at one level the realization that one's world is inhabited by persons who have committed murder, sexual assaults and various forms of violent crimes is of little reassurance for the inmate. Who does one pick for a friend from such company (Sykes, 1958)? Although some inmates maintain that their fellows are simply ordinary people (Walford, 1989: 43) their capacity for the execution of extreme violence sets them apart from their fellow citizens. Privacy, or the lack of it, is an issue for all lifers as well as the fragility of friendships which are intense given the limited nature of choice in such matters. There is little room for the expression of feelings when the audience remains essentially the same throughout one's life activities.

Time and Deterioration

All lifers undergo the terror that time can represent. While not wishing to overstate their case, their condition and fears are comparable to the fate of the subjects Oliver Sacks (1990: 223) described in his landmark work *Awakenings*. This book chronicled his work with post-encephalitic patients whom he "awakened" after decades of inactivity from their catatonic type state:

> The terrors...of losing ourselves and losing the world, are the most elemental and intense we know; and so too are our dreams of recovery and rebirth, of being wonderfully restored to ourselves and the world.

Inmates in this category spend a great deal of time, not only dealing with time, but trying to stop time in terms of their physical state of being. The intense activity of weightlifting is viewed as a way of stealing time back from the system, of emerging looking younger and fitter than one did at the beginning of one's sentence. Time is also worried about; how much time has passed? How much time is there to do? These concerns often become overwhelming as one's perception of time becomes warped within the prison environment. As Serge (1970: 56) observed:

> The unreality of time is palpable. Each second falls slowly. What a measureless gap from one hour to the next. When you tell yourself in advance that six months—or six years—are to pass like this, you feel the terror of facing an abyss. At the bottom, mists in the darkness.

Struggles with Authority

One of the methods that lifers (and other prisoners) use to give meaning to their lives is to engage in constant struggles with authority. This can take several forms: attempts to escape, letter writing, the filing of grievances, legal appeals against incarceration, or refusal to follow orders. Authorities respond to these challenges not by resort to brute force on a continual basis but rather by the use of measured concessions to the men. Even so there is little in the way of programming for life prisoners. The Infinity Lifers Group has pointed out the contradiction of the absence of such programs. Lifers are at a severe disadvantage when appearing before parole boards or for fifteen year reviews since they cannot benefit from programs that would demonstrate some form of "progress" to these bodies. Therefore, such reviews usually consist largely of correctional personnel offering their observations on the inmate's behaviour during the duration of his sentence or by reference to his disciplinary record.

The struggle may take the form of working for prisoners' rights both within and outside of the system. Just as the body may be built, so many inmates now choose to build the mind, taking secondary school credits, or attaining various university degrees (ILG, 1989). Whatever form it takes struggle seems to be an essential element that acts as a catalyst in producing the will to survive. Just as withdrawal will signal a victory of the forces that label, degrade and punish a man, so fighting signals the determination not to succumb and lose one's self to the system. This battle should not be conceived of in heroic terms, rather it is the fight of the individual against slipping into the abyss described by Serge and others. When there seems to be no hope of ever attaining release, then men will begin to seek means of expressing themselves, of protesting their inhumane treatment. Amongst lifers there is agreement that there are some who should never be released from the confines of the prison, those for example who engage in serial killing. However, this is not the prognosis for the majority of men serving life sentences, rather than are more than likely, given our knowledge of their post release behaviour, to be contributing citizens. In Canada, at present, there are serious attempts underway to establish halfway residences for men who are being released from life sentences into the community. Much of this effort as might be expected has been met with hostile community reaction. The sheer number of prisoners who are serving this form of sentence and the escalating numbers that may be eligible for release over the next decade mean that planning must proceed to establish graduated ways of providing for their re-entry into society.

Of course all of these problems of adaptation to long-term confinement are also veiled in the web of secrecy which pervades prison activities and makes it difficult for the academic researcher, let alone the layman, to have reasonable access to information concerning the operation of the prison system. If the individual responsible for the investigation of these conditions has expressed difficulty in effecting the inner workings of the prison and the correctional service, then it is reasonable to argue that the lay person must remain largely uninformed.

The true struggle for lifers may be facing the prospect of fifteen year reviews of their parole eligibility. The review can be a ray of hope or a harbinger of continued hopelessness. The remainder of this chapter provides an analysis of the fifteen year review and its application to various Canadian cases. It is suggested that the fifteen year review represents no more than another form of indeterminate sentencing one that may have the potential of increasing the potential for violence or inhumane punishment. Having now provided the reader with an overview of some of the current problems with the Canadian prison system, and an analysis of the specific problems which confront those serving long-term sentences, the reader is equipped to put the following analysis into a more realistic framework.

Vaillancourt: The Politics of Review

The abolition of the death penalty in 1976 was rightly heralded as a new and humane moment in Canadian legal history. However, as I have already noted this movement forward meant that a trade-off occurred and the losers were those who were convicted of first and second degree murder. First of all, mandatory life sentences were instituted for those convicted of murder that required premeditation or involved the death of a peace officer killed in the line of duty. Second degree murder convictions carried a minimum ten year prison term but the trial judge could increase the period of time spent before parole eligibility to twenty-five years. From 1961 through 1976 lifers generally served ten years before eligibility for parole consideration. The effect of the 1976 abolition was therefore to greatly increase the amount of time spent by those convicted of first and second degree murder behind bars. As a means of compensating for what was perceived as leniency on the part of Parliament in relegating the death penalty to the scrap heap of history, it is apparent that a new means of ensuring long prison sentences for those who kill their fellows has been initiated. The process which informs police decisions in this area is referred to as "upcrimeing," that is, charging accused at the highest level possible so that plea bargains are bound to result in guilty pleas to a more serious charge than the actions of the accused warrant. Walford (1989: 40) has presented compelling evidence on the progression of events that underscored this change in policing and charging:

> Between 1965 and 1971, while the death penalty was still in effect, police charged only six percent with first degree murder, twenty-eight percent with second degree, and the vast majority, sixty-five percent with manslaughter. Between 1977 and 1988, when the death penalty was replaced with the twenty-five year minimum sentence, police charged thirty-eight percent with first degree murder, fifty-two percent with second degree murder (almost double), and only nine percent with manslaughter.

Although one might assume that a greater number of people were committing first degree murder this is simply not supportable. As Walford (1989: 40) quite rightly notes, "...instead of making the laws more lenient or humane as it would first appear, laws and sentences became far more severe for over eighty percent of persons involved in homicide."

The Canadian Criminal Code provides for a review of life sentences under Section 745. This judicial mechanism can provide for a reduction in the period the inmate must wait before receiving parole eligibility. The jury who sits on this review may recommend three options two of which have dire implications for the life of the prisoner. First, the applicant may be granted immediate eligibility for parole review. Second, the period of eligibility before parole may be set at between a low of sixteen years or a high of twenty-five years. The final option is to allow the original sentence to remain in force.

The Vaillancourt case is instructive on a number of levels regarding the politicization of release and imprisonment. Rene Vaillaincourt's case was the first to be heard in Ontario under this section. While his is the first case to come before the courts in this province it will not be the last by any means. Canadian prisons now hold some 1,904 offenders who are serving a life sentence. In 1968, prior to the abolition of the death penalty there were only 768 such offenders in custody. Of this group 500 are eligible to have a judicial review at the fifteen year mark of their sentence (Ministry of the Solicitor General, 1989). This is far in excess of the figure estimated by Griffiths (1984) or Gaucher (1988) which reflects not the research skills of either of these criminologists but points once again to the inherent difficulties in retrieving solid information from correctional authorities in Canada, and the escalating number of people who have been subject to these sentences.

Rene Vaillancourt was a typical "hood" in east Toronto when he attempted to "go big time" and rob a bank at Coxwell and Danforth Avenue in Toronto. In 1972, Vaillancourt was an 18-year-old with a history of run-ins with the law, and not much of a future in sight. His inexperience showed when he fled the bank and was confronted by Constable Leslie Maitland, a police officer serving with the Metropolitan Toronto service. Maitland and Vaillancourt apparently got involved in a stand-off with each asking the other to drop their weapon. Vaillancourt panicked and fired two bullets into the young officer killing him. Maitland was a father and devoted family man.

Vaillancourt was convicted of the first degree murder of Maitland and sentenced to death, later commuted to life imprisonment. The 1970s were turbulent times both outside and within the prison. Society was still in the last stages of the hippie, drug and sex revolutions that had dramatically transformed the nature of Canadian society. Prisoners in US prisons regularly rioted, and Kingston had itself experienced a horrendous riot in 1971, a violent and bloody outburst of inmate anger against the conditions under which they were held

(Caron, 1985; Desroches, 1974a). It was during this early part of his sentence that Vaillancourt ran afoul of prison authorities for his involvement in drug trafficking within the institution. An interesting question which arises out of his case is how drugs are available in a prison to such an extent that they can be stockpiled for trafficking?

By 1984 Vaillancourt had been cited on a number of occasions for offences within the prison, the measure by which an inmate's progress is measured. Complacency is regarded as a virtue in the correctional world; the inmate who does his time without causing "trouble" will see the outside world sooner than someone who questions the arbitrary and unfair nature of much of what occurs on the inside. In 1984, Vaillancourt was sentenced to a period of solitary confinement during which he underwent a revelation of sorts which led to him becoming a model inmate. During the next few years he became proficient in the use of computers and used this as a means of preparing himself for eventual release. The fifteen year review offered an opportunity to escape from his living tomb before he was an old man. Though he had been in prison for many years, the latter half of his sentence was remarkable for its lack of citations for unwanted behaviours.

On June 6, 1988 Vaillancourt's review began before Chief Justice Callaghan. Under the rules which govern such reviews the hearing must take place in the original province in which the crime was committed. The jury was empanelled under special rules of practice which were developed by the Chief Justice within the context of the ongoing hearing, a sort of improvisational means of establishing precedent for future hearings. These rules, as I have written elsewhere (O'Reilly-Fleming, 1991), neither permitted Vaillancourt to obtain a fair hearing of his review case, nor do they represent anything more than an arbitrary, politically driven, and inequitable form of indeterminate sentencing. Let us examine some of the components of the review which are particularly distressing.

The rules developed in Vaillancourt's hearing limited the ability of the jury to determine the effects of their decision on a number of levels. The media coverage of the case is instructive for it notes not that Vaillancourt was denied consideration for *eligibility for parole*, but rather that he was denied *early parole*. There is an important and fundamental distinction to be drawn between these two forms of release. This misunderstanding and confusion is not limited to the media and the general public, but extends as well to serious concerns on the part of correctional officials and the Parole Board (Makin, 1988: 1). The opinion of The Solicitor General's Committee on Long-Term Imprisonment (1983: 4) and the National Parole Board was at best apprehensive regarding the potential misunderstanding that the review process was likely to produce. It was their perception that both the public and inmates could quite easily misunderstand the concept of the review in the sense that the verdict of the review court might be seen as a recommendation either for or against parole itself. This is not the case in one sense, but obviously a recommendation for a longer period before parole eligibility cannot be considered a positive sign in terms of the deliberation of some future parole board. The parole board can hardly ignore the obviously strong feelings of a community jury that has pronounced a man unfit to be even considered for parole after serving a fifteen year sentence in a prison setting. Thinking back to the position of lifers in the 1960s and early 1970s, prisoners who have served fifteen years have already served five more years before receiving their review. It would certainly be interesting to have comparative data—on the length of time served between the granting of parole eligibility and the gaining of parole—which compared the two groups. The problems of interpreting this review process are cause for a further review of the Vaillancourt case alone. Beyond this is the inhumanity of a review process which acts like a lottery, rewarding some with the right to seek for freedom while others are sent back for the equivalent of another life sentence.

Making Up Rules as You Go Along

The criminal justice system in Canada through its police, courts and prisons as well as the multiple forms of social control agencies available in the community reflects the need to reinforce and protect class-based interests (Mandel, 1986). I take it that part of these interests includes upholding the expressed needs of those who must administer the law, i.e., the police. It also implies that the courts will take a negative view predicatably of those who have or are seeking to challenge the legitimacy of that order, as in the case of the Mohawk warriors who have been convicted for their part in the Oka crisis, or will simply usurp the claim of the individual(s) before them to legitimacy as in the recent denial of land claims rights of natives in British Columbia. Women and children, similarly have been the recipients of rough justice handed out by the courts, both in the removal of rape shield laws during 1991 in Canada, and in the form of comments to sentencing made by judges in sexual assault cases. Prisoners, who as late as 1969 were informed by the courts that they were entitled to no civil rights after conviction other than those permitted under their own legislation The Penitentiary Act as arguably the most disenfranchised members of our society, as one might expect, fare no better.

The remarks made in the Vaillancourt review make it apparent that the court's attitude towards this review was not favourable and reflected some rather bizarre thinking. In the judgment which was given in the case the review is characterized within a law and order framework, re-emphasizing (as if this was required) the great kindness that is being done for the prisoner under S.745 which is seen as:

> *permissive* and it is the applicant who has the *option* of determining whether or not to bring the application. *There is nothing compelling the applicant to bring the application* (my emphasis).

The section, I beg to differ, is not *permissive*, rather it is a *right* under law of any prisoner serving such a sentence to be considered for review. Reasonably, what prisoner would voluntarily choose not to seek a review when the alternative is to spend another ten plus years in prison? The effect, of course, is to underscore the assertion that this is somehow a voluntary process and therefore applicants cannot expect the kind of treatment given for example, a defendant at trial who is brought to court against his/her will to answer charges. Think for a moment of the alternative again. The chief Justice is trying to argue that a thirty-year-old man who is sentenced to a mandatory life term would want to serve his full sentence of 25 years followed by perhaps a 4 year wait for parole. This would mean that he could be trained to pick up his pension check six years after getting out from behind bars! Certainly serious questions have to be raised about the kinds of job training, rehabilitation, and life skills programs that would be appropriate, or even relevant, over a lifetime of penitentiary life. It is only when we consider the Vaillancourt ruling from this perspective that we can give meaning and context to it in its impact on the applicant.

In advance of the hearing Chief Justice Callaghan formulated a number of rules which were the focus of challenges by defence counsels Cole and Manson. Specifically, they addressed several rules which they felt constituted a violation of their client's rights under Sections 7 and 11 of The Canadian Charter of Rights and Freedoms. Let us now examine these in some detail for they are instructive in terms of the ways that rules can be constructed in order to constrain the ability of an applicant to get a fair hearing.

1.   *All evidence and materials were to be disclosed at the preliminary inquiry.* While the disclosure of materials at a preliminary inquiry is normally held in order to eliminate the need for a jury trial in frivolous or unfounded cases this is arguably an issue under consideration for a 15 year review or should not be. The exchange of information between defence and prosecution forms an amicable part of the trial process that provides both sides with the essence of the case either for or against the defendant, but in the case of a 15 year review the applicant is not a defendant, rather he/she is a candidate for review. I would argue that the defendant has very few resources available to him to make his case, for the majority of the evidence, as we shall learn, that is heard,

arises from correctional authorities. What character references for example can normally be brought forward in support of the applicant's case?

Sapsford's (1978) research with lifers found that men who had served periods of six years or greater had developed problems which could reasonably be expected to impinge upon their ability to mount a case. These included a preoccupation in conversation with the past and things past and little thought of the future. Their interest in recreational and social activities had diminished severely, and they were becoming less and less involved with relationships on the outside. Those who fell within the two groups that had served longer periods of confinement (plus six or plus eleven years) had lost virtually all contact with their spouses or girlfriends.

Two of Sapsford's other observations are acutely relevant here. First, he discovered that the lifers had developed a pronounced inability to handle even the most trivial of decisions, let alone the will needed to mount a review in concert with counsel. Secondly, lifers formed a close identification with staff in his sample, which is arguably somewhat natural when one is dependent upon them for even the smallest of concessions and must spend the majority of one's life with them. However, the question this begs is, "What effect would this have on the inmate's ability to launch an effective review given the central part correctional authorities as witnesses play in this review, particularly if the applicant, as in the case of Vaillancourt, has not succumbed to the pressures to conform?" I believe it would be stretching our faith greatly to assume that Vaillancourt's captors can be expected to act impartially within what we have seen is a decidedly non-impartial bureaucracy. This first rule, then, I argue, is highly prejudicial to the applicant.

2.   *The applicant is required to lead his/her evidence first.*
This position is legally the equivalent of publicly committing suicide. When one leads evidence one permits the prosecution to listen to, evaluate, and form strategies after the fact for destroying one's evidence. The prosecution is also able to leave a more marked impression upon the court, as their witnesses, and their cross-examination of witnesses are the last evidence to be heard by the judge and jury. This is extremely advantageous to prosecution counsel, and is evidence of an unwillingness by the state to let the disadvantaged party, i.e., the applicant, have some advantage in terms of best presenting his case. For if this is a *review*, and that is questionable at best, why is there an individual charged as *prosecutor*. Again, the inmate may only receive *eligibility* for parole review if he/she is successful. The parole process could conceivably, if the person is a bad risk, take ten or fifteen years. As Culhane (1985, 1989) has consistently informed us, parole board hearing are like a big lottery wherein the inmate tries to play a role in order to get out. The inmate enrols in programs (whether he wants to or not, and whether they are of any benefit or not), finds a

"problem" (drugs, alcohol, relationships) and attends groups to obtain a certificate that he has dealt with "the problem," tries to keep a clean rap sheet in the joint, appears remorseful for past wrongdoings, and has made plans for the future. Long-term inmates realistically have so little in the way of suitable programs that they do not have the same sorts of personal ammunition to bring to the parole board. Neither does the lifer usually have a network of outside contacts to cite as persons who will assist with their readaptation and readjustment to the community. Thus, an eligibility for review and subsequent favourable decision by the parole board is again, almost exclusively, dependent upon the input of correctional officials.

3.   *The applicant is required to address the jury prior to the Crown.*
The pivotal importance of the final argument and the position that one occupies in regards to its effects upon the minds of the jury does not have to be argued at length.

4.   *No evidence on the practices and policies of The National Parole Board can be introduced.*
It is beyond belief that the counsel for an inmate seeking to be granted leave for parole review should be prevented from introducing evidence pertaining to the ministrations of the parole board itself! The central question here is the amount of time that an inmate who has been granted eligibility for parole consideration, with a similar institutional history, has to wait before receiving parole. If, for instance, the normal waiting period would be 7 years this could have a direct bearing on the jury's decision. So, a man who is returned to prison to await parole eligibility until the twenty-year mark might conceivably wait until his 27th year of confinement to be placed upon parole! Returning to Stewart's (1991) report, some idea of the delays, mismanagement and outright manipulation of the parole process by correctional officials is evident. The "doublespeak" of corrections talk is to provide reasons for parole waivers, cases in which the inmate does not apply for parole, which do not reflect on the inadequacy of correctional programming but rather seemingly on the personal shortcomings of the prison applicant.

Stewart (1991: 33) analysed the *3,000 waivers* that occurred during the *first half* of the fiscal year 1989/90. The reasons provided by correctional officials for the waivers are as follows; 1) 410 "other," 2) 238 "inmates not interested in early release," 3) 414 "inmates wish to continue programming," 4) 437 "inmate waived to avoid a negative recommendation" and 5) 430 as "inmate has incomplete release plans." A further 6) 272 waived their rights due to "outstanding case preparation." These figures are not only disturbing, they defy common sense. The second reason cited by inmates should give us some inkling that something is either seriously wrong with the parole system or with the preparation that inmates can reasonably make in terms of attaining parole. That is, if the reasons cited were truly representative of what transpires.

As complaints to Stewart's (1983: 33) office demonstrated, and as he concludes, "the Service's current information on waivers neither identifies nor reflects the actual cause of the delays." Inmates complained specifically that:

1. — there was unreasonable delay in referring them for treatments or assessments that resulted in waiver reasons #3 and #4.
2. — unreasonable delays in ordering of a Community Assessment results in the citing of reason #5.
3. — the failure of the case management team to prepare for the Board date results in a waiver under reasons #5 or #2.
4. — they were unable because of unreasonable backlogs in the assessment and treatment programs to participate before their scheduled hearing date and were therefore categorized as waiving under reasons #4 or #2.
5. — finally there were cases that involved several or all of the above elements and resulted in a classification of "other." These practices of the prison are cause for serious concerns about sentences being unduly long, and confirm MacLean's (1989) and Mandel's (1986) arguments concerning the ability of prison officials to make a success of keeping people in prison far longer than they need be there. Engaging in the unseemly practice of "blaming the victim" they rationalize the failures of the system and do an injustice to the concept of justice itself in our society.

Evidence on waiting times before parole once eligibility is attained, the problems with correctional programming in this area and the practices of the correctional service in this regard should be heard if this review is retained, and as I shall argue later in this chapter the foregoing and several other serious problems with it bode in favour of its abandonment. Finally, The Federal Solicitor General's Committee on Long-Term Imprisonment (1983: 3) was cognizant of these problems, although little, if nothing has been done to rectify the situation in the past eight years:

> Should the jury order that parole eligibility is to be terminated, it will by no means necessarily follow that the Board will be favourably inclined to a grant of parole...(there may be a need to...carry out psychological and psychiatric assessments (preceding parole). If the inmate were to believe that parole was an automatic or almost automatic consequence of the court

processings, the distress and resentment when this did occur can be imagined.

Indeed, this characterization in light of the previous discussion, of the approach of prison authorities to Parole should be seen for the nonsense it is. Men will wait for more years, and the tests, assessments, or programs (if they exist at all!) that they are waiting for may be unavailable to them. The prisoner who wants to gain release is thus effectively prevented from doing so. What human being in such dire straights would not also have to believe that they had a good chance at gaining at least the chance for consideration? If we cannot provide treatment or programming for prisoners when they desire and are in need of it, then we are simply punishing them unduly for their crimes.

Three other rules devised by Chief Justice Callaghan require commentary. *Viva voce* evidence, that is evidence related to the original offence committed by Vaillancourt, was ruled inadmissable. Rather the applicant was permitted only to read into the record a statement which had previously been voted on and agreed to by the Crown. The effect of this ruling was to exclude new evidence that, although it might not warrant a new trial, might shed some light on the character or actions of the applicant at the time of the offence. In terms of fairness to the inmate it seems reasonable that given their limited resources, although a retrying of original offence would not be in order, certainly new evidence should have some bearing on his/her eligibility for review. The case of David Milgaard in which key witnesses contradicted testimony given over 20 years ago is indicative of the importance of permitting reasonable leeway for the applicant's counsel.

Callaghan's final two rulings are arguably the most contentious. The first of these prohibited the defence counsel from questioning prospective jurors during the empanelling period on their attitudes toward capital punishment. They were not allowed to ask individuals how they viewed the killing of a police officer. The danger inherent in this extraordinary protection being allowed jurors rather than allowing such protection to fall to the applicant I have argued (O'Reilly-Fleming, 1991) elsewhere accomplished the following:

> This effectively tied the hands of the defence attorneys in this matter, and it can be argued that such a ruling allows jurors with strongly held views to be admitted to a jury situation where they might unduly prejudice the nature of the deliberations. This is somewhat akin to allowing perspective jurors with obvious racist viewpoints to judge a person who is the object of their prejudice.

The attempts of Manson and Cole to introduce key evidence concerning The Standing Committee on Justice and Legal Affairs (1976: 71: 50-61) were thwarted by another ruling. They would have argued, had the opportunity been made available to them, that the current sentence "minimum" (a rather poor choice of terms) was developed at the last minute by the Committee and not in a considered fashion. Chief Justice Callaghan's ruling was that "modern rules of statutory interpretation do not permit reference to these extrinsic aids" *(Criminal Reports,* 66 C.R. (3d) 1988). Were it to be demonstrable to the satisfaction of a jury that this minimum did not reflect sober reflection, and were rather chosen in a somewhat arbitrary fashion, it might give pause to the jury to consider the appropriateness of the current length of sentence a lifer must serve. These deliberations were brief given the severe ramifications for the lives of eventually thousands of Canadians who will be subject to them. The 1976 compromise, that is, the trade of the death penalty for the 25 year minimum is dated, struck within the context of a pre-abolition society (O'Reilly-Fleming, 1991).

The Return of Indeterminate Sentences

Rene Vaillancourt's 15 year review was not successful. He must now serve the remaining ten years of his original sentence before he is even eligible for parole. While his early institutional record was that of an inmate with some not inconsiderable problems, his offences which seem to be of significance in the world of prison management are somewhat less striking to the average observer. His "crimes" in prison were seemingly minor, "ranging from taking a shower at the wrong time to refusing to work," offences which seem more relevant to outdated ideas of high school behaviour than that which should grace the record of a federal inmate (Haliechuk, 1990: B5). When viewed from the context of relations in capitalist society, and if we follow Mandel's (1986) argument regarding the spilling over of the relations of production into the prison in Canada, then such offences can be seen as contrary to producing a productive citizen. Rebellion, as we have already deciphered, is a normal means of responding to and rebelling against a repressive prison environment. A large percentage of persons serving life sentences admit to having a drug or alcohol problem. In a survey conducted amongst 638 persons serving a life sentence in Ontario it was found that only 193 did not view themselves as being afflicted with one of these two problems (June, 1989). Vaillancourt it must be remembered spent 33 months on death row before being transferred to general population. Jackson (1983) has documented in chilling detail the abuses both psychological and physical which prisoners undergo in solitary confinement and in the Special Handling Units at Millhaven Penitentiary where the cells are lined with steel. The desolation that this treatment produces was termed by one prisoner, "Tomb city." From the repressive and bleak existence of awaiting death Vaillancourt was transferred into general population. From 1984 onwards he made serious efforts at self-rehabilitation given the limited resources available to him in prison.

Vaillancourt's crime, the killing of a police officer, is a serious offence. However it does not share the characteristics common to a first degree murder that is carefully calculated in advance. Few bank robbers expect to kill someone to get money, and banks since that time have instituted procedures to ensure that robbers are able to leave the bank with a small amount of cash rather than have them confronted and risk the life of anyone. Vaillancourt's actions in shooting Maitland were, I argue, spur of the moment. He did not torture, maim, rape, burn, bite, stab, or prolong the suffering of his victim. Compare his crime with that of Clifford Olsen who bludgeoned several child victims to death with a heavy object. Think of the planning that preceded the murders committed by Thatcher, Demeter or Buxbaum. Vaillancourt does not fit into this category of killer.

A comparison of Vaillancourt's case to several other cases involving homicide is instructive for it further calls into question both the length of his original sentence and the refusal of his eligibility for parole. In the case of *Regina v Jordan* the case involved a man who was put in charge of the child of a woman with whom he was sharing an intimate relationship. While on his own in a position of authority and isolation with the child he managed to batter the infant child to death quite methodically over a period of several weeks. The injuries to the body of the child were massive and included both internal and external injuries. In a second case, *Regina v Gourgon,* the accused along with his partner in crime decided to attack the manager of an inn, his wife and her mother. The husband was stabbed repeatedly until death ensued. The two men attempted to kill the wife but failed after having stabbed and strangled her. In the case of *Kivell,* the accused along with his accomplices spent months planning the kidnap and ransom of the wife of a grocery store manager. Something apparently went drastically wrong despite this planning. The woman was not ransomed but rather taken to a remote location and murdered. All three of these cases are of some importance to the argument being made in this paper, for each of these offenders received sentences that were dramatically shorter than Vaillancourt's. I think it can be reasonably contended that their crimes were more brutal, cruel and calculated.

There have been two recent decisions in the Manitoba court system which further underscore the arbitrariness and inequities in the 15 year review process. In both of the cases to be discussed the lifers were sentenced to 20 year mandatory sentences and had their period of eligibility before parole consideration reduced to 17 years. In 1973, Dwight Lucas was convicted of the axe slaying of a man outside of Winnipeg. He spent time at various locations in the correctional system but while in a British Columbia prison in 1976 he was involved in the abduction of a female correctional officer. The officer was shot to death accidentally. While originally he was cited as having had problems with prison rules he was eventually transferred due to good behaviour to Warkworth which is a minimum security institution.

Larry Sheldon, also sentenced to a twenty year minimum committed the crime of murdering a defenceless ten-year-old girl. He picked up the hitchhiking youngster near Gimli, Manitoba and then brutally killed her. However, during incarceration he had been a model prisoner and took advantage of a number of rehabilitative programs.

Scrapping the Fifteen Year Review

The second portion of this chapter has been devoted to an exploration of the inherent inequities which the 15 year review produces. The fifteen year review was a decision made in haste rather than in light of penological research on the appropriateness of punishments. In a very real sense, persons sentenced to the 25 year minimum became guinea pigs for what the effects might be of handing out such sentences. Every time a prisoner requires a review of his/her case they must be returned to the province in which the original offence was committed. The cost of bringing witnesses, counsel and others to these reviews is soon to become astronomical. By 1993 there will be over 40 persons a year that will become eligible for the review in Canada, reaching a peak of over 50 cases a year by the year 2002.

If we can learn anything from the Vaillancourt case and from the foregoing analysis of the operation of the prison system it is that "rules" can be made, bent, or ignored when criminal justice officials decide to do so, at all stages of the process. In the context of the 15 year review Mandel's (1986: 90) observation is appropriate, "It is probably most helpful in this context to think of judges as lawyers whose clients are the status quo." The Infinity Lifers Group (IFG, 1989: 49) similarly is able to comment from experience on the preferential treatment accorded those who co-operate with authorities, "We believe that people suddenly become credible and receive preferential treatment and favourable parole decisions for disclosing information to police and/or prison officials." One such inmate who benefited with an early release for co-operating with authorities before his conviction as a serial killer was Clifford Olsen (Mulgrew, 1991).

The comparison developed between those charged with brutal slayings in the second degree and who received favourable verdicts at review and/or at sentencing indicates quite clearly that there is an overreliance in these decisions on correctional misconduct, co-operation, and support of a corrupt system (by not lodging complaints) as the basis for recommendations. Rather than focussing the attention of such bodies upon the failures of the system generally the focus is upon the seeming continued pathology of the individual. What responsibility does the prison system have if after fifteen years a man is not even ready to be *reviewed* for *possible* parole? The description of the Infinity Lifers Group of the conditions under which they must live and their inability to work towards any meaningful measure of their readiness for release other than correctional whim rings true in the finding in the Vaillancourt review. The politics of control were also paraded in the Vaillancourt case. Twelve senior police officers sat in full dress regalia during the proceedings as a "secondary" jury to impress upon the jury that they wanted Vaillancourt to remain inside. The symbolic presence of the police was a not so subtle reminder that the police want the punishment for the murderers of police to be as harsh as is possible under the law (Manson, 1988). There was no such police presence when the murderer of a little girl came forward for his fifteen year review.

The fifteen year review represents no more than an indeterminate sentence which is imposed on the inmate after more than a decade and a half of his/her sentence has been served if they are not successful in their appeal. The fifteen year review only permits persons to *apply* for parole, it does not *grant parole*. A reasonable alternative might contain the following elements:

1. First, the current distinctions between first and second degree murder should be eliminated. The charge of murder should go forward to the court for a full hearing with an elimination of the plea bargain in these cases. Cases would then be heard on merit, and upcriming tendencies eliminated (Infinity Lifers Group, 1989: 49).
2. The period of eligibility for parole consideration should be dropped to ten years. In cases of serial murder or repeated acts of murder or extreme violence there should be a mandatory life sentence, to mean life.
3. All lifers (who do not fall into the two specific categories outlined above) should nonetheless appear before parole authorities at one year intervals so that their progress or lack of it can be discussed, and suggestions for treatment, counselling, or training can be given. In this way parole authorities will have a reasonable opportunity to become acquainted with the individual, and so be able to make an informed decision when he is eligible for a parole decision.
4. Appropriate programs must be made available to lifers. As Mike Fitzgerald (1987: 155) has argued, programs must recognize "the long-term nature of long-term imprisonment." While this assertion may seem simplistic it means that education and training must run throughout the length of confinement rather than be "stop and go" every few years, and that they must equip the inmate with "skills and

qualifications which they can make use of during later stages of their imprisonment." This implies, above all else that prisoners should not be subject to arbitrary withdrawal of privileges or programs, or subject to transfers or whimsical shifts in policy in order that rights may be protected (Jackson, 1983).

5.   If following five years of parole review the individual is not recommended there should be a mandatory mechanism for the review of the problems that the inmate is having, programs that might remedy this situation, and a review of prison programming in this area. In this way prisoners will have the opportunity to learn over the course of their sentence, rather than in the brief period preceding their review, or eventual parole, what problems are impeding his progress towards relative freedom.

The judicial review I have previously labelled a "Pandora's Box of Indeterminancy" (O'Reilly-Fleming, 1991). It is bound to provoke feelings of anger, mistreatment, and frustration in the several hundreds of men who will be awaiting their review in the coming decade. As a society we can no longer afford to support the exponential growth of a system which fails at the task society has assigned it, while ensuring that it prospers. More people are serving longer sentences in Canadian prisons than at any time in history. The prisoner who is able to withstand a decade of punishment for his/her actions in reasonably good mental and physical health deserves the opportunity to work towards eventual release in a constructive manner. To do less than consider their cases condemns them to a limbo from which many will eventually return to our society. If we ignore and mistreat them we make more than a sad commentary on our society, we lessen ourselves as human beings. As Foucault (1979: 232) has written, we will have to seek answers to our continued failures emanating from warehouses of punishment:

> We are aware of all the inconveniences of prison and that it is dangerous when it is not useless. And yet one cannot "see" how to replace it. It is the detestable solution, which one seems unable to do without.

Legal Cases Cited

Regina v Gourgon (1981), 58 C.C.C. (2d).

Regina v Jordan (1983), 7 C.C.C. (3d).

Regina v Kivel (1982), 321 C.C.C. (3d).

Regina v Vaillancourt (1988), 43 C.C.C. (3d).

Vaillancourt v Solicitor General of Canada, Attorney General of Canada and Attorney General of Ontario (1988), 66 C.R. (3d).

References

Abbott, Jack H., 1982. *In the Belly of the Beast.* New York: Vintage.

Amnesty International, 1983. *Report on Allegations of Ill-Treatment of Prisoners at Archambault Institution.* Quebec: Amnesty International Publications.

Bettleheim, B., 1960. *The Informed Heart.* New York: Free Press.

Bolton, N., et al., 1976. "Psychological Correlates of Long-Term Imprisonment," *British Journal of Criminology,* Vol. 16, pp. 38-47.

Burtch, Brian and R. Ericson, 1979. *The Silent System.* Toronto: Centre of Criminology.

Caron, Roger, 1985. *Go-Boy.* Toronto: Methuen.

Cohen, S. and L. Taylor, 1981. *Psychological Survival.* London: Penguin.

————, 1976. *Prison Secrets.* London: National Council for Civil Liberties, Radical Alternatives to Prison.

Coker, J. and J.P. Martin, 1985. *Licensed to Live.* Oxford: Basil Blackwell.

Committee on Long-Term Imprisonment, 1983. Judicial Review of Parole Eligibility Pursuant to Section 672 Criminal Code. Discussion Paper, Ottawa: Ministry of the Solicitor General.

Culhane, Clare, 1985. *Still Barred from Prison.* Montreal: Black Rose.

————, 1989. The Dick Award Lecture. Faculty of Law, University of Windsor.

Desroches, Fred, 1974a. "The April 1971 Kingston Penitentiary Riot," in *The Canadian Journal of Criminology and Corrections,* Vol. 16, pp. 317-351.

————, 1974b. "Patterns in Prison Riots," in *The Canadian Journal of Criminology and Corrections,* Vol. 16, pp. 332-351.

Douglas, Catherine, et al., 1980. "Administrative Contributions to Prison Disturbances," in *The Canadian Journal of Criminology,* Vol. 22, pp. 197-205.

Ericson, R.V., 1976. *Young Offenders and their Social Work.* Farnborough: Gower.

Ericson, R.V., et al., 1987. "Punishing for Profit: Reflections on the Revival of Privatization in Corrections," in *The Canadian Journal of Criminology,* Vol. 29, No. 4, Oct. pp. 355-387.

Evans, Peter, 1980. *Prison Crisis.* London: George Allen and Unwin.

Fox, J. and J. Levin, 1985. *Mass Murder: America's Growing Menace.* New York: Praeger.

Fitzgerald, Mike and Joe Sim (eds.), 1982. *British Prisons.* 2nd ed. Oxford: Basil Blackwell.

Fitzgerald, Mike, 1987. "The telephone rings: long-term imprisonment," in A.E. Bottoms and R. Light (eds.). *Problems of Long-Term Imprisonment.* Aldershot: Gower, pp. 142-157.

Foucault, M. 1979. *Discipline and Punish.* New York: Vintage.

Gaucher, R., 1988. "Doing Life in Canadian Penitentiaries." Address to The Faculty of Law, University of Windsor, March 29.

————, 1989. "Beyond Reasonable Doubt: Anatomy of A Murder Trial," in *The Windsor Yearbook of Access to Justice*, Vol. 9, pp. 277-292.

Goffman, E., 1961. *Asylums*. Garden City, New York: Doubleday.

Gosselin, Luc, 1982. *Prisons in Canada*. Montreal: Black Rose.

Haliechuk, R., 1990. "Lifers' good conduct key to jury verdicts on parole," *The Toronto Star*, March 25, B5.

Hogarth, John, 1970. *Sentencing as a Human Process*. Toronto: University of Toronto Press.

Home Office, 1966. Report of the Inquiry into Prison Escapes and Security (Montbatten Report). Cmnd 3175. London: HMSO.

————, 1984. Managing the Long-Term Prison System: The Report of The Control Review Committee. London: HMSO.

Infinity Lifers Group, 1989. "Can You Hear Us?" *The Journal of Prisoners on Prison*, Vol. 1, No. 2, Winter pp. 45-58.

Irwin, John, 1980. *Prisons in Turmoil*. Boston: Little Brown.

Jackson, M., 1983. *Prisoners of Isolation: Solitary Confinement in Canada*. Toronto: University of Toronto Press.

Lauzon, R., 1989. "Stonewalled," *The Journal of Prisoners on Prison*, Vol. 1, No. 2, pp. 17-38.

Leyton, E., 1985. *Hunting Humans: The Rise of the Modern Multiple Murderer*. Toronto: McClelland and Stewart.

Lowman, John, 1986. "Images of Discipline in Prison," in Neil Boyd (ed.). *The Social Dimensions of Law*. Scarborough: Prentice-Hall, 237-259.

Lunde, D., 1976. *Murder and Madness*. Stanford: Stanford University Press.

MacGuigan, Mark (Chair), 1977. Report to Parliament: The Sub-Committee on the Penitentiary System in Canada. Ottawa: Supply and Services.

MacLean, Brian, 1983. "Contradictions in Canadian Prisons: Some Aspects of Social Control Mechanisms," in Thomas Fleming and Livy Visano (eds.). *Deviant Designations: Crime, Law and Deviance in Canada*. Toronto: Butterworths, pp. 389-410.

————, 1989. "What is to be done about the correctional enterprise in Canada?" *The Journal of Prisoners on Prisons*, Vol. 1, No. 2, Winter pp. 59-74.

Makin, K., 1988. "Jury Rejects Police Killer's Bid for Early Parole," *The Globe and Mail*, September 13, p. 1.

Mandel, M., 1986. "The Legalization of Prison Discipline in Canada," in *Crime and Social Justice*, No. 26, pp. 79-94.

Manson, A., 1988. "15 Year Review Eligibility Hearings (Proceedings and Case Comments), Invited Address. Faculty of Law, University of Windsor, March 29.

Mathieson, Thomas, 1990. *Prison on Trial*. London: Sage.

Matthews, R., 1989. "Alternatives to and in Prison: A Realist Approach," in P. Carlen and D. Cook (eds.). *Paying for Crime*. Milton Keynes: Open University Press, pp. 128-150.

McKay, H.B. et al., 1979. *The Effects of Long-Term Incarceration and a Proposed Strategy for Future Research*. Ottawa: Ministry of the Solicitor General.

Melossi, D. and Pavarini, M., 1981. *The Prison and The Factory*. London: Macmillan.

Ministry of the Solicitor General, 1989. Unpublished statistics on life sentences.

Mitford, J., 1973. *Kind and Usual Punishment*. New York: Dell.

Morris, T. and L. Blom-Cooper, 1963. *A Calendar of Murder*. London: RKP.

Morris, T. and P. Morris, 1963. *Pentonville*. London: RKP.

O'Reilly-Fleming, Thomas, 1991. "The injustice of judicial review: Vaillancourt reconsidered," in *The Canadian Journal of Criminology*, October pp. 163-170.

Porporino, Frank and Ed Zamble, 1984. "Coping With Imprisonment," in *The Canadian Journal of Criminology*, Vol. 26, No. 4, pp. 403-421.

Ratner, R.S., 1986. "Parole Certificate as Dominant Hegemony," in D. Currie and B. MacLean (eds.). *The Administration of Justice*. Saskatoon: University of Saskatchewan Press, pp. 205-214.

Ratner, R.S. and J. McMullan, 1985. "The Exceptional State," in T. Fleming (ed.). *The New Criminologies in Canada*. Toronto: Oxford.

Richards, E., 1978. "The Experience of Long-Term Imprisonment," *British Journal of Criminology*, Vol. 18, pp. 162-68.

Sacks, Oliver, 1990. *Awakenings*. New York: Harper Perennial.

Sapsford, R.J., 1978. "Life-Sentence Prisoners: Psychological Changes During Sentence," *British Journal of Criminology*, Vol. 18, pp. 128-145.

————, 1983. *Life Sentence Prisoners: Reaction, Response and Change*. Milton Keynes: Open University Press.

Serge, V., 1970. *Men in Prison*. London: Gollancz.

Standing Committee on Justice and Legal Affairs, 1976. Minutes of the Standing Committee on Justice and Legal Affairs. 1st Session, 30th Parliament, 71: 50-61.

Stewart, R.L., 1991. Annual Report of the Correctional Investigator. Ottawa: Ministry of Supply and Services.

St. Leonard's House, 1989. Press release on life prisoners in Ontario prisons. June 1989.

Sykes, G., 1958. *The Society of Captives*. Princeton: Princeton University Press.

Walford, Bonnie, 1989. "Homicide in Canada," in *The Journal of Prisoners on Prison*, Vol. 1, No. 2, Winter pp. 39-44.

Walker, N., 1987. "The unwanted effects of long-term imprisonment," in A.E. Bottoms and R. Light, *Problems of Long-Term Imprisonment*. Aldershot: Gower, pp. 183-199.

Zubrycki, R.M., 1984. "Long-term Incarceration in Canada," in *The Canadian Journal of Criminology*, Vol. 26, No. 4, pp. 397-402.

Chapter 13

Shocked, Disciplined, and Inspected:
Shock Incarceration and Cultural Sensibilities

Kevin Haggerty

Basic training is "a feat of psychological manipulation on the grand scale which has been so consistently successful and so universal that we fail to notice it as remarkable" (Dyer 1985: 105).

Introduction

Visual images. Printed texts. The media impact on how we perceive both punishment and wider society through the presentation of recurring themes and the omission of potentially significant issues. The recent development of "boot camps" as a correctional reform in the United States has received wide attention from the mainstream media (Parent 1989: 1; Sechrest 1989: 16). The selective and limited presentations of punishment, labour, discipline, and human nature in the media accounts serve to reinforce and shape cultural conceptions. They tell a story highlighting the individual manifestations of deviance while failing to address structural antecedents of criminality.

This paper will examine the content of Shock Incarceration (SI) programs, the political factors contributing to their popularity and will detail the content of mass media accounts of SI programs. Drawing upon the work of D. Garland (1990) and his discussions concerning how forms of punishment are determined by, and simultaneously serve to form the dominant culture, an elaboration will be provided on the relationship between Shock Incarceration, the media and cultural sensibilities. However, as the visibility of SI programs is integral to both political aspirations and the forming of cultural values, Garland's argument that punishment increasingly occurs "behind the scenes" of social life will be contested. As Shock Incarceration is a comparatively new undertaking, some time will be spent providing an overview of its structure.

Shock Incarceration

The first American correctional program based on the military model began operation in 1888 at the Elmira Reformatory in New York where inmates were taught the basics of drill, military bearing, and tactical procedures. This military model was abandoned after WW I due to anti-military attitudes prevalent at the time (Smith 1988). A similar military emphasis has recently been rejuvenated in the United States and exists under a variety of names including RID (Regimented Inmate Discipline), IMPACT (Intensive Motivational Program of Alternative Correctional Treatment) and SAI (Special Alternative Incarceration). While there is variability among states on the degree to which factors such as life skills training, counselling, and educational achievement are stressed, the principal emphasis remains the same. Young inmates, generally between the ages of 17 and 24, exchange a longer period of incarceration in a regular penitentiary for shorter detainment in a military training environment, often followed by a period of probation. Programs usually extend between 90 to 120 days, with the longest lasting 6 months in Louisiana and New York State (Sechrest 1989: 15). Their maximum inmate capacity ranges from 60 in Orleans Parish (LA), to 500 in New York State.

Individuals in SI are usually first time felony offenders who have never been incarcerated (MacKenzie and Shaw 1990: 128). Admittance procedures vary between states and range from having SI as a court imposed sentence to an elaborate screening of prison-bound inmates, designed to ensure appropriate candidates. Participation is voluntary and offenders may choose to quit the SI and return to the general prison population to complete their sentence. During their stay at the SI facility, offenders are subjected to a regime reminiscent of the U.S. Marine basic training centre at Parris Island: hair is shaved, uniforms assigned, rudimentary drill procedures taught, and physical fitness stressed. All of this occurs under the scrutinizing authority of Drill Instructors (DIs), who are authorized to impose summary punishment for regulatory infractions. Shock Incarceration is designed to challenge the offender both physically and mentally. This has led to a high attrition rate with as many as 40% of selected participants being released for medical reasons or opting to complete the full length of their sentence in the general prison population (MacKenzie 1990: 49).

The genesis of contemporary SI can be traced to Georgia in the early 1970s where a local judge and the correctional department lobbied for a strict military regime for offenders (Parent 1989: 1). First implemented in Georgia and Oklahoma in 1983, SI programs have seen a steady increase in popularity. As of 1989, 21 SI units were in operation in 14 states, with another 13 considering, or in the process of, developing shock facilities (MacKenzie 1990: 44). Furthermore, an unspecified number of military-model facilities exist at the local level and hearings into the feasibility of adopting Shock Incarceration federally have recently been completed. Both President Bush and his drug czar William Bennett support SI as a procedure for dealing with narcotics offenders (MacKenzie 1990: 44; Morash and Rucker 1990: 205).

Correctional departments and administrators across the nation during the 1980s were facing similar economic and political factors which appear to have made shock incarceration a popular option for dealing with young offenders. Great concern existed about the "crisis of overcrowding" in prisons and the alarming escalation in the rate of imprisonment. The combination of a "get tough" attitude towards crime, changing demographics, the declining rehabilitative ideal, and the diminishing discretion of parole officials have contributed to the increases in the numbers of inmates in both federal and state institutions (Blumstein 1984: 207). Shortages of funds and fear of court intervention into the correctional realm prompted states to begin experimenting with procedures ranging from electronic monitoring to intensive parole supervision, all justified as methods to ease prison crowding. It was such a scenario which spawned the 1983 shock program in Georgia. Under court order to reduce overcrowding, officials faced the prospect of strict, court imposed regulations on the operation of the correctional system. In order to avert such a loss of autonomy, a wide variety of prison alternatives were implemented. Examples include intensive probation, diversion centres, and the newest experiment, Shock Incarceration.

More explicit political considerations also had an impact upon corrections during the 1980s, a period characterized by the rise of the New Right in the United States and England. Often invoking the rhetoric of "law and order," governments called for stiff and swift punishments for offenders. Rehabilitation was considered to be a bankrupt ideology; the best that could be hoped for was the incapacitation of offenders. Calls for longer sentences, especially in conjunction with the American "war on drugs," met with political and social approval.

The influence of Reagan economic policies also had an effect upon American corrections during the 1980s. The emphasis on "supply side economics" and calls for reductions in taxation, made the undertaking of large capital projects difficult. Despite a substantial prison building campaign, prisons continued to be overcrowded and politicians were wary to further burden tax-payers with the costs of incarcerating individuals (Koneazny and Schwartz 1984: 1). Some states also encountered difficulty in raising sufficient revenue to build prisons capable of housing the existing and projected numbers of persons facing incarceration.

These factors should be seen as the backdrop to the ascension of Shock Incarceration. Calls for harsher and longer periods of detainment, a rising fear of crime, escalating prison costs, and an increasing prison population all coinciding with diminishing resources to manage facilities. One potential solution was to punish offenders more intensely for a shorter period of time rather than increasing the length of imprisonment. The first contemporary manifestation of such an approach occurred in Britain during the early 1980s. Faced with similar expenditure increases and rising incarceration rates, the Thatcher government in 1982 introduced legislation aimed at persuading magistrates to reduce sentence length and in return, "the government would make this sojourn memorable" (Pitts 1988: 51). Entitled "Short Sharp Shock," these programs entailed a brief period of regimented incarceration—as short as three weeks—designed to "shock" young offender out of their criminal habits.

This rhetoric of "shocking" criminals was adopted in the United States with the advent of Shock Incarceration. SI proved to be a popular option among politicians, who by conducting interviews on the physical grounds of shock incarceration facilities, were able to show their constituents their commitment to cutting costs while being "tough on crime" (Turque et al. 1989: 43; MacKenzie 1990: 44). In some states, the SI program has so improved the stature of the department of corrections among judges, prosecutors, police, and politicians that correctional officials used this newly established support to advance further reforms (Parent 1989: 3).

The advent of Shock Incarceration can therefore be understood as a convenient method for politicians to punish offenders while simultaneously maintaining the appearance of being committed to cost reductions. Savings were predicted to emanate from a number of sectors. It was speculated that the shorter duration of incarceration would generate a reduction in prison populations while the harshness of SI would act as a deterrent, thereby further reducing costs. Others have posited that despite the relative lack of counselling in most shock incarceration units, the experience would have a rehabilitative effect on participants (Caldas 1990). The verdict as to the extent to which SI programs relieve prison crowding is still unclear. In examinations of Shock Incarceration, different authors have determined that the nature of the selection process in some programs may be contributing to a further expansion of the correctional system by drawing upon a population which would previously have been on probation (Parent 1989: 12).

Cultural Sensibilities

Both the United States and England have devised shorter and more rigorous terms of incarceration in order to be seen to be "tough on crime" while managing a reduced budget. One question arising in the American context is, "why a military environment?" At first glance, it would appear to be a rather peculiar proposition to place offenders in a structure designed to teach military recruits how to kill other human beings. It will be shown, however, that specific aspects of American culture have an affinity with the military establishment, formulating the notion that it is "common sense" to subject offenders to military-style training. Furthermore, the portrayal of SI in the media serves to both reinforce and aid in the creation of these dominant cultural assumptions.

Garland (1990) provides a useful starting point for examining the relationship between culture and the dominant forms of punishment. He commences from the proposition that culture exists in intellectual systems, forms of consciousness, structures of affect, and sensibilities in a given society. These cultural factors provide a framework for how punishment is conceived and removes from the realm of the possible those punishments that are culturally inappropriate. In connection with this understanding of culture, Garland outlines how within any society there are certain predominant sensibilities which change over time. Images and actions are responded to in a culturally and historically specific manner. For example, the re-introduction of the practice of quartering offenders would not constitute efficient penal strategy because of the likelihood that it would shock contemporary sensibilities.

Recognizing that sensibilities change, Garland applies to the study of punishment N. Elias' notion of a "civilizing process" that "produces individuals of heightened sensibilities..." (Garland 1990: 222). One important aspect of the civilizing process is the movement whereby certain spectacles and actions become "privatized"; that is, acts and rituals such as "sex, violence, bodily functions, illness, suffering and death" (Garland 1990: 222) are removed from view, occurring outside of public observation. Within the penal realm, Garland argues that the thesis presented by Elias on "privatization" is clearly applicable, concluding that "the administration of punishment is essentially a private affair conducted by professional agents out of sight of the public" (1990: 234-35). Visual displays of punishment are now recognized as inappropriate in the public sphere, evoking a negative emotional response from witnesses to the suffering.

While the idea that sensibilities and culture limit the boundaries of punishment provides an interesting avenue for exploration, there are shortcomings with the "privatization thesis" adopted by Garland. One factor he appears to neglect is the impact of the news media in contemporary society. The explosion of communications technology and its ability to reach substantial portions of the population clearly make it "one of the most important and powerful institutions in society" (Ericson, Baranek and Chan 1987: 10).

While the news media do not customarily provide extensive coverage of the punishment inherent in the day-to-day routine of prisons, this may relate more to the structure of the media than a desire to avoid offending sensibilities. As Ericson et al. have argued, the contemporary news media are geared towards examining deviance and the straying from organizational norms (1987: 4). It is not surprising then that the structured day-to-day activities of punishment in prisons are neglected in favour of more dramatic and "deviant" escape attempts or riots. The long-term nature of penal punishment is also not suited to the television medium which relies on dramatic film footage to support its stories.

However, when vivid visual images are available and the exacted punishment deviates from standard penal techniques, there appears to be little consideration given to the public's sensibilities against viewing punishment. If such sensibilities exist, the media has been able to overcome them in their portrayals of SI by linking punishment with dominant cultural themes such as the importance of work and the malleability of youthful offenders. Through the use of such cultural themes, Shock Incarceration is able to gain public acceptance where many of the arbitrary, degrading, and psychologically abusive aspects of SI "would be rejected as cruel and unusual punishment in other correctional settings" (Morash and Rucker 1990: 208).

Media representations do more than simply reflect reality, they serve as a dominant source of knowledge on matters of crime and criminality for the general population (Ericson et al. 1987: 15-18). This knowledge, however, is filtered through a selective process of observations and representations. The mainstream media can be perceived as a discriminating discourse containing rules serving to exclude some understandings of society and the subject matter under examination. Conceptions of reality falling outside of these unwritten boundaries are not subject to examination or comment. This not only reinforces certain cultural themes but can also aid in the construction of reality. In relation to punishment, the media, through its reliance on particular accounts of the "facts" concerning penal programs and the exclusion of other interpretations of such "facts," is able to shape a dominant cognitive framework for comprehending issues of punishment. The cognitive framework ultimately "eliminates conflict or divergence by rendering alternative definitions and solutions unthinkable" (Gusfield 1981: 7).

Media Portrayals

In order to ascertain how the media has portrayed Shock Incarceration, a review of three major American newspapers was undertaken. *The Washington Post*, *The New York Times* and *The Christian Science Monitor* were all searched for any article or editorial dealing with Shock Incarceration from 1983 to 1990. These newspapers were chosen both for reasons of access and circulation size. Printed material was also examined from sources such as *Newsweek* and *Life* and from clippings that were received from various correctional departments. In addition, one video dealing with Georgia's correctional system and one twenty minute account of Shock Incarceration on the Canadian news telecast *The Journal* were examined.

Before any article could be written or report filmed, however, reporters have to obtain access to both the SI site and to individuals deemed to be relevant to the story. While prisons pose a formidable problem for media access, this is not the case with SI. Indeed, it appears that shock programs have been designed specifically with access to the media and public visibility in mind. The community is able to see recruits in some units when they march in local parades (Parent 1989: 26) or participate in public long distance races (Caldas 1990: 73). Inmates on these excursions are provided with strict guidelines on the proper manner of interaction with any "free world people" (Louisiana Department of Public Safety and Corrections: IMPACT handbook; Mississippi Department of Corrections 1990: RID handbook).

Media access is also affected by the physical location of programs. In Louisiana, for example, it was perceived beneficial to operating SI within the confines of a penitentiary as that locality provided scrutiny by the news media (MacKenzie, Shaw and Gowdy 1990: 28). In order to overcome any legal barriers to filming, or conducting interviews, recruits in Mississippi and Louisiana are required to sign a form providing consent to the use of their image and comments in the print or television media (IMPACT handbook [Louisiana]; RID handbook [Mississippi]). Media reports are important for some correctional departments that see SI as a method of improving public relations (RID handbook [Mississippi]) or, as stated earlier, for underscoring a politician's commitment to fighting crime.

One aspect of American culture appearing to have contributed to the acceptance of boot camps as a correctional reform is the large military establishment in American society. With 130 million Americans who have served in the armed forces (Yarmolinsky and Foster 1983: 71) and a contemporary force of over two million men and women there is a large core of individuals who have undergone, or can personally relate to, military basic training. The military experience is customarily viewed as having been an important turning point in a person's life where meaningful lessons were learned (Stewart 1989: iii). Hollywood has also contributed to the largely positive associations related to military training through depictions in popular films, frequently portraying basic training as a difficult and at times brutal experience with constructive personal consequences for graduates. The classic contemporary example of this genre of film is *An Officer and a Gentleman* which portrayed how a lower class non-conformist was groomed to be a "gentleman" as a result of Air Force basic training. This association was emphasised by journalists of *Newsweek* who made reference to the film while providing a descriptive overview of different SI facilities (Turque et al. 1989: 42).

In a nation where individuals view boot camp as having had positive effects upon their own or a family member's life and where such beliefs are reinforced through entertainment depictions of boot camp, it is not difficult to understand the popular acceptance of SI. What this generally uncritical acceptance overlooks, however, is that for everyone except shock inmates, boot camp is the introductory stage to a lengthy career providing support, reinforcement, and some possibility of advancement. Outside of parole supervision for SI graduates, shock programs lack such post-program support.

The fact that basic training is an experience shared by such a large number of Americans also makes challenging SI difficult. As one editorial stated, these young men "...are essentially the same group that, in war time, would most likely be in boot camp anyway" (Milloy 1988: C3). Some commentators have been critical of SI, claiming that it constitutes little more than degradation of the offender (Shen 1990: B1). However, it is difficult for those opposed to SI to generate effective opposition framed in the constitutional discourse of "cruel and unusual punishment" when all branches of the armed forces are relying on essentially the same procedures to train recruits (Sechrest 1989: 18).

Once programs were in place and media access secured, a number of dominant themes became apparent in the media portrayals, one of which was punishment. The emphasis on the punishment inherent in SI should not be surprising considering the political desire for a more intensive form of penance. The media provides a valuable political service by stressing the harshness of SI. If boot camps were not explicitly portrayed as being severe, the reduced length of sentence for shock inmates could be interpreted as leniency towards offenders, a position upon which political opponents would seek to capitalize.

The imagery of harshness was decidedly more pronounced in the video and television reports examined. This likely results from the nature of the medium which can let images speak for themselves. SI provides powerful images. The production by *The Journal* showed repeated shots of Drill Instructors belittling and screaming at new arrivals and at inmates undergoing rigorous exercises. Visibly confused and anxious youths are shown arriving at the centre, clearly unsure of what to anticipate. There is often no narrative accompanying these scenes as the images tell the story: these offenders are being punished.

Punishment is also a recurring theme in newspaper and magazine accounts of SI. Of the nine descriptive accounts found in the print media, all commence with a vivid narrative of inmates being yelled at on arrival or leaping from their bunks before dawn for morning inspection or exercise. Physical exercises accent the punitive aspects of SI programs. Images and descriptions abound of offenders under the constant supervision of a drill instructor, running in formation or doing push-ups. The punitive component of these exercises is highlighted by the fact that two offenders deemed to be physically suitable for full participation in the shock training have died from participating in the preliminary exercise periods (Parent 1989: 18).

Perhaps the most frequently recurring theme in the media representations is "discipline." Editorials have commented that a lack of discipline is one of the contributing factors to offenders committing crimes (Raspberry 1987: H21) and the administrators of SI appear determined to reverse this situation. Some states go so far as to draw on the rehabilitative discourse, labelling the obedience to a detailed set of rules "disciplinary therapy" (Parent 1989: 25; RID handbook [Mississippi]). *The Journal's* report outlined that one of the components setting graduates apart from new recruits is their "easy acceptance of discipline" (*Journal* 1989). Politicians and correctional officials continually reinforce the emphasis on discipline, as witnessed by J. Welborn, chairperson of the Michigan Senate Committee on Criminal Justice, who described his state's boot camp as "a 90-day regimen of drill, exercise, hard labour and discipline, discipline, discipline" (Welborn 1989: 136). The *Washington Post* reported on the comments of Governor W. Schaeger of Maryland who bluntly proclaimed:

> The camp was not set up as a method to ease overcrowding: it was set up to teach inmates how to learn discipline (Shen 1990: B1).

Discipline is an inherent aspect of contemporary armed forces training. As Foucault (1977) has outlined, many of the disciplinary techniques originating in the military have become dispersed throughout society. Designed to create automatic docility in individuals (Foucault 1977: 169), military discipline is derived from attendance to minute components of personal behaviour, the "little things" that constitute a "political anatomy of detail" (1977: 139):

> Discipline
> ...aims to increase the efficiency of each movement and develop its co-ordination with others, exercising different forces and

building them up together. It does this by bringing to bear a constant, uninterrupted supervision which is alert to the slightest deviation, thereby allowing a meticulous control of the body which is being disciplined (Garland 1990: 144).

Perhaps nowhere is the meticulous disciplinary emphasis on "little things" and supervision more pronounced than in a military environment. Offenders in Shock Incarceration are subject to both a timetable detailing their activities between the time they get up until the time they go to bed and to a comprehensive set of regulations prescribing rules for almost all aspects of communication, dress, movement and hygiene. Behaviour as personal as showering and brushing teeth are part of the disciplinary code and subject to regular inspection (IMPACT handbook [Louisiana]; Caldas 1990: 72). Dyer (1985) has noted that within the U.S. Marine Corps, inspections:

> help to set up the pattern in the recruits of unquestioning submission to military authority: standing stock-still, staring straight ahead, while somebody else examines you closely for faults is about as extreme a ritual act of submission as you can make with your clothes on (1985: 113).

The disciplinary features of SI continue in the photographs that inevitably accompany printed accounts of these programs. Pictures of inmates standing in formation, being inspected by Drill Instructors, or parading in military formation accent the discipline inherent in SI. The discipline in such images is obvious. No aspect of the inmate is free from observation and criticism: posture must be maintained, communication forbidden, with eyes forward in a total respect for authority.

The distinction between disciplinary and punitive representations of SI, however, is often ambiguous because of the tremendous authority conferred upon Drill Instructors. These individuals are often former military personnel and are empowered to exact summary punishment for disciplinary infractions. Correctional authorities maintain that these forms of punishment are legal and not subject to due-process protection because SI is a "voluntary" program. Newspaper accounts often provide descriptions of summary punishments such as the performing of extra exercises, or, reminiscent of early penal practices, moving a large pile of rocks from one location to another (Yen 1989: C1). Techniques aimed at degrading or humiliating offenders, such as forcing inmates to shoulder a large log during drill (Martin 1988: C3), to carry an unfinished lunch in their pocket (Ross 1990: 7), or to partake in a mock marriage when caught fighting (Yen 1989: C1), are also recounted.

Another disciplinary practice stressed in media portrayals of SI is one which has existed since the earliest forms of incarceration: the importance of work. Inmates are continually portrayed cleaning their barracks or the surrounding compound, typically in the most time consuming and tedious manner possible. Outside of the institution, offenders are presented undertaking taxing forms of manual labour including digging ditches by hand (*Journal* 1989; Parent, 1989: 24), clearing brush, or breaking rocks (Dillin 1989: 7). The emphasis on work in SI is often contrasted with prison where offenders in the general population are displayed sitting idle in their cell or sleeping during the day (Innovations; Zagaroli 1990: 1B). The Correctional Commissioner for New York State in a *New York Times* report asserted that Shock Incarceration provides offenders with "an alternative to spending the day in idleness, watching TV or lying in their bunks" (Barron 1990: B2).

The existence of work programs in penitentiaries dates back to the earliest days of· contemporary incarceration (Foucault 1965; Ignatieff 1978; Rothman 1980). As Rusche and Kirchheimer (1939) argue in their classic work, *Punishment and Social Structure*, one of the principal functions of the penitentiary is to instil the work ethic into offenders. This process is manifest in shock programming. While vocational training is limited in SI programs (Parent 1989: 28), inmates are employed at a variety of manual tasks, as outlined above, fashioned around teaching them the importance of labour. The entire Oklahoma SI regime is designed to instil positive work habits in offenders (Oklahoma RID unit plan), while the Mississippi shock program has a list of "12 commandments" for inmates, one of which proclaims that manual labour is "inherently beneficial" (RID handbook: [Mississippi]). The media has been quick to highlight the importance of labour in SI. For example, the reporting in the *Christian Science Monitor* outlined the concerns of one correctional officer who was distressed that these inmates constitute the next labour market (Dillin 1989: 7).

Narratives on labour, summary punishment, discipline, and psychological berating provide insight into another cultural aspect emphasised by the media: the notion that offenders can be changed. In most programs, however, change in the offender is not anticipated to result from psychological counselling; rather, the military discipline and the harsh routine are understood to be integral catalysts for personal development. This is based on the presumption that youthful offenders are malleable. This is evident in the fact that one justification for not accepting offenders·over 40 years of age in the Louisiana program is because "most forty-year-olds are not sufficiently "unformed" for 180 days to make a great or lasting difference" (IMPACT handbook [Louisiana]).

In order to effectively convert offenders "into disciplined, authority-respecting men" (Raspberry 1987: H21), the media presents offenders as requiring the "stripping away" of their former personalities (Milloy 1988: C3). The discipline, hard work and summary punishment of SI are all aspects of this "stripping away" process. Staff psychologist A. Strong provides insight into these presumptions when he outlined in the *Washington Post* that inmates:

> Come to us as a vessel all filled up. We have to dump them out and fill them back up. All the yelling, screaming and humiliation is an effort to dump out all the negativity, the past patterns, the defence mechanisms (Yen 1989: C1).

Discussion

In summary, both the print and television media have dwelled upon specific aspects of SI. The punitive and work-related characteristics of SI programs are recurringly stressed. In addition, throughout the media reports, the emphasis is on disciplining offenders, providing the hope that the punitive and disciplinary aspects will combine to produce positive changes in individual inmates. Garland's notion of a "privatization" of punishment significantly overlooks the power of the media to bring depictions of punishment to people's living rooms and kitchen tables. Far from shocking sensibilities, it appears that through the linking of punishment with dominant cultural themes and shared cultural experience, punishments that in other social settings would morally offend are able to be efficiently packaged, sold, and accepted. However, there is more occurring in these reports than is apparent from a cursory reading.

The representations offered do not mirror reality but tell a story about the nature of deviance and the wider society. By selectively focussing on certain aspects of SI, while neglecting other potentially significant considerations, the media provides an unwritten moral sub-text. The emphasis on punishment not only describes the punishments being administered but also implicitly states that punishment is valid and necessary. If, as has been argued, one of the main impetuses for the development of SI was the desire to save tax dollars, one option neglected in the press is the placement of offenders, selected for SI, on parole or releasing them outright. While this may seem a fanciful suggestion, it should be remembered that elaborate screening mechanisms exist in many states to ensure suitable candidates for SI and that the majority of SI offenders are incarcerated for their first felony offence (MacKenzie and Shaw 1990: 128). Coincidentally, many of these criteria are those that would also indicate a low likelihood of recidivism. The focus on the nature and quantity of SI punishment in the media excludes such options from popular debate and consideration.

Such a selective analysis is also apparent in the media emphasis on discipline in SI. The significance of discipline in military institutions is that it is exacted by, and demands submission to, a higher authority. Throughout media portrayals of SI, inmates have no choice but to defer to the authority of Drill Instructors and correctional officials. Ultimately the discipline and deference to authority is expected to re-emerge in a respect for American values. As W. Bennett, one of the chief proponents of SI, has said of shock inmates' "attention to rituals like saluting the flag...will instil badly needed self-discipline in young-offenders" (Turque et al. 1989: 42).

The emphasis on a blind resignation to "superiors" also overlooks the desirability of having individuals so disciplined that they require directives or commands in order to conduct their daily affairs. This has proven to be a problem for the military establishment, particularly as it relates to officers who theoretically are groomed to be commanders:

> The central, ironic paradox of Academy life is that the institution attempts to build leaders by denying them room for individual choice, thought and initiative.... Under the present system, the most efficiently socialized cadets are also the dullest, the least independent, critical and creative—and the most addicted to a regulations book approach to life [Cadet Donald D. Cantlay 1971] (Ellis and Moore 1974: 93).

Another theme underlying the representations of SI in the media is the notion of individual pathologies leading to crime. This notion is apparent in the continued portrayals of inmates having the "work ethic" instilled in them through demanding physical labour. The cause of crime is attributed to the lack of a personal quality which presumedly exists in individuals who do not commit crimes. Structural considerations such as racial and economic inequities are ignored, or are presented as obstacles able to be overcome through hard work and self-discipline. The neglect of these structural variables serves to marginalize debate on issues concerning the nature of the contemporary labour market which has little demand for unskilled labour, and the fact that inmates may have little opportunity to exercise their newly acquired work ethic in depressed economic circumstances. Some stories portray SI graduates forsaking selling drugs for up to $3,000 a day in favour of a construction job paying $32 a day (Yen 1989: C1; *Journal*, 1989). These stories ignore the fact that the lack of economic opportunities for marginalized segments of society will ensure a steady flow of youths willing to occupy vacated positions in the drug trade.

The lack of consideration of structural variables and the accentuation of individual manifestations of crime are also apparent in the manner in which the media portrays offenders as malleable, capable of being "re-formed." By exhibiting discipline and hard work as therapeutic, punishment is effectively transformed into treatment. Offenders characterized as needing "re-form" also have a reassuring quality for the reader or viewer; criminals are shown to be somehow "different" from the rest of society and the intervention of criminal justice personnel preserves the possibility of a quick fix to crime. This process of focussing on the individual while neglecting structural considerations is summarized neatly by Gusfield:

> Such modern myths serve to symbolize complex events, as ways to understand social problems in personal terms. As such they redirect attention from structural and instrumental aspects and support a theory of social behaviour, and the policies related to it, that sees social policy as geared to remake the person (1989: 434).

Shock Incarceration can therefore be seen as operating simultaneously on at least three different levels: the personal, the political and the public. For individuals in SI programs, the opportunity of trading a more lengthy punishment for a shorter period of incarceration would seem to be an appealing option. Despite the media emphasis on the punitive aspects of SI, the possibility may also exist for personal benefit as new SI units, like that in New York, encourage counselling and educational upgrading. At the political level, the linking of increased punishment to the military institution which has positive personal connections for many Americans, has enabled politicians to appear to be "cracking down on crime" while simultaneously administering a restricted budget.

Public perceptions of SI are largely drawn from mainstream media representations of boot camp programs. The media are able to bring the punishment of Shock Incarceration into individual's homes and emphasise the dominant themes of hard work, discipline, and personal change. The knowledge that is presented, however, is limited by the manner in which the media define some stories and topics as acceptable or "newsworthy." At the same time, a moral sub-text is provided which distinguishes criminals from the rest of the population as individuals deserving of punishment or lacking in some personal attribute which can be changed through disciplinary intervention. By highlighting certain aspects of SI and neglecting other potentially important issues, the media serve to limit how crime, punishment and society are perceived. Structural issues are outside of the focus of media representations and their absence supports and helps to create the conception that crime is fundamentally an individual problem.

References

Barron, James. 1990. "Boot-Camp Jail to Begin in Fall at Rikers Island," *New York Times*, August 02, B2.

Blumstein, Alfred. 1984. "Planning for Future Prison Needs," *University of Illinois Law Review*, No. 2: 207-230.

Caldas, Stephen. 1990. "Intensive Incarceration Programs Offer Hope of Rehabilitation to a Fortunate Few: Orleans Parish Prison Does an 'About Face,'" *International Journal of Offender Therapy and Comparative Criminology*, 34, 67-75.

Dillin, John. 1989. "Hardship, Help for Drug Dealers," *Christian Science Monitor*, November 10, 7.

Dyer, Gwynne. *War*. New York: Crown, 1985.

Ellis, Joseph and Robert Moore. *School for Soldiers: West Point and the Profession of Arms*. Oxford: New York, 1974.

Ericson, Richard V., Patricia M. Baranek and Janet B.L. Chan. *Visualizing Deviance: A Study of News Organization*. Toronto: University of Toronto Press, 1987.

Foucault, Michel. *Madness and Civilization*. New York: Vintage, 1965.

———. *Discipline and Punish*. New York: Vintage 1977.

Garland, David. *Punishment and Modern Society: A Study in Social Theory*. Oxford: Oxford University Press, 1990.

Gusfield, John. 1989. "Constructing the Ownership of Social Problems: Fun and Profit in the Welfare State," *Social Problems*, 36, 431-439.

———. *The Culture of Public Problems*. Chicago: University Press, 1981.

Ignatieff, Michael. *A Just Measure of Pain: The Penitentiary in the Industrial Revolution 1750-1850*. New York: Pantheon, 1978.

Innovations. Georgia Department of Corrections, (video), 1985.

Journal. "Boot Camp," CBC News Broadcast, April 11, 1989.

Koneazny, Peter M. and Karl D. Schwartz. 1984. "Preface," *New York University Review of Law & Social Change: The Prison Overcrowding Crisis*, 12, 1-3.

Louisiana Department of Public Safety and Corrections *IMPACT handbook*

MacKenzie, Dorris L. 1990. "Boot Camp Prisons: Components, Evaluations and Empirical Issues," *Federal Probation*, 54, Sept., 44-52.

MacKenzie, Dorris L. and James W. Shaw. 1990. "Inmate Adjustment and Change During Shock Incarceration: The Impact of Correctional Boot Camp Programs," *Justice Quarterly*, 17, 125-146.

MacKenzie, Dorris L., James W. Shaw and Voncile B. Gowdy. *An Evaluation of Shock Incarceration in Louisiana*. Unpublished Manuscript, Final Report to the National Institute of Justice, Washington, D.C., 1990.

Martin, Douglas. 1988. "New York Tests a Boot Camp for Inmates," *New York Times*, March 4, B1.

Mississippi Department of Corrections Handbook: *Regimented Inmate Discipline* 1990.

Milloy, Courtland. 1988. "Louisiana's Correctional Boot Camp," *Washington Post*, December 27, C3.

Morash, Merry and Lila Rucker. 1990. "A Critical Look at the Idea of Boot Camp as a Correctional Reform," *Crime and Delinquency*, 26, 204-218.

Oklahoma *Unit Plan* Regimented Inmate Discipline, 1989.

Parent, Dale. *Shock Incarceration: An Overview of Existing Programs.* National Institute of Justice, U.S. Department of Justice, 1989.

Pitts, John. *The Politics of Juvenile Crime.* London: Sage, 1988.

Raspberry, William. 1987. "Boot Camp—In Prison," (editorial), *Washington Post*, March 21, H21.

Ross, Elizabeth. 1990. "At this Camp, It's Shape Up or Ship Out," *Christian Science Monitor*, July 24, 7.

Rothman, David. *Conscience and Convenience: The Asylum and Its Alternatives in Progressive America.* Boston: Little, Brown, 1980.

Rusche, Georg and Otto Kirchheimer. *Punishment and Social Structure.* New York: Columbia University Press, 1939.

Sechrest, Dale. 1989. "Prison 'Boot Camps' Do Not Measure Up," *Federal Probation*, 53 September, 15-20.

Shen, Fern. 1990. "Md.'s 1st 'Boot Camp' Gives Inmates a Taste of Military Discipline," *Washington Post*, August 07, B1.

Smith, Beverly. 1988. "Military Training at New York's Elmira Reformatory, 1888-1920," *Federal Probation*, 52, 33-40.

Stewart, James K. "Foreword," in Dale Parent, *Shock Incarceration: An Overview of Existing Programs.* National Institute of Justice, U.S. Department of Justice, 1989.

Turque, Bill, David Gonzalez and Frank Washington. 1989. "Experiments in Boot Camp," *Newsweek*, May 22, 42.

Welborn, Jack. 1989. "A Senator Speaks: Boot Camps Work in Michigan," *Corrections Today*, 51, 136.

World Defence Forces 1989. 2nd ed. Rose Schumacher ed., Santa Barbara: ABC-CLIO, 1989.

Yarmolinsky, Adam and Gregory Foster. *Paradoxes of Power: The Military Establishment in the Eighties.* Bloomington: Indiana University Press, 1983.

Yen, Marianne. 1989. "Shock Camp: Pride & Punishment," *Washington Post*, September 02, C1.

Zagaroli, Lisa. 1990. "U.S. Lawmaker Told of Boot Camp Successes," *Lansing State Journal*, [Illinois] January 30, 1B.

Chapter 14

Technology and Control: Generic Trends

Kevin McCormick and Livy Visano

Conceptual Overview

Throughout history, the creation and implementation of a technology has established a power dynamic between the device and those who attempt to harness its potential to liberate themselves from a litany of tedious tasks. From the introduction of papyrus in ancient Egypt, to the current proliferation of devices of global communication, technology has enacted itself directly upon the very nature of human existence. This phenomenon imposes frames of reference and articulation around the experiences of the those individuals who attempt to utilize the alleged emancipatory abilities of the device. Technology designates for the users the mechanical, linguistical and conceptual parameters in which they must develop and execute strategies of social interaction and articulation. It is the "power" which the device has over the user:

> ...that reaches into the very grain of the individual, inserting itself directly into their actions, attitudes, discourses, learning processes and everyday lives (Foucault, 1986: 39).

The disproportionate power dynamic between apparatus and user, mediates and defines human experiences within a technologically generated and perpetuated structure, a relationship which forces the user to unconditionally submit to the language and definitions which the device imposes. As a consequence of this technological intrusion, the user becomes a "servomechanism of the apparatus, substituting a language of codes of processed information for 'natural experience'" (McLuhan, 1964), which is internalized by the individual in order to successfully utilize the device. In internalizing the apparatus the user does not extend his/herself technologically, but rather the device internalizes the individual, becoming "an electronic extension of their central nervous system" (McLuhan, 1964). This technologically consuming relationship establishes a disproportionate power dynamic between the device and the user, where the apparatus becomes an electronic calculus by which to construct and de-construct individual and collective social realities. While any technology possesses manifest functions, such as increased speed, the latent repercussions of its social introduction are far more impacting upon the societal structure into which the device is introduced. In liberating the user from manual tasks, the individual must submit to the operational constraints which the apparatus imposes on them, structures which in turn imprison the user in "technological barriers." Thus, when examining the affiliation between any technology and its users, one must comprehend the asymmetric power relationship which exists and how this imbalance articulates social experiences through a technologically imposed and perpetuated set of languages and definitions. While these technological power differentials are evident in all facets of corrections, their effects become problematic as they impact directly on the process of social control. The process by which individuals become imprisoned in "technological barriers" and internalize their unique lexicons as methods of social articulation and definition, has long been overlooked in penological inquiries. While aiding the control function, technology transcends the "convenience function," imposing on the state agent an electronic conceptual framework through which to explore diverse social environments. For the most part, bureaucratic workers utilizing external devices in social control have disregarded their manipulative tendencies. Instead, they attribute any negative impact as a "small cost, for using such a powerful device." What is completely ignored in avoiding the negative impacts of a technology's implementation in social control is that by utilizing the device the user suspends his/her own language and definitions, submitting both their personal experiences and methodology to the seductive power offered by the specific device.

Various perspectives have been advanced in appreciating the role of technology. For example, "technological somnambulism" maintains that the computer is consciously manipulated as a tool for a specific function. Opposing this insidious manipulation technological deterministic perspective, has emerged which finds that technology is a powerful and autonomous agent that dictates in some detail the patterns of human, social and cultural life (Pfaffenberger, 1988: 14). "Technological determinists" argue that any apparatus sets upon its users agendas, definitions and lexicons, which in turn mediate and articulate their experiences, as well as those feelings captured within the data.

In an attempt to merge these two distinct perspectives, theorists such as Marshal McLuhan advocated a humanist study of the effects of technologies. McLuhan (1964) in this "technological humanist" perspective realized that an apparatus imposed itself upon the user and that this could result in an "internalization of the technology" (McLuhan, 1964). Nevertheless he found great liberating potential in the relationships between user and electronic device. Highlighting the positive aspects of this relationship, "McLuhan's project was to break the spell cast upon the human mind by electronic technologies—which operate in the language of seduction and power" (Kroker 1984: 54). By understanding the ways in which technologies dominate the user, individuals could develop successful strategies with which they could avail themselves of the emancipatory abilities of the technology. Once conscious of the "seductive language" of the computer, the user could utilize it without becoming imprisoned within its technologically imposed structures. While the "humanist" perspective would appear as the most valuable method by which to utilize computers without becoming consumed in the electronic experience, "technological somnambulism" (Winner, 1986: 5) remains dominant. To recognize the manipulative tendencies is to admit that the user has lost control of his/her work and becomes a "servomechanism of the apparatus" (McLuhan 1964: 16). The infatuation with computers has mesmerized the users into believing that qualities such as "speed, accuracy and convenience," are desirable attributes.

II — Technology and the Routine Work of Control: Transforming the Self

Presently, the introduction of such technologies into penology is observed as establishing a new mode of communication, a structure of social presentation and expectation far detached from the framework utilized in "face to face" and aural encounters. With interaction occurring in the physical presence of others, "performance cues" such as physical and aural gestures, are visible extensions of the individuals' perceptions of their audience's expectations. However, the introduction of electronic devices such as the computer, have shifted the techniques employed in the presentation of self, creating expectational structures premised on electronic criteria, rather than personally intimate signs. In presenting a role electronically, technology grants them the ability to communicate orally, indifferent to physical and geographical impediments to successful social interaction. While this relationship with a device may be seen to liberate an individual electronically, its latent effects radically alter the extent to which individuals interact within diverse technologically generated environments. Established is a new technologically constructed stage, upon which the examination of social interaction enters a new dimension, in which expectational structures and performance techniques assume an electronic articulation. Meyrowitz (1985: 16) suggests that these "media are not simply channels for conveying information between two or more environments, but are "cultural environments" in and of themselves." Individuals in these encounters are mediated as in any other social circumstance, by the language, social practices and obligations unique to any culture or social performance. In examining technologies, we note that their effects upon individuals are far greater than the increased convenience levels of the users. Rather, technologies have established a dynamic medium of communication and technological culture, in which an individual's ability to manipulate their presence is arbitrated by the specific characteristics of the device utilized. This in turn, establishes the foundation upon which the articulation of social self, may begin to be explored as a technological extension of the traditional perspectives of societal presentation.

Current research into the impact which a technology has upon social interaction, finds its origins in "the old "hypodermic needle theory," popular in the 1920s, which postulated a direct and universal response to a message stimulus" (Meyrowitz, 1985: 15). This perspective observed that there was a direct and calculable relationship between the device and the individual using it, based on the scientific model of stimulus and response. Any individual using a certain technology would be expected to receive the same stimulus from the interaction, a response which then could easily be generalized and applied generically to all others using a similar device. Perspectives such as the "hypodermic needle," overlooked that in the relationship between technology and society, one must realize that there is a distinct dichotomy between the manifest and latent social repercussions of the device's social introduction. While a computer may be observed as stimulating the individual by increasing their levels of communication, "there is a general tendency for scholars and researchers, to ignore or even deny the effects of invisible environments and the latent effects of technologies, simply because they are invisible" (Meyrowitz, 1985: 20). In an attempt to explore these "invisible environments," medium theorists "argued that the form in which people communicate has an impact beyond the mere choice of specific messages" (Meyrowitz, 1985: 20). This perspective stated that technologies are selected by users for reasons beyond the successful reception of a message, in that a device such as the computer is selected by individuals who desire alternative media of social presentation. Medium theorists attempted to address the effects which a device had upon social interaction, but considerations with respect to class and the ability to afford the technology were neglected, ignoring that only those with certain levels of financial resources would be able to present themselves via electronic media such as computers. Further, the specific electronic capabilities of a technology highlights the unique social make-up of its users, where only those with a degree of computer literacy would be able to physically manipulate a computer and would be aware of the language and social nuances of the "invisible electronic environment." While medium theorists began to expand the frameworks for examining technological communication, they were criticized, for it was noted that "missing from it, was any real attempt to link an analysis of media characteristics with the structure and dynamics of everyday social interaction" (Meyrowitz, 1985: 24). Given this weakness, researchers sought out other paradigms, through which technological interaction could be examined not as a static occurrence, but as part of the dynamic process of social interaction occurring upon electronic stages of social performance.

The theoretical perspective currently being used to examine the technological dynamic between computer users and the physical devices which they utilize, is the interactionist approach. Both McLuhan and Meyrowitz argue that the technological presentations of self occurring in electronic environments are not mutually exclusive from face to face interactions and in fact utilize many of the same techniques as those employed in more physically intimate encounters. In his work, Goffman (1959) constructs a "dramaturgical" paradigm for the study of interaction, drawing a theatrical analogy between the ways in which actors manipulate their staged roles, in an attempt to present a performance commensurate with the expectations of their audience and the fashions by which individuals construct roles within their daily lives. While an actor plays to an audience and receives applause for a successful performance, an individual in day to day encounters must also play to the expectations of their respective audiences receiving not applause, but acceptance within the respective social circumstance. He notes that "when an individual enters the presence of others, they seek to acquire information about them or to bring into play information about them already possessed" (Goffman, 1959: 27), expectations which are generated within a specific social context. In doing this, the individual becomes an "actor, implicitly requesting his/her observers to take seriously the impression that is fostered before them" (Goffman, 1959: 18), a social articulation of self which is mediated by two often adversarial social stances, those being the intent of the performance and its reception within the audience's system of expectations. While the performer possesses his/her own personal agenda, the audience to which they are presenting also has certain expectations of the presentation and only if the actions of the actor are consistent with the audiences anticipations, will the performer's agendas of "self interest or personal gain" (Goffman, 1959: 18) be realized. While this metaphor appears simplistic, in that all an individual has to do to succeed socially is merely perform for an audience, the scenario becomes complex when we begin to more closely examine the processes of social interaction and find that an actor is playing many roles simultaneously, that of performer and audience, conflicting roles existing within conflicting expectational structures. Thus, just as an actor has the difficulty of not being able to please everyone in the audience, an individual engaged in social performance can never completely satisfy or appease the personal expectational structures of all those individuals who comprise the countless audiences before which they present varying depictions of their self.

In exploring the various ways in which individuals manipulate their presence in order to achieve a successful social performance, Goffman engages a theatrical analogy, upon which he constructs a "dramaturgical" model of social interaction. This interactionist perspective views that an individual in any social setting exists within two physical areas of performance, the stage before the scrutinizing eye of the audience and that area behind the curtain, away from the audience's ability to observe any scenario of the performance. The first area is called the "'front region,' which refers to all the activity of an individual which occurs during a period marked by his/her continuous presence before a particular set of observers and which has some influence on these observers" (Goffman, 1959: 22), the socially constructed stage upon which the "performance" transpires. In this region the actor's presence must be consciously manipulated and directed, with a clear understanding of the audience's specific expectations of what constitutes a successful performance. Contrasting this public area, is the "back region" (Goffman, 1959: 28), the setting where the individual rehearses and prepares their performance, protected by a socially constructed curtain, away from the scrutiny of the audience. While these two performance areas are defined and bounded by physical and social barriers of perception or "curtains," in electronic interaction the performance stages are not as mutually exclusive. In dramaturgical interaction, Goffman noted that the individual is playing many roles simultaneously, in that while an individual is presenting one performance in the "front region," they are also simultaneously preparing other performances in various "back regions." Therefore, areas of performances must be considered as overlapping concentric circles and in the area where these two regions converge, the performance becomes convoluted, which may result in an unsuccessful social presentation.

In attempting to balance diverse expectations and personal agendas with the spectre of a failed presentation, the social actor must employ "dramaturgical techniques" according to Goffman, in order to negate any possibility of a failed performance. In attempting to present a successful performance, the social actors reinforce their performance with "'dramatic realization,' where in the presence of others they typically infuse their activity with signs which dramatically highlight and portray confirmatory facts about their role that might otherwise remain unapparent or obscure" (Goffman, 1959: 30) within the limited scope of the performance. Further, the social actor will attempt to "idealize" their performance, in that they "will incorporate and exemplify in their presentation, the officially accredited values of the society," (Goffman, 1959: 35), so that the audience observes the performance as within acceptable expectational structures. By utilizing the process of "idealization," the performance attempts to be presented in an "expected form," which aids in concealing to an extent, the personal agenda of the actor. To further control the social construction of their presence, the actor can "mystify their audiences, accentuating certain matters and concealing others" (Goffman, 1959: 68), distancing the audience by the "realization" or "mystification" of the intended message of the performance. Also, individuals engaged in performance may get together with others possessing similar agendas and present as a "team" (Goffman, 1959: 79), utilizing the dynamics of a group to present a favourable image. In both individual and "team" presentations the actor(s) manipulates his/her regions of performance, in an attempt to construct physical and temporal barriers around their performance, which limits their audience's ability to observe aspects of the performance which contradict the intended message. These dramaturgical devices are attempts to avoid a failed presentation, which occurs when an audience "accepts signs of performance as evidence of something greater than or different from the sign-vehicles themselves" (Goffman, 1959: 58). In that "sign-vehicles" are not presented properly and subsequently perceived by the audience as signifying something completely different from original intention of the performer. Thus, Goffman observes in face to face encounters the construction of the social self as possessing similar techniques of presentation as those employed by theatrical actors, who perform within the constraints imposed by the expectations of their audience.

In the dramaturgical perspective, social interaction is examined within physically intimate social circumstances, but it ignores the presentation of self which is constructed not upon physically intimate settings, but rather is achieved through diverse technological media. "While Goffman's model of 'back and front region' behaviour describes a static set of stages and is limited to face to face interaction, the principles implicit in it can be adapted to describe the changes in situations and behaviours brought about by a new media" (Meyrowitz, 1985: 46), as with the case of the computer. In contrasting the interaction occurring in physically intimate encounters with those observed in electronic interactions, a new social structure is highlighted, technological in nature, sharing similar roles and expectations traditionally attributed to face to face encounters. With electronic interaction, the actor via a technology performs in a similar fashion to his/her audience, as does the personally intimate actor. In negotiating this role with their audience, the actors utilize dramaturgical techniques which are not physically demonstrated, but highlighted through electronic impulses. These technologically mediated roles are framed within the appropriate cultural etiquette and language of the technological culture, performed not with a face to face encounter, but rather upon a electronically erected stage of social performance. It is this shift in focus which has led researchers in the study of technology and society to expand the interactionist paradigm, to include social interaction which is directly mediated by an electronic media.

While personal computer networks are a relatively new occurrence, the use of electronic bulletin boards has been prevalent since the first computer, with the use of internal electronic memo systems, such as the "E-Mail" program. This program was the forerunner to current "Echo Mailing" systems used by bulletin boards, used predominantly by large corporations and educational institutions to facilitate quick inter-office communication. Their basic functions were to act as a mainframe message posting base, where employees could send instantaneous memos, which expedited time and saved the financial costs incurred with conventional mailing systems. From its initial use, the increase in the number of larger systems, "mainframes," established complex electronic mail procedures, through which private messages could be sent to individuals within the institutional scope of the computer network. This communicative force was powerful, because it enabled all within the electronic network to be linked electronically, irrespective of financial and physical barriers. Instantaneous written communication and interaction had begun, "liberating" (Heise, 1981) the individual from traditional impediments to communication. While the computer had transcended geographical boundaries, the scope of interaction is now bounded institutionally.

Technology designates for the users the mechanical, linguistical and conceptual parameters in which they must develop and execute strategies of social interaction and articulation. As a result of this electronic relationship between the computer and the user a disproportionate power dynamic is initiated, which forces both the experiences of those being examined and the methodologies employed to be articulated within a technologically imposed structure. As a result the world of corrections is forced into a structure of electronic lexicons and definitions which express human experiences far differently from more traditionally employed investigative techniques. In submitting to these electronically constructed assumptions and definitions, corrections reduces human experiences to easily manipulatable units of analysis, a technological reduction which ignores in many instances the richness contained within diverse experiences.

III — Penal Prospects and Paradoxes

Throughout the 1980s, there have been radical transformations in the technical infrastructure of corrections. A rapid infusion of computational modalities oriented towards co-ordinated information systems, integrated data bases, immediate retrieval strategies, instant case analysis and human resources management, have had significant consequences on the nature of control. As the corrections bureaucracy strives to minimize uncertainty, discretionary practices of employees from correctional officers to parole supervisors have become increasingly subjected to closer scrutiny of distant administrative superiors thereby reducing discretionary activities that were once largely invisible. The decisions of parole officers, for example, are increasingly "based on reliable information" that is congruent with Case Management Manuals. Tasks are routinized with acceptable formats that can be easily reviewed by distant technocrats. For post suspension action, deferred decisions or recommendations are made by fax, notifying the National Parole Board of circumstances that are expected to be presented as brief formulations that satisfy the recipe-like formulae. Available information may be limited and critical details not clearly recorded especially in retrospective accounts. Irrespective of the ideological orientation of parole officials, decisions must be accountable to organizational criteria. The National Parole Board's Review Sheets are designed to homogenize if not minimize uncertainty of information requested. In the Ontario Region, for example, CSC has been involved in discussions with local police authorities regarding the establishment of a centralized Bail and Parole system interfaced with the Offender Management System and the Canadian Police Information Computer System to ensure the availability of up-to-date information on all offenders on conditional release. Efforts have been made to provide workers with laptop computers with access to mainframes, and facsimile machines for home use.

As identified earlier, in interaction with offenders, state officials employ a language that has become more distant, code information that fails to "capture" their experiences of dependent clients. This reliance on technology and its concomitant lexicon enhances the power of care/control delivery personnel, Technology conceals as much as it reveals the controlling mandate of the state.

Ideologically, the state justifies enhanced centralized technological strategies in terms of developing closer and supportive ties with the community, as an improvement of information-sharing, and surveillance.

In assessing the impact of technology on corrections, we concur with Franklin's assertion that prescriptive technologies are designs for compliance which is seen as "normal" and "necessary" (Franklin, 1990: 23). Moreover, as Franklin astutely concludes, technologies come with an enormous social mortgage;

> The mortgage means that we live in a culture of compliance, that we are ever more conditioned to accept orthodoxy as normal, and to accept that there is only one way of doing "it" (Franklin, 1990: 24).

References

Foucault, M. 1986. (Editor, C. Gordon) *Power/Knowledge*. New York: Pantheon.

Franklin, Ursula. 1990. *The Real World Of Technology*. Toronto: C.B.C. Enterprises.

Goffman, Erving. 1959. *The Presentation Of Self In Everyday Life*. New York: Doubleday Anchor Books.

Heise, David R. 1981. *Sociological Methods And Research* "Microcomputers And Social Research," Volume 9, 395-536.

Kroker, Arthur. 1984. *Technology And The Canadian Mind: Innis/McLuhan/Grant*. Montreal: New World Perspectives.

McLuhan, Marshall. 1969. *Counter Blast*. Toronto: McClelland and Stewart.

————. 1964. *Understanding Media: The Extensions Of Man*. New York: Mentor Books.

Meyrowitz, Joshua. 1985. *No Sense Of Place*. New York: Oxford University Press.

Pfaffenberger, Bryan. 1988. *Microcomputer Applications In Qualitative Research*. California, U.S.A.: Sage Publications Inc.

Winner, L. 1986. *The Whale And The Reactor*. Chicago: University of Chicago Press.

Chapter 15

Dare to Struggle...Political Prisoners and the Criminalization of Dissent in the United States: Insidious Implications for Canadians

Rick Lines

First of all, I think the use of RICO [Racketeer Influenced and Corrupt Organizations Laws] against the Puerto Ricans and then against us is basically an attempt to deny the fact that there are political prisoners, and ultimately that there is a need for political struggle in this country or in those areas which this country tries to dominate. The first aspect of criminalization is denying the justness of the struggle.[1] (Tom Manning, U.S. Political Prisoner)

They [the U.S. government] always tried to say that this was a criminal trial and that whole bit, but their treatment and actions towards us say something else. The repression, the psychological and physical torture that we suffer says everything to the contrary. Our treatment before the trial, during the trial, and during our incarceration is that of a political prisoner.[2] (Felix Rosa, Puerto Rican Independentista, Former Prisoner of War in the U.S.)

On December 19, 1991 the New York State Court of Appeals reversed a lower court decision of March 1990 vacating the conviction of Dhoruba bin-Wahad. Dhoruba, a former Field Secretary for the Black Panther Party in New York City, was arrested in 1971 for the attempted murder of two police officers and, after three trials, was convicted and sentenced to 25 years to life.

After serving over nineteen years in New York prisons, Dhoruba was finally released after his attorneys managed to obtain over 300,000 pages of government documents through the Freedom of Information Act. These documents detailed not only his own frame-up by the state, but also the extensive government and police covert operations designed to destroy the Black Liberation Movement. A key portion of the documents included the prior written statements of the main witness against Dhoruba, a witness who was held in police custody for over two years while the trials were going on. These statements completely contradicted the testimony which the witness had given in court. The fact that the prior testimony of the witness had been withheld by the prosecution was the basis upon which Justice Peter McQuillan vacated Dhoruba's conviction in 1990. This is the decision which was overturned by a narrow 4-3 margin by the Court of Appeals, effectively reinstating a twenty-year-old conviction for a crime which the government knows Dhoruba did not commit, and may again subject him to imprisonment. Says Robert Boyle, attorney for Dhoruba bin-Wahad:

> Although neither opinion, the majority nor the dissenting opinion, talked about Dhoruba's political involvement and how this [case] grew out of the era of the Black Panther Party, the majority's opinion was clearly a political one. They knew the nature of the case before them. They knew the consequences of it. Basically what they're saying is that if the prosecution does a good enough job of hiding evidence, and you only find out about it after your direct appeal has been decided, we're going to reward the prosecution by making it difficult for those individuals to get new trials. And where do they intentionally withhold evidence? They withhold evidence in those cases of a political nature, where there's more of an effort to get a conviction and to get a conviction against a particular person than there is in seeking any kind of justice. So it really gives a licence to the prosecution to engage in this kind of misconduct.[3]

Since his release, Dhoruba has travelled across North America and the world raising public awareness of the existence of the over 200 political prisoners and prisoners of war currently incarcerated in U.S. prisons and jails. These prisoners represent a broad cross-section of the various opposition movements and liberation struggles going on within the U.S. These activists are women and men from the Black Liberation Movement, the Puerto Rican Independence Movement, the American Indian Movement, and white anti-imperialists and nuclear disarmament protesters. Like Dhoruba, many are imprisoned on fabricated charges inspired by covert government operations aimed at destroying radical movements within the United States. People such as American Indian Movement leader Leonard Peltier and former Black Panther Party members Mumia Abu-Jamal, Herman Bell, Albert "Nuh" Washington, and Anthony Bottom have all been in prison for well over a decade, all framed for killing police officers in cases where the state fabricated prosecution evidence while withholding vital defence evidence. Still others are convicted of armed acts of political protest and self-defence for which, because of the political nature of the actions, they are serving inordinately long sentences under the most restrictive of conditions.

One thing they all share in common is having the full weight of state power directed against them for their political actions and associations. In their cases, we can see the U.S. government's counterinsurgency strategy manifested not only in overt and covert police attacks on the individuals and their political movements, but also through the manipulation of the judicial and the prison systems in order to further isolate and punish the political prisoners themselves and intimidate other activists. The decision in Dhoruba bin-Wahad's case, which overturned a long-standing legal precedent, is yet another example of the use of the courts (and perhaps again, in Dhoruba's case, the prisons) in this capacity. Says Robert Boyle:

> It's a very disturbing development not only for Dhoruba but for the other political prisoners in the United States. I think that one of the reasons why they issued this decision was that when Dhoruba was released in March of 1990 he became a spokesperson for the more than fifty Black political prisoners still in jail in the United States. He was living proof that they did frame-ups...and he was going around speaking about all of this. I don't think that went unnoticed by the people in power in this country. I think the reinstatement of his conviction is part of an attempt to really quell the movement to release the remaining political prisoners in the United States and also to re-silence him.[4]

While Dhoruba's case is certainly instructive, it is by no means unique in either a modern or historical context. Perhaps the most long-standing feature of U.S. government policy is the fear of domestic opposition. While supposed external threats and menaces have changed over time, as currently manifested in the movement away from global communism and towards global competitiveness as a public rationale for domestic and foreign policy decision-making, individuals and groups within the country who threaten the status quo have always been seen as enemies and subjected to intense repression.

This tradition dates back as far as first contact, when Europeans first came to this continent and began the systematic annihilation of the aboriginal populations of what are now North, Central, and South America and the Caribbean. In years past counterinsurgency and genocidal programs were used to continue the exploitation of African people who were brought to this continent to work as slaves. Likewise, there have been continuous assaults on working people who have tried to organize to protect themselves and promote their own interests, culminating in the murderous government attacks on trade unionists around the time of the First World War. Communists and socialists were similarly attacked by the state from the 1930s through the 1950s, effectively destroying their political organizing. During the 1960s and 1970s, the Black Liberation Movement, anti-war, and Native American movements were all subjected to intense political persecution by the government. During the 1980s, the state clamped down on Central American solidarity groups and people who opposed U.S. aggression against Nicaragua and El Salvador. Already in the 1990s, organized state repression has been exposed against the anti-Gulf War movement, environmental groups, and lesbian and gay activists and AIDS organizations. Attacks against the Puerto Rican Independence Movement have been constant throughout the twentieth century. Such is the history of political opposition in an "open society." Government attacks of this nature are certainly not restricted to the United States. Canada, while priding itself on being a more tolerant and well-mannered society than its often brutish neighbour to the south, has its own unflattering history of domestic repression. In fact, Canada has often revealed itself to be less hesitant than the U.S. to unleash the full weight of military power against militant political opposition. From the invocation of the War Measures Act in 1970 to the Oka Crisis in 1990, the Canadian government has certainly not conducted itself domestically with the same type of military moderation and compromise with which it likes to portray itself internationally. Canada has also not hesitated to use both the courts and the prisons as tools for quelling political opposition. As in the United States, racism has always been a significant factor in determining which groups are considered "dangerous" and are subjected to prosecution. In recent years, the Canadian government has focussed much of its wrath against the people of the First Nations who have organized to defend their territory against government and corporate encroachment. Whether its civil disobedience by the Innu people in Labrador or more militant armed defence against police attacks by the Peigan in Alberta or the Mohawks in Oka, governments at both the provincial and federal levels have acted quickly to prosecute and imprison Native activists. Yet while Canada certainly has a long record of domestic political repression, the history of the past twenty-five years of political struggles in the U.S. has provided that government with the opportunity to refine its counterinsurgency program to a much higher degree. Because of that level of sophistication, Canadian intelligence and police agencies look to their U.S. counterparts for leadership in domestic counterinsurgency strategies. Similarly, methods for isolating and repressing prisoners who are seen as being political leaders are shared on both sides of the border. Certainly the ideological framework used to justify these programs to the U.S. public are evident in Canada and in many ways are just as susceptible to manipulation. For these reasons, it is essential for activists in Canada to study and understand the U.S. situation, particularly as the two countries grow ever closer economically, legally and politically in pursuit of the "level playing field" promised by the Free Trade Agreement. Not only will this understanding contribute to building links between progressive and radical movements in both nations, but an awareness of the existence of political prisoners within the United States and the nature of the judicial and penal systems used to persecute them may lead to a broader recognition of the true obstacles facing opposition movements in supposedly democratic countries.

An essential point to note in the history of the repression faced by resistance movements in the U.S. is that these types of attacks were, for the most part, conducted legally. They were not perpetrated by a group of "loose cannons" operating without the knowledge of the political establishment. Nor were they the doings of a handful of paranoid politicians who, although overstepping their mandates, were only "doing what they thought was best for the country." Rather, this political persecution was carried out systematically with the backing of laws and court decisions which legalized these attacks. In effect, political organizing and protest were criminalized and dealt with as criminal matters.

This point is crucial because many people, including activists, continue to view the courts as places where "justice" can truly be served. While the government and the police are [correctly] scrutinized for their actions, somehow the judicial system is often spared the same critique. Although this is beginning to change somewhat with the realization that the Reagan/Bush administrations have appointed 70% of the federal court judges, there is still precious little recognition of the use of the courts and prisons themselves by the state as tools for counterinsurgency.

For this reason, this analysis will ignore, for the most part, the covert methods which have been used extensively against political opposition groups and activists. The most notable of these was the FBI's Counterintelligence Program (COINTELPRO), whose purpose was to "expose, disrupt, misdirect, discredit, or otherwise neutralize the activities...[the] leadership, spokesmen, membership, and supporters" of, among others, New Left, Puerto Rican Independence, and Black groups and organizations.[5] While these programs were approved by the White House, and therefore enjoyed a kind of "legal" authorization, this analysis will focus instead upon the use of the law, the courts, and the prisons themselves as counterinsurgency tools. This is in no way intended to minimize the scope and effectiveness of these covert programs, for they were and are used with deadly effectiveness, particularly against the Black Liberation Movement in general and the Black Panther Party in particular.[6] It is merely to focus upon a different arm of what is, in reality, the same overall program of repression.

Central to the propaganda framework in which the judicial and penal counterinsurgency systems operate is the notion of "criminality." One of the main ideological goals which the state has been pursuing for the past number of years is the broadening of the definition of "criminal activity" to encompass political activity. If this can be accomplished, it will provide the government with an almost limitless arsenal with which to prosecute and imprison any political activists deemed threatening to the interests of the state. This goal was articulated explicitly in 1969 by then U.S. Deputy Attorney General Richard Kleindienst.

> If [Students for a Democratic Society] or any group was organized on a national basis to subvert our society, then I think Congress should pass laws to suppress that activity. When you see an epidemic like this cropping up all over the country—the same kind of people saying the same kind of things—you begin to get the picture that this is a national subversive activity.... [SDS and other new left activists] should be rounded up and put in a detention camp.[7]

In the move towards criminalization, the courts fulfil essential functions. Operationally, they provide the arena and the mechanisms through which the prosecution operates. They also serve as political intelligence gathering tools, used to coerce testimony from activists themselves, and often their friends, families, and supporters. Ideologically, the courts are used to put a "civilized" face upon this repression. The society places its faith in the courts, in the "Rule of Law," and this faith is used to manipulate the opinions of not only the population as a whole, but even large segments of the left against whom this program is being directed. Through this process of criminalization, the state tries not only to isolate revolutionaries physically from their movements by imprisoning them for decades, but also to isolate and discredit any kind of radical political activity. Says Susan Rosenberg, a political prisoner currently serving a 58-year sentence in the federal women's prison in Marianna, Florida:

> I think that criminalization and isolation go hand in hand. It's a strategy that is part of the political repression that every government in power uses to say that its own radical base...has to be destroyed. And they have to be destroyed at what the government perceives as the root...by putting the rubric of criminal activity over us as "terrorists," which is the main form it has taken in the United States against the left in the 1980s.... I think the effect of that is to really try and isolate us and to intimidate anybody from seeing what commonality or common ground might exist between our actions and our politics and in fact what their own actions and politics are.[8]

Beginning in the late 1960s, the government embarked upon a program of legal manoeuvring designed to augment the successful extra-legal and covert operations of the FBI's Counterintelligence Program (COINTELPRO), as well as similar operations directed by the CIA and local police squads, against the radical movements of the era. The main purpose of this program was to use the courts as an offensive weapon against the movements in an effort to intimidate, tie-up, and bankrupt opposition leaders and organizations. The public manifestations of this campaign were a series of high publicity conspiracy prosecutions of selected opposition leaders, and the use of grand juries as instruments for intelligence gathering.

It should be noted that one of the results of the COINTELPRO-type activities by the various police agencies was the infiltration of informers and *agents provocateurs* into different movement organizations (a process which continues to this day). This infiltration was conducted on an unbelievable scale. Scott Camil, an organizer for Vietnam Veterans Against the War (VVAW) and a defendant in the Gainesville [Florida] 8 conspiracy trial remembers:

> I was so open that anybody could come to my house. And they just filled the place up with cops. There were over eleven government agencies in our organization. There was the Treasury Department, the Federal Bureau of Investigation, the Secret Service, the Florida Department of Law Enforcement, the Miami Police Department, the Dade County Metro Police Department, the Gainesville Police Department, the Alachua County Sheriff's Department, the New Orleans Police Department. At times more than half of those at our meetings were government agents. One Miami police informant said, "Darling, the spies were spying on the spies that were spying on the spies."[9]

With the high levels of infiltration of police operatives and paid informants into movement organizations, it was usually not difficult for the state to fabricate a conspiracy case, implicating movement leaders in conspiring to violate some law, and then have "witnesses" to back it up. [In fact, *agents provocateurs* within movement organizations were often used to encourage and promote activities which, if carried out, could form the basis of criminal prosecutions.] While such testimony would often be enough to bring the cases to court, the activists themselves were almost always acquitted. However, a conviction was just the icing on the cake as far as the government was concerned. The main reason for the prosecutions was to force the movements into a defensive posture, thereby neutralizing their organizing abilities.

Robert Justin Goldstein, in his book *Political Repression in Modern America*, notes:

The Nixon Administration instituted an extraordinary series of conspiracy trials against anti-war leaders—in fact, together with the [Dr. Benjamin] Spock-[William Sloane] Coffin trial of the Johnson administration, the Nixon administration prosecuted virtually every prominent anti-war leader. What was perhaps the most extraordinary thing about the prosecutions was that the major charges brought either all collapsed during the judicial process, or the cases were thrown out due to illegal government activities or refusal to disclose records of illegal wiretapping.... While the prosecutions failed in one sense...they succeeded sensationally in another. Namely, they succeeded in tying up huge amounts of time, money and energy that anti-war and radical movements could have used to expand rather than expend on protracted and costly defence struggles.[10]

Similar conspiracy cases were brought against the Black Panther Party. Perhaps the most notable of these was the Panther 21 trial in New York, in which Dhoruba bin-Wahad was a co-defendant. In 1969, the state of New York charged the entire New York BPP leadership with conspiracy to commit murder and arson and jailed them all on $100,000 bail each for the duration of the trial. This case is instructive in that the state charged the 21 with "conspiracy" to commit these acts rather than having physically committed them. Indeed, the prosecution never alleged that any acts of murder or arson had ever occurred. After a two-year trial, all the defendants were acquitted by the jury after less than two hours of deliberations.[11]

In 1970, the state also began to use the powers of the federal grand jury system as an instrument for harassing activists and gathering political intelligence. Says Michael Deutsch, a lawyer involved in defending Puerto Rican Independence activists in the U.S.:

...[the government] began to use a power we have here of a federal grand jury, which has the power to call people before it in secret session and ask people questions about their political movement, about their political activity, about their relationships with other people, and if they don't answer those questions they can actually send them to prison without charging them with any specific crime. And in the 70s we see the use of the federal grand jury to try and intimidate...activists, and many of them did go to jail, in fact, because they refused to give information and become informants.[12]

Because the witnesses called before the grand jury are given a form of immunity, they are compelled to answer every question asked of them or risk being charged with contempt and jailed indefinitely. In fact, activists have routinely been jailed for many months for refusing to co-operate with grand juries' investigations, including some defence attorneys who have been asked to inform on their own clients. Witnesses are also denied access to legal counsel during questioning. In political cases the government uses the grand jury more as a method for harassment, intimidation, and intelligence gathering than as a tool for specific prosecutions. Between 1970 and January 1973, grand juries probing opposition groups were convened in thirty-six states and eighty-four cities subpoenaing over one thousand people.[13] The use of the grand jury has proven itself a successful weapon in the domestic war on opposition movements and has been used during the last few years to investigate political activities ranging from the Armed Clandestine Movement to Central American solidarity groups.

With the inauguration of the Reagan/Bush Administration in 1981 came a renewed emphasis on domestic repression. It also began the manipulation of a new scourge which serves as the primary justification for political repression to this day. That scourge is "terrorism."

Terrorism actually made its debut as an important counterinsurgency rationale in 1972, immediately following the exposure of COINTELPRO and other similar programs which forced the FBI to publically announce the discontinuation of the operation. However, as has become abundantly clear in the intervening years, the FBI has merely continued identical operations under different names. The year 1972 is important because it marks the beginning of the use of the term "terrorist" to describe political activists in internal COINTELPRO-type FBI documents, rather than the previously used "agitator" or "key extremist."[14] Obviously, the decision had been made that while the government might suffer public disapproval for operations targeting political activity, the populace would be much more forgiving if the political activity could be carefully moulded into a violent threat. Armed with a new propaganda strategy, the FBI was able to continue and expand COINTELPRO-type activities, which were supposedly discontinued.

Despite the operational use of the term by police agencies in the middle to late 1970s, which enabled severe government attacks against the American Indian Movement, Black Liberation Movement and Puerto Rican Independence Movement, "terrorism" did not become a major public concern until the 1980s. Ronald Reagan came into office in 1981 declaring that the threat of international terrorism was going to be his government's overriding concern, replacing the Carter Administration's supposed concern for human rights, and the Reagan team began to play up terrorism as a main counterinsurgency strategy at home and abroad. These intentions were spelled out quite clearly in the New Right manifesto "Mandate for Leadership," prepared by the conservative think-tank, The Heritage Foundation. This document, upon which much of the first term agenda of the new government was based, states:

> Many of the current restrictions on internal security functions arose from legitimate but often poorly informed concerns for civil liberties of the citizen and the responsibility of the government. While these are legitimate concerns, *it is axiomatic that individual liberties are secondary to the requirements of national security and internal civil order;* without the latter, the former can never be secure. Moreover, much of the current legislation was adopted with little appreciation of the threat or the Modus Operandi of extremist, subversive, and violent groups[15] [emphasis mine].

Buoyed by a receptive and unsceptical media, the terrorism scare has been a major item on the national agenda ever since. Of particular concern was the threat of domestic terrorism, a threat which we see being used to harass political opposition as recently as the Gulf War.

To go into an extended examination of the manipulation of the "terrorist threat" by the U.S. is perhaps beyond the parameters of this paper. However, it is essential to cover a few basic facts both about the term itself, its relevance to political resistance in the U.S. context, and the judicial and penal penalties applied to those upon whom the label is thrust. Indeed, it is under the guise of the "terrorist threat" that the U.S. government has justified more and better armed police, more prisons, expanded use of the death penalty, and the manipulation of the legal system to criminalize political associations and to limit rights of due process.

"Terrorism," as it is commonly defined, denotes actions by political groupings (almost exclusively left-wing in application, as shall be demonstrated) to inflict violence upon a population in order to achieve the acceptance of a political goal. While this might be a common and acceptable definition to the population at large, it is not the way the definition is manipulated by the state. If we examine the acts of "violence" by clandestine left-wing groups in the U.S., we find that they are without exception directed against property rather than people. They are acts of armed propaganda; symbolic bombings of government, military, and corporate targets designed to draw public attention to U.S. violence against "Third World" nations, to corporate support for racist and fascist regimes, and to the manufacturers of the weapons of destruction. The single most important common denominator to these actions is that they caused no injuries, let alone deaths. The United Freedom Front (UFF), a revolutionary anti-imperialist organization to whom the U.S. government attributes eleven bombings or attempted bombings of corporate and military targets between December 1982 and September 1984, stated in their "Communique No. 6," which was distributed to the media, unions, workers groups, and community organizations,

> It is NOT the intention of the United Freedom Front to hurt any innocent civilians and workers and it has been our procedure, when applicable, to give sufficient warning for evacuation of buildings and to use other methods to minimize the chance of personal injury.[16] [emphasis in original]

This statement is supported by the fact that all UFF bombings, as well as those of the other clandestine anti-imperialist groups during the same period, occurred late at night when there would be few, if any, people in the buildings to be evacuated, and were preceded by warning calls. These actions were in no way meant to terrorize the U.S. population, except perhaps those elites occupying the seats of political and corporate power who have everything to lose from the awakening of public consciousness.

Despite what the government tries to imply, "terrorism" is not a neutral term applied equally to right-wing and left-wing actions. This is made quite clear by examining the FBI's own statistics on "terrorism." From 1984-1988, during Reagan's second term when the terrorism scare was still at its peak, FBI records show a total of 61 "terrorist" incidents in the United States. Of those, 35 incidents took place in Puerto Rico, where the independence movement is engaged in a national liberation struggle to end the U.S. colonial rule of the island, a struggle which is justified by International Law and cannot be defined as terrorism.[17] Of the remaining 26 incidents, half were by "Left-Wing Domestic" groups[18] and half were by various right wing elements (white supremacist, zionist, and anti-Castro Cuban).[19] The media coverage of the issue of domestic terrorism, and the way in which the government utilizes the label, certainly does not indicate that fully half of the officially acknowledged actions during this period were by elements of the right. Rather, we are given the impression that left-wing groups pose the threat, and they are therefore targeted for judicial and military counterinsurgency operations.

It is also important to note that the FBI, judging from these statistics, only considers crimes against government and corporate property to be "terroristic." There is no mention at all of the untold number of personal and property attacks against Jews, lesbians and gay men, and people of colour by white supremacist groups. Such acts of violence are truly terroristic in that they are designed to intimidate and terrify the communities, yet these attacks are ignored in the official statistics. In fact, even bombings of abortion clinics by right-wing elements are ignored in the FBI's statistics. As shall be explored later, the state's treatment of right-wing activists and white supremacists arrested for violent actions are wholly different than their treatment of elements of the left.

Despite the obvious disinformation "proving" the "terrorist threat," the fact remains that the issue has been successfully manipulated in such a way to become a credible justification for repressive social controls and counterinsurgency programs. A major focus of this social control is the use of "anti-terrorism" or "counter-terrorism" as a rationale for repressing dissident points of view and expanding the criminalization of opposition movements.

To further these ends, during the past ten years, the U.S. government has revived two old laws which have become the main "legal" tools to aid them in their program of judicial counterinsurgency. The first of these is the Seditious Conspiracy statute, which essentially bans opposition to the authority of the U.S. government by force. This law, which is more than 100 years old, was used to prosecute Industrial Workers of the World (IWW) leaders in the early part of the century. Since that time it has been used almost exclusively against Puerto Rican Independentistas, in the 1930s and 1950s, and then again in the 1970s and early 1980s.

As with many of the programs of judicial counterinsurgency, activists advocating the independence of Puerto Rico have been used to test the new applications of the laws. Independentistas were among the first to be attacked using the grand jury system in the early 1970s, and they were the only political activists subjected to seditious conspiracy prosecutions for more than fifty years (until the late-1980s when the government used the laws against white activists).

The seditious conspiracy law is essentially defined as "two or more people conspiring to oppose, by force, the government's authority or delay the execution of any law of the United States" [certainly an interesting charge to lay against Independentistas who are waging an anti-colonial struggle against U.S. occupation of their homeland]. The danger of this law for activists, both above ground and clandestine, and therefore its usefulness to the government, lies in its vagueness.

> ...seditious conspiracy is the only conspiracy statute which does not require an overt act by a member of the conspiracy, membership in an organization which agrees to use force to oppose U.S. [policies], without any act of violence or force taken in furtherance of the conspiracy, is enough for a conviction.[20]

Herein lies the danger of this law. It actually criminalizes *membership* in a political organization. The crime of sedition lies in the "conspiracy," or the agreement to oppose U.S. policies by force, rather than the act of doing so. It is effectively "thought crime." The state need only decide that a group's stated goals are "seditious" in order to be able to prosecute their leaders and members for seditious conspiracy. Says Michael Deutsch, a lawyer who has defended Independentistas in U.S. courts for twenty years,

> Essentially what the [Independentistas] were convicted of was being part of a conspiracy which was equated with being a member of a clandestine organization that was fighting for independence. But they [the state] didn't have to prove that this particular person did anything violent or used force. They just had to show that they agreed to be part of this organization. So you have a situation where you are really criminalizing membership in an organization and really making the membership itself the crime. In fact in [a] case in Chicago, the jury was instructed by the judge that if you believe the person was a part of this organization then you can convict them of seditious conspiracy, and that's really what they've done.[21]

After using the seditious conspiracy laws to prosecute and imprison a group of Independentistas in the early 1980s, the U.S. attempted to expand the use of conspiracy laws through the prosecution of a group of six white anti-imperialist activists in Washington, D.C. in the late 1980s.[22] Five of the six were already serving lengthy prison sentences stemming from convictions for such "crimes" as the possession of weapons and false identification, harbouring a fugitive, and liberating Black Liberation Army prisoner Assata Shakur. However, the government decided to try them, using conspiracy laws, for a series of bombings during the early 1980s, including the bombing of the U.S. Capitol Building in 1983 to protest the invasion of Grenada. The trial became known as the Resistance Conspiracy Case (RCC).

In a July 1988 statement from the RCC 6 defendants, they state:

> The charges are couched in a language that targets our politics and associations. The government makes no claim to know who actually did the bombings. The Reagan administration wants to stage a show trial that will...have a chilling effect on activists.[23]

In fact, not only did the government not claim to know who actually committed the bombings, but several of the defendants were actually in prison at the time when some of the bombings occurred. From the beginning of the case, it was obvious that the actual acts of constructing or delivering the bombs were irrelevant to the prosecution.

Here is where we can see the effectiveness, from the government's point of view, of conspiracy laws for attacking political opposition. Moving a step beyond the earlier cases of the Puerto Rican Independentistas, in which membership in an organization became the basis for conviction, in the RCC case the state sought to prosecute the activists for some sort of ideological solidarity or shared political objectives with the goals of the bombings. As Mary O'Melveny, one of the defence attorneys in the case, put it:

> The defendants' direct guilt or innocence...appears immaterial to the government, which has constructed an indictment to convict the six on charges of aiding and abetting and of "conspiracy to influence, change and protest practices of the United States...through the use of violent and illegal means."[24]

This kind of prosecution has obvious implications for political organizing, whether above ground or clandestine. As RCC 6 defendant Laura Whitehorn states, "Once anti-imperialist resistance is converted into 'terrorism,' it can be combatted with a wide variety of counter insurgency methods."[25]

The other major law which the state is using against political activists is the Racketeer Influenced and Corrupt Organizations Act (RICO). Again, this is an old law originally drafted to combat organized crime. It was created to enable the government to prosecute people for "crimes" resulting from what the state terms a "criminal enterprise." Conspiracy to take in this "criminal enterprise," whether or not there is evidence that a person has directly committed any of the specific alleged "crimes," is sufficient for conviction. As with the sedition law, RICO is conveniently vague enough to allow the government to prosecute just about anything.

During the 1980s, RICO laws were used to prosecute several major political cases. In the case of the OHIO 7, a group of seven white anti-imperialists who were tried under both seditious conspiracy and RICO laws, their prosecution stemmed from a series of bombings of U.S. corporate and military targets in the early 1980s.[26] These bombings were claimed by a clandestine group called the United Freedom Front (UFF). All of the seven were in prison at the time of the trial, having already been convicted of the UFF bombings, and several were serving sentences of over fifty years.

Having convicted them of the bombings themselves, the state also sought to convict them of conspiring to do the bombings. In the case of the OHIO 7, the use of the seditious conspiracy and RICO laws amounted to double jeopardy, that is being tried twice for the same crime. However the courts would not accept this argument, and, after two years of litigation, three of the activists were eventually tried and acquitted. However, the government has clearly demonstrated the direction they will take in future political cases. Says Tom Manning, a member of the OHIO 7:

The use of RICO against us, and originally against the Puerto Rican comrades, is a test. They used it successfully against the Puerto Ricans. They got convictions. They got big time. The next step, once you've used it successfully against people of colour, is to see if you can use it against white people. Basically, I think that's what their progression was. If they can successfully use it against us, this small group of white people being the OHIO 7, the next step would be to use it against people in above ground work. They can tailor it. All they've got to do is find two acts that have some kind of aspect to them that they can classify as "criminal." If they can find those two acts, then they can make a conspiracy out of any kind of organizing that you can imagine. Anywhere where you're putting out a message and an agenda, if they can attach two acts together that they can justify as "criminal" then they've got a RICO conspiracy.[27]

RICO laws were also used to prosecute Dr. Mutulu Shakur and Marilyn Buck, who were accused of being members of the Black Liberation Army, in the early 1980s. In a brief to the court filed by the defendants along with several other political prisoners, they stated:

The RICO statute has become a tool for criminalizing political movements that has enabled the government to define the New Afrikan Independence Movement as a criminal enterprise. Criminalizing the essentially political acts which are undeniably involved in the conflict between the New Afrikan Independence Movement/Black Liberation Struggle and the United States government such as riots, civil disorders, and rebellion, places the United States in violation of international law.[28]

Again it is important to emphasize that these laws are essential to the state not only as tools for prosecuting and imprisoning activists, but also for the labelling of their movements as "criminal." Defining revolutionary activities as being criminal enterprises facilitates the marginalization of these movements, as well as enabling the government to state that they have no political prisoners, only "criminals."

We can observe this process at work by the British during the past fifteen years as they have moved to criminalize the Republican struggle in the north of Ireland, and thereby attempt to strip any political legitimacy away from the movement. It was this strategy of criminalization by the British which prompted the well known blanket protest amongst Republican prisoners at Long Kesh, leading to the hungerstrike of 1980. If a government can convince the public that they are combatting a criminal organization rather than a political one, it provides them with an enlarged legal, military, and propaganda arsenal with which to attack the movement. This is the strategy which the United States government has been following for many years.

Political trials in the U.S. are also notable for the lengthy pre-trial imprisonment of defendants. This is accomplished through the use of the Preventive Detention Law, which is used to deny bail to defendants who are considered "dangerous." The extreme application of this law has again been justified through the manipulation of "terrorism" as a rationale. Says Michael Deutsch:

> The other aspect that's been used a lot against the Puerto Rican Independence Movement, whenever they do have a trial, is they've now used the Preventive Detention Law, which means you can be denied bail if you are considered dangerous. Well, if they believe that you're a member of a Puerto Rican Independence organization, that's per se almost a finding that you're dangerous. In [one] case, we had one of the people who was accused of being the leader of Los Macheteros [a clandestine Independence organization in Puerto Rico] who was in jail for four years awaiting trial without any conviction, just awaiting trial for four years because he was accused of being dangerous.[29]

Although that defendant, Filiberto Ojeda Rios, was eventually released after a court order, he remained under electronic house arrest, forcing him to wear an electronic transmitter around his ankle which monitored his every movement. Similar restrictive pretrial conditions were placed on Puerto Rican Independentista Felix Rosa after his capture in 1980. Says Rosa:

> Immediately after I was captured I was put in isolation and I stayed there for two years during my trial. Right off the streets. I was in 23-24 hour lock-up, in a cell that was 6' by 8'. They called it administrative detention. I was kept in a special unit where they kept people who were sentenced to the electric chair.[30]

During the Resistance Conspiracy Case, Laura Whitehorn, who was the only defendant not convicted of any previous "crimes," was also held under the Preventive Detention Law for more than four years. Such punitive pretrial imprisonment not only reinforces a propaganda image of the defendants being "dangerous terrorists" but also serves to disrupt preparations for their legal defence.

Richard Williams, one of the OHIO 7 prisoners who was retried the fall of 1991 for the shooting of a New Jersey state trooper, was held under the tightest security in Trenton State Prison while awaiting trial. Says Williams:

> In putting me here they labelled me Special Housing, basically a pre-trial status. With that Special Housing status they have suspended all my rights which I would normally have as a prisoner in Trenton State Prison.... Basically I'm in non-congregate status. What that means is that I'm not allowed to associate with any prisoner here. Basically that's solitary confinement, I'm even recreated alone. Being non-congregate status I'm not eligible for any hobby programs, meaning that in general population and even in MCU [Management Control Unit] if I wanted to paint or if I wanted to do different things for recreation in my cell, I'm not allowed to do that. I'm not allowed to associate with anybody, so I'm basically locked in my cell 24 hours a day except for two hours on alternate days when I'm put out for recreation. I'm put out into a yard all by myself and I'm recreated.... So this is basically to try and break my will and interfere with my frame of mind in getting ready for this trial. It hasn't worked yet, and it won't.[31]

Because Williams had not been convicted of a crime in New Jersey, he should have been held in a county jail while awaiting the retrial. In order to confine him in the maximum security prison in the state and under such restrictive conditions, the governor signed an executive emergency order, essentially declaring martial law in Williams' case and suspending his rights. The administration even took the unprecedented step of requiring Williams' visitors to apply weeks ahead of time so that a "security check" could be performed. [Visitors for all other prisoners need no appointments, they just come to the prison during designated visiting hours.] If the visitor was eventually approved (which was unlikely), s/he had to submit to being photographed and thumbprinted before being allowed a one hour window visit with Williams.

Another prosecution strategy which has developed during the past decade which, like the Preventative Detention Law, is a direct outgrowth of the manipulation of "terrorism," is the militarization of the courtrooms themselves. Certainly given the racism and fear of the "terrorist threat" ingrained into the minds of U.S. citizens, the hopes of obtaining an unbiased jury is by no means a given. Still, a jury trial has long been seen as the last hope for defendants in political cases, which is why jury trials have been abolished for political trials in the north of Ireland and South Africa. This new courtroom "security" is quite plainly a cynical attempt by the state to further prejudice the minds of the jurors.

This type of propaganda was first used in the trials of Puerto Rican Independentistas. Its manifestations include heavy courthouse security, including not only well armed marshals but snipers positioned on neighbouring buildings. People attending the trials are subjected to searches by police and with metal detectors. In some cases the public are photographed and forced to produce identification. Other props which the state uses in this "theatre of justice" include floor to ceiling walls of bullet-proof glass separating the spectators from the participants, surveillance video cameras directed at both the defendants and the spectators, and heavily armed convoys to transport the defendants to and from the courthouse. Says attorney Michael Deutsch:

> In the case in Connecticut, they actually built a concrete bunker, like a concrete wall, in front of the courthouse to give the impression that somehow there was going to be some bombing of the courthouse.[32]

In the first trial of OHIO 7 prisoners Richard Williams and Tom Manning in 1986-87 on the trooper shooting charge, all spectators attending the proceedings were made to give their social security numbers and submit to being photographed before being allowed to enter the courtroom. At the retrial at the end of 1991, spectators had to pass through a metal detector and anyone obviously supportive of the defendant was photographed by the police outside the courtroom and searched for identification. While security was apparently less strict than at the first trial, there were always upwards of twelve officers in the courtroom at any one time, as well as heavily armed troopers and snipers stationed outside.

As with most government operations, these tactics fulfil several functions at once. Most obviously, the heavy militarization serves to prejudice the jury. It provides the forgone conclusion that the defendants are dangerous "terrorists" because of the extreme security precautions. Similarly, it serves to implant this notion in the minds of the local community and reinforces it for the media. Finally, this militarization serves to attack the supporters of the defendants. It succeeds in intimidating some, effectively scaring them away from appearing in court to show their solidarity and expose the political nature of the trial. More importantly, the identification requirements to enter the courtroom and the use of photographic and video surveillance of the spectators facilitates the collection of political intelligence on the support community.

Another tactic used to eliminate any semblance of fairness in the trials is the use of anonymous juries. This again was tested in the trials of Puerto Rican Independentistas. Under this system, jurors are given numbers to identify themselves and told not to reveal their names, addresses, and places of employment because of the danger posed by the violent nature of the case. The jurors are then isolated in hotels throughout the trial, under armed guard, for their own "protection." Says Michael Deutsch:

> All these things create the image that these people are violent, they're dangerous and they're terrorists, and therefore the jurors...are already prejudiced by all this security. And then they're told by the government, in the media and through the media, that these are terrorists and these are violent people, and it's impossible to get a fair trial in the United States....[33]

Once convicted, political activists face inordinately long sentences under particularly harsh conditions. Political sentences during the past twenty years have the common feature of being as much as ten times longer than the identical "crime" in a non-political case.

For example, a group of Independentistas convicted in 1981 of seditious conspiracy charges stemming from actions attributed to the clandestine organization Fuerzas Armadas de Liberacion Nacional (FALN) received sentences ranging between 55 and 90 years, with an average sentence of over 70 years. The presiding judge in the case stated that he regretted the fact that he did not have the power to impose the death penalty. That same year, the next highest average sentence for all crimes except seditious conspiracy was 41 years and 3 months. This average includes all crimes including homicide, rape, kidnapping, bank robbery, etc. None of the thirteen had any previous criminal record.[34]

Defence attorney Mary O'Melveny compiled one of the most extensive studies on the subject in 1990 entitled Memorandum on Disparate Treatment of Political/POW Prisoners by United States Authorities on Sentencing and Parole Eligibility. She notes that "Virtually every political/P.O.W. prisoner serving time in prison today is serving a multiple-year sentence which amounts to life imprisonment in fact, if not in name."[35]

O'Melveny highlights cases such as that of anti-imperialist political prisoners and Resistance Conspiracy Case defendants Tim Blunk and Susan Rosenberg, who were both sentenced in 1984 to 58 years for illegally possessing dynamite. This sentence was more than *sixteen times* the average sentence for the offence and more than double the average federal sentence for first degree murder in 1985. Because of the absurd severity of their sentences, neither will be eligible for parole until they have served at least ten years. In 1989, the longest average prison time served by federal prisoners for "major offences" was 6 years and 5 months. Blunk and Rosenberg have both already served over 7 years.

Marilyn Buck, another RCC defendant and anti-imperialist political prisoner, was arrested in 1973 for using false identification to buy ammunition. She was later convicted and sentenced to 10 years, at the time the longest sentence ever given for such an offence. Her sentence amounted to one year in prison for each bullet confiscated by the police.

In 1986, former SDS organizer and anti-imperialist Linda Evans was sentenced in a Louisiana court for using false identification to purchase a firearm. Although the average sentence for this charge is 2 years, with many people receiving only probation, Evans was given 40 years, the longest sentence ever imposed for such an offence in the history of the U.S.

A telling comparison in Evans' case is the treatment afforded Alabama Ku Klux Klan leader Don Black during that same year. Black and nine other white supremacists, who were planning an invasion of the Caribbean island of Dominica, were arrested with a boatload of automatic weapons, explosives, and cash. Black was tried in the same court as Evans and received an 8 year sentence, 5 years of which were suspended, and was out on parole after serving only 24 months.

In fact, O'Melveny's study demonstrates quite vividly the leniency shown towards far-right and white supremacist extremists charged with violent acts, showing quite clearly that the government is only concerned with "terrorism" by the left. Compare the 58 year sentences given Blunk and Rosenberg for possession of dynamite, none of which was fashioned into bombs, to the case of far-right survivalist Edward Hefferman. Hefferman was convicted in the mid-1980s for possessing 1,000 pounds of dynamite and 18 fully constructed pipe bombs. He received a sentence between 6 months and two years and was released after 6 months.[36]

In 1985 Michael Donald Bray was convicted of ten bombings of abortion clinics, three of which occurred without warning calls while the buildings were occupied. He received a ten year sentence and was paroled after less than four. That same year, four people were charged in Florida with nine counts of conspiracy to bomb abortion clinics and with possession and use of explosives in four clinic bombings. Two of those convicted received ten years and are now awaiting parole while the other two were given suspended sentences. Interestingly, no such bombings of abortion clinics are recorded in the FBI's study of domestic terrorism examined earlier.

In 1987, three members of the Jewish Defence League received 10 years, 5 years, and 5 years probation respectively after being charged with "a pattern of terrorist acts, including bombings, arsons, extortions, and fraud." These sentences were handed down by the same judge who had earlier given the OHIO 7 prisoners sentences between 15 and 50 years for bombings in protest of U.S. aggression in Central America and U.S. support for the South African government.

The severity of the sentencing experienced by left activists makes it clear that they are being dealt with unusually harshly because of their involvement in revolutionary politics and national liberation struggles. Not only are their sentences many times heavier than those of other defendants charged with similar offences, they are also much more severe than those given to racist and fascist elements involved in violent acts. Obviously, these prisoners are being singled out for unusually long sentences because of their political beliefs and associations.

Of course, the weight of these sentences also means that political prisoners and prisoners of war must serve a large amount of time before being eligible for parole. Independentista Haydee Beltran Torres, for example, applied for parole in 1990 after serving ten years but was told by the parole board that she would have to serve at least another fifteen before she would even be considered.[37]

It has also been the experience of many political prisoners and prisoners of war that their political beliefs and associations are used by the state to deny their paroles. A clear example of this is evident in the treatment of MOVE prisoners by the Pennsylvania Board of Probation and Parole. The MOVE organization, whose members are predominantly Black, was subjected to intense state repression in the late 1970s and 1980s for their anti-authoritarian politics and their community activism around issues such as racism and police brutality in the city of Philadelphia. This repression culminated in two massive military-style police attacks on their communal homes in 1978 and 1985. During the 1985 attack the police dropped a heavy explosive charge on the roof of the MOVE house from a helicopter resulting in a fire which killed eleven MOVE people, five of whom were children.

Over a dozen MOVE people are currently imprisoned, most on fabricated charges of killing a police officer during the 1978 attack. One of the traditional conditions given to MOVE people for parole is that they "must not contact or associate with MOVE members for any reason."[38] This is quite clearly an example of penalizing the prisoners for their political associations. Ku Klux Klan leader Don Black was allowed to go straight back into white supremacist activities after parole, so if any such stipulation existed at all in his case it was certainly not enforced.

In the MOVE cases, such a condition is made even more vindictive by the fact that many of the MOVE political prisoners have husbands, wives, and children who are MOVE members. Such a parole restriction would thereby prohibit family contact. Because of this clearly politically motivated restriction, MOVE prisoners have historically refused parole rather than agree to such conditions and therefore are not released until they complete their maximum sentences.

Similarly, former Los Angeles Black Panther Party leader Geronimo Pratt, currently in his twentieth year of imprisonment on an FBI murder frame-up, has been denied parole over the years specifically because of his political commitment. Says Pratt:

> Well, I could be out tomorrow. All I'd have to do would be confess to a crime I didn't commit.... This would serve to prove the cops were right all along, provide a non-political justification for all the years I've spent behind bars, and help validate the government's pretence that the Black Panther Party was really just a bunch of criminals that deserved what was done to it.... But I'll never play that game.... Hell, if murder was what I was in for, I'd have been back on the street 15 years ago.[39]

Geronimo Pratt's experiences at parole hearings are also instructive in this context. At his first hearing in February 1978, the chairperson of the three-member panel was Ray Brown, who had formerly been the head of the Oakland Police Department's anti-BPP Squad from 1967-72. Brown refused to disqualify himself from hearing Pratt's case and parole was denied.[40] The political nature of his imprisonment became even less disguised in his November 1987 hearing, where L.A. Deputy District Attorney Diane Visanni argued successfully against his parole because Pratt is "still a revolutionary man."[41]

The final component of this model of counterinsurgency is the use of the prisons themselves as tools for brutalizing and torturing political prisoners in isolation units and "dead wings" in an attempt to break them, both as activists and as human beings. This process has been fairly well documented against Irish Republican prisoners in the British H-Blocks and Red Army Faction (RAF) prisoners in the Stammheim Prison in West Germany.

The use of isolation—isolation from friends, family, community, and other prisoners—is the common feature of the treatment of both female and male political prisoners and prisoners of war. The most instructive example of this is the Lexington High Security Unit (HSU) in Lexington, Kentucky. The Lexington HSU was essentially a prison within a prison, located in the basement of the larger Lexington Federal Prison. It was designed as an isolation unit and opened in October 1986 when political prisoner Susan Rosenberg and Puerto Rican P.O.W. Alejandrina Torres were moved there. In January 1987, a third political prisoner, Silvia Baraldini, was also brought to Lexington. A 1991 study entitled *Prison Conditions in the United States* by Human Rights Watch notes:

All three women had been convicted of politically motivated offences. Prior to their arrest they were members of radical leftist organizations.... None of the three had been transferred to Lexington because of a crime committed while in prison or a bad disciplinary record.[42]

Although the highest number of women ever housed in the HSU was seven, for most of the length of its operation it held only these three political prisoners.

Lexington was essentially an experimental facility testing the effects of isolation and sensory deprivation on the women imprisoned there. Says Mary O'Melveny, Rosenberg's attorney:

> The HSU prisoners lived in constant artificial light. Their only link to the world above was a television set, an occasional ten minute social telephone call, and less frequent visits from attorneys. The things we take for granted—natural light, fresh air, color, sound, human contact, variable smells—were conspicuously, intentionally absent from the lives of the women confined to the HSU. Also denied were those equally important, slightly more subtle human needs—privacy spheres, intellectual stimulation, comradeship, continuing connections to family, friends and caring others, undisturbed sleep, health care, educational and recreational options, and spiritual options.[43]

Video cameras monitored the women twenty-four hours a day, including when showering and using the toilet. They were also subjected to regular strip searches and cavity searches, often by male guards. They were harassed by sleep deprivation, as well as completely arbitrary rule changes.

The women were told that they would not be allowed to receive mail unless they submitted the names of fifteen persons to be investigated. Only those who passed this "security clearance" would be allowed to communicate with them. The women refused to co-operate with this obvious intelligence gathering operation. Later they were allowed to receive mail, but the names and addresses of all those who sent letters were recorded by the Bureau of Prisons (B.O.P.) and circulated to other police agencies. Similarly, all phone calls were carefully monitored and the callers names, as well as all names referred to during the conversation, were recorded.

The B.O.P. initially maintained that the women transferred to this facility were moved because they posed security risks. The B.O.P. stated that placement in the facility was due to "serious histories of assaultive, escape-prone or disruptive activity."[44] However, because none of the three women had any history of disciplinary problems, this rationale is obviously contrived.

Later, the B.O.P.'s criteria became expressly political. Assignment to Lexington was the result of:

> [A] prisoner's past or present affiliation, association or membership in an organization which has been documented as being involved in acts of violence, attempts to disrupt or overthrow the government of the U.S. or whose published ideology includes advocating law violations in order to "free" prisoners....[45]

Once the women were sent to Lexington, their relocation to a less secure facility was based upon the elimination of the "problems" which caused them to be sent there. In the case of these women, it was therefore quite obvious that in order to get out of the HSU they would have to change their political beliefs.

Says Susan Rosenberg:

> We were informed that we were permanently designated to the HSU, expected to serve our entire sentences of 35 to 58 years there. We were told that we had no due process because the director of the Bureau of Prisons, acting as an agent for U.S. Attorney General Meese, had personally approved our placement and only he could approve our removal. When we asked if there was any way for us to get out of the HSU we were informed that if we changed our associations and affiliations a change would be considered. The staff joke was you got a "one-way ticket" to the Lexington HSU.[46]

After a time, this kind of isolation and complete dependency had debilitating effects on the women, both physically and psychologically. They experienced insomnia and exhaustion because of sleep deprivation. The small area of their confinement severely limited the distance their eyes needed to focus, eventually causing impaired vision and hallucinations. They experienced "memory loss, inability to concentrate, loss of appetite and weight, and lethargy."

In March 1988, a lawsuit was launched which resulted in a court decision that Rosenberg and Baraldini were unlawfully confined in Lexington because of their political beliefs and affiliations. [As an Independentista, Torres did not participate in the suit because she does not recognize the jurisdiction of the U.S. courts.] In his decision, which was later overturned on appeal, Judge Barrington Parker stated that the government:

Specifically punish[es] Baraldini and Rosenberg for their "radical" political beliefs and their alleged associations with "revolutionary" political organizations.... Baraldini and Rosenberg have been singled out for advocating ideas disagreeable to the government.[47]

It is one thing to place persons under greater security because they have escape histories and pose special risks to our correctional institutions. But consigning anyone to a high security unit for past political associations they will never shed unless forced to renounce them is a dangerous mission for this country's prison system to continue.[48]

In the meantime, public opposition to the HSU was mounting and the American Civil Liberties Union and Amnesty International both issued reports condemning the Lexington facility. In addition to finding that the women were placed in the HSU because of their politics, the Amnesty International report stated:

The conditions and regime are deliberately and gratuitously oppressive. The constant and unjustified use of security chains, the repeated strip searching, the almost total lack of privacy, the claustrophobic lack of sensory stimuli, freedom of movement, possessions, choice of activities and incestuously small range of contacts cannot be other than debilitating.... There is no need for these prisoners to be at HSU.... There is overwhelming evidence that the prisoners at HSU have deteriorated physically and psychologically during their custody here. There has to be a prospect that one or more will finally resort to suicide should their custody at HSU be prolonged. I conclude therefore that HSU should close forthwith.[49]

The public pressure eventually led to the closure of the unit in August 1988 and the relocation of the women to other prisons. However, the negative publicity only hastened the closure of the Lexington HSU. The B.O.P. had decided a year earlier that Lexington would be closed because of the completion of a new and much larger women's facility in Marianna, Florida based upon the Lexington model. Marianna is operating presently and houses Rosenberg, Baraldini, and Marilyn Buck as well as dozens of other women.

Male political prisoners and prisoners of war are confined in similarly oppressive control units. The most restrictive is the federal prison at Marion, Illinois, which has also been condemned by Amnesty International for violating almost every condition of the United Nations Standard Minimum Rules for the

Treatment of Prisoners. Marion currently holds revolutionaries from the Puerto Rican Independence Movement, Black Liberation Movement, and Armed Clandestine Movement among others.

At Marion, prisoners are held in their individual cells for more than 22 hours a day and are given extremely limited access to telephones and visiting privileges. As with the Lexington HSU, the denial of meaningful human contact and sensory stimulation are focal parts of the Marion regime. The institution is also notorious for it's contaminated water supply, which is proven to contain more than twice the allowable levels of cancer-causing trihalomethanes (TTHM).

Many of the tactics for control, intimidation, and isolation used in the federal prisons such as Marion and Lexington have been adopted by the control units in state prisons in thirty-six states. Says political prisoner Tom Manning, currently held in the Management Control Unit (MCU) in Trenton State Prison in New Jersey along with several other political prisoners and P.O.W.s from the Black Liberation Army and the OHIO 7:

> You have to understand that this is part of a national move. The same shakedowns and moves and other stuff that they're doing here are also happening at Marion right now. I hear from Ray [Levasseur, a member of the OHIO 7 held in Marion] that they're moving people every ninety days, confiscating property and stuff, and that's also what they're doing here.... Eventually they want to turn the whole of Trenton State Prison into a lockdown unit for this state, and with each move they're doing that deeper and deeper.... What is left of the general population is getting cut down to basically a service corps of prisoners that serve all the other prisoners that are locked up, doing the cleaning up in the corridors and stuff like that. As a matter of fact, nobody gets to use the corridors these days except the crews that clean up, and basically that's what you see in places like Marion where the whole prison is locked down. The only movement is those prisoners who are in trustee status out there buffing the floors and stuff, and that's what it's coming to here.[50]

The official rationale not only for Marion but for control units generally is that they are designed to hold "the baddest of the bad," or in the words of former Marion warden Gary Henman "to provide a correctional setting for the most hostile, assaultive, and escape-prone inmates in the Bureau of Prisons."[51] However, this statement is no more accurate than the U.S. government's repeated claims that it holds no political prisoners.

Indeed, of the more than half dozen political prisoners and prisoners of war currently held in Marion, for example, none have histories of being "disciplinary problems," nor have they committed any acts of violence in other prisons. In fact, according the Human Rights Watch Report:

> A number of individuals who had not committed disciplinary infractions during their pre-trial detentions were sent to Marion directly after sentencing. They include prisoners convicted of politically motivated criminal offences, among them Yukik Umura [sic], Leonard Peltier, Raymond Levasseur, Sekou Odinga and Alan Berkman.[52]

According to a 1985 Congressional study, 80% of the people held in Marion did not have the "Level 6" security rating that is supposedly the requirement to be sent there [Marion is designated a level 6 institution, the B.O.P.'s highest security rating]. However, many prisoners in Marion do share the common characteristic of having participated in work stoppages and hungerstrikes in other prisons, or are known for filing "too many" lawsuits, or have steadfastly pursued their religious or political beliefs.[53]

Says Tom Manning:

> The kind of people they keep in control units are the people who they feel will have some influence on the general population. It's mainly ideas that they're trying to lock up here rather than individuals. There are few people locked up here for actually acting out anything that they call a "disciplinary problem." It's the people who have the ideas that they're afraid of.[54]

This is abundantly evident in cases such as that of former Black Panther Party member Bashir Hameed who, along with fellow ex-BPP member Abdul Majid, was framed for the 1981 killing of a New York City police officer. Since their conviction, Hameed has faced particularly harsh prison conditions, including a stretch of over two years and seven months in solitary confinement—locked in a 6' x 8' cell for 23 hours a day. Says Mark Gombiner, attorney for both Hameed and Majid:

> The reason which they [the prison administration] themselves gave, even in a written statement to Mr. Hameed, was that you are being held here because the other people in the prison look up to you too much and we think that you are a radical and have too much leadership ability.... [The conditions] were imposed purely because of who he was politically, not for anything he did

in prison.... It's just that they were afraid of him because they thought the other inmates looked up to him too much.[55]

The evidence supporting the use of the control units as punishment against political prisoners is particularly clear in Manning's own case. His "Criteria Record Sheet" prepared by the Trenton State Prison administration state the reasons for his placement in MCU quite explicitly.

This subject inmate has proven to be a leader toward anti-government establishment and authority figures. He has shown this terroristic attitude by using whatever resources available to attain his negative goals. Because of his established revolutionary dissident record, subject could use this position to negatively influence and manipulate the prison population.[56]

In September 1988, Manning appealed this decision to place him in MCU because of his political beliefs and affiliations. Howard L. Beyer, administrator of the prison, denied Manning's appeal, saying:

Information reveals that you are an avowed revolutionary, committed to the overthrow of the government through subversive and violent means. Additionally, you are a member and participant in terroristic organizations and activities.[57]

Manning is currently pursuing a civil rights lawsuit against the prison for violating his constitutional rights by placing him in the control unit. Says Manning, "The suit demonstrates clearly the fact that I'm treated differently because of my politics, because I'm identified as political."[58] With this suit, he hopes to challenge not only his confinement but the use of control units in general and expose their use as tools for oppressing political prisoners and prison leaders.

While Tom Manning's lawsuit awaits a hearing date, Dhoruba bin-Wahad waits to hear whether the state of New York plans to send him back to prison on the fabricated shooting charges. On the same day that the court was deciding that Dhoruba's innocence was merely a technicality standing in the way of his imprisonment, an appeal in the cases of former Black Panther Party members Bashir Hameed and Abdul Majid was rejected by the appellate division of the New York State Supreme Court. Says defence attorney Mark Gombiner:

Well, to put it bluntly, they just lied about what happened. This is a hard thing for most people to believe that a court would do, but if you read their decision they set out what they say are the facts of the case—and the facts that they set out in their opinion do not bear any relationship to what the transcript of the trial says. For example, they claim that when the prosecutor was striking all the Black jurors, they claim in their decision that the prosecutor offered race neutral explanations for why he was striking the Black jurors. In fact, exactly the opposite occurred. The prosecutor repeatedly and vociferously stated that he was not going to give any explanation for why he was striking the jurors and he did not give any explanation. And then in connection to the guns that were admitted, [the court] said that the guns matched the make and model numbers of the murder weapons—even though the record shows that the murder weapons were never recovered and there's no evidence as to what the make or model numbers of the weapons were. Those are just a couple of examples. Essentially what they did is that they grossly, well it's not just misstating the facts, they made up a new set of facts and then used the facts that they made up to justify the rejection of the arguments we made.[59]

The week before these decisions were released, revolutionary Richard Williams was convicted in New Jersey in his retrial. Certainly the dozen or more police officers "guarding" the defendant must have helped the jury conclude that Williams was at least as dangerous as the prosecution's weak circumstantial evidence made him out to be. Pieces of key defence evidence from the first trial which were mysteriously "lost" while in federal custody probably made their decision easier as well.

At the same time in California, former BPP leader Geronimo Pratt was again denied parole. He now enters his twentieth year in prison for a murder conviction in which the main witness against him was a paid police informant, and in which the police's own records of surveillance of Pratt, verifying his alibi, were "lost" by the FBI.

In Canada, the first of the trials of Mohawks for defending their lands against invasion by the Quebec Provincial Police and Canadian Armed Forces wound down in Montreal, resulting in the conviction and sentencing of Native activists Ronald Cross and Gordon Lazore. In the spring of 1992, several dozen more Mohawks will be tried for their actions during the standoff. In February 1992, a Toronto judge sentenced Canadian Union of Postal Workers members Andre Kolompar, Jim Lawrence, and Ron Pollard to prison for violating a court order which barred them from picketing during a 1991 postal strike. Control units have been opened in several Canadian prisons, including Prince Albert in Saskatchewan and the Prison for Women (P4W) in Kingston, Ontario.

The new unit in P4W currently houses members of the Native Sisterhood who the administration blames for leading a hungerstrike in the prison in 1991.

As economic and political repression continue to tighten in the U.S. and Canada, the courts and prisons are going to play an ever expanding role in quelling any resistance activities. That repression will mean the incarceration of even more political prisoners and prisoners of war. Says attorney Robert Boyle:

> Although as a lawyer I'm still going to be going to court and fighting my best, and we have to do that if just to expose the hypocrisy of the court system, the freedom of political prisoners is not going to come necessarily through the courts—only if the courts are forced to do it. And there's going to have to be a movement to free political prisoners and that movement has to be a grassroots movement within the United States, within Canada certainly where's there's a lot of awareness of the situation in the United States, and people have to demand it. That's the only way these people are going to be freed.[60]

While the state continues to prosecute opposition and national liberation struggles under the guise of criminal activity and bury political activists for the rest of their lives in the dungeons of the modern era, we have the choice to either recognize the situation and act—or turn our heads, or retreat into our privilege and wait quietly while the "chickens come home to roost"—if in fact they are not already here.

I would like to express my respect and thanks to the many people in the U.S. and Canada whose work has directly or indirectly contributed to this piece. I would also like to express special gratitude to my friends and comrades Tom Manning and Richard Williams who continue to do active political work and to provide me with both inspiration and information while struggling under the oppressive conditions in the control unit at Trenton State Prison.

Endnotes

1. Tom Manning, interview with author, April 19, 1991.
2. Felix Rosa, interview with Marie Caloz, January 11, 1992.
3. Robert Boyle, interview with author, January 6, 1992.
4. Robert Boyle, interview with author, January 6, 1992.
5. Quoted from an internal FBI document from Director J. Edgar Hoover dated August 25, 1967. Document reprinted in Ward Churchill and Jim Vander Wall, *The COINTELPRO Papers: Documents from the FBI's Secret War Against Dissent in the United States* (Boston: South End Press, 1990), p.92.
6. As quoted in internal FBI documents reprinted in the books below, some of the stated aims of COINTELPRO were to ...disrupt, misdirect, discredit, or otherwise neutralize the activities of black nationalist hate-type organizations and groupings, their leadership, spokesmen, membership, and supporters....

    Prevent the *coalition* of militant black nationalist groups.... Prevent the *rise of a "messiah"* who could unify, and electrify, the militant black nationalist movement.... Prevent militant black nationalist groups from gaining *respectability* by discrediting them...prevent the long-range *growth* of militant black nationalist organizations....

    And some of the less deadly tactics included...the instigating and taking advantage of personal conflicts or animosities existing between New Left [and Black] leaders;...creating of impressions that certain New Left [and Black] leaders are informants;...[use of] co-operative press contacts...to emphasize that disruptive elements constitute a minority...and do not represent the convictions of the majority;...use of cartoons, photographs, and anonymous letters which will have the effect of ridiculing the New Left [and Black Liberation Movement];...confuse and disrupt New Left [and Black] activities by misinformation....

    For information on the specific activities of the FBI's Counterintelligence Program, see Ward Churchill and Jim Vander Wall, *Agents of Repression: The FBI's Secret Wars Against the Black Panther Party and the American Indian Movement* (Boston: South End Press, 1988) and *The COINTELPRO Papers: Documents from the FBI's Secret Wars Against Dissent in the United States* (Boston: South End Press, 1990) among others.
7. Cited in Churchill and Vander Wall, p. 165.
8. Susan Rosenberg, interview with Shannonbrooke Murphy, July 28, 1990.

9.   Scott Camil, "Undercover Agents' War on Vietnam Veterans" in *It Did Happen Here: Recollections of Political Repression in America*, Bud Shultz and Ruth Schultz, ed. (Berkeley: University of California Press, 1989), p. 328.
10.   Robert Justin Goldstein, *Political Repression in Modern America: From 1870 to the Present* (Boston: Schenkman Publishing, 1978), p. 487.
11.   Robert J. Boyle, "COINTELPRO: The 19-Year Ordeal of Dhoruba bin-Wahad" in *Covert Action Information Bulletin* (Number 36, Spring 1991), pp. 13-14.
12.   Michael Deutsch, interview with author, November 6, 1989.
13.   Goldstein, p. 493.
14.   Churchill and Vander Wall, p. 306.
15.   Cited in Chip Berlet, "The Hunt for the Red Menace" in *Covert Action Information Bulletin* (Number 31, Winter 1989), p. 7.
16.   United Freedom Front, "Communique No. 6" reprinted in *Build a Revolutionary Resistance Movement: Communiques from the North American Armed Clandestine Movement 1982-1985* (New York: Committee to Fight Repression, 1985), p. 22.
17.   Resolution 3103 (XXVIII) of the United Nations General Assembly, adopted December 12, 1972, states "The struggle of people under colonial and alien domination and racist regimes for the implementation of these rights to self-determination and independence is legitimate and in full accordance with the principles of international law."
18.   Of the 13 actions by the left, eight were bombings and five were acts of sabotage by animal rights and environmental groups.
19.   Statistics from *Terrorism in the United States 1988* compiled by the Terrorist Research and Analytical Center, Counterterrorism Section, Criminal Investigative Division of the FBI, December 31, 1988.
20.   Michael E. Deutsch and Richard J. Harvey, "Repression Against the Independentistas" in *Covert Action Information Bulletin* (no. 31, Winter 1989), pp. 44-5.
21.   Michael Deutsch, interview with author, November 6, 1989.
22.   These activists were Dr. Alan Berkman, Tim Blunk, Marilyn Buck, Linda Evans, Susan Rosenberg, and Laura Whitehorn.
23.   Alan Berkman, et al., "Statement from the Resistance Conspiracy Case Defendants/July 1988" reprinted in *Resistance Conspiracy* (Toronto: Anarchist Black Cross), July 1990.
24.   Churchill and Vander Wall, p. 314.
25.   Laura Whitehorn, "The Resistance Conspiracy Case" in *Covert Action Information Bulletin* (no. 31, Winter 1989), p. 47.

26. An eighth defendant, Kazi Toure (formerly Christopher King) was initially charged as well. He later pleaded guilty to seditious conspiracy, making him the first person of African descent to be convicted under this law in the twentieth century. It had been used in the 1800s to prosecute, among others, Denmark Vesey, Nat Turner, and those Africans hanged with John Brown.

27. Tom Manning, interview with author, April 19, 1991.

28. *United States of America v. Mutulu Shakur*, SSS 82 Cr. 312 (CSH), *United States of America v. Marilyn Buck*, 84 Cr. 220, "Defendants Memorandum in Reply to the Government's Response to the January 19, 1988 Order of Judge Charles S. Haight," April 12, 1988, p. 20.

29. Michael Deutsch, interview with author, November 6, 1989.

30. Felix Rosa, interview with Marie Caloz, January 11, 1992.

31. Richard Williams, interview with author, July 30, 1991.

32. Michael Deutsch, interview with author, November 6, 1989.

33. Michael Deutsch, interview with author, November 6, 1989.

34. Sentencing information provided by Jan Susler of the People's Law Office in Chicago, Illinois.

35. Mary O'Melveny, Memorandum on Disparate Treatment of Political/POW Prisoners by United States Authorities on Sentencing and Parole Eligibility, November 19, 1990, p. 20. The following statistics on sentencing are all taken from this report except where noted otherwise.

36. Ward Churchill, "The Third World at Home: Political Prisoners in the U.S." in *Z Magazine*, July 1990, p. 91.

37. Information provided by Jan Susler, People's Law Office, Chicago, Illinois.

38. Quoted from parole document from Hermann Tartler, Board Secretary, Commonwealth of Pennsylvania, Penna. Board of Probation and Parole to MOVE member Carlos Perez Africa dated February 19, 1991.

39. Ward Churchill, "A Person Who Struggles for Liberation: An Interview with Geronimo Pratt" in *New Studies on the Left* (vol. XIV, no. 1-2, Spring/Summer 1989), p. 93.

40. Ward Churchill and Jim Vander Wall, "The Case of Geronimo Pratt" in *Covert Action Information Bulletin* (no. 31, Winter 1989), p. 39.

41. Cited in Churchill, "A Person Who Struggles for Liberation: An Interview with Geronimo Pratt," p. 85.

42. Human Rights Watch, *Prison Conditions in the United States: A Human Rights Watch Report*, (New York, Human Rights Watch, 1991), p. 78.

43. Mary O'Melveny, "Lexington Prison High Security Unit" in *Covert Action Information Bulletin* (no. 31, Winter 1989), p. 49. The account of the conditions for the women within the Lexington HSU contained herein is derived from this source.

44.   Cited in O'Melveny, "Lexington Prison High Security Unit," p. 51.
45.   Cited in O'Melveny, "Lexington Prison High Security Unit," p. 51.
46.   Susan Rosenberg, "Reflection on Being Buried Alive" in *New Studies on the Left* (vol. XIV, no. 1-2, Spring/Summer 1989), p. 40.
47.   Quoted in David Fathi, "U.S. Punishes Political Dissenters" in *The National Prison Project Journal* (vol. 5, no. 4, Fall 1990), p. 8.
48.   Cited in Human Rights Watch, p. 80.
49.   Cited in Michael E. Deutsch and Jan Susler, "Political Prisoners in the United States: The Hidden Reality" (unpublished document), pp. 8-9.
50.   Tom Manning, interview with author, October 18, 1991.
51.   "Inside Marion: Warden Gary Henman Talks about the BOP's Most Secure Prison" in *Corrections Today*, vol. 50, no. 4, July 1988, p. 93.
52.   Human Rights Watch, p. 77.
53.   Committee to End the Marion Lockdown, "Florence, Colorado Update" in *Walkin' Steel* (vol. 1, no. 2, Fall 1991), p. 8.
54.   Tom Manning, interview with author, October 18, 1991.
55.   Mark Gombiner, interview with author, January 20, 1992.
56.   "Criteria Record Sheet, State Prison Trenton" of Thomas Manning, dated September 6, 1988, exhibit 1.2 in *Thomas William Manning, Plaintiff, v. Howard L. Beyer, et al.*
57.   "Memorandum" from Howard L. Beyer to Thomas Manning dated September 28, 1988, exhibit 4 in *Thomas William Manning, Plaintiff, v. Howard L. Beyer, et al.*
58.   Tom Manning, interview with author, October 18, 1991.
59.   Mark Gombiner, interview with author, January 20, 1992.
60.   Robert Boyle, interview with author, January 6, 1992.

Appendices

Appendix A

Proposals for a Corrections Act

Short Title
1.   This Act may be cited as the Corrections Act.

Interpretation
2.   In this Act *"contraband"* means an item that could jeopardize the safety
of an individual or the security of a penitentiary, including
(a)   an intoxicant,
(b)   a weapon, a part thereof, ammunition for a weapon, and anything
that is designed to kill, injure or disable a person,
(c)   an explosive or bomb, and a part thereof, and
(d)   currency over the limit prescribed by a schedule to the
regulations;

"inmate" means a person under sentence who
(a)   is in penitentiary pursuant to
(i)   a sentence or committal to penitentiary, or
(ii)   a transfer to penitentiary under the authority of this Act or
any other Act of Parliament, or
(b)   is outside penitentiary by reason of
(i)   statutory release where a residency requirement has been
imposed,
(ii)   day parole, or
(iii)   a temporary absence, or
(c)   is outside penitentiary subject to the authority of a staff member;

"institutional head" means the person responsible, under the direction of
the Commissioner, for
(a)   the care, custody and control of all inmates in a penitentiary, or
offenders supervised by a parole office,
(b)   the management, organization, safety and security of a
penitentiary or parole office, and
(c)   the direction and welfare of staff members of a penitentiary or
parole office, and in the event of his or her absence or inability
to act, the person who assumes his or her authority;

"intoxicant" means any substance that if ingested has the potential to
impair or alter judgment, behaviour, the capacity to recognize reality or

ability to meet the ordinary demands of life, but does not include caffeine, nicotine, or any authorized medication used in accordance with directions given by a staff member or a health care professional;

"Minister" means the Solicitor General of Canada;

"offender" means inmates and released inmates;

"parole office" means a facility that is operated by the Service for the supervision of released inmates;

"penitentiary" means a facility of any description, including all lands connected therewith, that is operated by the Service for the custody, treatment or training of inmates, and any place declared to be a penitentiary pursuant to this Act;

"regional head" means the person responsible, under the direction of the Commissioner, for a regional headquarters of the Service;

"released inmate" means an individual under sentence who has been released from penitentiary
(a)   on parole other than day parole, or
(b)   on statutory release where a residency requirement has not been imposed;

"Service" means the Correctional Service of Canada;

"staff member" means an employee of the Correctional Service of Canada;

"working day" means a day on which offices of the Public Service of Canada are generally open.

Declaration of Purpose and Principles of Federal Corrections
3.   It is hereby recognized and declared that
(a)   the purpose of federal corrections is to contribute to the maintenance of a just, peaceful and safe society by
(i)   carrying out the sentence of the court through the imposition of appropriate measures of custody and control; and
(ii)   contributing to the rehabilitation and reintegration of offenders into the community as law-abiding citizens

through the provision of programs in penitentiaries and in the community; and

(b)   the principles that shall guide correctional staff members in achieving the above purpose are

(i)   offenders under sentence retain the rights and privileges of all members of society, except those that are necessarily removed or restricted as a consequence of the sentence;

(ii)   the sentence should be carried out having regard to all relevant information, including the stated reasons and recommendations of the sentencing judge, information from the trial or sentencing process, and the release policies of, and any comments from, the National Parole Board;

(iii)   correctional authorities should use the least restrictive measures necessary to protect the public, staff members and offenders;

(iv)   correctional authorities should ensure effectiveness and openness through the timely exchange of relevant information with other components of the criminal justice system, and through the public communication of information about correctional policies, programs and resources;

(v)   correctional decisions should be made in a forthright and fair manner, with access to effective grievance mechanisms;

(vi)   correctional policies, programs and practices should respect gender, ethnic and cultural differences, and should be responsive to the needs of women and Aboriginal Peoples, as well as the needs of other groups of offenders with special needs; and

(vii)   correctional staff should be properly selected and trained, and supported by appropriate personnel development opportunities, good working conditions, and opportunities to participate in correctional policy and program development.

Correctional Service of Canada

4.   There shall be an agency known as the Correctional Service of Canada, and it shall be responsible for

(a)   the care and custody of inmates;

(b)   the provision of programs that contribute to the rehabilitation and reintegration of offenders;

(c)   subject to subsection 21(1) of the *Parole Act,* the supervision of offenders;

(d)   the timely provision of all relevant information under its control to the National Parole Board, for the purpose of release decision making;

(e)   establishing and maintaining a program of public education about corrections and the operation of the Service; and

(f)   carrying out this Act and the regulations hereunder in accordance with the purpose and principles set out in section 3.

Commissioner

5.   (1)   The Governor-in-Council may appoint a person to be known as the Commissioner of Corrections who, under the direction of the Minister, has the control and management of the Service and all matters connected therewith.

(2)   The Commissioner may issue rules to facilitate the carrying out of this Act and the regulations thereunder, and they shall be known as Commissioner's Directives and shall be accessible to inmates and staff members and publicly available.

Headquarters

6.   (1)   The headquarters of the Service and the offices of the Commissioner shall be in the National Capital Region.

(2)   The Commissioner may establish regional headquarters of the Service and fix the location of regional offices.

Penitentiary

7.   (1)   Subject to subsection (3), the Commissioner may, by order, declare any prison as defined in the *Prisons and Reformatories Act* or any hospital to be a penitentiary in respect of any person or class of persons.

(2)   Subject to subsection (3), the Governor-in-Council may, by order, declare any place to be a penitentiary.

(3)   No prison, hospital or place administered or supervised under the authority of an Act of the legislature of a province may be declared a penitentiary under subsection (1) or (2) until an officer designated by the Lieutenant-Governor of the province in which the prison, hospital or place is located gives his or her approval.

Lawful Custody

8. A person is in the lawful custody of the Service where

    (a) having been sentenced, transferred or committed to penitentiary or a provincial institution, he or she is in transit to penitentiary in the custody of a staff member;

    (b) having been sentenced or committed to penitentiary, or transferred to penitentiary pursuant to this Act or the *Criminal Code,* he or she is in penitentiary; or

    (c) he or she is an inmate outside a penitentiary subject to the authority of a staff member.

9. In any proceedings before a court in Canada in which a question arises concerning the location or dimension of lands alleged to constitute a penitentiary, a certificate, purporting to be signed by the Commissioner, setting out the location or description of the said lands as constituting a penitentiary, is admissible in evidence and in the absence of any evidence to the contrary is proof that the lands as located or described in the certificate constitute a penitentiary.

Community Involvement

10. To promote openness and accountability in the operation of the Service, the Commissioner shall ensure the existence of mechanisms that facilitate the involvement of members of the community in federal corrections in accordance with the regulations.

Staff Members Duties

11. Every staff member shall

    (a) familiarize himself or herself with this Act, the regulations made pursuant to this Act, and written policy directives;

    (b) make his or her best effort to achieve the purpose and to uphold the principles set out in this Act, and perform his or her duties impartially and diligently, in accordance with the law; and

    (c) encourage and assist offenders in becoming law-abiding persons.

Peace Officer Status

12. The Commissioner may, in writing, designate any staff member of the Service or each member of a class of staff members of the Service to be a peace officer, and a staff member so designated is a peace officer in every part of Canada and has all the powers, authority, protection and privileges that a peace officer has by law.

Investigations — General

13.   (1)   The Minister or the Commissioner may appoint a person or persons to
- (a)   investigate any matter within the jurisdiction of the Commissioner, and
- (b)   submit a report with respect to an investigation under paragraph on his or her direction.

     (2)   A person appointed under subsection (1) has the powers of a commissioner under Part II of the *Inquiries Act,* and subject to subsection (1), Part II of the *Inquiries Act* applies to investigations carried out under the authority of this section.

Injury or Death of an Inmate

14.   Where an inmate suffers death or serious bodily injury, the institutional head shall cause an investigation to be made and shall make a report to the Commissioner of
- (a)   the findings of the investigation; and
- (b)   the recommendations, if any, arising out of the investigation.

Committal

Warrant of Committal and Reasons for Sentence

15.   Where a person is sentenced to serve a term of imprisonment that, in accordance with the *Criminal Code,* is required to be served in a penitentiary
- (1)   he or she may be received into any penitentiary whether or not the warrant of committal specifies that the person is sentenced to a particular penitentiary; and
- (2)   the court that sentenced the person shall order that a copy of the reasons for sentence and any relevant reports considered by the court during the trial or sentencing be forwarded to the Service.

Reception

16.   (1)   A person who has been sentenced or committed to penitentiary shall not be received in penitentiary until after the expiration of 30 days from the date of sentence, unless the person waives his or her entitlement to remain in provincial custody, and thereupon that person may, subject to subsection (2), be received in a penitentiary.

     (2)   The institutional head may refuse to accept a person into custody where there is not a certificate of a duly qualified medical practitioner as to whether the person is suffering from a dangerous, contagious or infectious disease.

17. (1) A person who by reason of section 16 is not received into a penitentiary shall be confined in any prison, common jail or other place, not being a penitentiary, in which persons who are charged with or convicted of offences are usually kept in custody.

(2) The keeper of any prison, common jail or other place referred to in subsection (1) to whom a person referred to in that subsection is delivered shall, on sufficient authority, receive, safely keep and detain that person under custody in the prison, common jail or other place until that person is returned to or transferred to a penitentiary or discharged from custody in accordance with law.

(3) The original of the warrant or other instrument by which a person referred to in subsection (1) is committed or is to be imprisoned in a penitentiary, or a copy thereof duly certified by any judge or provincial court judge or by the clerk of the court in which that person was convicted, is sufficient authority for that person's detention in accordance with subsection (2).

Newfoundland

18. (1) Notwithstanding anything in this Act or any other Act of Parliament, every person sentenced by a court in Newfoundland to imprisonment for life, or for a term of not less than two years, shall be sentenced to imprisonment in the prison operated by the Province of Newfoundland at the city of St. John's, known as Her Majesty's Penitentiary, and shall be subject to the statutes, rules, and regulations, pertaining to the management and control of the said prison.

(2) Where a person is imprisoned in accordance with subsection (1), no transfer to a federal penitentiary may be authorized without the approval of an officer designated by the Lieutenant-Governor of Newfoundland.

(3) Subject to the approval of the Governor-in-Council, the Minister may enter into an agreement with the Province of Newfoundland providing for the payment to the Province of the cost of maintaining the persons who are or have been sentenced or committed to penitentiary.

Exchange of Service Agreements

19. (1) The Minister may, with the approval of the Governor-in-Council, enter into an agreement on behalf of the Government of Canada with the government of any province for

(a) the confinement in penitentiary of persons sentenced or committed to imprisonment for less than two years for offences under any Act of Parliament or any regulations made thereunder, but any such agreement shall include provisions whereby such persons shall be confined at the expense of the provincial government concerned; and

(b)   the confinement in prisons or hospitals in that province of persons sentenced or committed to penitentiary, but any such agreement shall include provisions whereby such persons shall be confined at the expense of the federal government.

(2)   A person who is confined in or transferred to a penitentiary, prison or hospital pursuant to an agreement made under subsection (1) is lawfully confined during the term of his or her sentence or period of committal, and is subject to all the statutes, regulations, and rules applicable in the penitentiary, prison or hospital to which he or she is transferred.

Inmates Participating in Judicial Proceedings
20.   (1)   Where the institutional head is ordered by a court of competent jurisdiction to bring an inmate before a court, he or she shall produce the inmate in accordance with the order, and in accordance with any Act of Parliament that applies thereto.

(2)   Where an inmate is an applicant, pursuant to section 745 of the *Criminal Code,* for a reduction in his or her number of years of imprisonment without eligibility for parole, the Commissioner or his or her delegate shall produce him or her in court for the purpose of attending the proceeding.

(3)   To facilitate an inmate's attendance at court or a Coroner's inquest, the Commissioner or his or her delegate may authorize a transfer to another penitentiary or a prison for that purpose.

Release of Inmates
Place of Release
21.   An inmate may be released from a penitentiary or from any other place designated by the Commissioner.

Timing of Release
22.   (1)   Subject to subsection (2), where an inmate is entitled to be released as a result of the operation of law, he or she shall be released during the daylight hours of the last working day prior to the day that he or she is entitled to be released.

(2)   Where an institutional head believes that a release under subsection (1) would not satisfactorily facilitate an inmate's re-

entry into the community, he or she may release the inmate up to five days prior to the day he or she is entitled to be released by operation of law, and he or she shall be deemed to be released by operation of law.

(3)   Where an inmate is granted a temporary absence and the day on which he or she is due to be released by operation of law falls within the period of that temporary absence, he or she shall be deemed to have been released by operation of law on the day on which the temporary absence commenced.

Temporary Accommodation
23.   Where it is the opinion of an institutional head or his or her delegate that it would assist the rehabilitation of a released inmate to be temporarily accommodated in a penitentiary, he or she may, on the request of the released inmate, allow him or her to stay temporarily in the penitentiary, and he or she shall be deemed to be an inmate for the duration of the temporary stay.

Temporary Absence
Escorted Temporary Absence
24.   Where, in the opinion of the Commissioner or the officer in charge of a penitentiary, it is necessary or desirable that an inmate should be absent, with escort, for medical or humanitarian reasons or to assist in the rehabilitation of the inmate, the absence may be authorized by

(a)   the Commissioner, for an unlimited period for medical reasons and for a period not exceeding fifteen days for humanitarian reasons or to assist in the rehabilitation of the inmate; or

(b)   the officer in charge, for a period not exceeding fifteen days for medical reasons and for a period not exceeding five days for humanitarian reasons or to assist in the rehabilitation of the inmate.

Temporary Absence Without Escort
25.   (1)   Subject to section 26, where, in the opinion of the Commissioner, it is necessary or desirable for an inmate to be absent without escort for medical, community service, socialization, personal development or humanitarian reasons including parenting, the Commissioner may, subject to subsection (3), authorize the absence on being satisfied that

(a)   the inmate will not present an undue risk of committing an offence during the absence;

(b)   the inmate's institutional behaviour warrants the absence; and

(c)   a structured plan for the temporary absence has been prepared.

(2)   Not later than six months following the reception of an inmate into a penitentiary, the Service shall determine whether the inmate is a person to whom paragraphs 21.3(2)(a) and (b) of the *Parole Act* apply and shall notify the inmate in writing of the determination.

(3)   An application for a temporary absence without escort by an inmate who is serving a sentence of imprisonment for life that was imposed as a maximum punishment or who has been determined pursuant to subsection (2) to be a person described therein shall, before it is considered by the Commissioner, be referred to the National Parole Board if

(a)   the application is the first application for temporary absence without escort made by the inmate during the inmate's term of imprisonment;

(b)   the last preceding application for a temporary absence without escort during the inmate's term of imprisonment was refused by reason of an order made pursuant to paragraph (4)(a) or by reason of a decision made pursuant to section 25.1 or 25.2 of the *Parole* Act as it read immediately before the coming into force of this section; or

(c)   the application is the first such application made by the inmate following the termination of a temporary absence without escort during the inmate's term of imprisonment or following the conviction of the inmate during that term of imprisonment for an offence.

(4)   On referral to the National Parole Board of an application for temporary absence without escort, the Board shall

(a)   order that the application be refused if it is satisfied that the inmate will, having regard to the circumstances, present an undue risk of committing an offence during the absence; or

(b)   if the Board is satisfied that the inmate will not present such a risk, return the application to the Commissioner for a determination in accordance with subsection (1).

(5)   Temporary absences without escort may be authorized for an unlimited period for medical reasons and for a period not exceeding fifteen days in any other case.

(6)   The Commissioner may delegate to a designated person the power to authorize temporary absences without escort and to terminate such absences.

(7)   Where, pursuant to an agreement under subsection 19(1), an inmate or a class of inmates has been admitted to a mental hospital or other institution operated by a provincial government in which the liberty of patients is normally subject to restrictions, the Commissioner may delegate to the person in charge of the hospital or institution the power to authorize and terminate temporary absences without escort.

(8)   The Commissioner may terminate a temporary absence without escort authorized pursuant to subsection (1) and cause the issuing of a warrant in writing authorizing the apprehension of the inmate and the recommitment of the inmate to custody as provided in this Act.

(9)   The Commissioner may fix the terms and conditions under which a power may be exercised pursuant to this section by a person designated by the Commissioner for that purpose.

26.   (1)   Subject to subsection (2), the portion of the term of imprisonment that an inmate must serve before temporary absence without escort may be authorized is as follows:

(a)   where the inmate is serving a sentence of imprisonment for life, the period of time required to be served by the inmate to reach the inmate's full parole eligibility date, minus three years;

(b)   where the inmate is serving a term of imprisonment other than a sentence of imprisonment for life, one sixth of the sentence or six months, whichever is the greater; or

(c)   where the inmate has been sentenced to detention in a penitentiary for an indeterminate period, three years.

(2)   Subsection (1) does not apply

(a)   to an inmate admitted to a penitentiary prior to May 4, 1978; or

(b)   to an inmate whose life or health is in immediate danger and temporary absence without escort is required in order to administer emergency medical treatment.

Compensation for Disability or Death

27.   (1)   In accordance with the regulations, the Minister may pay compensation to

(a)   a person who was an inmate for physical disability attributable to his or her participation in an approved program of a penitentiary; and

(b)   the surviving spouse or dependent children of a person who was an inmate for death of the person attributable to his or her participation in an approved program of a penitentiary.

Information

28.   For the purpose of sections 30-33, "information" means information about an identifiable offender recorded in any form, and includes factual information and opinion.

29.   Nothing in this Act limits a person's right of access, correction or complaint under the *Access to Information Act* or the *Privacy Act,* or the regulations thereunder.

Collection of Information

30.   When a person is sentenced, committed or transferred to penitentiary, as soon as practicable the Service shall take reasonable steps to obtain

(a)   relevant information about the circumstances of the offence and the person, including his or her criminal and young offender history; and

(b)   the reasons and recommendations of the sentencing court, and reports relevant to sentencing submitted to that court.

31.   The Service shall take reasonable steps to ensure that information that is used by it is as accurate, up-to-date and complete as possible.

Sharing of Information with Other Components of the Criminal Justice System

32.   The Service shall provide relevant information

(a)   to the National Parole Board, contracting agencies, provincial governments, and police, for the purpose of release decision making or the supervision of the offender on conditional release; and

(b)   before warrant expiry, to the police force in the jurisdiction where an inmate is to be released on warrant expiry, where the Commissioner or his or her delegate has reasonable grounds to believe that the inmate would pose a threat to the safety or security of the public upon release.

Disclosure of Information to Victims

33.   (1)   The Commissioner or his or her delegate may authorize the release to victims of the following information:

(a) the offender's name and age;
(b) court of conviction;
(c) the nature of the current offence;
(d) date and length of sentence;
(e) probable date for release on mandatory supervision;
(f) parole eligibility dates;
(g) the initial review date for unescorted temporary absences, day parole and parole;
(h) the date and type of release;
(i) the destination of the offender;
(j) whether the offender might be in the vicinity of the victim while in transit;
(k) certain terms and conditions attached to the release where this may reduce the victim's fear; and
(l) whether an offender is in custody or is unlawfully at large, where he or she is satisfied that the victim's need for the information clearly outweighs the offender's interest in privacy.

(2) For the purpose of subsection (1), "victim"
(a) means a person who suffers physical, mental or economic harm as a result of the commission of an offence by an offender; and
(b) where the person described in paragraph (a) is not able to apply for information due to death, illness or other reason, includes the spouse, common law spouse, or other person who has an interest in the information by virtue of his or her relationship with a person described in paragraph (a).

(3) An offender shall be notified of a disclosure under subsection (l) unless the Commissioner or his or her delegate is satisfied that notification thereof would jeopardize the safety of an individual or the security of a penitentiary.

Disclosure of Information to Offenders
34. (1) Where an offender is entitled to reasons for and an opportunity to respond to a decision taken or to be taken about him or her, subject to subsection (2), he or she shall be provided with all the information relied upon or to be relied upon in the making of the decision.
(2) Where the Commissioner or his or her delegate is satisfied that full disclosure of information under subsection (l) would
(a) jeopardize the safety of an individual;
(b) jeopardize the security of a penitentiary; or

(c)   be injurious to the conduct of an ongoing criminal investigation,

he or she may authorize the withholding from the offender of as much information as is strictly necessary to protect the interest identified in paragraph (a), (b), or (c), and give the offender specific grounds for withholding the information.

Custody and Control of Inmates
General
35.   Every inmate shall be confined in a penitentiary that provides the least restrictive measure of custody and control appropriate in all the circumstances, taking into account
   (a)   the degree and kind of custody and control considered necessary;
   (b)   accessibility to the inmate's home community or a compatible cultural and linguistic environment;
   (c)   the availability of appropriate programs and services, including health care services, and the inmate's willingness to participate in appropriate programs;
   (d)   the availability of cell space; and
   (e)   the inmate's need for special protection.

Placement and Transfer
36.   The Commissioner or his or her delegate may in accordance with section 35 and the regulations, authorize the placement of an inmate in a penitentiary or the transfer of an inmate to
   (a)   another penitentiary; or
   (b)   a provincial institution pursuant to an agreement entered into under the authority of paragraph 19 (l)(b).

Administrative Segregation
37.   Where an inmate must be kept from associating with other inmates, he or she may be confined in administrative segregation, in a secure and humane fashion, in accordance with a fair decision making process, and shall be returned to the general population as soon as possible, in accordance with this Act and the regulations thereunder.
38.   The institutional head or his or her delegate may order that an inmate be placed in administrative segregation where placement therein is in accordance with section 35 and there are reasonable grounds to believe
   (a)   that the inmate has acted, attempted to act, or plans to act in a manner that jeopardizes the security of the penitentiary or the safety of an individual, and that his or her presence in the general

population would jeopardize the security of the penitentiary or the safety of an individual;

(b)   that the presence of the inmate in the general population would interfere with the investigation of a criminal or serious disciplinary offence; or

(c)   that the inmate would be in danger in the general population.

39.   Where an inmate is involuntarily placed in administrative segregation, a segregation review board constituted by the institutional head shall

(a)   conduct an in-person hearing to review the case of the inmate;

(b)   conduct regular reviews of the case of the inmate if he or she is kept in administrative segregation after the hearing referred to in paragraph (a); and

(c)   advise him or her whether the inmate should remain in administrative segregation or be released therefrom, in accordance with the regulations.

40.   Where the institutional head does not intend to follow the advice of the segregation review board to release an inmate from administrative segregation, he or she shall meet in person with the inmate to explain the reasons for the proposed decision, and give the inmate an opportunity to respond in person, or in writing if the inmate prefers.

41.   Where the institutional head or his or her delegate refuses to authorize the voluntary placement of an inmate in administrative segregation, he or she shall give the inmate written reasons for his or her decision and an opportunity to respond.

42.   Every inmate in segregation shall be visited by a health care staff member at least once every day and the institutional head or his or her delegate at least once every eight hours.

43.   Inmates in administrative segregation shall be accorded the same rights, privileges, and conditions of confinement as the general population, except for those that

(a)   can only be enjoyed in association with other inmates; or

(b)   cannot reasonably be granted having regard to the physical limitations or the security requirements of the administrative segregation area.

Inmate Discipline

44.   In this Part "disciplinary offence" means a disciplinary offence as prescribed by regulation.

Establishment of Disciplinary System

45.   (1)   There shall be in each penitentiary a fair and reasonable disciplinary system to foster an environment in which inmates are

expected to conduct themselves according to acceptable standards of behaviour, thereby promoting the good order of the institution and contributing to their successful reintegration into the community.

(2)   Inmates shall only be disciplined in accordance with this Part and the regulations hereunder.

Disclosure of Information

46.   Notwithstanding anything in this Act, information shall not be withheld from an inmate under this Part.

Reporting to Police

47.   Where there are reasonable grounds to believe that an inmate has committed a disciplinary offence that is also a criminal offence, the conduct may be dealt with under this Part unless it is in the public interest to have the matter dealt with through the criminal process, in which case the institutional head or his or her delegate shall refer the matter to the police force having jurisdiction.

Informal Resolution or Issue of Charge

48.   Where there are reasonable grounds to believe that an inmate is committing or has committed a disciplinary offence, the institutional head or his or her delegate shall reasonably attempt to informally resolve the matter, where possible, but where an informal resolution is not possible he or she may, depending upon the seriousness of the conduct, issue a charge of a minor or a serious disciplinary offence.

Notice of Charge

49.   An inmate charged with a disciplinary offence shall receive a notice of the charge in writing as soon as practicable, in accordance with the regulations.

Hearing

50.   Every inmate charged with a disciplinary offence shall be entitled to an in-person hearing of the charge, in accordance with the regulations, and shall not be found guilty of a disciplinary offence unless the person presiding over the hearing is satisfied that the inmate committed the disciplinary offence with which he or she is charged.

Disciplinary Sanctions

51.   (1)   An inmate who is found guilty of a minor offence is liable, in accordance with the regulations, to

(a) a warning or reprimand;
(b) a loss of privileges;
(c) make restitution;
(d) a fine; or
(e) perform extra duties, with his or her consent.

(2) An inmate who is found guilty of a serious offence is liable, in accordance with the regulations, to
(a) a warning or reprimand;
(b) a loss of privileges;
(c) make restitution;
(d) a fine;
(e) perform extra duties, with his or her consent;
(f) be dissociated from other inmates for a maximum of 30 days; or (g) any combination of the sanctions in (a), (b), (c), (d), (e) and (f).

Factors to be Considered in Imposing Sanctions

52. In imposing a sanction, the person presiding over the disciplinary hearing shall consider
(a) the seriousness of the offence and the degree of responsibility of the inmate for the offence;
(b) the least restrictive alternative appropriate in the circumstances;
(c) all relevant aggravating and mitigating circumstances;
(d) the sanctions that have been imposed on other inmates for similar offences committed in similar circumstances;
(e) the nature and duration of any other sanction imposed on the inmate, to ensure that the combination of the sanctions is not excessive;
(f) any measures taken by the Service before the disposition of the charge, and any recommendations as to the appropriate sanction.

Summary Conviction Offences

53. (1) Every person commits an offence who
(a) possesses contraband beyond the visitor control point within the penitentiary facility, as specified in the regulations;
(b) possesses contraband as defined in paragraph (b) or (c) of the definition of contraband, in a penitentiary;
(c) delivers or attempts to deliver contraband to an inmate;
(d) receives or attempts to receive contraband from an inmate;

      (e)   without prior authorization, delivers or attempts to deliver jewellery to an inmate;

      (f)   without prior authorization, receives or attempts to receive jewellery from an inmate;

      (g)   trespasses upon penitentiary lands; or

      (h)   assists a person to do anything in paragraph (c), (d), (e), (f), or (g).

(2)   Every inmate who possesses contraband in a penitentiary commits an offence.

(3)   For the purpose of this section, "prior authorization" means the written permission of the institutional head or his or her delegate.

(4)   Every person who commits an offence under subsections (1) or (2) is guilty of a summary conviction offence and is liable to imprisonment for a term not exceeding one year, or to a fine of one thousand dollars, or to both.   .

Search and Seizure Definitions

54.   In this Part

Personal search includes the following:

Non-intrusive search by technical or other means, as specified in the Regulations.

Frisk search, a hand search of the clothed body, and search of personal possessions the person may be carrying, as specified in the Regulations.

Urinalysis, a procedure in which a person is required to provide a urine sample by the normal excretory process for scientific analysis by an approved instrument.

Strip search, a visual search of the naked body, as well as a search of all clothing and things in the clothing, as specified in the Regulations.

Body cavity search, a procedure in addition to a strip search which includes the physical probing of the rectum or vagina, as specified in the Regulations.

X-rays, as specified in the Regulations.

Routine search or inspection means the power to conduct a search of a person, place or vehicle without individualized suspicion.

Power to Seize

55.   Subject to section 58(5) and 58(6)(b), a staff member may seize contraband or evidence of a disciplinary or criminal offence during the course of a lawful search under this Part.

Routine Non-intrusive Searches and Frisk Searches

56. A staff member may conduct routine non-intrusive searches or frisk searches of inmates, visitors and staff members, where reasonably required for security purposes, as specified in the regulations.

Search of Inmates

57. A staff member of the same sex as the inmate may conduct a routine strip search of an inmate where he or she has had access to items which may constitute contraband that may be secreted on the body, as specified in the Regulations, or where he or'she is entering or leaving dissociation or segregation.

58. (1) A staff member of either sex may conduct a frisk search of an inmate where he or she has a reasonable suspicion that the inmate is carrying contraband or there is evidence of an offence, including a disciplinary offence.

   (2) Subject to subsection (3), where a staff member believes on reasonable grounds that the inmate is carrying contraband or there is evidence of an offence and that a strip search is necessary to detect the presence of the contraband or evidence, and he or she first satisfies the institutional head or his or her delegate, a staff member of the same sex as the inmate may conduct a strip search.

   (3) Where a staff member believes on reasonable grounds that an inmate is carrying contraband of a dangerous nature, or that is in danger of loss or destruction, and that the delay necessary to obtain prior approval for a strip search or to comply with the gender requirement in subsection (2) would result in danger to human life or safety, he or she may conduct the strip search.

   (4) Where during a strip search a staff member has reasonable grounds to believe contraband is secreted in an intimate body cavity, he or she shall advise the institutional head.

   (5) A body cavity search

   (a) shall only be authorized where the institutional head is satisfied that there are reasonable grounds to believe that an inmate is carrying contraband within his or her body and that such a search is necessary to detect and seize the contraband, and

   (b) shall only be performed by a qualified medical practitioner who has obtained the consent of the inmate.

   (6) Where the institutional head is satisfied that there are reasonable grounds to believe that an inmate has ingested contraband or is

carrying contraband in a body cavity, he or she may authorize, in writing,

(a)   the detention of the inmate in a cell without plumbing fixtures, with notice to medical staff, on the expectation that the contraband will be expelled, or

(b)   the use of an x-ray machine by a qualified technician to detect the contraband where the consent of the inmate and a qualified medical practitioner has been obtained.

Exceptional Power for General Search of Inmates

59.   The institutional head may authorize a general frisk search or strip search of all the inmates in the institution or part thereof, where he or she believes on reasonable grounds that there exists a clear and substantial danger to human life or safety and that such a search is necessary to seize contraband to avert the danger.

Urinalysis

60.   Subject to section 61, a staff member may require an inmate to submit a urine sample for urinalysis

(a)   where the staff member believes on reasonable grounds that the inmate has committed or is committing a disciplinary offence and that a urine sample is necessary to provide evidence of the offence, and he or she obtains the prior authorization of the institutional head or his or her delegate;

(b)   as part of a random selection urinalysis program conducted without individualized grounds on a periodic basis in accordance with the regulations;

(c)   where the inmate has a documented history of substance abuse and the urinalysis is necessary to meet the eligibility requirements for participation in a community contact program as defined in the regulations; or

(d)   as a requirement of a substance abuse treatment program as defined in the regulations.

61.   (1)   Where an inmate is requested to submit a urine sample, prior to submitting the sample, he or she shall be advised in writing of

(a)   the reason for the request; and

(b)   the consequences of non-compliance with the request.

(2)   Where an inmate is requested to submit a urine sample pursuant to subsection 60(a), he or she shall be provided with an opportunity to respond to the institutional head or his or her delegate prior to submitting the sample.

Search of Cells and Other Areas

62.   Searches of cells and activity areas may be conducted in accordance with the regulations.

Search of Visitors

63.   (1)   A staff member of the same sex as a visitor may conduct a frisk search of the visitor where he or she suspects on reasonable grounds that the visitor is carrying contraband in circumstances constituting an offence and he or she first obtains the prior authorization of the institutional head or his or her delegate.

        (2)   Where a staff member suspects on reasonable grounds that a visitor is carrying contraband in circumstances constituting an offence and that a strip search is necessary to detect it, he or she may inform the visitor that he or she may either

                (a)   leave the institution and be denied the visit; or

                (b)   be strip searched if prior authorization of the institutional head has been obtained, or upon obtaining the authorization of the institutional head.

        (3)   Where a staff member has reasonable grounds to believe that a visitor is carrying contraband in circumstances constituting an offence and that a strip search is necessary to detect it, he or she may detain the visitor in order to seek authority from the institutional head

                (a)   to have the visitor strip searched by a staff member of the same sex; or

                (b)   to inform the police force having jurisdiction.

        (4)   Where a visitor is detained under subsection (1) or (3), he or she shall

                (a)   be informed promptly of the reasons therefore; and

                (b)   be given a reasonable opportunity to retain and instruct counsel without delay and be informed of that right before being searched.

        (5)   Where the institutional head is satisfied that there are reasonable grounds to suspect under subsection (2) or to believe under subsection (3) that a visitor is carrying contraband in circumstances constituting an offence and that a strip search is necessary to detect the contraband, he or she may authorize, in writing, a staff member of the same sex as the visitor to conduct a strip search.

        (6)   There shall be a sign posted at the entrance to penitentiary property, in a conspicuous position, to give warning that all

vehicles and persons on institutional property are subject to being searched in accordance with this Act and the regulations.

Search of Vehicles on Penitentiary Property

64. (1)   Routine searches of vehicles on penitentiary property may be conducted in accordance with the regulations.

(2)   A staff member who believes on reasonable grounds that contraband is located in a vehicle on penitentiary property in circumstances constituting an offence may, with prior authorization from the institutional head or his or her delegate, search the vehicle.

(3)   Where a staff member in subsection (2) believes on reasonable grounds that the delay necessary to obtain prior authorization would result in danger to human life or safety, he or she may search the vehicle without prior authorization.

Search of Staff Members

65. (1)   Where a staff member has reasonable grounds to believe that another staff member is carrying contraband in circumstances constituting an offence, he or she may detain the staff member in order to advise the institutional head.

(2)   Where a staff member is detained under subsection (1), he or she has the right

(a)   to be informed promptly of the reasons therefore; and

(b)   to retain and instruct counsel without delay and to be informed of that right.

(3)   Where the institutional head is satisfied that there are reasonable grounds to believe that a staff member is carrying contraband in circumstances constituting an offence, he or she may inform the police force having jurisdiction, or may authorize, in writing, a frisk search or a strip search of the staff member where he or she believes that such a search is necessary to detect the contraband.

Search of Offenders in Community-based Residential Facilities

66. (1)   Where an offender is in a community-based residential facility, an employee of the facility of either sex may

(a)   conduct a frisk search of the offender where he or she has a reasonable suspicion that the offender is violating a condition of his or her release, and that such a search is necessary to confirm it; and

(b)   search an offender's room where he or she has a reasonable suspicion that the offender is violating a condition of his or her release, and that such a search is necessary to confirm it.

(2)   For the purpose of this section, "community-based residential facility" means a facility offering accommodation or treatment to offenders on day parole, parole or statutory release pursuant to a contract with the Service.

Post-search

67.   (1)   Anyone who seizes an item during the course of a search under this Part

(i)   shall make and submit a report and receipt in accordance with the regulations; and

(ii)   shall submit the item to the institutional head or person specified in the Regulations.

(2)   A staff member who conducts a strip search under section 58, 63, or 65, in which nothing is seized, shall file a report in accordance with the Regulations.

(3)   Where the institutional head authorizes a general search of inmates pursuant to section 59, he or she shall make and submit a report to the Regional Deputy Commissioner in accordance with the Regulations.

Conditions of Confinement
Prohibited Treatment

68.   Instruments of restraint shall not be applied as punishment.

69.   Every staff member is prohibited from administering, instigating, consenting to, or acquiescing in the cruel, inhuman or degrading treatment or punishment of an offender who is or has been incarcerated in a penitentiary.

Physical Conditions

70.   The institutional head shall ensure that the penitentiary environment is maintained in a healthful and safe state.

Communications with the Public

71.   (1)   To promote relationships between offenders and the community through the maintenance and development of contacts with family, friends, community members and community resources, every inmate shall in accordance with the regulations, have reasonable access to telephones, the postal service and visits, subject to reasonable limits for maintaining the security of a penitentiary or the safety of an individual.

(2)   In accordance with the regulations
 (a)   an inmate's communications with members of the public may be intercepted, monitored, or prevented; and
 (b)   a visit between an inmate and a member of the public may be refused, suspended or restricted, where it is reasonable to do so to maintain the security of a penitentiary or the safety of an individual.

72.   (1)   There shall be posted at the entrance of each penitentiary a list of items that a visitor is permitted to have in his or her possession in the visiting area of the penitentiary.

 (2)   A visitor shall not have in his or her possession in the visiting area of a penitentiary an item that is not on a list of permitted items posted at the entrance of the penitentiary, unless he or she has obtained the permission of a staff member to possess the item.

 (3)   Where contrary to subsection (2) a visitor has in his or her possession an item mentioned in subsection (2) without having obtained the permission of a staff member to possess it, his or her visit may be suspended or restricted.

Inmate Association and Assembly

73.   The Service may limit the entitlement of an inmate to associate and assemble in order to maintain the security and good order of a penitentiary, the safety of an individual, or because of reasonable time, space or resource requirements.

74.   To the extent possible and appropriate, inmate committees and organizations shall on a continuing basis be provided with a reasonable opportunity to contribute to decisions concerning the inmate population as a whole.

Religion

75.   Every inmate shall be given reasonable opportunities to freely and openly participate in, and express his or her religion or spirituality, subject to reasonable limits for maintaining the security of a penitentiary or the safety of an individual in accordance with the regulations.

76.   The Service shall ensure that Aboriginal spirituality and spiritual leaders are accorded the same status, protections and privileges as other religions and religious leaders, and where numbers warrant, make a reasonable attempt to provide a penitentiary with an Aboriginal Elder who has been selected in consultation with the appropriate Aboriginal community.

Programs and Health Care

77. (1) The Service shall make available a range of programs designed to promote the reintegration of offenders and to address their special needs.

(2) Every offender is expected to actively participate in appropriate programs, subject to their availability.

Inmate Pay

78. The Commissioner shall with the approval of Treasury Board, authorize payments to inmates, which shall be designed to encourage them to participate in the programs of the penitentiary and may be subject to deductions and forfeitures in accordance with the regulations.

Female Offenders

79. The Service shall
(a) provide programs particularly suited to serving the needs of female offenders; and
(b) regularly consult with women's groups and persons with experience and expertise on female offenders about the provision of correctional programs to female offenders.

Aboriginal Offenders

80. For the purpose of this Act "Aboriginal community" means a nation, tribal council, band, organization or other group of predominantly Indian, Inuit or Metis people;
"Aboriginal correctional authority" means a body or an individual that is providing or is designated by an Aboriginal community to provide correctional services, and is, to the extent possible, staffed by Aboriginal persons; and "correctional services" means services or programs appropriate for offenders, including their care and custody.

81. Correctional services shall be responsive to the needs of Aboriginal offenders, in accordance with this Act.

82. (1) The Minister or his or her delegate may enter into an agreement
(a) with an Aboriginal community; or
(b) with an Aboriginal correctional authority, for the provision of correctional services to Aboriginal offenders.

(2) An agreement entered into under subsection (1) may provide for payment to the Aboriginal community or the Aboriginal correctional authority in consideration for the provision of correctional services to an offender or offenders.

(3) Pursuant to an agreement entered into under subsection (1), the Commissioner or his or her delegate may place an offender under

the care and custody of the Aboriginal community or Aboriginal correctional authority

(a)   with the consent of the offender; and

(b)   following consultation with the relevant Aboriginal community or Aboriginal correctional authority.

(4)   The Service shall consult with Aboriginal communities and Aboriginal correctional authorities providing correctional services pursuant to an agreement entered into under subsection (1), about the provision of correctional services, the exercise of powers, and other matters affecting the offenders to whom they are providing correctional services.

83.   The Service shall establish a National Aboriginal Advisory Committee and, where appropriate, regional or local committees to

(a)   regularly consult with Aboriginal communities and persons with experience and expertise on Aboriginal offenders, customs and laws; and

(b)   provide advice to the Service about the provision of correctional services to Aboriginal offenders under the care and custody of the Service.

84.   The Service shall provide programs that are particularly suited to serving the needs of Aboriginal offenders.

85.   With the offender's consent, and where he or she has expressed an interest in being released to an Aboriginal community with a regular and recognized leadership, the Service shall give adequate notice to the Aboriginal community of the offender's parole application or approaching date of release on mandatory supervision, and shall give the Aboriginal community the opportunity to present a plan for the return of the offender and his or her reintegration into the Aboriginal community.

Health Care

86.   In this Part

(a)   "health care services" means professionally designed medical, dental and mental health care services administered to inmates by registered professionals; and

(b)   "mental health care" means the treatment of a disorder of thought, mood, perception, orientation or memory that significantly impairs judgment, behaviour, the capacity to recognize reality or ability to meet the ordinary demands of life.

87.   (1)   The Service shall provide every inmate with the essential health care services that he or she requires, which includes reasonable

access to mental health care services that will assist him or her to reintegrate into the community.

(2) The provision of health care services shall conform to professionally accepted standards of treatment.

88. (1) Subject to subsections (4) and (5), health care treatment shall only be provided to an inmate where he or she has the capacity to understand the consequences of accepting or rejecting the treatment, and gives his or her informed consent thereto.

(2) For the purpose of subsection (1), an inmate's consent to treatment is informed where it is voluntary and he or she has been advised

(a) of the likely effects of the treatment including possible side effects;

(b) of the likelihood and degree of improvement, remission, control or cure under the treatment;

(c) of the degree of uncertainty of the benefits and hazards of the treatment;

(d) of the reasonable alternatives to the treatment; and

(e) that he or she may refuse the treatment or withdraw from the treatment at any time.

(3) For the purpose of subsection (2), an inmate's consent to treatment shall not be considered involuntary only because the treatment is stipulated as a requirement for a conditional release program.

(4) Health care treatment under a therapeutic research program shall not be provided to an inmate unless an independent committee constituted in accordance with the regulations has

(a) approved the program as clinically sound and in conformance with accepted ethical standards; and

(b) reviewed the consent of the inmate thereto, and has determined that it has been given in accordance with subsections (1), (2), and

(5) Where an inmate does not have the capacity to understand the consequences of accepting or rejecting treatment, health care treatment shall be governed by the applicable provincial legislation.

89. The Service shall not authorize the force feeding of an inmate who had the capacity to understand the consequences of not eating at the time he or she made the decision not to eat.

90. Significant institutional decision making, including placement, classification, transfers, administrative segregation, disciplinary and

release decision making, shall involve reasonable consideration of an offender's health care needs.

Grievances

91. (1)   There shall be an inmate grievance procedure at each penitentiary for fairly and expeditiously resolving inmates' grievances on matters that, subject to subsection (2), are within the jurisdiction of the Commissioner, and it shall operate in accordance with this Act and the regulations.

(2)   The operation of the inmate grievance procedure shall not extend to matters relating to the discipline of staff members.

92. Every inmate shall have free access to the inmate grievance procedure without punitive consequences.

Annual Report

93. The Minister shall, on or before the 31st day of January next following the end of each fiscal year or, if Parliament is not then sitting, on any of the first five days next thereafter that Parliament is sitting, submit to Parliament a report showing the operations of the Service for that fiscal year.

Regulations

94. The Governor-in-council may make regulations

(a)   for the organization, training, discipline, efficiency, administration and good management of the Service;

(b)   for promoting and maintaining the security and good order of penitentiaries;

(c)   for the custody, treatment and supervision of offenders including but not restricted to regulations for

(i)   the organization, association and assembly of inmates,

(ii)   the religion of inmates,

(iii) inmates' access to reading and legal materials, and a commissioner of oaths,

(iv)   the provision of appropriate programs for offenders,

(v)   the discipline of inmates,

(vi)   the communication of inmates with members of the public,

(vii) the access of inmates to legal counsel and legal materials,

(viii) the transfer of inmates to federal and provincial institutions, and

(ix)   the administrative segregation of inmates;

(d)   for the search of offenders, staff members, visitors, cells, other parts of penitentiaries, and rooms in community-based residential facilities, and the seizure of items found thereon or therein;

(e)   for the return and forfeiture of items seized;

(f)   for inmate pay;

(g)   for the delivery of the estates of deceased inmates to their personal representatives in accordance with the applicable provincial laws;

(h)   for paying compensation for the disability or death of an offender;

(i)   for an inmate grievance procedure;

(j)   for the involvement of members of the community in the operation of the Service; and

(k)   generally, for carrying into effect the purpose, principles and provisions of this Act.

Chapter P-5
An Act Respecting Penitentiaries

SHORT TITLE

Short title

1. This Act may be cited as the *Penitentiary Act*. R.S., c. P-6, s. 1.

INTERPRETATION

Definitions

2. In this Act,

"Commissioner"

"Commissioner" means the Commissioner of Corrections referred to in section 5;

"inmate"

"inmate" means a person who, having been sentenced or committed to a penitentiary, has been received and accepted at a penitentiary pursuant to the sentence or committal and has not been lawfully discharged therefrom or from any other place pursuant to section 23.1;

"Minister"

"Minister" means the Solicitor General of Canada;

"penitentiary"

"penitentiary" means an institution or facility of any description, including all lands connected therewith, that is operated by the Service for the custody, treatment or training of persons sentenced or committed to penitentiary, and includes any place declared to be a penitentiary pursuant to subsection 3(1) or (2);

"Service"

"Service" means the Correctional Service of Canada referred to in section 4. R.S., 1985, c. P-5, s. 2; R.S., 1985, c. 35 (2nd Supp.), s. 15.

PENITENTIARIES

Place declared a penitentiary

3. (1) The Commissioner may, by order, declare any prison as defined in the *Prisons and Reformatories Act* or any hospital to be a penitentiary in respect of any person or class of persons.

Idem

(2)   The Governor in Council may, by order, declare any place to be a penitentiary.

Provincial approval required

(3)   No prison, hospital or place administered or supervised under the authority of an Act of the legislature of a province may be declared a penitentiary under subsection (1) or (2) until an officer designated by the lieutenant governor of the province in which the prison, hospital or place is located gives his approval.

Extended meaning of penitentiary

(4)   For the purposes of any law of Canada relating to escapes and rescues of prisoners, a penitentiary shall be deemed to include any place at or in which an inmate, prior to the inmate's lawful discharge from custody, is required by this Act or the regulations, or by an officer of the Service, to be or remain.

Lands constituting penitentiary

(5)   In any proceedings before a court in Canada in which a question arises concerning the location or dimension of lands alleged to constitute a penitentiary, a certificate, purporting to be signed by the Commissioner, setting out the location or description of the lands as constituting a penitentiary, is admissible in evidence and in the absence of any evidence to the contrary is proof that the lands as located or described in the certificate constitute a penitentiary.

Custody

(6)   Where an inmate is temporarily outside a penitentiary but under the direct charge, control or supervision of a member of the Service, the inmate is in custody for the

purposes of this Act and any other Act of Parliament. R.S., 1985, c. P-5, s. 3; R.S., 1985, c. 35 (2nd Supp.), S. 16.

CORRECTIONAL SERVICE OF CANADA

Correctional Service of Canada

4. There shall continue to be a penitentiary service in and for Canada, to be known as the Correctional Service of Canada. R.S., 1985, c. P-5, s. 4; R.S., 1985, c. 35 (2nd Supp.), s. 17.

COMMISSIONER

Commissioner

5. The Governor in Council may appoint an officer to be known as the Commissioner of Corrections who, under the direction of the Minister, has the control and management of the Service and all matters connected therewith. R.S., c. P-6, s. 4; 1976-77, c. 53, s. 36.

Administration of Parole Service

6. The portion of the staff of the National Parole Board known as the National Parole Service shall be under the control and management of the Commissioner who, in addition to the duties described in section 5, is responsible, under the direction of the Minister, for the preparation of cases of parole and the supervision of inmates to whom parole has been granted or who have been released on mandatory supervision pursuant to the *Parole Act*. 1976-77, c. 53, s. 37.

OFFICERS AND EMPLOYEES

Directors

7. (1) The Minister may appoint officers of the Service to be known as Directors of Divisions and Regional Directors.

Maximum number		(2)	The maximum number of officers in each class and their salaries shall be as prescribed by the Treasury Board. R.S., c. P-6, s. 5.
Other officers and employees	8.	(1)	The Commissioner, under the direction of the Minister, may appoint such other officers and employees of the Service as are necessary for the administration of this Act, and, in respect of those appointments, the preferences provided in the *Public Service Employment Act* in respect of military service apply.
Ranks and grades		(2)	The ranks and grades of officers and employees appointed by the Commissioner under subsection (1), the maximum number of persons to be appointed to each of those ranks and grades and their salaries shall be as prescribed by the Treasury Board. R.S., c. P-6, s. 6.
Oath	9.	(1)	Every officer and employee of the Service shall, before entering on the duties of his office, take the oath of allegiance and, in the case of an officer, an oath of office in the following form:

I, ..., solemnly swear that I will faithfully, diligently and impartially execute and perform the duties required of me as an officer of the Canadian Penitentiary Service and will well and truly obey and perform all lawful orders that I receive as such, without fear, favour or affection of or toward any person. So help me God.

Authority to administer	(2)	The oath prescribed by subsection (1) and any other oath or declaration that may be necessary or required may be taken by the Commissioner before any judge, magistrate or justice of the peace having jurisdiction in any part of Canada, and by any other officer of the Service before the Commissioner or any officer in charge of an institution or any person having authority to administer oaths or take or receive affidavits. R.S., c. P-6, s. 7.
Tenure	10. (1)	Officers and employees of the Service hold office during pleasure.
Suspension	(2)	The Commissioner may, where the Commissioner considers it in the interests of the Service, suspend from duty any officer or employee of the Service.
Idem	(3)	The officer in charge of a penitentiary may, where that officer considers it in the interests of the Service, suspend from duty any officer or employee of the Service who is under his jurisdiction. R.S., c. P-6. s. 8.
Member of Service	10.1	All officers and employees of the Service shall be deemed to be members of the Service. R.S., 1985, c. 35 (2nd Supp.), s. 18.
When Commissioner and Deputy Commissioner absent	11.	In the event that the Commissioner and Deputy Commissioner are absent or unable to act or their offices are vacant, the senior Divisional Head at the headquarters of the Service has the control and management of the Service and all matters connected therewith, and

for those purposes the senior Divisional Head may exercise all the powers of the Commissioner under this Act or any other Act of Parliament. R.S., c. P-6, s. 9.

Peace officer

12. The Commissioner may, in writing, designate any member of the Service or each member of a class of members of the Service to be a Peace officer and a member so designated is a peace officer in every part of Canada and has all the powers, authority, protection and privileges that a peace officer has by law. R.S./, 1985, c. P-5, s. 12; R.S., c. 35 (2nd Supp.), s. 19.

HEADQUARTERS

Headquarters

13. (1) The headquarters of the Service and the offices of the Commissioner shall be at Ottawa.

Regional headquarters

(2) The Commissioner may establish regional headquarters of the Service and fix the location of regional offices. R.S., c. P-6, s. 11.

INVESTIGATIONS

Investigations

14. The Commissioner may, from time to time, appoint a person to investigate and report on any matter affecting the operation of the Service and, for that purpose, the person so appointed has all of the powers of a commissioner appointed under Part II of the Inquiries Act, and section 10 of that Act applies, with such modifications as the circumstances require, in respect of investigations carried on under the authority of this section. R.S., c. P-6, s. 12.

COMMITTAL, RECEPTION AND TRANSFER OF INMATES

Warrant of committal

15. (1) Where a person is sentenced or committed to imprisonment for life, for an indeterminate period or for any term that is required to be served in a penitentiary, it is sufficient compliance with the law, notwithstanding anything in the Criminal Code, if the warrant of committal states that the person was sentenced for life, for an indeterminate period or for the term in question, as the case may be, without stating the name of any penitentiary to which the person is sentenced or committed.

Rules

(2) The Commissioner may make rules naming the penitentiaries in which, in the first instance, persons sentenced or committed in any part of Canada to penitentiary shall be received.

Transfer

(3) Where a person has been sentenced or committed to penitentiary, the Commissioner or any officer directed by the Commissioner may, by warrant under the hand of the Commissioner or that officer, direct that the person shall be committed or transferred to any penitentiary in Canada, whether or not that person has been received in the relevant penitentiary named in rules made under subsection (2).

(4) [Repealed, R.S., 1985, c. 35 (2nd Supp.), s. 20.

Custody in transit

(5) A person shall be deemed to be in lawful custody anywhere in Canada if, (a) having been sentenced or committed to penitentiary, that

person is in the custody of a person acting under the authority of the court that sentenced or committed him; or

(b) having been directed to be transferred to another penitentiary, that person is in the custody of a person acting under the authority of the officer who directed the transfer. R.S., 1985, c. P-5, s. 15; R.S., 1985, c. 35 (2nd Supp.), s. 20.

Newfoundland   16. (1) Notwithstanding anything in this Act, every person who is sentenced by any court in Newfoundland to imprisonment for life, or for a term of years not less than two, shall be sentenced to imprisonment in the penitentiary operated by the Province of Newfoundland at the city of St. John's for the confinement of prisoners, and shall be subject to the statutes, rules, regulations and other laws pertaining to the management and control of that penitentiary.

Transfer from   (2) Subsection 15(3) applies in respect
Newfoundland   of persons imprisoned under subsection (1), except that such a person shall not be transferred from the penitentiary mentioned in subsection (1) without the approval of an officer designated by the Lieutenant Governor of Newfoundland.

Agreement   (3) The Minister may, with the approval of the Governor in Council, enter into an agreement with the Province of Newfoundland providing for the payment to the Province of the cost of maintaining the persons who are or have been sentenced or committed to penitentiary. R.S., 1985, c. P-5, s. 16; R.S., 1985, c. 35 (2nd Supp.), s. 21.

YUKON TERRITORY AND NORTHWEST TERRITORIES

Arrangements with provinces

17. (1) The Minister may, with the approval of the Governor in Council, arrange with the lieutenant governor of any province for the confinement, in the prisons or reformatories of that province, of persons convicted in the Yukon Territory or the Northwest Territories and for the compensation to be paid by the Government of Canada to the government of the province in respect of persons so confined.

Transfer

(2) Where an arrangement has been made under subsection (1), the Commissioner or any officer directed by the Commissioner may, by warrant under the hand of the Commissioner or that officer, direct the transfer of a person convicted in the Yukon Territory or the Northwest Territories to a prison or reformatory in a province in respect of which the arrangement applies, and the person shall, while being escorted to that prison, be deemed to be in a lawful custody.

Deeming

(3) A person who is confined in a prison or reformatory outside the Yukon Territory or the Northwest Territories pursuant to an arrangement made under subsection (1) shall, during the term of that person's sentence or period

of committal, be deemed to be lawfully confined. R.S., c. P-6, s. 14.

SENTENCES OF LESS THAN TWO YEARS

Agreements with provinces

18. (1) The Minister, with the general or special approval of the Governor in Council, may on behalf of the Government of Canada enter into an agreement with the government of any province for the confinement in penitentiaries or any other institutions under the direction or supervision of the Service of persons sentenced or committed to imprisonment for less than two years for offences under this Act or any other Act of Parliament or any regulations made thereunder, but any such agreement shall include provisions whereby those persons shall be confined at the expense of the provincial government concerned.

Effect of confinement in penitentiary

(2) A person who is confined in a penitentiary or other institution pursuant to an agreement made under subsection (1) shall, during committal, be deemed to be lawfully confined and is subject to all the statutes, regulations, rules and orders applicable in the penitentiary or in the institution. R.S., c. P-6, s. 15; 1976-77, c. 53, s. 39.

RECEPTION OF INMATES

Time when persons may be received

19. (1) A person who has been sentenced or committed to penitentiary shall not be received in a penitentiary until after the expiration of the time limited by law for an appeal, and thereupon that person may be

Election not to appeal

Transfer for
preparation or
presentation of appeal

received in a penitentiary whether or not that person has entered an appeal.

(2) A person referred to in subsection (1) may, before the expiration of the time limited by law for an appeal, give written notice to the court that sentenced or committed that person that he elects not to appeal or abandons his appeal, as the case may be, and thereupon the time limited for appeal shall be deemed to have expired.

(3) Where the Commissioner or an officer of the Service designated by the Commissioner is satisfied that attendance of an inmate is required away from the penitentiary into which the inmate has been received, for the purpose of the preparation or presentation of an appeal from the inmate's conviction or sentence, the Commissioner or the officer designated by the Commissioner may issue a written direction to the officer in charge of the penitentiary into which the inmate has been received directing that officer, for that purpose, to transfer the inmate to a prison, common jail or other place, not being a penitentiary, in which persons who are charged with or convicted of offences are usually kept in custody. R.S.. c. P-6. s. 16.

Medical certificate 20. Subject to any relevant agreement that may be made under section 22, the officer in charge of a penitentiary is not required to accept a person into custody under a warrant of committal unless there is, in relation to that person, a certificate of a duly qualified medical practitioner that certifies that the person is free from dangerous, contagious or infectious disease. R.S., c. P-6, s. 17.

Custody before being received in penitentiary

21. (1) A person who by reason of subsection 19(1) is not received into a penitentiary or who by reason of section 20 is not accepted into custody shall be confined in any prison, common jail or other place, not being a penitentiary, in which persons who are charged with or convicted of offences are usually kept in custody.

Custody by keeper of prison, common jail or other place

(2) The keeper of any prison, common jail or other place referred to in subsection (1) or 19(3) to whom a person referred to in either of those subsections is delivered shall, on sufficient authority, receive, safely keep and detain that person under custody in the prison, common jail or other place until that person is returned to or transferred to a penitentiary or discharged from custody in accordance with law.

Sufficient authority

(3) The original of the warrant or other instrument by which a person referred to in subsection (1) or 19(3) is committed to or is to be imprisoned in a penitentiary, or a copy thereof duly certified by any judge or magistrate or by the clerk of the court in which that person was convicted, is sufficient authority for that person's detention in accordance with subsection (2). R.S., c. P-6, s. 18.

TEMPORARY ACCOMMODATION

Assisting person's rehabilitation

21.1 Subject to the Commissioner's directives, where in the opinion of the member in charge of a penitentiary it would assist the rehabilitation of a person who has been released on parole or subject to mandatory supervision pursuant to the *Parole Act* to allow that person to be temporarily accommodated in that penitentiary, the member in charge may, on the request of the person, allow the person to stay temporarily in the penitentiary for such period of time and subject to such conditions as are specified by the member in accordance with the Commissioner's directives. R.S., 1985, c. 35 (2nd Supp.), s. 22.

TEMPORARY ACCOMMODATION

Mentally Ill Inmates

22. (1) The Minister may, with the approval of the Governor in Council, enter into an agreement with the government of any province to provide for the custody, in a mental hospital or other appropriate institution operated by the province, of persons who, having been sentenced or committed to penitentiary, are found to be mentally ill or mentally defective during confinement in penitentiary.

Idem

(2) Where no agreement has been made under subsection (1) between the Minister and the government of any province from which a mentally ill or mentally defective person is sentenced or committed to penitentiary, the officer in charge of the penitentiary may, on the advice of the penitentiary physician or psychiatrist, refuse to accept

custody of that person under the sentence or committal or, if custody of that person has been accepted, may, under the authority of a written direction by the Commissioner, return that person to the prison or other place of confinement from which that person was received.

Diseased inmates (3) The Minister may, with the approval of the governor in Council, enter into an agreement with the government of any province to provide for the custody, in penitentiary hospitals, of persons who, having been sentenced or committed to a provincial prison, are found to be suffering from any dangerous, contagious or infectious disease during the sentence.

Deeming (4) A person who, pursuant to subsection (1), is confined in a provincial hospital or other institution shall, during the term of his confinement therein, be deemed to be confined in a penitentiary.

Idem (5) A person who, pursuant to subsection (3), is confined in a penitentiary hospital shall, during the term of his confinement therein, be deemed to be confined in a provincial prison. R.S., c. P-6, s. 19.

Discharge of diseased inmates 23. Where, on the day appointed for the lawful discharge of an inmate from a penitentiary, the inmate is found to be suffering from a disease that is dangerous, contagious or infectious, the inmate shall be detained in the penitentiary until such time as the officer in charge has made appropriate arrangements for the treatment of the inmate in an appropriate provincial institution or until the inmate is cured, whichever is the earlier. R.S., c. P-6, s. 20.

DISCHARGE OF INMATES GENERALLY

Place of discharge

23.1 An inmate may be discharged from a penitentiary or from any other place designated by the Commissioner's directives. R.S., 1985, c. 35 (2nd Supp.), s. 23.

Date of release

23.2 (1) An inmate, other than a paroled inmate as defined in the *Parole Act*, who is entitled to be released shall be released during the daylight hours of the last working day prior to the ordinary release date of the inmate.

Definition of "working day"

(2) For the purposes of subsection (1), "working day," in a province, means a day on which offices of the Public Service of Canada are generally open in that province. R.S., 1985, c. 35 (2nd Supp.), s. 23.

YOUNG INMATES

24. [Repealed, R.S., 1985, c. 24 (2nd Supp.), s. 48]

EARNED REMISSION

Remission

25. (1) Subject to this section and section 26.1, every inmate shall be credited with fifteen days of remission of the sentence of the inmate in respect of each month and with a number of days calculated on a pro rata basis in respect of each incomplete month during which the inmate has been industrious, as determined in accordance with any Commissioner's directives made in that behalf, with regard to the

program of the penitentiary in which the inmate is imprisoned.

Computing remission credits

(2) The first credit of earned remission pursuant to subsection (1) shall be made not later than the end of the month next following the month the inmate is received into a penitentiary, and thereafter a credit of earned remission shall be made at intervals of not more than three months.

Idem

(3) Where an inmate was received into a penitentiary before July 1, 1978, the date of the first credit of earned remission referred to in subsection (2) is August 31, 1978 and the subsequent intervals run from that date.

References to expiration of sentence according to law

(4) For the purposes of this section and section 26.1, a reference to the expiration of a sentence of an inmate according to law shall be read as a reference to the day on which the sentence expires, without taking into consideration any remission standing to the credit of the inmate.

Effect of remission

(5) An inmate is not entitled to be released from imprisonment, solely as a result of remission,

(a) prior to the expiration according to law of the sentence the inmate is serving at the time an order is made in respect of the inmate pursuant to paragraph 21.4(4)(a) of the *Parole Act*, as determined in accordance with section 20 of that Act at the time the order is made; or

(b)   where the case of the inmate is referred to the Chairman of the National Parole Board pursuant to subsection 21.3(3) of the *Parole Act* during the six months immediately preceding the presumptive release date of the inmate, prior to the rendering of the decision of the Board in connection therewith.

Effect of direction not to be released as a result of remission

(6)   Where an order is made in respect of an inmate pursuant to paragraph 21.4(4)(a) of the *Parole Act*, the inmate shall forfeit all statutory and earned remission standing to the credit of the inmate, whether accrued before or after the coming into force of this section.

Idem

(7)   Any remission of sentence forfeited pursuant to subsection (6) shall not thereafter be recredited pursuant to subsection 24(3) of the *Parole Act.* R.S., 1985, c. P-5, s. 25; R.S., 1985, c. 34 (2nd Supp.). s. 10.

Forfeiture of earned remission

26.   Every inmate who, having been credited with earned remission, is convicted in disciplinary court of any disciplinary offence is liable to forfeit, in whole or in part, the earned remission that stands to the credit of the inmate and that accrued after July 1, 1978 but no such forfeiture of more than thirty days shall be valid without the concurrence of the Commissioner or a member of the Service designated by the Commissioner, or of more than ninety days without the concurrence of the Minister. R.S., 1985, c. P-5, s. 26; R.S., 1985, c. 35 (2nd Supp.), s. 24.

No remission on
revocation of
mandatory supervision

26.1 (1) Where, following an order of the Board made pursuant to paragraph 21.4(4)(a) or (b) of the *Parole Act* or an order declaring that, at the time the case was referred to the Board, the inmate was serving a term of imprisonment that included a sentence imposed in respect of an offence mentioned in the schedule to the *Parole Act* that had been prosecuted by indictment and declaring that, in the opinion of the Board, the commission of the offence caused the death of or serious harm to another person, the inmate was released subject to mandatory supervision and the mandatory supervision is revoked, the inmate

(a) shall, except in respect of a consecutive sentence or portion thereof imposed after the inmate's release subject to mandatory supervision and served prior to the revocation of the mandatory supervision, forfeit all statutory and earned remission standing to the credit of the inmate, whether accrued before or after the coming into force of this section; and

(b) is not entitled to be released from imprisonment, solely as a result of remission, prior to the expiration according to law of the sentence, as determined in accordance with section 20 of the *Parole Act*, that the inmate was serving on the date of release.

Idem   (2)   Any remission of sentence forfeited pursuant to subsection (1) shall not thereafter be remitted or recredited pursuant to paragraph 25(2)(c) or (d) or subsection 25(3) of the *Parole Act*. R.S., 1985, c. 34 (2nd Supp.), s. 11.

PAROLE
27.   [Repealed, R.S., 19485, c. 35 (2nd Supp.), s. 25.

TEMPORARY ABSENCE

Escorted temporary absence   28.   Where, in the opinion of the Commissioner or the officer in charge of a penitentiary, it is necessary or desirable that an inmate should be absent, with escort, for medical or humanitarian reasons or to assist in the rehabilitation of the inmate, the absence may be authorized by

(a)   the Commissioner, for an unlimited period for medical reasons and for a period not exceeding fifteen days for humanitarian reasons or to assist in the rehabilitation of the inmate; or

(b)   the officer in charge, for a period not exceeding fifteen days for medical reasons and for a period not exceeding five days for humanitarian reasons or to assist in the rehabilitation of the inmate. R.S., c. P-6, s. 26; 1976-77, c. 53, s. 42.

Where inmate transferred to provincial institution   29.   (1)   Where, pursuant to an agreement made ;under subsection 22(1), an inmate has been admitted to a provincially operated mental hospital or to any other provincially operated institution in which the liberty of the patients is normally subject to restriction, the officer in charge of the provincial institution may permit temporary absences with escort from that institution, within the limits prescribed in paragraph 28(b), when the officer is delegated that authority by the member in charge of the penitentiary in which the inmate was last confined.

Delegation of authority

(2)   For the purposes of subsection (1), the member in charge of a penitentiary may delegate the authority to grant temporary absences to the officer in charge of the provincial institution described in subsection (1) either generally or for specific cases. R.S., 19485, c. P-5, s. 29; R.S., 19485, c. 35 (2nd Supp.), s. 26.

30.   [Repealed, R.S., 1985, c. 35 (2nd Supp.), s. 26.

Effect on date of release

31.   Where an inmate is granted a temporary absence and the day on which he is due to be released falls within the period of that temporary absence, the inmate shall, for the purpose of all entitlements accruing to him on release, be deemed to have been released on the day on which the temporary absence commenced. 1976-77, c. 53. s. 42.

PENITENTIARY INDUSTRY

Advisory Committee

32.   (1)   There shall be a committee called the Advisory Committee on Penitentiary Industry, to be appointed by the Minister and to

consist of not more than nine persons chosen from the fields of industry, labour, government and the general public, to advise the Commissioner concerning industrial operations to be carried on by inmate labour in connection with the Service.

Expenses (2) Members of the Advisory Committee appointed pursuant to subsection (1) shall serve without remuneration but are entitled to be paid reasonable travel and living expenses incurred by them while absent from their ordinary place of residence in connection with the work of the Committee. R.S., c. P-6, s. 27.

BUILDING AND WORKS

Commissioner's powers 33. The repair and maintenance of buildings and works in relation to penitentiaries and, to the extent specified by any order of the Governor in Council, the construction of those buildings and works, are under the control and direction of the Commissioner. R.S., c. P-6, s. 28.

COMPENSATION FOR DISABILITY OR DEATH

Minister may pay compensation 34. (1) Subject to and in accordance with any regulations made under subsection 37(1), the Minister may pay compensation

(a) to a discharged inmate for physical disability attributable to the inmate's participation in the normal program of a penitentiary; and

(b) to the surviving spouse or dependent children of a

discharged inmate or an inmate who died before the expiration of his sentence whose death is attributable to his participation in the normal program of a penitentiary.

Definition of "discharged inmate"

(2)   In this section, "discharged inmate" means an inmate who has been released as a result of the expiration of his sentence or the operation of remission or who has been released on parole other than day parole. 1976-77, c. 53, s. 43.

FORFEITURE OF CONTRABAND

Forfeiture

35.   (1)   Subject to subsections (2) and (3), where an inmate is convicted in disciplinary court of possession of contraband, the contraband in respect of which the inmate is convicted is forfeited to Her Majesty in right of Canada.

Expiration

(2)   Where, on application made by an inmate in accordance with the regulations within three months after a forfeiture referred to in subsection (1), it is established to the satisfaction of the Commissioner or a member of the Service designated by the Commissioner that the forfeiture would cause undue hardship to the inmate, the Commissioner or that member shall, if possession of the object forfeited by the inmate would be lawful, cancel the forfeiture and order that the object be delivered to the inmate.

Idem

(3)   Where, within three months after a forfeiture referred to in subsection (1), it is established to the

satisfaction of the Commissioner or an officer of the Service designated by the Commissioner that a person other than the inmate has title to or an interest in an object forfeited and is innocent of any complicity in the events that resulted in the forfeiture, the Commissioner or that officer shall, if possession of the object forfeited by that person would be lawful, cancel the forfeiture and order that the object be delivered to that person.

Definition of "contraband"

(4) For the purposes of this section, "contraband" means anything that is in an inmate's possession in circumstances in which possession thereof is forbidden by any Act, regulation or Commissioner's directive, or by an order of general or specific application within the penitentiary in which the inmate is imprisoned. R.S., 1985, c. P-5, s. 35; R.S., 1985, c. 35 (2nd Supp.), s. 27.

ADMINISTRATION OF DECEASED INMATES' ESTATES

Service may administer estate

36. (1) Subject to and in accordance with any regulations made under subsection 37(1), the Service may, if the appropriate authority of the province in which the inmate was incarcerated does not do so, collect, administer and distribute the estate of a deceased inmate.

Definition of "estate of a deceased inmate"

(2) For the purposes of this section, "estate of a deceased inmate" means the following parts of the estate of an inmate who dies while serving a term of imprisonment in a penitentiary:

(a) any pay that, under the regulations, was due or otherwise payable to the inmate at the time of the inmate's death;

(b) any moneys standing to the inmate's credit at that time in any fund maintained or controlled by the Service; and

(c) any personal belongings, including cash, found on the inmate or in the possession of the inmate at the time of death or that are in the care or custody of the Service at that time. 1976-77, c. 54, s.43.

REGULATIONS AND RULES

Regulations

37. (1) The Governor in Council may make regulations

(a) for the organization, training, discipline, efficiency, administration and good government of the Service;

(b) for the custody, treatment, training, employment and discipline of inmates;

(c) prescribing the compensation that may be paid pursuant to section 34, the terms and conditions in accordance with which the compensation is to be paid and the manner of its payment;

(c.1) prescribing the manner in which an inmate applies for cancellation of a forfeiture of property under subsection 35(2);

(d) defining the term "spouse" and the expression "dependent child" for the purposes of section 34;

(e) for the collection, administration and distribution of estates of deceased inmates;

(f) providing for the appointment by the Governor in Council or by the Minister of a person to preside over a disciplinary court, prescribing the duties to be performed by that person and fixing that persons' remuneration; and

(g) generally, for carrying into effect the purposes and provisions of this Act.

Punishment for contravention (2) The Governor in Council may, in any regulations made under subsection (1) other than paragraph (b) thereof, provide for a fine not exceeding five hundred dollars or imprisonment for a term not exceeding six months, or both, to be imposed on summary conviction for the contravention of any such regulation.

Rules and orders of Commissioner (3) Subject to this Act and any regulations made under subsection (1), the Commissioner may make rules, to be known as Commissioner's directives, for the organization, training, discipline, efficiency, administration and good government of the Service, and for the custody, treatment, training, employment and discipline of inmates and the good government of penitentiaries. R.S., 1985, c. P-5,

s. 37; R.S., 19485, c. 35 (2nd Supp.), s. 28.

ANNUAL REPORT

Annual report

38. The Minister shall, on or before January 31 next following the end of each fiscal year, or if parliament is not then sitting on any of the first five days next thereafter that either House of Parliament is sitting, submit to Parliament a report showing the operation of the Service for that fiscal year. R.S., c. P-6, s. 30.

RELATED PROVISIONS

R.S., 19485, c. 34 (2nd Supp.), s. 14:

Review of Act after three years

14. (1) Three years after the coming into force of this Act, a comprehensive review of the provisions and operation of sections 21.2 to 21.6 of the *Parole Act* and the schedule thereto, as enacted by sections 5 and 9 of this Act, and subsections 25(5) to (7) and section 26.1 of the *Penitentiary Act*, as enacted by subsection 10(2) and section 11 of this Act, shall be undertaken by such committee of the House of Commons or of both Houses of Parliament as may be designated or established by Parliament for that purpose.

Report to Parliament

(2) The committee referred to in subsection (1) shall, within one year after a review is undertaken pursuant to that subsection or within such further time as Parliament may authorize, submit to Parliament a report on the review, including a statement of any changes the committee recommends.

R.S., 1985, c. 35 (2nd Supp.), s. 15(2):

References to "Correctional Service of Canada"	"(2) Whenever the 'Canadian Penitentiary Service' is referred to in any Act of Parliament other than this Act or in any document, regulation or statutory instrument made thereunder, there shall in every case, unless the context otherwise requires, be substituted the 'Correctional Service of Canada.'"

R.S., 19485, c. 35 (2nd Supp.), s. 18(2):

References to members	"(2) Whenever, with respect to the Correctional Service of Canada, the word 'officer' or 'employee' occurs in any Act of Parliament other than this Act or any document, regulation or statutory instrument made thereunder, there shall in every case, unless the context otherwise requires, be substituted the word 'member.'"

Chapter P-20
An Act Respecting Public and Reformatory Prisons

SHORT TITLE

Short title

1. This Act may be cited as the *Prisons and Reformatories Act*. R.S., c. P-21, s.1.

INTERPRETATION

Definitions

"lieutenant governor"

"Minister"

"prison"

"prisoner"

2. (1) In this Act,

"lieutenant governor" means lieutenant governor in council;

"Minister" means the Solicitor General of Canada;

"prison" means a place of confinement other than a penitentiary as defined in the *Penitentiary Act*;

"prisoner" means a person, other than

(a) a child within the meaning of the *Juvenile Delinquents Act*, chapter J-3 of the Revised Statutes of Canada, 1970, as it read immediately prior to April 2, 1984, with respect to whom no order pursuant to section 9 of that Act has been made, or

(b) a young person within the meaning of the *Young Offenders Act* with respect to whom no order pursuant to section 16 of that Act has been made,

who is confined in a prison pursuant to a sentence for an offence under an Act of Parliament or any regulations made thereunder.

Custody

(2) Where a prisoner is temporarily outside a prison but under the direct charge, control or supervision

of an officer or employee of a prison, the prisoner is in custody for the purposes of this Act and any other Act of Parliament. R.S., 1985, c. P-20, s. 2; R.S., 1985, c. 35 (2nd Supp.), s. 29.

COMMITTAL, RECEPTION AND TRANSFER OF PRISONERS

Warrant of committal

3. Where a person is sentenced or committed to imprisonment in a prison, it is sufficient compliance with the law, notwithstanding anything in the *Criminal Code*, if the warrant of committal states that the person was sentenced or committed to imprisonment in a prison for the term in question, without stating the name of any particular prison. R.S., c. P-21, s. 3; 1976-77, c. 53, s. 45.

4. (1) [Repealed, R.S., 1985, c. 35 (2nd Supp.), s. 30]

Transfers between provinces

(2) The governments of the provinces may enter into agreements with one another providing for the transfer of prisoners from a prison in one province to a prison in another province.

Effect of transfer

(3) A prisoner transferred under an agreement made pursuant to subsection (2) shall be deemed to be lawfully confined in the receiving prison and is subject to all the statutes, regulations and rules applicable in the receiving prison. R.S., 1985, c. P-20, s. 4; R.S., 1985, c. 35 (2nd Supp.), s. 30.

Transfers from penitentiaries to prisons

5. (1) The Minister may, with the approval of the Governor in Council, enter into an agreement with the government of any

province for the transfer of inmates from any penitentiary in Canada to any prison in that province.

Idem   (2) The Commissioner of Corrections or a member of the Canadian Penitentiary Service designated by the Commissioner may direct transfers of inmates in accordance with agreements entered into under subsection (1).

Effect of transfer   (3) An inmate transferred under this section or under an agreement made pursuant to any other lawful authority shall be deemed to be lawfully confined in the receiving prison and is subject to all the statutes, regulations and rules applicable in the receiving prison. R.S., 1985, c. P-20, s. 5; R.S., 1985, c. 35 (2nd Supp.), s. 31.

EARNED REMISSION

Remission   6. (1) Every prisoner serving a sentence shall be credited with fifteen days of remission of the sentence in respect of each month and with a number of days calculated on a pro rata basis in respect of each incomplete month during which the prisoner has applied himself industriously, as determined in accordance with any regulations made by the lieutenant governor of the province in which the prisoner is imprisoned, to the program of the place of confinement in which the prisoner is imprisoned.

Computing remission credits   (2) The first credit of earned remission pursuant to subsection (1) shall be made not later than the end of the month next following the month the prisoner is received into a prison and thereafter a credit of earned remission shall be made at intervals of not more than three months.

Idem   (3)   Where a prisoner was received into a prison before July 1, 1978, the date of the first credit of earned remission referred to in subsection (2) is August 31, 1978 and the subsequent intervals run from that date.

Forfeiture   (4)   Every prisoner who, having been credited with earned remission, commits any breach of the prison rules is, at the discretion of the person who determines that the breach has been committed, liable to forfeit, in whole or in part, the earned remission that stands to the credit of the prisoner and that accrued to the prisoner after July 1, 1978.

R.S., 1985, c. P-20, s. 6; R.S., 1985, c. 35 (2nd Supp.), s. 32.

TEMPORARY ABSENCE

Temporary Absence   7.   (1)   Where, in the opinion of an officer designated by the lieutenant governor of the province in which a prisoner is confined, it is necessary or desirable that a prisoner should be absent, with or without escort, for medical or humanitarian reasons or to assist in the rehabilitation of the prisoner, subject to subsection (2), the absence may be authorized by that officer for an unlimited period for medical reasons and for a period not exceeding fifteen days for humanitarian reasons or to assist in the rehabilitation of the prisoner.

Approval of provincial parole board

(2) Where, in a province, a provincial parole board has been appointed pursuant to section 12 of the *Parole Act*, the lieutenant governor of the province may order that no absence without escort be authorized except under that authority and with the approval of the provincial parole board.
R.S., c. P-21, s. 8; 1976-77, c. 53, s. 45.

Effect on date of release

8. Where a prisoner is granted a temporary absence and the date on which he is due to be released falls within the period of that temporary absence, the prisoner shall, for the purposes of all entitlements accruing to him on release, be deemed to have been released on the day on which the temporary absence commenced.
R.S., c. P-21, s. 9; 1976-77, c. 53, s. 45.

YOUNG OFFENDERS

9. [Repealed, R.S., 1985, c. 24 (2nd Supp.), s. 49]

10. and
11. [Repealed, R.S., 1985, c. 35 (2nd Supp.), s. 33]

12. [Repealed, R.S., 1985, c. 1 (1st Supp.), s. 1]

13. [Repealed, R.S., 1985, c. 1 (1st Supp.), s. 2]

Mission Statement

The Correctional Service of Canada, as part of the criminal justice system, contributes to the protection of society by actively encouraging and assisting offenders to become law-abiding citizens, while exercising reasonable, safe, secure and humane control.

Core Value 1
We respect the dignity of individuals, the rights of all members of society and the potential for human growth and development.

Core Value 2
We recognize that the offender has the potential to live as a law-abiding citizen.

Core Value 3
We believe that our strength and our major resource in achieving our objectives is our staff, and that human relationships are the cornerstone of our endeavour.

Core Value 4
We believe that the sharing of ideas, knowledge, values and experience, nationally and internationally, is essential to the achievement of our Mission.

Core Value 5
We believe in managing the Service with openness and integrity and we are accountable to the Solicitor General.

Constitution Act, 1982
Schedule B
Part I

Canadian Charter of Rights and Freedoms

Whereas Canada is founded upon principles that recognize the supremacy of God and the rule of law:

Guarantee of Rights and Freedoms

Rights and freedoms in Canada

1. The *Canadian Charter of Rights and Freedoms* guarantees the rights and freedoms set in it subject only to such reasonable limits prescribed by law as can be demonstrably justified in a free and democratic society.

Fundamental Freedoms

Fundamental freedoms

2. Everyone has the following fundamental freedoms:
    (a) freedom of conscience and religion;
    (b) freedom of thought, belief, opinion and expression, including freedom of the press and other media of communication;
    (c) freedom of peaceful assembly; and
    (d) freedom of association.

Democratic Rights

Democratic rights of citizens

3. Every citizen of Canada has the right to vote in an election of members of the House of Commons or of a legislative assembly and to be qualified for membership therein.

Maximum duration of legislative bodies

4. (1) No House of Commons and no legislative assembly shall continue for longer than five years from the date fixed for the return of the writs at a general election of its members.

Continuation in special circumstances
(2)   In time of real or apprehended war, invasion or insurrection, a House of Commons may be continued by Parliament and a legislative assembly may be continued by the legislature beyond five years if such continuation is not opposed by the votes of more than one-third of the members of the House of Commons or the legislative assembly, as the case may be.

Annual sitting of legislative bodies
5.   There shall be a sitting of Parliament and of each legislature at least once every twelve months.

Mobility Rights

Mobility of citizens
6.   (1)   Every citizen of Canada has the right to enter, remain in and leave Canada.

Right to move and gain livelihood
(2)   Every citizen of Canada and every person who has the status of a permanent resident of Canada has the right
(a)   to move and take up residence in any province; and
(b)   to pursue the gaining of a livelihood in any province.

Limitation
(3)   The rights specified in subsection (2) are subject to
(a)   any laws or practices of general application in force in a province other than those that discriminate among persons primarily on the basis of province of present or previous residence; and
(b)   any laws providing for reasonable residency requirements as a qualification for the receipt of publicly provided social services.

Affirmative action programs
(4)   Subsection (2) and (3) do not preclude any law, program or activity that has as its object the amelioration in a province of conditions of individuals in that province who are socially or economically disadvantaged if the rate of employment in that province is below the rate of employment in Canada.

Legal Rights
Life, liberty and security of person
7. Everyone has the right to life, liberty and security of the person and the right not to be deprived thereof except in accordance with the principles of fundamental justice.

Search or seizure
8. Everyone has the right to be secure against unreasonable search or seizure.

Detention or imprisonment
9. Everyone has the right not to be arbitrarily detained or imprisoned.

Arrest or detention
10. Everyone has the right on arrest or detention
    (a) to be informed promptly of the reasons therefor;
    (b) to retain and instruct counsel without delay and to be informed of that right; and
    (c) to have the validity of the detention determined by way of *habeas corpus* and to be released if the detention is not lawful.

Proceedings in criminal and penal matters
11. Any person charges with an offence has the right
    (a) to be informed without unreasonable delay of the specific offence;
    (b) to be tried within a reasonable time;
    (c) not to be compelled to be a witness in proceedings against that person in respect of the offence;
    (d) to be presumed innocent until proven guilty according to law in a fair and public hearing by an independent and impartial tribunal;
    (e) not to be denied reasonable bail without just cause;
    (f) except in the case of an offence under military law tried before a military tribunal, to the benefit of trial by jury where the maximum punishment for the offence is imprisonment for five years or a more severe punishment;
    (g) not to be found guilty on account of any act or omission unless, at the time of the act or omission, it constituted an offence under Canadian or international law or was criminal according to the general principles of law recognized by the community of nations;

    (h)   if finally acquitted of the offence, not to be tried for it again and, if finally found guilty and punished for the offence, not to be tried or punished for it again; and

    (i)   if found guilty of the offence and if the punishment for the offence has been varied between the time of commission and the time of sentencing, to the benefit of the lesser punishment.

Treatment or punishment
12.   Everyone has the right not to be subjected to any cruel and unusual treatment or punishment.

Self-crimination
13.   A witness who testified in any proceedings has the right not to have any incriminating evidence so given used to incriminate that witness in any other proceedings, except in a prosecution for perjury or for the giving of contradictory evidence.

Interpreter
14.   A party or witness in any proceedings who does not understand or speak the language in which the proceedings are conducted or who is deaf has the right to the assistance of an interpreter.

Equality Rights
Equality before and under law and equal protection and benefit of law
15.   (1)   Every individual is equal before and under the law and has the right to the equal protection and equal benefit of the law without discrimination and, in particular, without discrimination based on race, national or ethnic origin, colour, religion, sex, age or mental or physical disability.

Affirmative action programs
    (2)   Subsection (1) does not preclude any law, program or activity that has as its object the amelioration of conditions of disadvantaged individuals or groups including those that are disadvantaged because of race, national or ethnic origin, colour, religion, sex, age or mental or physical disability.

Official Languages of Canada

Official languages of Canada

16. (1) English and French are the official languages of Canada and have equality of status and equal rights and privileges as to their use in all institutions of the Parliament and government of Canada.

Official languages of New Brunswick

(2) English and French are the official languages of New Brunswick and have equality of status and equal rights and privileges as to their use in all institutions of the legislature and governments of New Brunswick.

Advancement of status and use

(3) Nothing in this Charter limits the authority of Parliament or a legislature to advance the equality of status or use of English and French.

Proceedings of Parliament

17. (1) Everyone has the right to use English or French in any debates and other proceedings of Parliament.

Proceedings of New Brunswick legislature

(2) Everyone has the right to use English or French in any debates and other proceedings of the legislature of New Brunswick.

Parliamentary statues and records

18. (1) The statutes, records and journals of Parliament shall be printed and published in English and French and both language versions are equally authoritative.

New Brunswick statues and records

(2) The statutes, records and journals of the legislature of New Brunswick shall be printed and published in English and French and both language versions are equally authoritative.

Proceedings in courts established by Parliament

19. (1) Either English or French may be used by any person in, or in any pleading in or process issuing from, any court established by Parliament.

Proceedings in New Brunswick courts
(2)   Either English or French may be used by any person in, or in any pleading in or process issuing from, any court of New Brunswick.

Communications by public with federal institutions.
20.   (1)   Any member of the public in Canada has the right to communicate with, and to receive available services from, any head or central office of an institution of the Parliament or government of Canada in English or French, and has the same right with respect to any other office of any such institution where
        (a)   there is a significant demand for communications with and services from that office in such language; or
        (b)   due to the nature of the office, it is reasonable that communications with and services from that office be available in both English and French.

Communications by public with New Brunswick institutions
(2)   Any member of the public in New Brunswick has the right to communicate with, and to receive available services from, any office of an institution of the legislature or government of New Brunswick in English or French.

Continuation of existing constitutional provisions
21.   Nothing in sections 16 to 20 abrogates or derogates from any right, privilege or obligation with respect to the English and French languages, or either of them, that exists or is continued by virtue of any other provision of the Constitution of Canada.

Rights and privileges preserved
22.   Nothing in sections 16 to 20 abrogates or derogates from any legal or customary right or privilege acquired or enjoyed either before or after the coming into force of this Charter with respect to any language that is not English or French.

Minority Language Educational Rights
Language of instruction
23.   (1)   Citizens of Canada
        (a)   whose first language learned and still understood is that of the English or French linguistic minority population of the province in which they reside, or

(b) who have received their primary school instruction in Canada in English or French and reside in a province where the language in which they received that instruction is the language of the English or French linguistic minority population of the province,

have the right to have their children receive primary and secondary school instruction in that language in that province.

Continuity of language instruction
(2) Citizens of Canada of whom any child has received or is receiving primary or secondary school instruction in English or French in Canada, have the right to have all their children receive primary and secondary school instruction in the same language.

Application where numbers warrant
(3) The right of citizens of Canada under subsections (1) and (2) to have their children receive primary and secondary school instruction in the language of the English or French linguistic minority population of a province

(a) applies wherever in the province the number of children of citizens who have such a right is sufficient to warrant the provision to them out of public funds of minority language instruction; and

(b) includes, where the number of those children so warrants, the right to have them receive that instruction in minority language educational facilities provided out of public funds.

Enforcement of guaranteed rights and freedoms
24. (1) Anyone whose rights or freedoms, as guaranteed by this Charter, have been infringed or denied may apply to a court of competent jurisdiction to obtain such remedy as the court considers appropriate and just in the circumstances.

Exclusion of evidence bringing administration of justice into disrepute.
(2) Where, in proceedings under subsection (1), a court concludes that evidence was obtained in a manner that infringed or denied any rights or freedoms guaranteed by this Charter, the evidence shall be excluded if it is established that, having regard to all the circumstances, the admission of it in the proceedings would bring the administration of justice into disrepute.

General

Aboriginal rights and freedoms not affected by Charter

25.   The guarantee in this Charter of certain rights and freedoms shall not be construed so as to abrogate or derogate from, any aboriginal treaty or other rights or freedoms that pertain to the aboriginal peoples of Canada including

(a)   any rights or freedoms that have been recognized by the Royal Proclamation of October 7, 1763; and

(b)   any rights or freedoms that now exist by way of land claims agreements or may be so acquired.

Other rights and freedoms not affected by Charter

26.   The guarantee in this Charter of certain rights and freedoms shall not be construed as denying the existence of any other rights or freedoms that exist in Canada.

Multicultural heritage

27.   This Charter shall be interpreted in a manner consistent with the preservation and enhancement of the multicultural heritage of Canadians.

Rights guaranteed equally to both sexes

28.   Notwithstanding anything in this Charter, the rights and freedoms referred to in it are guaranteed equally to male and female persons.

Rights respecting certain schools preserved.

Canadian Bill of Rights

An Act for the Recognition and Protection of Human Rights and Fundamental Freedoms.

8-9 Elizabeth II, c. 44 (Canada)

[Assented to 10th August 1960]

Preamble

The Parliament of Canada, affirming that the Canadian Nation is founded upon principles that acknowledge the supremacy of God, the dignity and worth of the human person and the position of the family in a society of free men and free institutions;

Affirming also that men and institutions remain free only when freedom is founded upon respect for moral and spiritual values and the rule of law;

And being desirous of enshrining these principles and the human rights and fundamental freedoms derived from them, in a Bill of Rights which shall reflect the respect of Parliament for its constitutional authority and which shall ensure the protection of these rights and freedoms in Canada:

Therefore her Majesty, by and with the advice and consent of the Senate and House of Commons of Canada, enacts as follows:

PART I
Bill of Rights

Recognition and declaration of rights and freedoms

1. It is hereby recognized and declared that in Canada there have existed and shall continue to exist without discrimination by reason of race, national origin, colour, religion or sex, the following human rights and fundamental freedoms, namely,

   (a) the right of the individual to life, liberty, security of the person and enjoyment of property, and the right not to be deprived thereof except by due process of law;

(b)   the right of the individual to equality before the law and the protection of the law;

(c)   freedom of religion;

(d)   freedom of speech;

(e)   freedom of assembly and association; and

(f)   freedom of the press.

Construction of law

2. Every law of Canada shall, unless it is expressly declared by an Act of Parliament of Canada that it shall operate notwithstanding the *Canadian Bill of Rights*, be so construed and applied as not to abrogate, abridge or infringe or to authorize the abrogation, abridgment or infringement of any of the rights or freedoms herein recognized and declared, and in particular, no law of Canada shall be construed or applied so as to

(a)   authorize or effect the arbitrary detention, imprisonment or exile of any person;

(b)   impose or authorize the imposition of cruel and unusual treatment or punishment;

(c)   deprive a person who has been arrested or detained

(i)   of the right to be informed promptly of the reason for his arrest or detention,

(ii)   of the right to retain and instruct counsel without delay, or

(iii) of the remedy by way of *habeas corpus* for the determination of the validity of his detention and for his release if the detention is not lawful;

(d)   authorize a court, tribunal, commission, board or other authority to compel a person to give evidence if he is denied counsel, protection against self-crimination or other constitutional safeguards;

(e) deprive a person of the right to a fair hearing in accordance with the principles of fundamental justice for the determination of his rights and obligations;

(f) deprive a person charged with a criminal offense of the right to be presumed innocent until proved guilty according to law in a fair and public hearing by an independent and impartial tribunal, or of the right to reasonable bail without just cause; or

(g) deprive a person of the right to the assistance of an interpreter in any proceedings in which he is involved or in which he is a party or a witness, before a court, commission, board or other tribunal, if he does not understand or speak the language in which such proceedings are conducted.

Duties of Minister of Justice

3. The Minister of Justice shall, in accordance with such regulations as may be prescribed by the Governor in Council, examine every proposed regulation submitted in draft form to the Clerk of the Privy Council pursuant to the *Regulations Act* and every Bill introduced in or presented to the House of Commons, in order to ascertain whether any of the provisions thereof are inconsistent with the purposes and provisions of this Part and he shall report any such inconsistency to the House of Commons at the first convenient opportunity.

Short title

4. The provisions of this Part shall be known as the *Canadian Bill of Rights*.

PART II

Savings

5. (1) Nothing in Part I shall be construed to abrogate or abridge any human right or fundamental freedom not enumerated therein that may have existed in Canada at the commencement of this Act.

"Law of Canada" defined

(2) The expression "law of Canada" in Part I means an Act of the Parliament of Canada enacted before or after the coming into force of this Act, any order, rule or regulation thereunder, and any law in force in Canada or in any part of Canada at the commencement of this Act that is subject to be repealed, abolished or altered by the Parliament of Canada.

Jurisdiction of Parliament

(3) The provisions of Part I shall be construed as extending only to matters coming within the legislative authority of the Parliament of Canada.